The Philosopher's Guide

To Sources, Research Tools, Professional Life, And Related Fields

Richard T. De George

THE REGENTS PRESS OF KANSAS
LAWRENCE

The preparation of this volume was made possible by a grant
from the Program for Research Tools and Reference Works of the
National Endowment for the Humanities, an independent federal
agency.

Z
7125
D445
Ref.

PREFACE

This volume is a successor to an earlier one entitled a *Guide to Philosophical Bibliography and Research.*

In 1976 the American Philosophical Association's Subcommittee on Research and Publication surveyed the field of Philosophy to determine the research tools needed by the profession. Among the initial needs was a comprehensive guide to the existing tools. The Subcommittee asked me to provide a ten-year supplement to my earlier guide, and the National Endowment for the Humanities awarded me a grant to carry through the work. It soon became evident to me, however, that what was needed was more than simply a ten-year supplement. The present volume contains in up-dated form much of the material which appeared in the previous volume. The contents have been reorganized for easier use by philosophy students and teachers. I have not only added recent material. I have also added some kinds of material, for example biographies of major philosophers, not present in the earlier volume. There is also a new part on research tools in fields related to philosophy.

This book is so organized that it can be used systematically by those who wish to find their way through the various kinds of philosophical writing and the tools available to the philosopher or to the philosophy student. It can also be used piecemeal to find the basic sources in an area of philosophy or to find material related to a particular philosopher.

Each chapter begins with a general introduction. Annotations have been added to those entries that are not self-explanatory and for which more information seemed desirable to help the reader evaluate the usefulness of the item listed. I have added evaluations in a number of cases, but only where I felt there was some consensus among scholars on the item in question. Where I have quoted someone else's opinion of an item, I have indicated the source. For the most part rare items, dated and superseded works, and bibliographies compiled before 1900 have been omitted, unless they have been reprinted recently or are still of general use. By utlizing the speciaized guides and bibliographies contained herein, the reader should be able to locate unlisted specialized and older material with relative ease. "See also" references will lead the reader to additional items on a topic, and this device has been used to avoid reprinting items that could correctly be listed under more than one heading. The Index is an author, subject, and title index and can be used as a means of unifying material on a topic or author which may be spread through various sections and chapters.

Since this guide was prepared primarily for English-speaking students and scholars, items in English are given fullest and most prominent treatment. Entries in other languages have—with a certain few obvious exceptions—been restricted to those written in French, German, Italian, Latin, Russian, and Spanish. There are, however, abundant sources listed for locating works in other languages. Where the number of items in a section is considerable, and where appropriate, entries have been grouped by language.

In addition to the general guidelines of selection enumerated here, I have attempted to indicate in the various introductions the additional criteria of selection that I have employed in choosing the items for that section. As is inevitable, my choice of criteria and my employment of those criteria will not meet with universal approval. There is ample room for individual scholars to lament the omission of some particular work or class of works. I can only hope that my selection has included a large majority of the basic sources and research tools, and sufficiently specific references to where other sources and tools can be found, so that this guide may be of general usefulness to readers with a variety of philosophic interests and inclinations.

The style I have employed for listing entries is basically that of the Library of Congress, with slight modifications where these seemed called for, and items have been checked against the Library of Congress Catalogue for accuracy and uniformity whenever this was appropriate.

I wish to express my thanks to the many colleagues and friends who have made suggestions on the work as a whole and on particular entries. My special thanks go to Debra Nails who helped me with many details of the present version, and to my wife, Dr. Fernande M. De George, who did most of the work on the related fields. I am grateful for the financial support I received from the University of Kansas General Research Fund (Grant no. 3119-5038) and from the National Endowment for the Huanities (Grant no. RT-27317-78-27). The evaluations and views expressed herein do not, of course, necessarily represent the views of either the University of Kansas or the National Endowment for the Humanities.

CONTENTS

GENERAL RESEARCH TOOLS

RELATED FIELDS

PHILOSOPHY

I
General

1. GENERAL HISTORIES AND TOOLS

Certain tools are basic to a wide variety of philosophical research. They are general rather than specialized. Included in this chapter are general histories of philosophy, bibliographical guides and general bibliographies, and general philosophical dictionaries and encyclopedias.

Histories of philosophy can provide a summary introduction to a philosopher's thought, interpretations of particular authors and works, background material on individuals, works and movements, and bibliographies. The histories listed here include the more important, scholarly histories of philosophy published in English or in major European languages. Many of them are standard reference works, and most of them contain bibliographies and bibliographical references to more specialized studies on particular philosophers and periods. The histories listed in this section are for the most part multivolumed and cover two or more periods of the history of philosophy. The appropriate volumes are not relisted in later sections, but the work as a whole is referred to by its number.

There are a great many undergraduate texts and popular presentations of the history of philosophy. No attempt has been made to list them here and such English language works which are still in print can be found by consulting *Subject Guide to Books in Print* (15.3.6). Additional works in special periods of philosophy, in special branches of philosophy, and on individual philosophers can be found in other chapters of this book.

The bibliographies contained in histories of philosophy, encyclopedias and dictionaries serve as useful introductions to the pertinent literature, but they are seldom complete. Through the systematic use of the proper bibliographical tools, however, it is possible to compile a reasonably complete list of books and articles dealing with any philosophical topic or any philosopher. The compilation of a bibliography should not be a hit-or-miss endeavor and need not involve the search of an endless number of sources. The items in 1.2.18 through 1.2.31 are especially important for developing a bibliography or for completing an already published bibliography. Bibliographies have already been compiled and published on a great many philosophers and philosophical topics. Knowledge of their existence can save a great deal of time. The pertinent chapters of this book should be consulted for such bibliographies.

General philosophical dictionaries (1.3) provide definitions and explanations of philosophical terms, often with references to their use by prominent philosophers and to their development in the history of philosophy, and frequently with brief bibliographies. The discussions are usually much more detailed than in unabridged general dictionaries.

Philosophical encyclopedias are able to cover items in more detail than either philosophical dictionaries or general encyclopedias. Of the philosophical encyclopedias listed in 1.4, the *Encyclopedia of Philosophy* (1.4.1.) deserves special mention, since it is the most recent, comprehensive and reliable of the encyclopedias, and can be recommended as a general reference for most philosophical topics.

1.1 GENERAL HISTORIES OF PHILOSOPHY

1.1.1 **Bréhier, Emile**. The history of philosophy. Chicago, Chicago University Press, 1963-69. 7v.

A translation of 1.1.13.
Vol. I, The Hellenic age, trans. by Joseph Thomas, 1963;
vol. II, The Hellenistic and Roman age, trans. by Wade Baskin, 1965;
vol. III, The Middle Ages and the Renaissance, trans. by Wade Baskin, 1965;
vol. IV, The Seventeenth Century, trans. by Wade Baskin, 1966;
vol. V, The Eighteenth Century, trans. by Wade Baskin, 1967;
vol. VI, The Nineteenth Century; period of systems, 1800-1850, trans. by Wade Baskin, 1968;
vol. VII, Contemporary philosophy—since 1850, trans. by Wade Baskin, 1969.
Excellent bibliographies.

1.1.2 **Caponigri, A. Robert**, and **Ralph McInerny**. A history of Western philosophy. Notre Dame, Ind., University of Notre Dame Press, 1964-71.

Vol. 1, From the beginnings of philosophy to Plotinus, 1964;
vol. 2, From St. Augustine to Ockham, 1970;
vol. 3, From the Renaissance to the romantic age, 1964;
vol. 4, From the romantic age to the age of positivism, 1971;
vol. 5, From the age of positivism to the age of analysis, 1971.
Bibliographical references conclude each chapter.

1.1.3 **Copleston, Frederick Charles**. A history of philosophy. Westminster, Md., Newman Press, 1946-66. 8v.

Vol. I, Greece and Rome;
vol. II, Mediaeval philosophy: Augustine to Scotus;
vol. III, Ockham to Suarez;
vol. IV, Descartes to Leibniz;
vol. V, Hobbes to Hume;
vol. VI, Wolff to Kant;
vol. VII, Fichte to Nietzsche;
vol. VIII, Bentham to Russell;
vol. IX, Maine de Biran to Sartre.
Reliable and objective. This is one of the best general histories of philosophy available in English. There is some criticism from a Thomistic point of view. The bibliographies are good for both sources and secondary works.

1.1.4 **Ferm, Vergilius**, *ed.* History of philosophical systems; contributions by forty-one professors of America, Canada, Europe, and Asia. New York, Philosophical Library, 1950. 642 pp.

Essays on 47 schools, systems, and branches of philosophy.
Includes bibliographies.

1.1.5 **Gilson, Etienne**, *general ed.* A history of philosophy. New York, Random House, 1962- .

In progress.
4 vol. projected.
See 4.1.5, 5.1.4, 6.1.2.

1.1.6 **Jaspers, Karl**. The great philosophers. Ed. by Hannah Arendt, trans. by Ralph Manheim. New York, Harcourt Brace & World, 1962-66. 2v.

Vol. 1, Part I: Socrates, Buddha, Confucius, Jesus; Part II: Plato, Augustine, Kant;
vol. 2, Anaximander, Heraclitus, Parmenides, Plotinus, Anselm, Nicholas of Cusa, Spinoza, Lao-Tzu, Nagarjuna.
Includes bibliographies.

1.1.7 **Jones, W. T.** A history of Western philosophy. New York, Harcourt, Brace, Jovanovich, 1969-1975. 5v.

Vol. I, The classical mind, 2nd ed., 1969;
vol. II, The medieval mind, 2nd ed., 1969;
vol. III, Hobbes to Hume, 2nd ed., 1969;
vol. IV, Kant and the nineteenth century, 2nd ed., revised, 1975;
vol. V, The twentieth century to Wittgenstein and Sartre, 2nd ed., revised, 1975.

1.1.8 **O'Connor, Daniel J.**, *ed.* A critical history of Western philosophy. New York, Free Press, 1964. 604 pp.

Twenty-nine scholarly studies by various philosophers of figures and periods in the history of philosophy from the early Greeks to the present.
Good bibliographies, pp. 576-594.

1.1.9 **Radhakrishnan, Sir Sarvepalli**, *ed.* History of philosophy, Eastern and Western. London, Allen and Unwin, 1952-53. 2v.

Essays on the history of Eastern and Western philosophy by various scholars.
Bibliographies throughout.

1.1.10 **Randall, John Herman.** The making of the modern mind; a survey of the intellectual background of the present age. Rev. ed. Cambridge, Mass., Houghton Mifflin, 1954. 696 pp.

A history of cultural development.
Bibliographies at the end of each chapter.

1.1.11 **Randall, John Herman.** The career of philosophy. New York, Columbia University Press, 1962-77. 3v.

Vol. 1, From the Middle Ages to the Enlightenment, 1962;
vol. 2, From the German Enlightenment to the age of Darwin, 1965;
vol. 3, Philosophy after Darwin, 1977. (Edited by Beth J. Singer.)
Bibliographical footnotes.

1.1.12 **Windelband, Wilhelm.** A history of philosophy. Trans. by James Tufts. Rev. ed., New York and London, Macmillan, 1901. 2v.

1st ed. 1893.
Reprinted: N. Y., Harper, 1958.
A translation of *Geschichte der Philosophie*, 1889.
Idealist in outlook. The ample bibliographical sections throughout the text have not been updated.

See also: 10.5.59.

French

1.1.13 **Bréhier, Emile.** Histoire de la philosophie. Paris, Presses Universitaires de France, 1926-32. 2v. in 7.

9th ed., revised with an updated bibliography by Pierre-Maxime Schuhl, 1967- .
See 1.1.1. Also later editions of each of the parts.
The French edition includes two supplementary volumes: Paul Masson-Oursel, *La philosophie en Orient*, 3. éd., 1948, and Basile Tatakis, *Philosophie Byzantine*, 1949.
A standard work. Excellent bibliographies.

1.1.14 **Chevalier, J.** Histoire de la pensée. Paris, Flammarion, 1955-66. 4v.

Vol. 1, La pensée antique, 1955;
vol. 2, La pensée chrétienne, des origines à la fin du XVIe siècle, 1956;
vol. 3, De Descartes à Kant, 1961;
vol. 4, De Hegel à Bergson, 1966.
Full bibliographies throughout.

1.1.15 **Histoire de la philosophie.** Paris, Hachette, 1972-73. 8v.

Vol. 1, La philosophie païenne (du VIe siècle avant J.-C. au IIIe siècle après J.-C.) par Pierre Aubenque, Jean Bernhardt, et François Chatelet, 1972;
vol. 2, La philosophie médiévale (du I au XVe siècle) par Anouar Abdel-Malek et al., 1972;
vol. 3, La philosophie du monde nouveau (XVIe et XVIIe siècles) par Ferdinand Alquié et al., 1972;
vol. 5, La philosophie et l'histoire (1780-1880) par Wanda Bannour et al., 1973;
vol. 6, La philosophie du monde scientifique et industriel (1860-1940) par Jean Bernhardt et al., 1973;
vol. 7, La philosophie des sciences sociales, de 1860 à nos jours, par André Akoun et al., 1973;
vol. 8, Le XXe (i.e. Vingtième) siècle par Jacques Bouveresse et al., 1973.

1.1.16 **Parain, Brice** et **Y. Belaval.** Histoire de

la philosophie (Enclylopédie de la Pléiade). Paris, Gallimard, 1969-74. 3v.

Vol. 1, Orient, Antiquité, Moyen Age;
vol. 2, De la Renaissance à la révolution Kantienne;
vol. 3, Du XIXe siècle à nos jours.

1.1.17 **Rivaud, Albert**. Histoire de la philosophie. Paris, Presses Universitaires de France, 1948-67. 5v. in 6.

Vol. 1, Des origines à la Scolastique, 1948;
vol. 2, De la Scolastique à l'époque classique, 1950;
vol. 3, L'époque classique, 1950;
vol. 4, Philosophie française et philosophie anglaise de 1700 à 1830, 1962;
vol. 5, Philosophie allemande, de 1700 à 1850: Ptie. 1, De l'Aufklarung à Schelling, 1968; Ptie. 2, De Hegel à Schopenhauer, 1968.
General bibliography in v. 1 and bibliographies at end of most chapters.

German

1.1.18 **Schilling, Kurt**. Geschichte der Philosophie. München, Reinhardt, 1951-53. 2v.

Vol. 1, Die alter Welt; das christlich-germanische Mittelalter, 1951;
vol. 2, Die Neuzeit, 1953.
Useful bibliographies.

1.1.19 **Ueberweg, Friedrich**. Grundriss der Geschichte der Philosophie. 11. and 12. Aufl. Berlin, Mittler, 1923-28. 5v.

1st ed. 1862-66, 3v. The 11th and 12th editions are famous for their extremely full bibliographies.
Reprinted: v. 1-3, Bâle, B. Schwabe, 1951-60.
Vol. 1, Die Philosophie des Altertums, 12. Aufl., herausgegeben von Karl Praechter, 1926;
vol. 2, Die patristische und scholastische Philosophie, 11. Aufl., herausgegeben von Bernhard Geyer, 1928;
vol. 3, Die Philosophie der Neuzeit bis zum Ende des 18. Jahrhunderts, 12. Aufl., herausgegeben von Max Frischeisen-Köhler und Willy Moog, 1924;

vol. 4, Die deutsche Philosophie des neunzehnten Jahrhunderts und der Gegenwart, 12. Aufl., herausgegeben von Traugott Konstantin Osterreich, 1923;
vol. 5, Die Philosophie des Auslandes vom Beginn des 19. Jahrhunderts bis auf die Gegenwart, 12. Aufl. herausgegeben von Traugott Konstantin Osterreich, 1928.
Though a standard reference for historical research, there is no systematic index. Bibliographies are massive, but not exhaustive. They cover the period of roughly up to 1920.
The two-volume English translation, *History of Philosophy, from Thales to the Present Time*, 1887, is from the 4th German edition, and does not have the bibliographical data which makes the history so useful.
A new German edition, in 8 series, under the direction of Paul Wilpert, has been announced by Schwabe (Basel).

Italian

1.1.20 **Abbagnano, Nicola**. Storia della filosofia. Torino, Unione Tipografico-Editrice Torinese, 1949-50. 2v. in 3.

Vol. 1, Filosofia antica; filosofia patristica; filosofia scolastica;
vol. 2, pt. 1, Filosofia moderna sino all fine del secolo XVII; pt. 2, Filosofia del romanticismo; filosofia contemporanea.
Includes bibliographies.

1.1.21 **De Ruggiero, Guido**. Storia della filosofia. Bari, Laterza, 1920-34. 14v.

Written from a neo-Hegelian point of view.
Bibliographies.

1.1.22 **Geymonat, Ludovico**. Storia del pensiero filosofico e scientifico. Milano, Garzanti, 1970-72. 6v.

Russian

1.1.23 **Akademiia nauk SSSR**. Institut filosofii. Istoriia filosofii. V shesti tomakh. Moskva, 1957-65. 6v. in 7.

Bibliography: vol. VI, pp. 474-544.

1.2 GENERAL PHILOSOPHICAL BIBLIOGRAPHIES

Bibliographical Guides

1.2.1 **Bertman, Martin A.** Research guide in philosophy. Morristown, N. J., General Learning Press, 1974. 252 pp.

1.2.2 **Borchardt, Dietrich Hans.** How to find out in philosophy and psychology. Oxford, Pergamon Press, 1968. 97 pp.

A descriptive guide to some of the basic reference works and bibliographies in philosophy.
The bibliography, pp. 75-94, contains a "List of works referred to."

1.2.3 **De George, Richard T.** A guide to philosophical bibliography and research. New York, Appleton-Century-Crofts, 1971. 141 pp.

Includes sections on dictionaries, encyclopedias, histories of philosophy, sources (i.e., bibliographies, standard editions and collected works of individual philosophers), bibliographies, library catalogs, serials, guides to writing and publishing, biographies and professional life. Annotated. Updated by the present work.

1.2.4 **Gerber, William.** "Philosophical bibliographies," Encyclopedia of Philosophy (1.4.1), vol. VI, pp. 166-169.

An historico-descriptive account of philosophical bibliographies.

1.2.5 **Guerry, Herbert,** *ed.* A bibliography of philosophical bibliographies. Westport, Conn. and London, Greenwood Press, 1977. 332 pp.

A list of philosophical bibliographies in all countries from 1450-1974. "The first list (1-1395) contains bibliographies on the works of, and literature about, individual philosophers. The second list (1396-2353) contains bibliographies on philosophical topics."

1.2.6 **Higgins, Charles L.** The bibliography of philosophy; a descriptive account. Ann Arbor, Mich., Campus Publishers, 1965. 29 pp.

A brief guide to some of the most important bibliographical tools in philosophy.

1.2.7 **Jasenas, Michael.** A history of the bibliography of philosophy. Hildesheim, Olms, 1973. 188 pp.

1.2.8 **Matczak, Sebastian A.** Philosophy: a select, classified bibliography of ethics, economics, law, politics, sociology. *See* 7.2.10.

1.2.9 **Pesce, Domenico.** Bibliographic review of the history of philosophy—extracted from magazines. Vol. 1, (covering 1966), Padova, Liviana Editrice, 1969- .

"The objective is to provide researchers with the most efficient instrument for discovering what has been published every year in the principal magazines throughout the world concerning the history of philosophy by way of articles, notes, and reviews."

1.2.10 **Plott, J. C.** and **P. D. Mays.** Sarva-Darsana-Sangraha: a bibliographical guide to the global history of philosophy. Leiden, Brill, 1969. 305 pp.

A guide for students. Full annotations. Suggests secondary works on major philosophers.

1.2.11 **Tobey, Jeremy L.** The history of ideas: a bibliographical introduction. Santa Barbara and Oxford, Clio Press, 1975- .

Vol. 1, Classical antiquity, 1975;
vol. 2, Medieval and early modern Europe, 1977.
An excellent bibliographical narrative covering not only philosophy but also science, religion, and aesthetics.

French

1.2.12 **Hoffmans, Jean.** La philosophie et les philosophes; ouvrages généraux. Bruxelles, Van Oest, 1920. 395 pp.

Reprinted: N. Y., Burt Franklin, 1968. Lists dictionaries, manuals, histories, editions and translations, journals and bibliographies. Neoscholastic in emphasis. Now dated but useful for older works.

1.2.13 Le Senne, René. Introduction à la philosophie. 4. éd. Paris, Presses Universitaires de France, 1958. 480 pp.

Has approximately 21 pages of bibliography and philosophically useful works.

1.2.14 Raeymaeker, Louis de. Introduction à la philosophie. 5. éd. Louvain, Publications Universitaires de Louvain, 1964. 320 pp.

Pp. 197-304 list many useful books and bibliographies and contain a great deal of information on philosophical centers and organizations.

1.2.15 Varet, Gilbert. Manuel de bibliographie philosophique. Paris, Presses Universitaires de France, 1956. 2v.

Vol. 1, pp. 1-39 list basic reference works in philosophy; pp. 45-494 list books dealing with classical philosophy, historically ordered (Orient, antiquity, Christian philosophy, Descartes, Cartesianism, English classical philosophy, Rousseau, Kant and Kantianism).

vol. 2, lists works on philosophical ideologies, culture, philosophy of history, of religion, of art, logic, epistemology, philosophy of the sciences, social philosophy, philosophy of law, of education, of being and value, and ethics.

Not only a guide but a bibliography which is particularly full in its coverage of the period 1914-34, which corresponds to the hiatus between the literature covered by Ueberweg (1.1.19) and De Brie (1.2.22).

German

1.2.16 Bochenski, Innocentius M. Bibliographische Einführungen in das Studium der Philosophie. Bern, Francke, 1948-1953.

A collection of small booklets, each dedicated to a particular philosopher or movement. Not exhaustive in any instance, but useful as an introduction and guide to the study of the authors and movements included.

No. 1: I. M. Bochenski and F. Monteleone, Allgemeine philosophische Bibliographie, 1948, 42 pp.

No. 2: R. B. Winn, Amerikanische Philosophie, 1948, 32 pp.

No. 3: E. W. Beth, Symbolische Logik und Grundlegung der exakten Wissenschaften, 1948, 28 pp.

No. 4: R. Jolivet, Kierkegaard, 1948, 33 pp.

No. 5: O. Gigon, Antike Philosophie, 1948, 52 pp.

No. 6: P. J. DeManasce, Arabische Philosophie, 1948, 49 pp.

No. 7: M. F. Sciacca, Italienische Philosophie der Gegenwart, 1948, 48 pp.

No. 8: M.-D. Philippe, Aristoteles, 1948, 48 pp.

No. 9: R. Jolivet, Französische Existenzphilosophie, 1948, 36 pp.

No. 10: M. F. Sciacca, Augustinus, 1948, 32 pp.

No. 11: K. Dürr, Der logische Positivismus, 1948, 24 pp.

No. 12: O. Gigon, Platon, 1950, 30 pp.

No. 13/14: P. Wyser, Thomas von Aquin, 1950, 78 pp.

No. 15/16: P. Wyser, Der Thomismus, 1951, 120 pp.

No. 17: F. Van Steenberghen, Philosophie des Mittelalters, 1950, 52 pp.

No. 18: O. Perler, Patristische Philosophie, 1950, 44 pp.

No. 19: G. Vajda, Jüdische Philosophie, 1950, 40 pp.

No. 20/21: C. Regamey, Buddhistische Philosophie, 1950, 86 pp.

No. 22: O. Schäfer, Johannes Duns Scotus, 1953, 34 pp.

No. 23: O. F. Bollnow, Deutsche Existenz-philosophie, 1953, 40 pp.

Italian

1.2.17 Ferro, Carmelo. Guida storico-bibliografica allo studio della filosofia. Milano, "vita e Pensiero," 1949. 196 pp.

Bibliographies of "sources" and "studies" in the history of philosophy.

See also: 1.2.5, pp. 219-32.

The Basic Bibliographies

These are the most important sources for working up a bibliography in philosophy. They are listed in the order of their coverage, and so in the order in which they would generally be used in developing a retrospective bibliography. Some of them supply summaries of books or articles. The summaries are especially useful in breaking down a complete bibliography into a working bibliography of works actually to be consulted.

1.2.18 **Rand, Benjamin**. Bibliography of philosophy, psychology and cognate subjects. New York, Macmillan, 1905. 1v. in 2.

> Reprinted: N. Y., Peter Smith, 1949.
> This is vol. III of Baldwin (1.3.1).
> Pt. 1 deals with general works and the history of philosophy. Pt. 2 deals with systematic philosophy. It is espcially good in its 16th, 17th, 18th, and 19th century references. Though not exhaustive in its coverage, which goes up to 1902, it is extremely comprehensive.
> Supplements appeared in the *Psychological Index* from 1901-08.

1.2.19 **Ueberweg, F.** Grundriss der Geschichte der Philosophie. 11.-12. Aufl. See 1.1.19.

> Covers the period of roughly up to 1920. Extremely full bibliographical information, with some emphasis on German scholarship. Some duplication with Rand.

1.2.20 **Totok, Wilhelm**. Handbuch der Geschichte der Philosophie. Frankfurt, Klostermann, 1964- .

> Vol. I, Altertum; Indische, Chinesische, Griechisch-Romische Philosophie. Very full bibliographies from 1920 on, and so vol. 1 completes Ueberweg (1.1.19) for Ancient Indian, Chinese, and Greek and Roman philos-

ophy. Pp. 1-11 are a systematic bibliographical overview of the history of philosophy.
> vol. II:1, Die Philosophie des Mittelalters, 400 pp. Full data on all figures—bibliographies, dictionaries, texts, festschriften, collected and other works, studies, etc.
> vol. II:2, Die Philosophie des Mittelalters, pp. 401-676. Patristic and various schools of philosophy and movements in the middle ages.
> vol. III:1, Die Philosophie der frühen Neuzeit, 384 pp. Italian Renaissance movements and figures.

1.2.21 **Varet, Gilbert**. Manuel de bibliographie philosophique. See 1.2.15.

> By intent, especially full for the period between Ueberweg (1.1.19) and De Brie (1.2.22).

1.2.22 **De Brie, G. A.** Bibliographia philosophica 1934-1945. Bruxellis, Editiones Spectrum, 1950-1954. 2v.

> Vol. I, "Bibliographia historiae philosophiae," contains a chronological list of works on and by philosophers. Vol. II, "Bibliographia philosophiae," is divided by branches of philosophy. Though the headings are in Latin, the "Introduction" and other service material are in six languages, including English. Included are books, articles (over 400 philosophical journals searched), and reviews, published during 1934-45 in Danish, Dutch, English, French, German, Italian, Latin, Norwegian, Portuguese, Spanish, Catalan, and Swedish. Vol. II ends with an index of names appearing in the two volumes.

1.2.23 **Répertoire bibliographique de la philosophie**. 1949- .

> From 1934-49 it appeared as a supplement to the *Revue néoscolastique de philosophie* (*see* 10.3.19). Since 1949 it has been issued separately, though still an annex to the *Revue philosophique de Louvain* (called the *Revue néoscolastique* until 1945). It contained the "Sommaire idéologique des ouvrages et des revues de philosophie" which appeared under varying titles 1895-1905, 1906-07,

1908-14. Not published 1915-33, 1941-45. Since 1939 the *Répertoire* has also appeared with Dutch headings as "Bibliographisch Repertorium" in *Tijdschrift voor Philosophie.* This appeared during the war when the *Revue néoscolastique* was suspended.

A quarterly listing books and articles in philosophy. Divided like De Brie (1.2.22), two sections in each issue. The fourth (Nov.) issue carries a list of book reviews and an index of names.

1.2.24 Bibliographie de la philosophie. Institut international de philosophie. 1937-52/53. Paris, Vrin, 1937-58. 10v.

Lists books and articles. Vol. I (1) catalog of editors; (2) catalog of philosophical journals; (3) catalog of names of authors. Vol. II (1) historical (by period) and geographical (by country); (2) philosophers (on whom books and articles have been written); (3) topics (based on Lalande, 1.3.19). It provides a brief résumé in the language of the book in question where the title is not self explanatory. It did not appear from July 1939-December 1945. After 1953 it was continued as 1.2.25.

1.2.25 Bibliography of philosophy; a quarterly bulletin. Published under the auspices of the International Institute of Philosophy and with the aid of UNESCO. U. S. Director: Paul Kurtz, Dept. of Philosophy, SUNY at Buffalo, 4244 Ridge Lea Rd., Amherst, N. Y. 14226. A continuation of 1.2.24.

Title also in French. Text in several languages.

It lists only books (no articles) and provides abstracts of new philosophical books published throughout the world and comprehensive bibliographical information of reeditions. Divided into nine subject (topical) headings. Alphabetical classification according to author under each of the subject headings. The last issue each year has an author index and an analytic subject index.

1.2.26 Bulletin analytique: philosophie. Paris, Centre de documentation du C. N. R. S., 1944-55. Vols. 1-9.

Lists journal articles only, and provides a brief noncritical résumé of each. Continued as 1.2.27.

1.2.27 Bulletin signalétique: sciences humaines, philosophie. Paris, Centre de documentation de C. N. R. S., Vol. 10, 1956- . Quarterly.

A continuation of 1.2.26. Series 19 (1961-63); series 19-23 (1964); series 19-24 (1965-). Lists abstracts in French of philosophical articles and reviews. Coverage is worldwide and attempts to be exhaustive.

Title varies.

1.2.28 The philosopher's index; an international index to philosophical periodicals. 1967-to date. Quarterly (Jan., Apr., July, Oct.). Ed., Richard H. Lineback, Bowling Green University, Bowling Green, Ohio. 43402.

A keyword subject and author index to more than 300 major American and British philosophical periodicals, selected foreign journals, and related interdisciplinary publications. Also includes information on the *Philosophy Research Archives* (10.2.105). Cumulations in hardback: every two years until 1971, annually thereafter. From vol. 3 includes abstracts written by authors of articles indexed. Later vols. include a book review index and translations in progress.

See 1.2.29 and 1.2.30.

1.2.29 The philosopher's index: a retrospective index to U.S. publications from 1940. Bowling Green, Ohio, Philosophy Documentation Center, 1978- .

Indexes U. S. philosophy articles 1940-66, and U. S. philosophy books from 1940-76 (ca. 16,000 articles and 3,500 books). Author and subject indexes. Many abstracts included.

See 1.2.28 and 1.2.30.

1.2.30 The philosopher's information retrieval system (PIRS). Bowling Green, Ohio, Philosophy Documentation Center.

Provides, on demand, custom bibliographies with abstracts on any logical combination of philosophical topics. The data goes back to 1940 and includes information published in *The Philosopher's Index* (1.2.28 and 1.2.29).

1.2.31 **Tijdschrift voor Filosofie.** Vols. 1-25. Louvain, 1939-64.

> Reprinted: N. Y., Kraus Reprints.
> *See* 1.2.23.

Auxiliary Bibliographies

1.2.32 **Bibliographie critique.** Paris, G. Beauchesne, 1924- . 1922-29, annual; 1930- , biennial.

Contains reviews of the principal philosophical works of the year or biennium. A supplement to *Archives de philosophie* (10.3.2).

1.2.33 **Bibliography of current philosophical works** published in North America. St. Louis, St. Louis University, 1948- .

May 1948-May 1955, January 1959- issued as a section of *The Modern Schoolman* (10.2.77). Nov. 1955-May 1958 issued as separately paged supplement. Title varies slightly.

1.2.34 **Bibliography of philosophy,** 1933-36. New York, Journal of Philosophy, 1934-37.

An annual bibliography which appeared in the *Journal of Philosophy* (10.2.57). It included books and articles published in English, French, German, and Italian, but was selective in its coverage.

1.2.35 **Decennial index to philosophical literature,** 1939-50. New York, Russell F. Moore, 1952. 115 pp.

Author, title, and subject list of "important books" in philosophy and cognate fields. Prepared in connection with 1.2.40.

1.2.36 **Dissertations in philosophy** accepted at American universities, 1861-1975. Com-

piled by Thomas C. Bechtle and Mary F. Riley. New York, Garland, 1979. 577 pp.

1.2.37 **Index philosophique;** philosophie et science. Année 1-2 (1902-03). Paris, Chevalier, 1903-05. 2v.

Indexes both articles and books for the years indicated.

1.2.38 **Kleine philosophische Bibliographien** aus dem philosophischen Institut der Universität Düsseldorf, edited under the direction of Alwin Diemer. Düsseldorf, Philosophia Verlag.

Vol. I, Bibliographie der Hermeneutik und ihrer Anwendungsbereiche seit Schleiermacher—Bibliography of Hermeneutics (Theory of Interpretation and Understanding) and Their Fields of Application Since Schleiermacher, ed. Norbert Henrichs (1968), 250 pp.

vol. II, Internationale Gesamtbibliographie der philosophischen Zeitschriften seit dem 17. Jahrhundert, ed. Gert König.

1.2.39 **McLean, George F.** Philosophy in the 20th century; Catholic and Christian. New York, Frederick Ungar, 1967. 2v.

Vol. I, An annotated bibliography of philosophy in Catholic thought 1900-64. Restricted to entries in English; primarily American.

vol. II, A bibliography of Christian philosophy and contemporary ideas. International in coverage.

Both volumes interpret "Catholic and Christian" in a very broad sense, and include the writings of non-Christians if they bear on religion.

1.2.40 **Philosophic abstracts.** New York, Philosophic Abstracts, 1939-54.

Contains English abstracts of books from many countries and lists of periodical articles. Decennial Index to Philosophical Literature, 1939-1950, New York, R. F. Moore, 1952, is an index of vols. 1-12.

Reprinted: N. Y., Kraus Reprints.

1.2.41 Philosophical books. Leicester University Press, 1960- . *See* 10.2.88.

A review of books, foreign and English. Selective in its coverage.

1.2.42 Philosophie; chronique des années de guerre, 1939-1945; d'après guerre, 1946-1948. Publié par l'Institut International de Philosophie. Editeur, Raymond Bayer. Paris, Hermann, 1950. 5v.

Covers history of philosophy, metaphysics, philosophy of value, philosophy of science, psychology, phenomenology, and existentialism.

1.2.43 Die Philosophie der Gêgenwart: eine internationale Jahresübersicht. Heidelberg, Weiss, 1910-15.

Annotated lists of books and periodical articles, especially German, covering the years 1908-13. Edited by Arnold Ruge.

1.2.44 Philosophischer Literaturanzeiger. Meisenheim/Glan, Anton Hain KG, 1949- .

Published in conjunction with *Zeitschrift für philosophische Forschung* (10.3.38). Contains reviews of the most significant books of the preceding period. Appears six times a year. In 1959 it absorbed *Deutsche philosophische Bibliographie*. A section entitled "Neue Bucher" lists new books in philosophy published in German.

1.2.45 Referateblatt Philosophie; an abstract journal. Zentralstelle für die philosophische Information und Dokumentation im Institut für Gesellschaftswissenschaften beim ZK der SED. J. Dieckman-Str. 19-23, 108 Berlin, D.D.R.

A series. Individual titles vary. Includes: *Bibliographie Philosophie mit Autoren und Sach Register*, quarterly, 1967—.

1.2.46 Répertoire bibliographique de philosophie des sciences. Paris, 1950- .

A supplement of the *Bulletin de l'Académie internationale de philosophie des sciences* (Actualités scientifiques et industrielles. Archives de l'Institut international des sciences théoriques).

1.2.47 Revue internationale de philosophie. *See* 10.3.17.

Each issue dedicated to one subject, e.g., no. 6 (Aug. 1948) "Liberté"; no. 9 (July 1949) "Existentialisme."

1.2.48 Schweizerische Philosophische Gesellschaft. Bibliographie der philosophischen, psychologischen und pädagogischen Literatur in der deutschsprachigen Schweiz, 1900-1940, hrsg. von E. Heuss, (u. A.). Basel, Verlag für Recht und Gesellschaft, 1944. 207 pp.

Supplement, 1941-1944, von Hans Zantop, 1945, pp. 218-78.

Lists books and periodical articles on philosophy, psychology, and education published in German-speaking Switzerland. The supplement covers German, French, and Italian works.

1.2.49 Scripta recenter edita. Nijmegen, Netherlands, 1959- .

Issued 10 times a year. Lists books on philosophy and theology. Each issue contains about 400 entries, with some emphasis on theology.

1.2.50 Verzeichnis von Inedita Philosophica des 19. und 20. Jahrhunderts. Düsseldorf, Philosophia Verlag, 1973. 86 pp.

Catalogue, index, inventory.

1.3 GENERAL PHILOSOPHICAL DICTIONARIES

This list is restricted to the more important, the widely used, and the relatively recent philosophical dictionaries. For a history of philosophical dictionaries, together with descriptive listings of such dictionaries in all languages, see William Gerber's article "Philosophical Dictionaries and Encyclopedias" in the *Encyclopedia of Philosophy* (1.4.1), vol. VI, pp. 170-99.

1.3.1 Baldwin, James M., *ed.* Dictionary of philosophy and psychology, including many of the principal conceptions of ethics, logic, aesthetics, philosophy of religion, mental pathology, anthropology, biology, neurology, physiology, economics, political and social philosophy, philology, physical science, and education, and giving a terminology in English, French, German, and Italian. New York, Macmillan, 1901-05. 3v. in 4.

A 2d ed., 1910, simply contains minor corrections.
Reprinted: Gloucester, Mass., Peter Smith, 1960. 2v.
Entries cover both terms and persons. An index of Greek, Latin, French, German, and Italian terms gives the equivalent in these languages of English terms. Vol. III (in 2 parts) is devoted to bibliographies (*see* 1.2.18).
Though long a standard reference work, the first two volumes, except for historical purposes, have been superseded by the *Encyclopedia of Philosophy* (1.4.1).
Contributors included J. Dewey, W. James, G. E. Moore, C. Peirce, and J. Royce.

1.3.2 Bruckmann, William D. Keystones and theories of philosophy; a handbook to aid in the study of philosophy containing definitions of terms, and a brief historical conspectus, with a chart "General diagrammatic survey of philosophy." New York, Benzinger Brothers, 1946. 230 pp.

Primarily scholastic in outlook.

1.3.3 Brugger, Walter, *ed.* Philosophical dictionary. Kenneth Baker, trans. and ed. Spokane, Wash., Gonzaga University Press, 1972. 460 pp.

A translation and adaptation of 1.3.25.
Bibliographies are omitted. Some articles have been omitted and some added for the Anglo-American reader.

1.3.4 A dictionary of philosophy. By M.M. Rozental and P.F. Iudin. *See* 1.3.46.

1.3.5 Dictionary of the history of ideas; studies of selected pivotal ideas. Ed. by Philip P. Wiener. New York, Scribner's, 1973-74. 4v. and index.

Substantial articles by well-known scholars. Bibliographies.

1.3.6 The great ideas; a syntopicon of great books of the Western world. Mortimer Adler, ed. in chief. Chicago, Encyclopaedia Britannica, 1952. 2v.

Vols. II and III of *Great Books of the Western World.*
The *Syntopicon* covers 102 ideas, with exposition, references to the Great Books series, and lists of additional readings.

1.3.7 Gutmann, James, *ed.* Philosophy A to Z. Based on the work of Alwin Diemer, Ivo Frenzel, and others. (Translation by Salvatore Altanasio.) New York, Grosset & Dunlap, 1963. 343 pp.

Based on 1.3.28. Contains long articles on broad topics; includes bibliographies.

1.3.8 Lacey, A. R. A dictionary of philosophy. London, Henley and Boston, Routledge & Kegan Paul, 1976. 239 pp.

Also in paperback: New York, Scribner's, 1977. 248 pp.

1.3.9 Runes, Dagobert D., *ed.* Dictionary of philosophy. 16th rev. ed. New York, Philosophical Library, 1960. 342 pp.

1st ed. 1942.
Useful, despite the fact that a number of its distinguished contributors objected to the final form of the published volume.

1.3.10 Urmson, James Opie, *ed.* The concise encyclopedia of Western philosophy and philosophers. London, Hutchinson and New York, Hawthorn, 1960. 431 pp.

Reliable, informative articles by a number of different scholars on concepts, terms, and philosophers.
Contributors include A. J. Ayer, I. Berlin,

A. C. Ewing, E. Nagel, G. Ryle, and P. F. Strawson; but individual articles are not signed.

1.3.11 Voltaire, François Marie Arouet de. Philosophical dictionary. Translated, with an introduction and glossary by Peter Gay. New York, Basic Books, 1962. 2v.

See 1.3.22. The latest of the English editions. More popular than technical, the work is now only of historical interest.

French

1.3.12 Auroux, Sylvain and Yvonne Weil. Dictionnaire des auteurs et des thèmes de la philosophie. Paris, Hachette (Faire le Point), 1975. 287 pp.

1.3.13 Auroux, Sylvain and Yvonne Weil. Nouveau vocabulaire des études philosophiques. Paris, Hachette (Faire le Point), 1975. 256 pp.

1.3.14 Cuvillier, Armand. Nouveau vocabulaire philosophique. 3. éd. Paris, Colin, 1958. 204 pp.

1st ed. 1956.
Supersedes his *Petit vocabulaire de la langue philosophique*, 1st ed., 1925.

1.3.15 Didier, Julia. Dictionnaire de la philosophie. Paris, Larousse, 1964. 319 pp.

Covers both terms and philosophers, but more popular than scholarly.

1.3.16 Foulquié, Paul. Dictionnaire de la langue philosophique. Avec la collaboration de Raymond Saint-Jean. 2e éd. rev. et augm. Paris, Presses Universitaires de France, 1969. 778 pp.

A useful dictionary which gives etymologies, definitions, synonyms, and quotations from individual philosophers. 1st ed. 1962.

1.3.17 Jerphagnon, Lucien. Dictionnaire des grandes philosophies. Toulouse, Privat, 1973. 397 pp.

1.3.18 Jolivet, Régis. Vocabulaire de la philosophie, suivi d'un tableau historique des écoles de philosophie. 4. éd. Lyon-Paris, Emmanuel Vitte, 1957. 227 pp.

1st ed. 1942.
Also in Spanish translation: Buenos Aires, 1953.
Somewhat dated.

1.3.19 Lalande, André. Vocabulaire technique et critique de la philosophie. 10. éd. Paris, Presses Universitaires de France, 1967. 1324 pp.

1st ed., in parts, 1902-22.
French terminology with Greek, Latin, German, English, and Italian definitions.
Excellent, but no bibliography. The best of the French philosophical dictionaries.

1.3.20 La philosophie. Les idées, les oeuvres, les hommes. Paris, Centre d'Etude et de Promotion de la Lecture, 1969. 544 pp.

A dictionary of contemporary philosophy. Index of English terms with their French equivalents.

1.3.21 Legrand, Gérard. Dictionnaire de philosophie. Paris, Bordas (Coll. Hippo-Bordas), 1973. 271 pp.

1.3.22 Voltaire, François Marie Arouet de. Dictionnaire philosophique, comprenant les 118 articles parus sous ce titre du vivant de Voltaire, avec leurs suppléments parus dans les Questions sur l'Encyclopédie. Avec introduction, variants et notes par Julien Benda. Paris, Garnier, 1936. 2v.

The best of the many varying editions. *See* 1.3.11.

German

1.3.23 Apel, Max. Philosophisches Wörterbuch. Berlin, de Gruyter, 1958. 5 völlig neubearbeitete von Peter Ludz. 315 pp.

1st ed. 1930.
Includes some short bibliographies.

1.3.24 **Austeda, Franz.** Wörterbuch der Philosophie. 2 Aufl. Berlin und München, Lebendiges Wissen, 1962. 270 pp.

1st ed., *Kleines Wörterbuch der Philosophie,* 1954.
Contains short articles and biographical sketches.

1.3.25 **Brugger, Walter.** Philosophisches Wörterbuch. 13., uberarb. u. erw. Aufl. Freiburg, Herder, 1967. 578 pp.

1st ed. 1948.
Spanish translation: Barcelona, 1953; Italian translation: Turin, 1961.
Explanations of terms, bibliographies, and a historical survey of philosophy.

1.3.26 **Eisler, Rudolf.** Handwörterbuch der Philosophie. 2. Aufl. neuhrsg. von R. Müller-Freienfels. Berlin, Mittler, 1922. 785 pp.

1st ed. 1913.
Neudr. Mikro-Aufg.: Dusseldorf, Microbuch und Film Gessels., 1949.
A condensation of 1.3.27. Gives bibliographical references.

1.3.27 **Eisler, Rudolf.** Wörterbuch der philosophischen Begriffe. 4. Aufl. Berlin, Mittler, 1927-30. 3v.

1st ed. of Vol. I, 1889.
Vols. II and III completed by K. Roetz. Will be superseded by 1.3.30.
Comprehensive, with good bibliographies. One of the better philosophical dictionaries. Revised and updated by 1.3.34.

1.3.28 **Das Fischer Lexikon,** Enzyklopädie des Wissens. Bd. II, Philosophie. Hrsg. von Alwin Diemer und Ivo Frenzel. Frankfurt und Hamburg, Fischer, 1958. 376 pp.

A collection of 26 articles on broad topics. See 1.3.7.

1.3.29 **Herders kleines philosophisches Wörterbuch.** Hrsg. von Max Muller und A. Halder. 7. Aufl. Freiburg in Br., Herder, 1965. 206 pp.

1st ed. 1958.
Contains a bibliographical appendix and some biographical articles.

1.3.30 **Historisches Wörterbuch der Philosophie.** Basel, Benno Schwabe, Vol. 1, 1971- .

9 or 10v. projected.
4v. to date. An important scholarly work in the history of technological terms and ideas in the German language.
A new edition of 1.3.27.

1.3.31 **Hoffmeister, Johannes.** Wörterbuch der philosophischen Begriffe. 2. Aufl. Hamburg, Meiner, 1955. 687 pp.

1st ed. 1944.
A revised edition of a work edited by Friedrich Kirchner and Carl Michaelis, 1st ed. 1886; 6th ed., by C. Michaelis, 1911.
Includes terms, concepts, and some bibliography; no biography.

1.3.32 **Klaus, Georg,** und **Manfred Buhr.** Philosophsiches Wörterbuch. 6., überarb. u. erw. Aufl. Berlin, Das Europäische Buch, 1969. 2v. 1221 pp.

1st ed. 1964.
Includes terms, categories, concepts. Marxist-Leninist in orientation.

1.3.33 **Neuhäusler, Anton Otto.** Grundbegriffe der philosophischen Sprache. München, Ehrenwirth, 1963. 275 pp.

Brief bibliographies after each article.

1.3.34 **Ritter, Joachim.** Historisches Wörterbuch der Philosophie. Basel and Stuttgart, Schwabe, 1971- . 8v. projected.

"Completely revised edition of Eisler's *Wörterbuch der philosophischen Begriffe*— successor of the 3 vol. work, 4th ed. 1927-30 (1.3.27). Philosophical concepts, including terminology from various branches of the sciences relevant to philosophy, numerous concepts from Asiatic thought, psychology, mathematical logic, theory of sets, cybernetics, information theory." When completed, will be the most comprehensive in any language.

1.3.35 Rothacker, Erich. Archiv für Begriffsgeschichte; Bausteine zu einem historischen Wörterbuch der Philosophie. Bonn, H. Bouvier, 1955- .

In progress. Vols. II, Part II (1958), III (1958), IV (1959), V (1960), VII (1962), VIII (1963) have already appeared.
Encyclopedic in scope and execution.

1.3.36 Schmidt, Heinrich. Philosophisches Wörterbuch. 18. Aufl., neubearb. von Georgi Schischkoff. Stuttgart, Kröner, 1969. 690 pp.

1st ed. 1912.
Treats concepts and philosophers (biographies and bibliographies) in alphabetical order.
A widely used German work.

Italian

1.3.37 Abbagnano, Nicola. Dizionario di filosofia. Ristampa riveduta. Torino, Unione Tipografico-Editrice Torinese, 1968. 908 pp.

The best of the Italian philosophic dictionaries.

1.3.38 Biraghi, A. Dizionario di filosofia. Milano, Communita, 1956. 787 pp.

Includes a dictionary of Greek and German terms.

1.3.39 Dizionario dei filosofi (a cura del) Centro di studi filosofici di Gallarate. Firenze, Sansoni, 1976. 1301 pp.

1.3.40 Lamanna, Eustachio Paolo, e Francesco Adorno. Dizionario di termini filosofici. 9 ed. Firenze, Le Monnier, 1960. 104 pp.

1st ed. 1951.
Entries are very brief.

1.3.41 Miano, V. (in collaborazione con alcuni professori). Dizionario filosofico. Torino, Società Editrice Internazionale, 1952. 693 pp.

Thomistic in orientation.

1.3.42 Ranzoli, Cesare. Dizionario di scienze filosofiche. 5. ed. augmentata e rev. da Maria Pigatti Ranzoli. Milano, Hoepli, 1952. 1313 pp.

1st ed. 1905.
Updated periodically.

1.3.43 Semprini, Giovanni. Nuovo dizionario di coltura filosofica e scientifica. Torino, Società Editrice Internazionale, 1951. 470 pp.

Primary emphasis is on philosophy.

Russian

1.3.44 Blauberg, I. V., P. V. Kopnin, i I. K. Pantin. Kratkii slovar' po filosofii. Moskva, Izd. politicheskoi literatury, 1966. 359 pp.

Marxist-Leninist in orientation.

1.3.45 Rozental', M. M., i P. F. Iudin. Kratkii filosofskii slovar'. 5 izd. Moskva, Gos. Izd. politicheskoi literatury, 1955. 567 pp.

1st ed. 1939.
English adaptation by Howard Selsam, New York, International Publishers, 1949, 128 pp. Also translated into many other languages.
Marxist-Leninist orientation of the Stalinist era.
Superseded by 1.3.46.

1.3.46 Rozental', M. M., i P. F. Iudin. Filosofskii slovar'. Moskva, Izd. politicheskoi literatury, 1963. 544 pp.

English translation and adaptation by R. R. Dixon and M. Saifulin, Moscow, Progress Publishers, 1967, 494 pp.

Spanish

1.3.47 Ferrater Mora, José. Diccionario de filosofía. 5. ed. Buenos Aires, Editorial Sudamericana, 1965. 2v.

1st ed. 1941.
Covers concepts, movements, schools, and persons. Bibliographies.

Reliable and useful, one of the better philosophical dictionaries.

1.3.48 Menchaca, José A. Diccionario bio-bibliográfico de filósofos. (Publicaciones de la Universidad de Deusto. Sección de Filosofía). Bilbao, El Mensajero del Corazón de Jesus, 1965- .

1.3.49 Pallares, Eduardo. Diccionario de filosofía. México, Editorial Porrúa, 1964. 652 pp.

Bibliography: pp. 641-52.

1.3.50 Zaragüeta Bengoechea, Juan. Vocabulario filosófico. Madrid, Espasa-Calpe, 1955. 571 pp.

Usually indicates German, French, English, and Italian equivalents.
Generally scholastic in orientation.

1.4 GENERAL PHILOSOPHICAL ENCYCLOPEDIAS

For an historical and detailed review of philosophical encyclopedias, see William Gerber's article "Philosophical Dictionaries and Encyclopedias" in the *Encyclopedia of Philosophy* (1.4.1), Vol. VI, pp. 170-99.

1.4.1 Encyclopedia of philosophy. Ed. in chief, Paul Edwards. New York, Macmillan and Free Press, 1967. 8v.

Contains 1450 articles, written by 500 scholars from 24 nations. An excellent source for almost any topic in philosophy. Detailed and annotated bibliographies follow each article.
The best single reference book in philosophy.

1.4.2 Encyclopaedia of religion and ethics. Ed. by James Hastings. Edinburgh, Clark, 1908-26. 12v. and Index.

Reprinted: N. Y., Scribner, 1955.
Aims "at containing articles on every religious belief or custom, and on every ethical movement, every philosophical idea, every moral practice" (p. v). Bibliographies.
An excellent reference work, despite its age.

1.4.3 Grooten, J. and G. Jo. Steenbergen. The new encyclopedia of philosophy (trans. from the Dutch and ed. by Edmond Den Bossche). New York, Philosophical Library, 1972. 468 pp.

German

1.4.4 Krings, H., H. M. Baumgartner, and Ch. Wild. Handbuch philosophischer Grundbegriffe. München, Kosel, 1973. 3v.

Italian

1.4.5 Enciclopedia filosofica. 2. ed. interamente rielaborata. Firenze, Sansoni, 1968-69. 6v.

1st ed. 1957-58.
An excellent reference work on philosophers and philosophy. International bibliographies.
A German revised edition, *Lexikon der Philosophie,* ed. by W. Brugger, H. G. Gadamer, R. Guardini, H. Kuhn, and L. Landgrebe, Freiburg, Herder, 1969- , is also in progress.

Russian

1.4.6 Filosofskaia entsiklopediia. Moskva, "Sovetskaia Entsiklopediia," 1960-70. 5v.

Bibliographies.
Marxist-Leninist in orientation.

2. PHILOSOPHICAL BIOGRAPHIES AND COLLECTIONS

The biographies of the more important figures in the history of philosophy are usually available in the major encyclopedias or histories of philosophy. In many cases the biography is available in book form, and such entries are listed in this volume under the individual philosopher's name. But it is often difficult to find biographical information for relatively minor figures or for contemporary or near-contemporary philosophers. General and philosophical biographies help supply this information. Philosophical directories supply the smallest amount of information, but are the most inclusive of the biographical sources. The *Directory of American Philosophers* (2.1.1) is especially useful in locating contemporary American philosophers and in learning something about the philosophy department of a given university.

The philosophical collections listed in 2.2 are some of the larger libraries in philosophy and some of the general published collections. In addition to these, special collections and centers are listed under the appropriate sections in other portions of this book.

2.1 PHILOSOPHICAL BIOGRAPHIES

2.1.1 **Directory of American philosophers**, 1978-79. Ninth ed. Ed. Archie J. Bahm. Bowling Green, Philosophy Documentation Center, 1978.

Revised every two years.
Covers U. S. and Canada. Information on philosophy department faculties; names, addresses and specialties of philosophers; data on colleges and universities, philosophical societies, centers, institutes, journals, publishers, fellowships, and assistantships; and statistics on the profession.
A companion volume to 2.1.3.

2.1.2 **Directory of American scholars**; a biographical dictionary. 6th ed. Ed. by the Jacques Cattel Press, Inc. New York, Bowker, 1974. 4v.

Vol. IV, Philosophy, Religion and Law,

includes some 6800 biographies. It lists name, personal data, education, positions, society memberships, research, publications, and address. Extremely useful for finding information on a large number of contemporary American philosophers.

2.1.3 **International directory of philosophy and philosophers**, 1978-81. 4th ed. Ed. by Gilbert Varet, Ramona Cormier, Richard H. Lineback, and Paul Kurtz. Bowling Green, Philosophy Documentation Center, 1978.

Covers Europe, Central and South America, Asia, Africa, and Australia. Provides names, addresses and specialties of philosophers; data on colleges, universities, philosophical societies, philosophical institutes, philosophical journals, and publishers of philosophical works.
A companion volume to 2.1.1.

2.1.4 **Kiernan, Thomas P.** Who's who in the

history of philosophy. New York, Philosophical Library, 1965. 185 pp.

"The ultimate design of this book is to acquaint rather than instruct the reader" (p. v).

2.1.5 Lewes, George Henry. A biographical history of philosophy. London, Routledge, 1900. 656 pp.

1st ed. 1845-51.

2.1.6 Runes, Dagobert D. Pictorial history of philosophy. Paterson, N. J., Littlefield Adams, 1959. 406 pp.

Includes biographical sketches of hundreds of philosophers, and nearly 1000 photographs and drawings.

2.1.7 Runes, D. D. Who's who in philosophy. New York, Philosophical Library, 1942. 243 pp.

Includes only Anglo-American philosophers.

2.1.8 Thomas, Henry. Biographical encyclopedia of philosophy. Garden City, N. Y., Doubleday, 1965. 273 pp.

Short biographical sketches; no bibliographies.

2.1.9 Thomas, Henry, and **Dana Lee Thomas.** Living biographies of great philosophers. Freeport, N. Y., Books for Libraries Press, 1972. 335 pp.

1st printing 1941.

2.1.10 Urmson, J. O., *ed.* The concise encyclopedia of Western philosophy and philosophers. *See* 1.3.10.

Bibliography: pp. 421-31.

2.1.11 Directory of women in philosophy, 1976-77. Ed. by Caroline Whitbeck. Bowling Green, Philosophy Documentation Center, 1977.

Lists basic information on women in philosophy and provides an index of registrants by field of specialization.

See also: 3.1.3, 16.1.2.

French

2.1.12 Dictionnaire des philosophes. Paris, Seghers, 1962. 376 pp.

2.1.13 Palharies, Fortune. Vies et doctrines des grands philosophes à travers les âges. Paris, Lamore, 1928-29. 3v.

German

2.1.14 Decurtins, Carl. Kleines Philosophenlexikon, von den Vorsokratikern bis zur Gegenwart. Affoltern, Aehren, 1952. 312 pp.

2.1.15 Eisler, Rudolf, *ed.* Philosophen-Lexikon: Leben, Werken und Lehren der Denker. Berlin, Mittler und Sohn, 1912.

Special emphasis on German philosophy.

2.1.16 Ziegenfuss, Werner. Philosophen-Lexikon; Handwörterbuch der Philosophie nach Personen. Unter Mitwerk von Gertrud Jung, verf. u. hersg. von Werner Ziegenfuss. Berlin, de Gruyter, 1949-50. 2v.

Biographies and short bibliographies of works of and about philosophers. Includes some contemporary philosophers. The best known of the philosophical biographies.
Replaces earlier biographies by Eisler and Hauer.

Spanish

2.1.17 Menchaca, José A. Diccionario bio-bibliográfico de filósofos. Bilbao, El Mensajero del Corazón de Jesus, 1965- .

In progress.

For each author: biographical note, bibliographies in which he is listed, list of author's writings and their translations, and list of studies on the author.

2.2 PHILOSOPHICAL COLLECTIONS

2.2.1 The Hoose Library of Philosophy. University of Southern California, Los Angeles. Catalog of the Hoose Library of Philosophy. Boston, G. K. Hall, 1968. 6v.

37,000 vols. The Library is strongest in German and classical philosophy, but all fields of philosophy are covered.

2.2.2 The Husserl Archive. *See* 5.2.107.

2.2.3 Library of the Pontifical Institute of Medieval Studies. Toronto. Dictionary catalogue of the Library of the Pontifical Institute of Medieval Studies. Boston, G. K. Hall, 1972.

83,000 entries. In addition to early printed volumes and facsimile manuscripts there are manuscripts on microfilm drawn from more than 160 different libraries.

2.2.4 Monastic Manuscript Microfilm Library. St. John's Abbey and University, Collegeville, Minnesota.

Contains microfilm of the manuscript collections of 36 monasteries and other non-monastic institutions. A numerical checklist is available from the Library's curator.

2.2.5 Open Court Archives of Philosophy. Morris Library, Southern Illinois University.

60,000 letters and manuscript pages. Dr. Paul Carus, former editor of the Open Court, and his associates conducted voluminous correspondence with philosophers, scientists, and men of letters throughout the world; the Archives offer a major source for the historical study of philosophy from 1888 to 1920. Archivist Kenneth Duckett is in charge of organizing the papers and making them available for use to all qualified scholars without regard to university affiliation.

2.2.6 Russell Archives. McMaster University, Hamilton, Ontario. Detailed catalogue of the Archives of Bertrand Russell. 343 pp.

Also publishes a journal (6.2.83).

2.2.7 Edwards, Paul, and **Richard H. Popkin,** *general eds.* Readings in the history of philosophy. New York, Free Press, 1966-69. 7v.

A collection of writings of philosophers:
Vol. 1, Thales to Aristotle;
vol. 2, Greek and Roman philosophy after Aristotle;
vol. 3, Medieval philosophy;
vol. 4, The philosophy of the 16th and 17th centuries;
vol. 5, 18th century philosophy;
vol. 6, 19th century philosophy;
vol. 7, 20th century philosophy: the analytic tradition.

II
The History of Philosophy: Sources

3. ANCIENT PHILOSOPHY

This chapter is divided into three sections. 3.1 lists the general histories, bibliographies and dictionaries dealing with this period. Some excellent works dealing with this period are part of larger collections dealing with the whole of the history of philosophy. These works are referenced in the "See also" annotations.

The Presocratic philosophers form the subject of 3.2.

Section 3.3 contains information on individual ancient philosophers, who are listed in alphabetical order. All of the items dealing with a given philosopher have been grouped together under his name.

For some major philosophers there are several different collections of their complete works and care should be taken to use the most accurate, which is often the most recent. Critical editions note variant readings, anomalies in the text, and so on. "Complete works" should be distinguished from "collected works" (which make no claim to completeness), and both of these should be distinguished from "selected works." Any of these, as well as individual works, may be "critical editions." A "standard" text or edition is the one generally cited in secondary sources.

3.1 GENERAL: HISTORIES, BIBLIOGRAPHIES, DICTIONARIES

Histories

3.1.1 **Armstrong, Arthur Hilary,** ed. The Cambridge history of later Greek and early medieval philosophy. Cambridge, The University Press, 1967. 711 pp.

A scholarly work by eight contributors covering a period from the 4th century B. C. to the beginning of the 12th centruy A. D.
Bibliography: pp. 670-91.

3.1.2 **Burnet, John.** Early Greek philosophy. *See* 3.2.2.

3.1.3 **Diogenes Laertius.** Lives of eminent philosophers, with an English translation by R. D. Hicks. Loeb classical library. Cambridge, Mass., Harvard University Press, 1958-59. 2v.

Greek and English on facing pages. First printed 1925.

For a critical edition of the Greek text see, *Diogenes Laertius, Vitae philosophorum; recognovit brevisque adnotatione critica instruxit H. S. Long,* Oxonii, E. Typographeo Clarendoniano, 1964, 2v.

An account, by a third century writer, of the lives and doctrines of the chief Greek philosophers, containing biographical data and fragments of their work, culled primarily from secondary sources.

3.1.4 **Fuller, Benjamin Apthorp Gould.** History of Greek philosophy. New York, Holt, 1923-31. 3v.

Reprinted: Westport, Conn., Greenwood Press.
A general, introductory work.

3.1.5 **Furley, David J.,** and **R. E. Allen.** Studies in presocratic philosophy. Atlantic Highlands, N. J., Humanities Press, 1970-75. 2v.

Vol. I, The beginnings of philosophy, 1970;
vol. II, The eleatics and pluralists, 1975.

3.1.6 Gomperz, Theodor. Greek thinkers; history of ancient philosophy. New York, Scribner's, 1901-12. 4v.

Reprinted: N. Y., Humanities Press, 1955. A translation of *Griechische Denker; eine Geschichte der antiken Philosophie*, Leipzig, Veit, 1893-1909. 3v.

3.1.7 Guthrie, William Keith Chambers. A history of Greek philosophy. Cambridge, The University Press, 1962-78. 5v.

Vol. 1, The earlier presocratics and the Pythagoreans, 1962;
vol. 2, The presocratic tradition from Parmenides to Democritus, 1965;
vol. 3, The fifth-century enlightenment, 1969;
vol. 4, Plato: the man and his dialogues: earlier period, 1975;
vol. 5, The later Plato and the academy, 1975.
Bibliographies at the end of each volume.

3.1.8 Kirk, G. S., and J. E. Raven. The presocratic philosophers. *See* 3.2.5.

3.1.9 Owens, Joseph. A history of ancient Western philosophy. New York, Appleton-Century-Crofts, 1959. 434 pp.

Includes bibliography.

3.1.10 Robinson, John Mansley. An introduction to early Greek philosophy; the chief fragments and ancient testimony with connecting commentary. Boston, Houghton Mifflin, 1968. 339 pp.

Includes a bibliographical essay and notes on sources.

3.1.11 Zeller, Eduard. A history of Greek philosophy from the earliest period to the time of Socrates. Trans. by S. F. Alleyne. London, Longmans, Green, 1881. 2v.

Translation of the first part of *Die Philosophie der Griechen* (3.1.18).

3.1.12 Zeller, Eduard. Outlines of the history of Greek philosophy. 13th rev. ed. Trans. by L. R. Palmer. New York, Meridian, 1955. 349 pp.

1st American ed. 1931; 1st German ed. 1883; 13th ed. 1928.
A translation of *Grundriss der Geschichte der griechischen Philosophie*.

See also: 1.1.1, 1.1.2, 1.1.3, 1.1.6, 1.1.7, 10.5.44.

French

3.1.13 Revel, Jean-François. Histoire de la philosophie occidentale (Coll. Livre de poche). Paris, Librairie Générale Française, 1975. 2v.

Vol. 1, Penseurs grecs et latins;
vol. 2, La philosophie classique. Humanistes et cartésiens.

3.1.14 Rivaud, Albert. Les grands courants de la pensée antique. 4. éd. Paris, Colin, 1941. 220 pp.

1st ed. 1929.

See also: 1.1.13-1.1.17.

German

3.1.15 Capelle, Wilhelm. Die griechische Philosophie. New York and Berlin, de Gruyter, 1971. 2v.

Vol. 1, Von Thales bis zum Tode Platons;
vol. 2, Von den Sokratikern bis zur hellenistischen Philosophie .

3.1.16 Diels, Hermann. Kleine Schriften zur Geschichte der antiken Philosophie. Hrsg. von Walter Burkert. Hildesheim, Olms, 1969. 467 pp.

3.1.17 Kranz, Walther. Die griechische Philosophie. 4 Aufl. Brême, Schünemann, 1958. 353 pp.

1st ed. 1950.

3.1.18 **Zeller, Eduard.** Die Philosophie der Griechen in ihrer geschichtlichen Entwicklung. 7 Aufl. Leipzig, Reisland, 1920-23. 3v. in 6.

Reprinted: Hildesheim, Olms, 1963. 1st ed. 1844-52.
English translation: *Philosophy of the Greeks*, trans. by S. F. Alleyne and others, 1881-88, 9v. *See also* 3.1.11.
Ample bibliographical notes.

See also: 1.1.18, 1.1.19.

Italian

3.1.19 **Zeller, Eduard,** and **R. Mondolfo.** La filosofia dei greci nel suo sviluppo storico. 5. ed. Firenze, La Nuova Italia, 1961. 4v.

Monumental, with many references.

See also: 1.1.20.

Bibliographies

3.1.20 **L'année philologique:** bibliographie critique et analytique de l'antiquité gréco-latine. Paris, Soc. d'Edit. Vol. 1, (1924)-to date. Continues 3.1.26.

An annotated index. Includes references to works on philosophy.

3.1.21 **Bibliography on the survival of the classics.** Ed. by the Warburg Institute. London, Warburg Institute, 1934-38. 2v.

3.1.22 **Engelmann, W. V.** Bibliotheca scriptorum classicorum . . . 1700-1878. 8. Aufl. Leipzig, Engelmann, 1880-82. 2v.

Reprinted: Hildesheim, Olms, 1959.
Bibliography of editions, translations, and commentaries.
Continued by 3.1.23.

3.1.23 **Klussmann, Rudolf.** Bibliotheca scriptorum classicorum et graecorum et latinorum. Die Literatur von 1878-1896. Leipzig, Reisland, 1909-13. 2v. in 4.

Reprinted: Hildesheim, Olms, 1961.
Continued by 3.1.25.

3.1.24 **Kristeller, Paul Oskar,** ed. in chief. Catalogus translationum et commentariorum; Medieval and Renaissance Latin translations and commentaries. Annotated lists and guides. Washington, D. C. Catholic University of America Press, Vol. I (1960); vol. II (1971).

Lists and describes the Latin translations of ancient Greek authors and the Latin commentaries on ancient Latin and Greek authors up to 1600.

3.1.25 **Lambrino, Scarlat.** Bibliographie de l'antiquité classique de 1896 à 1914. Paris, Soc. d'Edit. "Les Belles Lettres," 1951- .

In progress.
Vol, 1, "Auteurs et textes"; vol. 2, "Matières et disciplines," has not appeared.
Continued by 3.1.26.

3.1.26 **Marouzeau, J.** Dix années de bibliographie classique, bibliographie critique et analytique de l'antiquité gréco-latine pour la période 1914-1924. Paris, Soc. d'Edit. "Les Belles Lettres," 1927-28. 2v.

Reprinted: N. Y., Burt Franklin, 1969.
Vol. 1, "Auteurs et textes"; vol. 2, "Matières et disciplines."
Continued by 3.1.20.

3.1.27 **Mondolfo, Rodolfo.** Guia bibliográfica de la filosofía antigua. Buenos Aires, Editorial Losada, 1959. 102 pp.

See also: 1.2.11, 1.2.16 (No. 5), 1.2.20.

Dictionaries and Encyclopedias

3.1.28 **Goclenius, Rudolf.** Lexicon philosophicum quo tamquam clave philosophiae fores aperiuntur. Marburg, Rudolf Hutwelcker, 1615. 2v.

Reprinted: Hildesheim, Olms, 1964.
Latin definitions and explanations of Greek terms. Still useful.

3.1.29 **Peters, Francis E.** Greek philosophical terms: a historical lexicon. New York, New York University Press, 1967. 234 pp.

Includes translations, definitions, and references to use by specific philosophers; it has an English-Greek index with cross-references, making knowledge of Greek unnecessary for its use.

3.1.30 **Schwartz, George T.** Index zu philosophischen Problemen in der klassischen griechischen Literatur. Bern, Francke Verlag, 1956. 109 pp.

Gives references to pre-Aristotelian Greek literature and philosophy.

See also: 10.2.9, 12.1.43.

3.2 PRESOCRATICS

3.2.1 **Diels, Hermann.** Die Fragmente der Vorsokratiker. 12. Aufl. hrsg. von Walther Kranz. Zürich, Weidmann, 1966-67. 3v.

Greek texts with German translations.
This is the standard collection and best edition of the fragments of the Presocratics. Vol. 3 is a *Wort-index*, by W. Kranz.

Translations and Commentaries

3.2.2 **Burnet, John.** Early Greek philosophy. 4th ed. London, Macmillan, 1930. 375 pp.

Reprinted: N. Y., Meridian, 1957. London, A. & C. Black, 1975. 1st ed. 1892.
Translations and commentaries. A basic and standard reference work.

3.2.3 **Freeman, Kathleen.** Ancilla to the Pre-Socratic philosophers; a complete translation of the fragments in Diels' *Fragmente der*

Vorsokratiker (3.2.1). Cambridge, Mass., Harvard University Press, 1948. 162 pp.

3.2.4 **Freeman, Kathleen.** The Pre-Socratic philosophers; a companion to Diels, *Fragmente der Vorsokratiker* (3.2.1). Cambridge, Mass., Harvard University Press, 1947. 486 pp.

Gives first a summary of what is known of the life, then of the teaching of each thinker, with references for every statement made.

3.2.5 **Kirk, G. S.,** and **J. E. Raven.** The Presocratic philosophers; a critical history with a selection of texts. Cambridge, The University Press, 1962. 486 pp.

Selected quotations in Greek and English with scholarly interpretations and discussions. It contains the most important texts. Bibliography: pp. 446-49.

See also: 14.3.3.

Bibliography

3.2.6 **Mourelatos, Alexander Phoebus Dionysiou,** *ed.* Pre-Socratics; a collection of critical essays. New York, Doubleday, 1974. 559 pp.

Bibliography: pp. 527-42.

3.3 INDIVIDUAL PHILOSOPHERS, ALPHABETICALLY FROM ARISTOTLE TO SEXTUS EMPIRICUS (COLLECTED AND STANDARD WORKS, BIBLIOGRAPHIES, BIOGRAPHIES)

Aristotle
(384-322 B. C.)

Bibliography

3.3.1 **Cranz, Ferdinand E.,** *ed.* A Bibliography of Aristotle Editions: 1502-1600. Baden-Baden, Koerner, 1971. 187 pp.

3.3.2 **Lacombe, Georgius.** Aristoteles Latinus. Roma, La Libreria dello stato, 1939. 763 pp.

Reprinted: Cambridge, The University Press, 1955. Paris and Bruges, de Brouwer, 1957.
Lists locations of extant manuscripts.

3.3.3 **Mioni, Elpidio.** Aristotelis codices graeci qui in bibliothecis venetis adservantur. Miscellanea erudita, vol. VI. Patavii, In Aedibus Antenoreis, 1958. 162 pp.

3.3.4 **Moraux, Paul.** Les listes anciennes des ouvrages d'Aristote. Louvain, Editions universitaires de Louvain, 1951. 391 pp.

3.3.5 **Schwab, Moïse.** Bibliographie d'Aristote. Paris, Welter, 1896. 380 pp.

Reprinted: Dubuque, Iowa, W. C. Brown, and N. Y., Burt Franklin.

See also: 1.2.16 (No. 8), and 1.2.5, pp. 7-11.

Dictionary and Index

3.3.6 **Bonitz, Hermanus.** Index Aristotelicus. Vol. 5 of 3.3.11.

Reprinted separately: Berlin, de Gruyter, 1961. 878 pp.
A complete concordance of the Greek texts.

3.3.7 **Kappes, Matthias.** Aristoteles-lexicon, erklaerung der philosophischen termini technici des Aristoteles in alphabetischer reihenfolge. Paderborn, F. Schöningh, 1894. 70 pp.

Reprinted: N. Y., Burt Franklin.
"Valuable adjunct to Bonitz's *Index Aristotelicus* (3.3.6) (1870) which is a concordance, not a lexicon explaining technical terms."

3.3.8 **Kiernan, Thomas P.** Aristotle dictionary. New York, Philosophical Library, 1962. 524 pp.

Lists each subject word in English, with references to the Greek text.
Based on 3.3.11.

3.3.9 **Delatte, Louis, Christian Rutten, Suzanne Govaerts,** and **Joseph Denooz.** La métaphysique d'Aristote, index verborum, listes de fréquences, relevés statistiques. Hildesheim, Olms, 1977.

Contains an index of words and a frequency list; an index of philosophical terms and of co-occurrences with other terms, and their frequencies; also other frequency lists.

3.3.10 **Organ, Troy W.** An index to Aristotle in English translation. Princeton, Princeton University Press, 1949. 181 pp.

Reprinted: N. Y., Gordian Press, 1966.
Based on 3.3.12.

Works

3.3.11 **Aristotelis opera.** I. Bekker (ed.). Berlin, Prussian Academy, 1831-70.

This is the edition usually cited in scholarly works. Vol. 5 includes the *Index Aristotelicus* (3.3.6). A new edition of vols. I, II, IV, and V, ed. by Olof Gigon, was printed: Berlin, de Gruyter, 1960-61.
See also: 3.3.8.

3.3.12 **The works of Aristotle**; translated into English. Ed. by J. A. Smith and W. D. Ross. Oxford, The University Press, 1908-52. 12v.
See also: 3.3.10 and 3.3.13.

3.3.13 **The basic works of Aristotle.** Ed. by Richard McKeon. New York, Random House, 1941. 1487 pp.

Includes the Oxford translation (3.3.12) of the major works in their entirety, and selections from minor works.
Bibliography: pp. xxxv-xxxix.

3.3.14 **Aristotle.** Works. Loeb classical library. Cambridge, Mass., Harvard University Press, 1933-69. 23v.

Greek and English on facing pages.

See also: 10.5.48, 10.5.53.

Biography

3.3.15 Chroust, Anton-Hermann. Aristotle: new light on his life and on some of his lost works. Notre Dame, Ind., University of Notre Dame Press; and London, Routledge & Kegan Paul, 1973. 2v.

Vol. I, Some novel interpretations of the man and his life, 441 pp.
vol. II, Observations on some of Aristotle's lost works, 488 pp.

3.3.16 Jaeger, Werner. Aristotle; fundamentals of the history of his development. Trans. by Richard Robinson. 2nd enlg. ed. Oxford, Clarendon Press, 1948. 475 pp.

"Still the best" (L. R. Lind in *Classical Journal*, XXXI).

3.3.17 Randall, John Herman, Jr. Aristotle. New York and London, Columbia University Press, 1962. 309 pp.

"I have no hesitation in saying that Professor Randall's new book is the most important work on Aristotle published since the publication of Jaeger's work in 1923" (Sir W. D. Ross in *Philosophical Review*).

Epictetus
(c. 50-c. 130)

Bibliography

3.3.18 Oldfather, William Abbott. Contributions toward a bibliography of Epictetus. Urbana, University of Illinois Press, 1927. 201 pp.

See also: A Supplement, ed. by Marian Harman, with a preliminary list of Epictetus manuscripts by W. H. Friedrich and C. U. Faye, Urbana, University of Illinois Press, 1952, 177 pp.

Works

3.3.19 Epictetus. Trans. by W. A. Oldfather. Loeb classical library. Cambridge, Mass., Harvard University Press. 2v.

1st published, 1926-28.
Text with English translations. For the works of Epictetus see also the edition by H. Schenkl, Leipzig, Teubner, 1916, 740 pp.

Epicurus
(341-270 B. C.)

Bibliography

3.3.20 De Lacy, Phillip. "Some Recent Publications on Epicurus and Epicureanism (1937-1954)," Classical Weekly, XLVIII (1955), 169-77.

Works

3.3.21 Epicurea. Edidit H. Usener. Leipzig, Teubner, 1887. 445 pp.
Text and commentary. Standard edition.

3.3.22 Epicurus, the extant remains with short critical apparatus, translation and notes. Ed. by C. Bailey. Oxford, Clarendon Press, 1926. 432 pp.

Greek texts with English translations. The Bailey translation is also available in W. J. Oates, *The Stoic and Epicurean Philosophers*, New York, Random House, 1957.

Biography

3.3.23 DeWitt, N. W. Epicurus and his philosophy. Minneapolis, University of Minnesota Press, 1954. 388 pp.

"A sympathetic and at times extravagant account, emphasizing Epicurus' saintly character and his opposition to Platonism" (P. H. De Lacy in 1.4.1).

Lucretius
(c. 99-55 B. C.)

Bibliography and Index

3.3.24 Gordon, Cosmo Alexander. A bibliography of Lucretius. London, Hart-Davis, 1962. 318 pp.

3.3.25 **Paulson, J.** Index Lucretianus. Gotoburgi, W. Zachrisson, 1911. 177 pp.

Works

3.3.26 **De rerum natura.** Ed. and trans. by C. Bailey. Oxford, Clarendon Press, 1947. 3v.

A critical edition with full English commentary and translation.

Biography

3.3.27 **Regenbogen, Otto.** Lukrez, seine Gestalt in seinem Gedicht. Leipzig und Berlin, B. G. Teubner, 1932. 87 pp.

3.3.28 **Valle, Guido della.** Tito Lucrezio Caro e l'epicureismo Campano. Napoli, 1933. 314 pp.

Marcus Aurelius Antoninus
(121-180)

Works

3.3.29 **Farquharson, Arthur Spenser Loat,** *ed.* The meditations of the Emperor Marcus Antoninus. Oxford, Clarendon Press, 1944. 2v.

A critical edition with English translation. The translation was published separately as *Meditations,* N. Y., Dutton, 1965, 237 pp.

Biography

3.3.30 **Sedgwick, Henry D.** Marcus Aurelius. New Haven, Yale University Press, 1921. 309 pp.

" . . . a useful historical study of his life and times, including an examination of his attitude toward Christianity . . ." (Maxwell Staniforth in 1.4.1).

Plato
(c. 428-347 B. C.)

Bibliography

3.3.31 **Cherniss, H. F.** "Plato Studies, 1950-57," Lustrum, IV (1959), 5-308; V (1960), 323-648.

3.3.32 **McKirahan, Richard D., Jr.** Plato and Socrates; a comprehensive bibliography, 1958-1973. New York, Garland, 1978. 630 pp.

3.3.33 **Plato manuscripts:** a catalogue of microfilms in the Plato microfilm project, Yale University Library. Edited by Robert S. Brumbaugh and Rulon Wells, with the assistance of Donna Scott and Harry V. Botsis. New Haven, Yale University Library, 1962. 2v.

Part I: Mss. in Belgium, Denmark, England, Germany and Italy.
Part II: Mss. in Austria, Czechoslovakia, France, Holland, and Spain; post-1600 mss. in Belgium, Denmark, England, Germany, and Italy; addenda to Part I.

3.3.34 **The Plato manuscripts;** a new index, prepared by the Plato microfilm project of the Yale University Library under the direction of Robert S. Brumbaugh and Rulon Wells. New Haven, Yale University Press, 1968. 163 pp.

Based on the Yale microfilm collection (3.3.33), it lists all the pre-1500 manuscript material held by libraries throughout the world. It includes an Index by Library, an Index by Dialogue, Collations, and a List of Papyri.

3.3.35 **Rosenmeyer, Thomas Gustav.** "Platonic Scholarship, 1945-1955," Classical Weekly, L (1957), 172-182, 197-201, 209-211.

3.3.36 **Sciacca, Michele Federico.** Platone. (Guide bibliografiche.) Milano, Vita e Pensiero, 1945. 58 pp.

See also: 1.2.16 (No. 12).

Dictionaries

3.3.37 **Ast, Fred** (Astius, D. Fredericus). Lexikon Platonicum sive vocum Platonicarum index. Bonn, Habelt, 1956. 3v. in 2. Leipzig, Weidmann, 1835-38. 3v.

Reprinted: N. Y., Burt Franklin.

3.3.38 **Stockhammer, Morris.** Plato dictionary. New York, Philosophical Library, 1963. 287 pp.

Based on the Jowett translation (3.3.42).

Works

3.3.39 **Platonis opera.** Ed. by J. Burnet. Oxford, Clarendon Press, 1899-1906. 5v.

Complete Greek text of Plato's works. The standard, critical edition.
Modern editions refer to the pagination of Plato's works edited by J. Serranus and H. Stephanus, 3v., with Latin translation, Paris, 1578.

3.3.40 **Platon.** Oeuvres complètes. Collection des Universités de France publiée sous le patronage de l'Association Guillaume Budé. Paris, Société d'édition "Les belles lettres," 1920-64. 14v. in 27.

Also published in 12v. in 19, 1951-66.
Greek text and French translation. Editors for individual volumes vary.
The critical apparatus is fuller than that found in 3.3.39.

3.3.41 **Plato.** The collected dialogues of Plato, including the letters. Ed. by Edith Hamilton and Huntington Cairns, with an introduction and prefatory notes. New York, Pantheon Books, 1961. 1743 pp.

Translations are by L. Cooper, B. Jowett, A. E. Taylor, and others.

3.3.42 **The dialogues of Plato.** Trans. by Benjamin Jowett. 4th ed., revised by D. J. Allan and H. E. Dale. Oxford, The University Press, 1952.

1st ed. 1871.
Also published by New York, Random House.
A complete and somewhat poetic translation of the dialogues.

3.3.43 **Plato.** (Selected works.) Trans. by Francis Macdonald Cornford, with running commentaries.

Translations of individual works, including the *Timaeus, Parmenides, Republic, Theaetetus,* and the *Sophist,* in separate volumes.
Publishers vary.

3.3.44 **Plato.** [Selected works.] Trans. by G. M. A. Grube. Indianapolis, Hackett, 1974- .

The Republic, The Trial and Death of Socrates, The Meno, The Phaedo, The Symposium, in separate volumes.

3.3.45 **Plato.** Works. Loeb classical library. Cambridge, Mass., Harvard University Press. 12v.

First published 1921-53.
Greek and English on facing pages.

Biography

3.3.46 **Taylor, A. E.** Plato: the man and his work. London, Methuen, 1926. 522 pp.

The standard reference work in the secondary literature.

3.3.47 **Randall, John Herman, Jr.** Plato: dramatist of the life of reason. New York and London, Columbia University Press, 1970. 274 pp.

A popular account.

See also: 10.5.48, 10.5.53.

Plotinus
(205-270)

Bibliography

3.3.48 **Marien, B.** Bibliografia critica degli studi Plotiniani con rassegna delle loro recensioni, rev. e curata da V. Cilento. Bari, Laterza, 1949. 668 pp.

Pt. 2 of vol. III of the Italian translation of and commentary on the *Enneads* by V. Cilento.
Reprinted separately: Wm. C. Brown, 1949.

Works

3.3.49 Plotini opera. Ediderunt P. Henry et Hans R. Schwyzer. Oxonii, e Typ. Clarendoniano, 1964-73. 3v.

A critical edition which supersedes all other editions.
The preface has a comprehensive bibliography.

3.3.50 Plotinus. With an English translation by A. H. Armstrong. Loeb classical library. Cambridge, Mass., Harvard University Press, 1966- .

In progress.
6v. projected.
Greek and English on facing pages. The Greek text is essentially that of P. Henry and H. R. Schwyzer (3.3.49).

3.3.51 Enneads. Translated by Stephen MacKenna. 4th ed., rev. and enl. by B. S. Page. London, Farber and Farber, 1969. 638 pp.

1st ed. 1927-30. 5v.
English translation without Greek texts.

3.3.52 Ennéades . . . . texte établi et trad. par Emile Bréhier. Paris, Soc. d'édit. "Les Belles Lettres," 1924-38. 6v.

Good for its notes, but not for its Greek text. Pp. 200-97 of vol. VI contain an index of Greek words and an analytic index of subject matter.

3.3.53 O'Brien, Elmer, S. J., *ed.* The essential Plotinus. Indianapolis, Hackett, 1975. 236 pp.

Biography

3.3.54 Turnbull, Grace H., *comp.* The essence of Plotinus; extracts from the six Enneads and Porphyry's life of Plotinus. New York, Oxford University Press, 1934. 303 pp.

Reprinted: Westport, Conn., Greenwood Press, 1976.

Series

3.3.55 Etudes Plotiniennes. Leiden, E. J. Brill.

I. Les états du texte de Plotin. 2e éd., 1961 (réimpression envisagée), 426 pp.;
II. Les manuscrits des Ennéades. 2e éd., 1948, 356 pp.;
III. L'enseignement oral de Plotin sur les catégories d'Aristote d'après Dexippe et Simplicius (in preparation).

Sextus Empiricus
(late 2nd, early 3rd c.)

Works

3.3.56 Sexti Empirici opera. Recensuit H. Mutschmann et J. Mau. Leipzig, Teubner, 1958-62. 4v.

3.3.57 Sextus Empiricus. Trans. by R. G. Bury. Loeb classical library. Cambridge, Mass., Harvard University Press. 4v.

First published 1933-49.
Greek text with English translation.

4. MEDIEVAL AND RENAISSANCE PHILOSOPHY

Listed in 4.1 are not only bibliographies, dictionaries and encyclopedias dealing with medieval and renaissance philosophy but also information about learned societies and journals.

The collections listed in 4.2 are important for the scholar who wishes to go to the original sources. The translated collections should be used with some care. In some cases better translations of an individual work by an individual author are available.

The entries in 4.3 pertain to individual philosophers, listed alphabetically. Individual works in translation are not usually listed. These can often be found by consulting the *Encyclopedia of Philosophy* (1.4.1), histories of philosophy, or the appropriate trade bibliographies (15.3).

4.1 GENERAL: HISTORIES, BIBLIOGRAPHIES, DICTIONARIES

Histories

4.1.1 Gilson, Etienne. History of Christian philosophy in the Middle Ages. New York, Random House, 1955. 829 pp.

Translation of 4.1.8.
A basic reference work. Bibliography, pp. 552-804.

4.1.2 Gilson, Etienne. The spirit of mediaeval philosophy. Trans. by A. H. C. Downes. London, Sheed and Ward, 1936. 490 pp.

Gifford Lectures, 1931-32.
A translation of *L'esprit de la philosophie médiévale*, Paris, Vrin, 1932.

4.1.3 Husik, I. A history of mediaeval Jewish philosophy. New York, Meridian, 1958. 466 pp.

1st ed. 1916.
Bibliography: pp. 433-37.

4.1.4 Kristeller, Paul Oskar. Studies in Renaissance thought and letters. Roma, Edizioni di Storia e Letteratura, 1956. 680 pp.

Bibliography: pp. 591-628.
A collection of essays, rather than a systematic history.

4.1.5 Maurer, Armand. Medieval philosophy. New York, Random House, 1962. 435 pp.

Bibliography and notes: pp. 380-426.

4.1.6 Wolfson, Harry Austryn. The philosophy of the Church Fathers. 3d rev. ed. Cambridge, Mass., Harvard University Press, 1970. 635 pp.

1st ed. 1956.
Includes bibliographies.

4.1.7 Wulf, Maurice de. History of mediaeval philosophy. 3d ed. London, Longmans, Green, 1935-37. 2v.

English translation by E. E. Messenger of first 2v. of 4.1.10.
Reprinted: New York, Dover, 1952-59.
A standard work. Excellent bibliographies.

MEDIEVAL AND RENAISSANCE PHILOSOPHY

See also: 1.1.1-1.1.3, 1.1.7.

French

4.1.8 Gilson, Etienne. La philosophie au moyen âge des origines patristiques à la fin du XIVe siècle. 3. éd. Paris, Payot, 1952. 782 pp.

1st ed. 1922.
Its bibliographies supplement those of de Wulf (4.1.10). *See* 4.1.1.

4.1.9 Vajda, Georges. Introduction à la pensée juive du Moyen Age. (Coll. Etudes de philos. médiév.) Paris, Vrin, 1947. Suppl. bibliog. arrêté en 1975.

4.1.10 Wulf, Maurice de. Histoire de la philosophie médiévale. 6. éd. Louvain, Institut Supérieur de Philosophie, 1934-47. 3v.

Its annotated bibliographies supplement those in Ueberweg (1.1.19).

See also: 1.1.13-1.1.16.

German

4.1.11 Grabmann, Martin. Mittelalterliches Geistesleben; Abhandlungen zur Geschichte der Scholastik und Mystik. München, Max Hueber, 1926-56. 3v.

A standard reference work. Bibliography: v. 3, pp. 10-35.

4.1.12 Grabmann, Martin. Die Geschichte der scholastischen Methode. Freiburg, Herder, 1909-11. 2v.

Reprinted: Basel/Stuttgart, 1961.

4.1.13 Kaulich, Wilhelm. Geschichte der scholastischen philosophie. Prag, F. Tempsky, 1863. 475 pp.

Reprinted: Minerva.

See also: 1.1.19.

Bibliographies

Medieval

4.1.14 Bibliographia patristica; internationale patristiche bibliographie. Berlin, de Gruyter, 1959- . Annual.

Lists works about the early Christian Fathers and related topics from c. 900 journals.

4.1.15 Chevalier, Cyr Ulysses Joseph. Répertoire des sources historiques du Moyen Age. Nouv. éd. Paris, Picard, 1894-1907. 2v. in 4.

Reprinted: N. Y., Kraus, 1960.
Vol. 1, Bio-bibliographie; vol. 2, Topobibliographie.
An important general reference work on the Middle Ages.

4.1.16 Farrar, Clarissa P., and **Austin P. Evans.** Bibliography of English translations from medieval sources. New York, Columbia University Press, 1946. 534 pp.

An annotated list of translations up to 1943 of works produced during the period from Constantine the Great to 1500. Supplemented by 4.1.17.

4.1.17 Ferguson, Mary Anne Heyward, *comp.* Bibliography of English translations from medieval sources, 1943-67. New York, Columbia University Press, 1974. 274 pp.

A supplement to 4.1.16.

4.1.18 McGuire, Martin R. P., and **Hermigild Dressler.** Introduction to Medieval Latin studies: a syllabus and bibliographical guide. 2nd ed. Washington, D. C., Catholic University of America Press, 1977. 406 pp.

1st ed. 1964.

See also: 1.2.16 (No. 17 and 18), 1.2.20, 12.1.18.

Renaissance

4.1.19 Kristeller, Paul Oskar. Catalogus

translationum et commentariorum; medieval and Renaissance Latin translations and commentaries. Annotated lists and guides. Washington, D. C., Catholic University of America Press, 1960- .

In progress.
Lists Latin translations and commentaries of Greek and Latin authors up to 1600.

4.1.20 **Kristeller, Paul Oskar**. Iter Italicum. A finding list of uncatalogued or incompletely catalogued humanistic manuscripts of the Renaissance in Italian and other libraries. London, Warburg Institute, 1965- .

4 or 5v. projected.
Lists philosophical and literary manuscripts of scholars active between 1300 and 1600.

4.1.21 **Kristeller, Paul Oskar**. Latin manuscript books before 1600; a list of printed catalogues and unpublished inventories of extant collections. 3d ed. New York, Fordham University Press, 1965. 284 pp.

4.1.22 **Riedl, John Orth** [et al]. A catalogue of Renaissance philosophers (1350-1650). Milwaukee, Marquette University Press, 1940. 179 pp.

Reprinted: Hildesheim, Olms.

See also: 1.2.20.

Dictionaries and Encyclopedias

4.1.23 **Dictionary catalogue** of the Library of the Pontifical Institute of Mediaeval Studies, Toronto and Boston, G. K. Hall, 1972. 5v.

83,000 entries, L. C. classification "catalogue describing 40,000 monographs, 40,000 microfilm frames, and the contents of 130 different periodicals."

4.1.24 **Du Cange, Charles Du Fresne**, Sieur. Glossarium mediae et infimae latinitatis conditum a Carolo Du Fresne, domino Du Cange; auctum a monachis Ordinis S. Benedicti, cum supplementis integris D. P. Car-

penterii, Adelungii, aliorum, suisque digessit G. A. L. Henschel; sequuntur Glossarium gallicum, Tabulae, Indices auctorum et rerum, Dissertationes. Ed. nova, aucta pluribus verbis aliorum scriptorum a Léopold Favre. Niort, L. Favre, 1883-87. 10v. il.

Reprinted: Paris, Librairie des Sciences et des Arts, 1937-38; Graz, Akademische Druck- & Verlagsanstalt, 1954. 10v.
"The great dictionary of medieval Latin" (Sheehy in 13.1.6).
Supplemented by *Petit Supplément au Dictionnaire de Du Cange* par Charles Schmidt, Strasbourg, Heitz, 1906, 71 pp.

4.1.25 **Michaud-Quantin, Pierre**. Etudes sur le vocabulaire philosophique du Moyen Age. Roma, Edizioni dell'Ateneo, 1970. 253 pp.

Learned Society

4.1.26 **Société Internationale pour l'Etude de la Philosophie Médiévale**. Founded 1959. Bulletin, Sécrétariat de la S. I. E. P. M., Kardinal Mercierplein 2, B-3000, Louvain, Belgique.

Publishes *Le bulletin de philosophie médiévale* (10.5.1).

Journals

4.1.27 **Bulletin de philosophie médiévale**. See 10.5.1.

4.1.28 **Mediaeval studies**. See 10.2.72

4.1.29 **Proceedings of the International Congress of Medieval Philosophy**.

Congresses are sponsored by Société Internationale pour l'étude de la philosophie médiévale (4.1.26).
The Fifth Congress took place in Madrid in 1972.

4.1.30 **Vivarium**. See 10.2.136.

See also: 1.2.4.

4.2 GENERAL COLLECTIONS

4.2.1 Beiträge zur Geschichte der Philosophie und Theologie des Mittelalters, Texte und Untersuchungen. Münster, Aschendorff, 1891- . Neue Folge, 1970- .

In progress.
An important and extensive collection on the philosophy of the Middle Ages. 42v. to date.

4.2.2 Corpus Christianorum. Series Latina. Turnholti, Typographi Brepols, 1953- . Vol. 1- .

In progress.
Critical texts. Designed to replace 4.2.5.

4.2.3 Corpus scriptorum ecclesiasticorum latinorum. Vienna, Hoelder-Pichler-Tempsky; Leipzig, Akademische Verlagsgesellschaft, 1866- .

In progress.
Contains critical editions of selected works of the Latin Fathers. 77v. to 1978.
Johnson Reprint Corp. has reprinted a large part of the series.

4.2.4 Gilson, Etienne, *ed.* Etudes de philosophie médiévale. Paris, 1922-47. 35v.

Monographs on patristic and medieval philosophers, with some critical texts.

4.2.5 Migne, Jacques Paul, *ed.* Patrologiae cursus completus. Series ecclesiae graecae. Paris, J.-P. Migne, 1857-66. 162v.

Works of Greek ecclesiastical writers from 1st to 15th centuries, with Latin translations.
Indices digessit Ferdinandus Cavallera. Paris, Garnier, 1912. 218 pp.

4.2.6 Migne, Jacques Paul, *ed.* Patrologiae cursus completus. Series ecclesiae latinae. Paris, J.-P. Migne, 1844-64. 221v. (of which the last four are indices).

Contains uncritical editions of works of Latin ecclesiastical writers from 2nd through

12th centuries. It is the basic source for this period of medieval philosophy.
Supplementum. A. Hamman, ed. Paris, Garnier, 1958.

Translated Collections

4.2.7 Ancient Christian writers; the works of the Fathers in translation. New York, Newman Press, 1946-78. 40v.

Key selections from the literature of early Christianity in English translation with contemporary commentaries and introductions for each volume.

4.2.8 The Fathers of the church. Ed. dir., Roy J. Defarrari. Washington, D. C., Catholic University of America Press. 1947- .

English translations.
100v. projected of which 67 had appeared by 1978.
The collection was founded by Ludwig Schopp.
Publisher varies.

4.2.9 Mediaeval philosophical texts in translation. Published by Marquette University. 1942-to date. Irregular.

Monograph-length translations.

4.2.10 Select library of Nicene and post-Nicene Fathers. New York, The Christian Literature Co., 1886-1900. 28v.

2 series of 14v. each. English translations with notes.
Reprinted: Grand Rapids, Mich., Eerdmans, 1961.

4.2.11 Hyman, Arthur, and **James J. Walsh,** *eds.* Philosophy in the Middle Ages: the Christian, Islamic and Jewish traditions. New York, Evanston and London, Harper & Row, 1967. 747 pp.

Bibliography: pp. 723-728.
An anthology.

4.2.12 McKeon, Richard., *ed.* and *trans.* Selections from Medieval philosophers. New York, Scribner, 1929-30. 2v.

An anthology.

4.3 INDIVIDUAL PHILOSOPHERS, ALPHABETICALLY FROM ABELARD TO WILLIAM OF OCKHAM (COLLECTED AND STANDARD WORKS, BIBLIOGRAPHIES, BIOGRAPHIES)

Abelard, Peter
(1079-1142)

Works

4.3.1 **Opera omnia.** Accurante J.-P. Migne. Paris, 1855. Vol. CLXXVIII of 4.2.6.

The most complete collection available, but should be used with later, critical editions when possible.

Includes the "biographical" *Historia Calamitatum.*

4.3.2 **Ouvrages inédits d'Abelard.** Publiés par V. Cousin. Paris, Imprimerie royale, 1936. 677 pp.

4.3.3 **Peter Abelards philosophische schriften.** Hrsg. von Bernhard Geyer. Münster, Aschendorff, 1919-33. 4v.

Vol. XXXI, 14 of 4.2.1.
Critical edition of Abelard's logical works.

4.3.4 **Petri Abaelardi opera.** [Accurante] V. Cousin, C. Jourdain et E. Despois. Parisiis, A. Durand, 1849-59. 2v.

Reprinted: Hildesheim, Olms.

4.3.5 **Abailard, Peter.** Sic et non, a critical edition. Ed. by Blanche Boyer and Richard McKeon. Chicago, University of Chicago Press, 1976. 192 pp.

" . . . 84 page introduction on the manuscript tradition and previously printed editions; Abailard's own prologue; and 41 questions (with the remaining 117 questions still to be published . . ." (*Cross Currents*, Spr. 77).

4.3.6 **De Rijk, L. M.,** *ed.* Petrus Abaelardus Dialectica; first complete edition of the Parisian manuscript. 2nd rev. ed. Assen, Van Gorcum, 1970. 623 pp.

Biography

4.3.7 **Remusat, Charles Francois Marie de.** Abelard; sa vie, sa philosophie, et sa théologie. 2. éd. Paris, 1855. 2v.

The most important biography of Abelard.

4.3.8 **Sikes, Jeffrey G.** Peter Abailard. Cambridge, The University Press, 1932.

Albertus Magnus, Saint
(c. 1193-1280)

Bibliography

4.3.9 **Catania, Francis J.** "A bibliography of St. Albert the Great," The modern schoolman, XXXVII (1959), 11-28.

Addenda: XXXIX (1961), pp. 61-64.

4.3.10 **Schooyans, Michel.** "Bibliographie philosophique de saint Albert le grand (1931-1960)," Revista da Universidade Católica de Sao Paulo, XXI (1961), 36-88.

4.3.11 **Weiss, Melchior.** Primordia novae bibliographiae b. Alberti Magni. . . . Edito secunda. Parisiis, Ludovicum Vives, 1905. 120 pp.

4.3.12 **Walz, A.,** and **A. Pelzer.** Bibliographia S. Alberti Magni indagatoris rerum naturalium.

Some 300 studies on various aspects of Albertus Magnus' scientific thought.

See also: 1.2.5, p. 2.

Works

4.3.13 **Alberti Magni . . . Opera omnia.** Münster, Aschendorff, 1951- .

In progress.

40v. projected.

New critical edition of the complete works by the Albertus-Magnus-Institute of Cologne.

Earlier edition of the works edited by P. Jammy, 21 folio volumes, 1651. Reprinted: A. Borgnet. Paris, Vives, 1890-99. 38v.

Biography

4.3.14 **Schwertner, T. M.** St. Albert the Great. New York and Milwaukee, Bruce, 1932. 375 pp.

St. Anselm of Canterbury
(1033-1109)

Works

4.3.15 **Sancti Anselmi** . . . opera omnia. Ad fidem codicum recensuit F. S. Schmitt. Sekau-Rome-Edinburgh, 1938-61. 6v.

Reprinted: Stuttgart, Frommann-Holzboog, 1968-69. 7v. in 2.

The standard, critical edition of Anselm's works. Supersedes the complete works ed. by G. Gerberon (1675) and reproduced in vols. CLVIII-CLIX of 4.2.6.

4.3.16 **Saint Anselm's basic writings.** Trans. by Sidney Deane. 2d ed. La Salle, Ill., Open Court, 1962. 288 pp.

1st ed. 1903

Contains English translations of the *Proslogium, Monologium, Liber pro Insipiente* of Gaulino, and *Cur deus homo.*

Biography

4.3.17 **Southern, Richard William.** St. Anselm and his biographer. Cambridge, The University Press, 1963. 389 pp.

Augustinus, Saint
(354-430)

Bibliography

4.3.18 **Andresen, Carl.** Bibliographia Augustiniana. Darmstadt, Wisseschaftliche Buchgesellschaft. 2. völlig neubearb. Aufl., 1973. 317 pp.

Includes works by and about Augustine. The best of the bibliographies.

For later works see the bibliographical supplements of the *Revue des études augustiniennes* (10.3.14).

4.3.19 **Bavel, Tarsicius van.** Répertoire bibliographique de Saint Augustin 1950-1960. Instrumenta Patristica, vol. III. The Hague, Nijhoff, 1963. 992 pp.

4.3.20 **Institut des études augustiniennes.** Augustine bibliography. (Réproduction des fichiers bibliographiques de l'Institut des Etudes Augustiniennes). Boston, Hall, 1972. 4v.

2 vols., Fichier Auterus; 2 vols., Fichier Matières.

60,000 cards reproduced.

4.3.21 **Nebreda del Cura, Eulogio.** Bibliographia Augustina seu Operum collectio quae divi Augustine vitam et doctrinam quadantenus exponunt. Romae, Typ. Pol. "Cuore de Maria," 1928. 272 pp.

Reprinted: Brown.

A critical bibliography of St. Augustine's works, collected editions, and books about him; indexes.

4.3.22 **Revue des études Augustiniennes** (10.3.14). Carries a running bibliography, "Bulletin Augustinien."

See also: 1.2.16 (No. 10) and 1.2.5, pp. 13-15.

Concordance

4.3.23 **Lenfant, D.** Concordantiae augustinianae. Parisiis, 1656-65. 2v.

Works

4.3.24 **Sancti Aurelii Augustini** . . . opera omnia. Paris, 1679-1700. 11v.

Benedictine edition of the Maurists.
Reprinted in 4.2.6, vols. XXXII-XLVII.
Paris, 1845-49.

This is the basis of a critical edition being published with a French translation in *Bibliothèque augustinienne* (Paris, Desclée de Brouwer).

4.3.25 Oeuvres de Saint Augustin. Paris, Desclée de Brouwer, 1976. 9 series, 72v.

4.3.26 Writings of Saint Augustine. 14v. in 4.2.8.

Includes bibliographies.

4.3.27 Basic writings of Saint Augustine. Ed. by W. J. Oates. New York, Random House, 1948. 2v.

A convenient collection of texts primarily from 4.2.8.

4.3.28 Bourke, Vernon J., *ed.* The essential Augustine. Indianapolis, Hackett, 1974. 274 pp.

Biography

4.3.29 G. Bonner. St. Augustine of Hippo; life and controversies. London, S. C. M. Press; and Philadelphia, Westminster, 1963. 428 pp.

". . . survey and guide to Augustine's career and literary output" (R. A. Markus in 1.4.1).

4.3.30 Brown, P. Augustine of Hippo. A biography. Leiden, E. J. Brill, 1975. 463 pp.

Reprint of the 1969 ed.

4.3.31 Marrou, H.-I. St. Augustin et la fin de la culture antique. Paris, E. de Boccard, 1938. 620 pp.

Retractatio: Paris, 1949.
". . . essential to understanding Augustine in the setting of contemporary education and culture" (R. A. Markus in 1.4.1).

Serials

4.3.32 Augustinian Studies. Vol. 1- , 1970- . Annual publication of the Augustinian Institute, Villanova University, Villanova, Pa. 19085.

4.3.33 Revue des études Augustiniennes. Vol. 1- , 1955- . Quarterly. Paris. Supersedes *Année théologique Augustinienne*, Vol. 1-14 (1940-54).

Averroes
(c. 1126-c. 1198)

Bibliography

4.3.34 Vennebusch, Joachim. "Zur Bibliographie des psychologischen Schriftums des Averroes," Bulletin de Philosophie Médiévale, VI (1964), 92-100.

See 1.2.5, pp. 15-16.

Works

4.2.35 Aristotelis opera cum Averrois commentariis. Venice, 1562-74. 12v.

Reprinted: Frankfurt am Main, 1962.
A Latin translation of Aristotle with commentaries by Averroes.
A new edition is in preparation by the Mediaeval Academy of America. 11v. published by 1978.

4.3.36 Müller, M. J. Philosophie und Theologie von Averroes. München, Franz, 1859-75. 2v.

Arabic text and German translation.

Avicenna
(980-1037)

Bibliography

4.3.37 Anawati, G. C. Essai de bibliographie avicennienne. Cairo, Dar-al-Maaref, 1950. 20 pp. (French text), 31-435 pp. (Arabic text).

Section 4 lists works about Avicenna in languages other than Arabic.

4.3.38 Ergin, Osman. Ibni Sina bibliŏgrafyasi. Bibliographie d'Avicenne. Istanbul, O. Yalçin Matbassi, 1956. 168 pp.

4.3.39 Nafisy, Said. Bibliographie des principaux travaux européens sur Avicenne. Téhéran, Université de Téhéran, 1953. 30 pp.

295 entries.

See also: 1.2.5, pp. 16-17.

Lexicon

4.2.40 Goichon, A.M. Lexique de la langue philosophique d'Ibn Sina (Avicenne). Paris, Desclée de Brouwer, 1938. 496 pp.

Works

4.3.41 Opera philosophica. Venetiis, 1508. 320 pp.

Reprinted: N. Y., Johnson Reprint Co., 1961; Frankfurt, Minerva, 1971-72.

There is no collected edition in the original.

4.3.42 Avicenna Latinus. Edition crit. par S. Van Riet. Introd. G. Verbeke. Leiden, E. J. Brill, 1968- .

3v. projected; v.3 to be a lexicon.

Biography

4.3.43 Afnan, S. M. Avicenna, his life and works. London, Allen and Unwin, 1958. 298 pp.

4.3.44 Gohlman, William E., *ed.* The life of Ibn Sina: a critical edition and annotated translation. Albany, State University of New York Press, 1974. 163 pp.

Bacon, Francis
(1561-1626)

Bibliography

4.3.45 Gibson, Reginald W. Francis Bacon: a bibliography of his works and of Baconiana to the year 1750. Oxford, Scrivener Press, 1950. 369 pp.

4.3.46 Patrick, John Max. Francis Bacon. British Council; British book news; bibliographical series of supplements (no. 131), 1961. 43 pp.

4.3.47 Vickers, Brian. Essential articles for the study of Francis Bacon. London, Sidgwick and Jackson, 1972. 323 pp.

4.3.48 Woodward, Parker. Francis Bacon's works (acknowledged, vizared, or suspected). London, Sweeting, 1912. 105 pp.

Works

4.3.49 The works of Francis Bacon. Collected and ed. by James Spedding, R. L. Ellis and D. D. Heath. London, Longmans, 1857-74. 14v.

Reprinted: Stuttgart, Frommann, 1962.

The last 7v. are *The Letters and Life of Francis Bacon* including all his occasional works.

This is the standard edition of his works.

4.3.50 Robertson, John M., *ed.* Philosophical works of Francis Bacon. Freeport, N.Y., Books for Libraries Press (Library of English Renaissance Literature), 1970. 920 pp.

Reprint of 1905 ed.

Concordance

4.3.51 Davies, David W., and **Elizabeth S. Wrigley,** *eds.* A concordance to the essays of Francis Bacon. Detroit, Gale Research, 1973. 392 pp.

Serials

4.3.52 Bacon Society, London. Journal. Vols. 1 and 2 (all publ.). London, 1886-91.

Reprinted: Kraus Reprints.
Superseded by: *Baconiana* (4.3.53).

4.3.53 Bacon Society, London. Baconiana.

Vol. 1, (all publ.). London, 1892.
Vols. 1-10, (i.e. nos. 1-40; all publ.). London, 1893-1901.
Vols. 1-42, (i.e. nos. 1-159). London, 1903-1959.
Vols. 43-53, (i.e. nos. 160-170). London, 1960-1970. Orig. ed.
Reprinted: Kraus Reprints.

Biography

4.3.54 Nichol, John. Francis Bacon, his life and philosophy. Edinburgh and London, Blackwood & Sons (Philosophical Classics for English Readers), 1901. 2v.

"Chiefly of biographical interest" (Maurice Cranston in 1.4.1).

4.3.55 Sturt, Mary. Francis Bacon: a biography. New York, Morrow, 1932. 246 pp.

"The best . . ." (Tobey in 1.2.11).

Bacon, Roger
(c. 1220-1292)

Bibliography

4.3.56 Alessio, F. "Un seculo di studi su Ruggero Bacone (1848-1957)," Revista critica di storia della filosofia, XIV (1959), 81-108.

4.3.57 Easton, S. C. Roger Bacon and his search for a universal science; a reconsideration of the life and work of Roger Bacon in the light of his own stated purposes. Oxford and New York, Blackwell, 1952. 255 pp.

Contains an extensive, annotated bibliography.

Works

4.3.58 The "Opus Majus" of Roger Bacon. Ed. with an introduction and analytical table,

by John Henry Bridges. Oxford, Clarendon Press, 1897-1900. 3v.

Reprinted: Johnson Reprint Co., 1964; Frankfurt, Minerva, 1971-72.

4.3.59 Opera hactenus inedita Fratris Rogeri Baconis. Edidit Robert Steele. Oxford, Clarendon Press, 1905-40. 16v.

4.3.60 The Opus Majus of Roger Bacon. Trans. by Robert Belle Burke. Philadelphia, University of Pennsylvania Press, 1928. 2v.

Reprinted: N. Y., 1962.
English translation of 4.3.58.

Biography

4.3.61 Easton, S. C. Roger Bacon and his search for a universal science. *See* 4.3.57.

Bernard of Clairvaux, St.
(1090-1153)

Works

4.3.62 S. Bernardi . . . Opera omnia. Paris, 1844-64.

Vol. CLXXXII-CLXXXV of 4.2.6.
A nine-volume critical edition by Dom Jean Leclerq is in preparation.

Biography

4.3.63 Vascandard, E. Vie de Saint Bernard. Paris, 1895. 2v.

Often reprinted.

Boethius, Anicius Manlius Severinus
(c. 480-524)

Concordance

4.3.64 Cooper, Lane. A concordance of Boethius; the five theological tractates and the Consolation of philosophy. Cambridge, Mass., The Mediaeval Academy of America, 1928. 467 pp.

Works

4.3.65 **Opera omnia.** Paris, 1847.

Vol. LXIII-LXIV of 4.2.6.

4.3.66 **Boethius.** De consolatione philosophiae. Edidit L. Bieler. Turnholti, Brepols, 1957. 124 pp.

Vol. XCIV of *Corpus Christianorum Series Latina.*
Another edition, edited by G. Weinberger, Vienna, Tempsky, 1934, 229 pp., is vol. LXVII of 4.2.3.

4.3.67 **Boethius.** The theological tractates, with an English translation by H. F. Stewart, and E. K. Rand, and S. J. Tester. The consolation of philosophy, with an English translation by S. J. Tester. New ed., Cambridge, Mass., Harvard University Press, 1973. 441 pp.

First published 1918.
Latin and English on facing pages.

4.3.68 **Boethius.** In Isagogen Porphyrii commenta. Copiis a G. Scheps comparatis suisque usus recensuit S. Brandt. Lipsiae, G. Freytag, 1906. 423 pp.

Vol. XLVIII of 4.2.9.

Bonaventure, St.
(c. 1217-1274)

Bibliography

4.3.69 **Bibliographia Franciscana.** Rome, 1962- .

Published as part of *Collectanea Franciscana*, 1931- ; published separately since 1942; contains current bibliographies.
See also pp. 929-944 of E. Gilson, *Der heilige Bonaventura*, Leipzig, J. Hegner, 1929; and vol. 1 of L. Amoros (and others) *Obras de S. Buenaventura*, Madrid, Biblioteca de Autores Cristianos, 1945-59, 6v.

4.3.70 **Bougerol, Jacques Guy,** et al. S. Bon-

aventura (1274-1974), V: Bibliographia Bonaventuriana (c. 1850-1973). Grottaferrata, Collegio S. Bonaventura, 1974. 704 pp.

4.3.71 **Vicenza, Antonio Maria da, O. F. M., et Joannes a Rubino, O. F. M.** Lexikon Bonaventurianum philosophico-theologicum in quo termini theologici distinctiones et effata praecipua scholasticorum a Seraphico Doctore declarantur. Venice, 1880. 338 pp.

Works

4.3.72 **S. Bonaventurae . . . Opera omnia.** [Ed. by] I. Jeiler, O. F. M., et al. Quaracchi, Ex Typographia Collegii S. Bonaventurae, 1882-1902. 10v.

A critical edition.

4.3.73 **The works of St. Bonaventure.** Trans. by José de Vinck. Paterson, N. J., St. Anthony Guild Press, 1960- .

In progress.
An English translation.

Thesaurus and Lexicon

4.3.74 **Thesaurus Bonaventurianus.** Sous la direction de Christian Wenin. Louvain, Publications du Cetedoc, 1972- .

Vol. 1, Hamesse, J. S. Bonaventure, itinerarium mentis in Deum. De reductione artiam ad theologiam. Concordance, indices. 195 pp.

4.3.75 **Lexique Saint Bonaventure.** Publié sous la direction de Jacques-Guy Bougerol. Paris, Editions franciscaines, 1969, 144 pp.

Includes bibliographies.

Bruno, Giordano
(1548-1600)

Bibliography

4.3.76 **Salvestrini, Virgilio,** e **Luigi Firpo.** Bibliografia de Giordano Bruno 1582-1950. Firenze, Sansoni, 1958. 407 pp.

Works

4.3.77 **Jordani Bruni Nolani opera latine conscripta.** Recensebat Francisco Fiorentino, Vittorio Imbriani, C. M. Tallarigo, Felice Tocco et Girolamo Vitelli. Neapoli, D. Morano, 1879-91. 3v.

Reissue: 1962.

4.3.78 **Le Opere italiane de Giordano Bruno,** con noti di Giovanni Gentile. Bari, Laterza, 1907-08. 2v.

Biography

4.3.79 **Spampanato, Vincenzo,** *ed.* Documenti della vita di Giordano Bruno. Firenze, Leo S. Olschki, 1933. 233 pp.

Cajetan, Cardinal (Thomas de Vio)
(1468-1534)

Bibliography

4.3.80 **Congar, M.-J.** Bio-bibliographie de Cajétan. Saint-Maximin (Var), Edit. de la Revue thomiste, 1935. 47 pp.

Originally appeared in the *Revue thomiste*, XVII, 1934-35, 3-39.

See also: 1.2.5, pp. 33-34.

Works

4.3.81 **Cajetanus, Thomas de Vio.** Opera omnia quotquot in Sacrae Scripturae expositionem reperiuntur cura atque industria insignis collegii S. Thomae Complutensis. Hildesheim, Olms. 5v.

Reprint of the 1639 Lyon Edition.

4.3.82 **Cajetanus, Thomas de Vio.** Opuscula omnia. Hildesheim, Olms. 3v. in 1.

Index rerum et verborum, que in opusculis Caietani continentur.
Reprint of the 1587 Lyon edition.

Duns Scotus, John
(c. 1266-1308)

Bibliography and Lexicon

4.3.83 **Schafer, Odulfus.** Bibliographia de vita, operibus et doctrina Iohannis Duns Scoti, doctoris subtilis ac Mariani, saec. XIX-XX. Romae, Orbis Catholicus-Herder, 1955. 223 pp.

For recent works see the continuing bibliography in *Bibliographia Franciscana.* (4.3.69)

4.3.84 **Schafer, Odulfus.** "Resenha abreviada da bibliografia escotista mais recente (1954-1966)," Revista portuguesa de filosofia, XXIII (n. 3, 1967).

4.3.85 **Fernandez Garcia, Marianus, O. F. M.** Lexicon scholasticum philosophico-theologicum in quo termini, definitiones, distinctiones et effata seu axiomaticae propositiones philosophiam ac theologiam spectantes a B. Joanne Duns Scoto exponuntur, declarantur. Ad Claras Aquas (Quarracchi), Collegium S. Bonaventurae, 1910. 1056 pp.

See also: 1.2.16 (No. 22).

Works

4.3.86 **Opera omnia.** Studio et cura Commissionis Scotisticae ad fidem codicum edita, praeside Carlo Balić. Civitas Vaticana, Typis polyglottis Vaticanis, 1950- .

In progress.
Complete and critical edition. Includes bibliographies
Will supersede the *Opera omnia*, ed. by L. Wadding, Lyons, 1639, 12v. (reprinted: Vives, 1891-95, 26v.), which contains some spurious works.

Biography

4.3.87 **Emden, A. B.** A biographical register of the University of Oxford to A. D. 1500. Vol. 1. Oxford, Clarendon, 1957, pp. 607-10.

Society

4.3.88 International Scotistic Society/Societatis Internationalis Scotisticae. *See* 12.1.12.

See also: 12.1.35.

Erasmus, Desiderius (1466-1536)

Bibliography

4.3.89 Haeghen, Ferdinand van der. Bibliotheca Erasmiana: répertoire des oeuvres d'Erasme. Nieuwkoop, B. de Graff, 1961. 3 pts. in 1v.

Reprint of the Gand, 1893 ed.
See also other volumes published by Ghent University, 1897- .

4.3.90 Margolin, Jean Claude. Quatorze années de bibliographie érasmienne, 1936-1949. Paris, Vrin, 1969. 431 pp.

Annotated.

4.3.91 Margolin, Jean Claude. Douze années de bibliographie érasmienne, 1950-1961. Paris, Vrin, 1963. 204 pp.

Annotated.

4.3.92 Devereux, E. J. A checklist of English translations of Erasmus to 1700. (Oxford Bibliographical Society. Occasional Publication no. 3.) Oxford, Oxford Bibliographical Society, 1968. 40 pp.

4.3.93 The collected works of Erasmus. Toronto, University of Toronto Press, 1972- .

In progress.
English translations, with introductions and notes. Complete correspondence and other principal writings, plus a Biographical Register.

Works

4.3.94 Opera omnia. [Ed.] Beatus Rhenanus.

Basilea, H. Frobenium et N. Episcopium, 1540-42. 9v.

4.3.95 Opera omnia emendatiora. [Ed.] Joannes Clericus. Leyden, P. Vander Aa, 1703-06. 11v.

Reprinted: Hildesheim, Olms, 1961-62. A new edition is in progress, edited by Dr. C. Reedijk.

4.3.96 A supplement to the Opera omnia. Ed. with intr. and notes by Wallace K. Ferguson. The Hague, Nijhoff, 1933. 373 pp.

4.3.97 Opus epistolarum. [Ed. by] P. S. Allen, H. M. Allen, and H. W. Garrod. Oxford, Clarendon Press, 1906-58. 12v.

This contains the complete correspondence.

For an English translation of the letters up to 1517 see *The Epistles of Erasmus*, ed. and trans. by F. M. Nichols, New York, Longmans, Green, 1901-08, 3v.

Reprinted: N. Y., 1962.

4.3.98 Erasmi. Opera omnia, recognita et adnotatione critica instructa notisque illustrata. Amsterdam, North-Holland, 1969- .

In progress. 30v. projected.

Biography

4.3.99 Huizinga, Johan. Erasmus and the age of reformation. Trans. by F. Hopman, with a selection from the letters of Erasmus. New York and London, Scribner's Sons, 1924. 276 pp.

Reprinted: N. Y., Harper, 1957.
"Excellent intellectual biography" (Richard H. Popkin in 1.4.1).

4.3.100 Phillips, Margaret M. Erasmus and the northern renaissance. New York, Macmillan; and London, English Universities Press, 1959. 236 pp.

4.3.101 Bainton, Roland H. Erasmus of

Christendom. New York, Scribners, 1969. 308 pp.

" . . . emphasizes the inwardness of Erasmus's religion and his religious tolerance in an age of controversy" (Tobey in 1.2.11).

Erigena, John Scotus
(c. 810-c. 877)

Works

4.3.102 Joannis Scoti opera quae supersunt omnia. Edidit H. J. Floss, 1853.

Vol. CXXII (1853) of 4.2.6.

Bio-bibliography

4.3.103 Cappuyns, M. Jean Scott Erigene, sa vie, son oeuvre, sa pensée. Louvain, Abbaye du Mont César; Paris, Desclée de Brouwer, 1933. 410 pp.

Reprinted: Brussels, Culture et Civilisation, 1964.

Farabi, Al-
(c.870-950)

Bibliography

4.3.104 Rescher, Nicholas. Al-Farabi; an annotated bibliography. Pittsburgh, University of Pittsburgh Press, 1962. 54 pp.

For corrections and additions see the review by W. I. Quinn in *The New Scholasticism*, XXXVII (1963), 528-33.

Ficino, Marsilio
(1433-1499)

Works

4.3.105 Marsilii Ficini opera. Basilea, Per Henricum Petri, 1576. 2v.

Reproduced: Torino, Bottega d'Erasmo, 1959.
See also: Supplementum Ficinianum, ed.

by P. O. Kristeller, Florence, Olschki, 1937, 2v., which lists manuscripts and editions and gives a chronology of Ficino's works.

Biography

4.3.106 Della Torre, Arnaldo. Storia dell'Accademia Platonica di Firenze. Florence, Carnesecchi, 1902. 858 pp.

Still the basic account of Ficino's life.

Kindi, Yakub ibn Ishak al-
(Ninth Century)

Bibliography

4.3.107 Rescher, Nicholas. Al-Kindi; an annotated bibliography. Pittsburgh, University of Pittsburgh Press, 1964. 55 pp.

4.3.108 Al-Kindi. Al-Kindi's metaphysics; a translation of Ya'qub ibn Ishaq al-Kindi's treatise "On first philosophy" (fi al-Falsafah al-ula) with introd. and commentary by Alfred L. Ivry. Albany, State University of New York Press, 1974. 207 pp.

Bibliography: pp. 191-200.

Machiavelli, Niccolo
(1469-1527)

Bibliography

4.3.109 Gerber, Adolph. Niccolò Machiavelli; die Handschriften, Ausgaben und Übersetzungen seiner Werke im 16. und 17. jahrhundert, mit 147 Faksimiles und zahlreichen Auszugen. Eine kritisch-bibliographische Untersuchung. Gotha, F. A. Perthes, Aktiengesellschaft, 1912-13. 3v. in 1.

Reprinted: 1973.

4.3.110 Lenger, Marie Thérèse. Contribution à la bibliographie des éditions anciennes, XVIe et XVIIe siècles, des oeuvres de Machiavel. Catalogue critique des exemplaires conservés dans les bibliothèques belges. (Archives et Bibliothèques de Belgique. No.

spécial, 9) Bruxelles, (bd. de l'Empereur, 4), 1973. 87 pp.

Works

4.3.111 Opere. A cura di Sergio Bertelli e Franco Gaeta, ed. Milano, Feltrinelli, 1960- .

In progress.

A critical edition which supersedes all earlier editions, none of which was complete.

4.3.112 Machiavelli; the chief works and others. Ed. by Allan Gilbert. Durham, N. C., Duke University Press, 1965. 3v.

The best English translation.

Supersedes the earlier edition in 4v., ed. by E. Farneworth, 2d ed., 1775.

Biography

4.3.113 Ridolfi, Roberto. Vita di Niccolò Machiavelli. Rome, 1954. Trans. by Cecil Grayson as The life of Niccolò Machiavelli, Chicago, University of Chicago Press, 1963. 337 pp.

The best of the biographies.

Maimonides
(1135-1204)

Bibliography

4.3.114 Gorfinkle, Joseph I. "A bibliography of Maimonides," *in* I. Epstein, ed., Moses Maimonides (1135-1204), London, Sancino, 1935, pp. 229-48.

Works

4.3.115 The guide of the perplexed. Trans., introduction and notes by S. Pines. Chicago, University of Chicago Press, 1963. 658 pp.

4.3.116 Le guide des égarés. Ed. par Salomon Munk. 2. éd. Paris, A. Franck, 1960. 3v.

1st ed. 1856-66. Arabic text and French translation.

4.3.117 Code of Maimonides. Yale Judaica Series. New Haven, Yale Unviersity Press, 1948- .

In progress. 15v. projected. 11 bks. in 12v. to date.

An extensive introductory volume will analyze the Code and trace its influence.

Important in the systematization of biblical, talmudic, and geonic law and jurisprudence as well as on the history of codification.

More, Thomas
(1478-1535)

Bibliography

4.3.118 Sullivan, Frank, and **M. P. Sullivan.** Moreana: materials for the study of Saint Thomas More. Los Angeles, Loyola University of Los Angeles Press, 1964. 4v.

Annotated.

Works

4.3.119 The complete works of St. Thomas More. New Haven, Yale University Press, 1963- .

In progress. 15v. projected, plus a 1v. Index and Bibliography.

Concordance

4.3.120 Concordance to Thomas More's Utopia. Ed. by Ladislaus J. Bolchazy. In collaboration with Gregory Gichan and Fred Theobald. Hildesheim, Olms, 1978. 388 pp.

Includes an Index Verborum.

Nicholas of Cusa
(1401-1464)

Bibliography

4.3.121 Kleinen, H., und **R. Danzer.** "Cusanus-Bibliographie, 1920-1961," Mitteilungen und Forschugensbeiträge der Cusanus-Gesellschaft, I (1961), 95-126.

4.3.122 **Danzer, R.** "Cusanus-bibliographie. Fortsetzung (1961-1964) und Nachtrage," Mitteilungen und Forschungsbeiträge der Cusanus-Gesellschaft, III (1963), 223-37.

Works

4.3.123 **Nicolai Cusae cardinalis opera.** Parisiis, 1514. 3v.

Reprinted: Frankfurt, Minerva, 1962.

4.3.124 **Nicolaus Cusanus-Edition.** Hamburg, Meiner.

Includes:
Nicolai de Cusa opera omnia. 1959- . 20v. projected. Philosophical theological, mathematical and church politico-historical writings. A critical edition.
Schriften des Nikolaus von Kues in deutscher übersetzung. 1952- .
Acta Cusana. 1974- . Cusanus-Texte und Cusanus-Studien.

4.3.125 **Philosophisch-theologische Schriften (von) Nikolaus von Kues.** Hrsg. und eingeführt von Leo Gabriel. Wien, Herder, 1964-67. 3v.

A jubilee edition with Latin and German texts.

4.2.126 **Opera omnia.** Ed., E. Hoffmann and P. Wilpert. Lipsiae, Meiner, 1932- .

19v. projected.

Concordance

4.3.127 **Zellinger, Eduard.** Cusanus-Konkordanz. München, Huber, 1960. 331 pp.

Biography

4.3.128 **Vansteenberghe, Edmond.** Le Cardinal Nicolas de Cues. Paris, H. Champion, 1920. 506 pp.

4.3.129 **Bett, Henry.** Nicholas of Cusa. London, Methuen, 1932. 210 pp.

4.3.130 **Volkmann-Schluck, K. H.** Nicolaus Cusanus. Frankfurt am Main, Klostermann, 1957. 190 pp.

Peter Lombard
(c. 1095-1160)

Works

4.3.131 [**Works.**] Contained in 4.2.6, vols. CXCI and vol. CXCII.

Biography

4.3.132 **Delhaye, Philippe.** Pierre Lombard, sa vie, ses oeuvres, sa morale. Montréal, Inst. d'Études Médiévales; and Paris, Vrin, 1961. 111 pp.

Pico della Mirandola, Count Giovanni
(1463-1494)

Bibliography

4.3.133 **Ludovici, Sergio Samek.** Catalogo della mostra delle opere di Giovanni Pico della Mirandola. Modena, Biblioteca communale, 1963. 71 pp.

Works

4.3.134 **Opera omnia.** Basileae, Henricpetrina, 1557-73. 2v.

Reprinted: Hildesheim, Olms.

4.3.135 **Commentationes Joannis Pici Mirandulae.** Eugenio Garin, ed. Firenze, Vallecchi, 1942- .

In progress.
A critical edition.

Biography

4.3.136 **Giovanni Pico della Mirandola;** his life by his nephew. Trans. by Sir Thomas More. Ed. with introduction and notes by J. M. Rigg. London, D. Nutt, 1890.

Also contains three of Pico's letters and some of his short religious works.

Suarez, Francisco
(1548-1617)

Bibliography

4.3.137 **Múgica, Plácido**. Bibliografía suareciana, con una introd. sobre el estado actual de los estudios por Eleuterio Elorduy. Granada, Universidad de Granada, Cátedra Suárez, 1948. 103 pp.

4.3.138 **Scorraille, Raoul de**. François Suarez de la compagnie de Jésus, d'après ses lettres, ses autres écrits inédits et un grand nombre de documents nouveaux. Paris, P. Lethielleux, 1912-13. 2v.

The most complete bibliography up to its time.

4.3.139 **Smith, Gerard**. "A Suarez bibliography," in Jesuit thinkers of the Renaissance, ed. by Gerard Smith, Milwaukee, Marquette University Press, 1939, pp. 227-238.

Works

4.3.140 **Opera omnia**. Paris, Vives, 1856-78. 28v. in 30.

An incomplete edition. A complete, critical edition is in progress.

Thomas Aquinas, St.
(c. 1225-1274)

Bibliography

4.3.141 **Eschmann, I. T.** "A Catalogue of St. Thomas's Works: Bibliographical Notes," in E. Gilson, The Christian philosophy of St. Thomas Aquinas. New York, 1956, pp. 381-439.

A complete list of Aquinas's works with editions, chronology, and translations.

See also: 1.2.16 (Nos. 13/14 and 15/16), and 1.2.5, pp. 4-7.

Index, Lexicons, and Dictionaries

4.3.142 **Defarrari, Roy Joseph**. A Latin-English dictionary of St. Thomas Aquinas, based on the Summa Theologica and selected passages of his other works. Boston, St. Paul, 1960. 1115 pp.

An abridged edition of 4.3.144.

4.3.143 **Defarrari, Roy Joseph**, and **Sister M. I. Barry**. A complete index of the Summa Theologica of St. Thomas Aquinas. Washington, D. C., The Catholic University of America Press, 1956. 386 pp.

A list of terms and where they appear.

4.3.144 **Defarrari, Roy Joseph, Sister M. Involata**, and **Ignatius McGuiness**. A lexicon of St. Thomas Aquinas based on the Summa Theologica and selected passages of his other works. Washington, D. C.; Catholic University of America Press, 1948-53. 5v.

Arranged by Latin words, with English meanings, Latin quotations, and indication of source.

4.3.145 **Schutz, Ludwig**. Thomas-lexikon. 2. Aufl. Paderborn, Schöningh, 1895. 889 pp.

Reprinted: New York, F. Ungar, 1957. 1st ed. 1881.
A useful concordance.

4.3.146 **Stockhammer, Morris**. Thomas Aquinas dictionary. New York, Philosophical Library, 1965. 219 pp.

4.3.147 **Thomas Aquinas**: Codices Manuscripti Operum Thomae de Aquino. Ed. by H. F. Dondaine, H. V. Schooner. Rome, Editori di S. Tommaso, 1967.

4v. projected. V.1 lists and describes 1,000 of the more than 4,000 known manuscripts of the works of Thomas Aquinas, classified alphabetically by the libraries in which they are found.

Works

4.3.148 Opera omnia.

There are many different editions. The Leonine edition (Rome, 1882-) is a critical edition. Prior to 1950, 16v. were published. A new critical edition began with vol. XVII and is in progress at Rome, Le Saulchoir (France), Ottawa, Torrente (Spain), and Yale University.

The Parma edition (1852-73, 25v., reprinted N. Y., 1948-50) is not a critical edition but is almost complete.

Other famous editions are the Piana edition of 1570 (Pius V), and the Vives edition of Paris, 1871-80, 34v.

4.3.149 Summa theologiae. New York, McGraw-Hill, 1964- .

In progress.
60v. projected.
A critical edition with Latin and English on facing pages.

4.3.150 Thomas Aquinas, Saint. Basic writings. Edited and annotated, with an introduction, by Anton C. Pegis. New York, Random House, 1945. 2v.

The text is a revision of the English Dominican Translation of St. Thomas (by Father Laurence Shapcote, O. P.) begun in 1911.

Biography

4.3.151 Foster, Kenelm. Life of St. Thomas Aquinas: biographical documents. London, Longmans, Green, and Baltimore, Helicon, 1959. 172 pp.

4.3.152 Walz, Angelus. Saint Thomas d'Aquin. French adaptation by Paul Novarina. Louvain, Publications Universitaires, 1962. 243 pp.

"One of the best biographies" (Vernon J. Bourke in 1.4.1).

See also: 10.5.48.

William of Ockham
(1285-1349)

Bibliography and Lexicon

4.3.153 Baudry, L. Guillaume d'Occam, sa vie, ses oeuvres, ses idées sociales et politiques. vol. I: L'Homme et les oeuvres. Paris, Vrin, 1949. 317 pp.

4.3.154 Heynck, V. "Ockham-Literatur 1919-1949," Franziskanische Studien, XXXII (1950), 164-83.

Continued by 4.3.155.

4.3.155 Reilly, James P. "Ockham bibliography: 1950-1967," Franciscan Studies, XXVIII (1968), 197-214.

Continues 4.3.154.

4.3.156 Ghisalberti, Allessandro, ed. "Bibliografia su Guglielmo di Occam dal 1950 al 1968," Rivista di Filosofia Neo-Scolastica, 61 (1969), 273-84, 545-71.

4.3.157 Baudry, Léon. Lexique philosophique de Guillaume d'Ockham. Etude des notions fondamentales. Paris, Lethielleux, 1958. 298 pp.

Works

4.3.158 Opera plurima. Lyon, Johannes Trechsel, 1492-96. 4v.

Reprinted: London, Gregg Press, 1962.
Contains the major political and theological works.

4.3.159 Opera omnia philosophica et theologica. St. Bonaventure, New York, The Franciscan Institute, 1967- .

In progress.
25v. projected.
Under the general editorship of E. M. Buytaert. A critical edition of the nonpolitical works.

4.3.160 **Guillelmi de Ockham opera politica**. Accuravit G. Sikes (et al.). Manchester, University Press, 1940-63. 3v.

Complete, critical Latin edition of the political works.

4.3.161 **Ockham**. Philosophical writings; a selection edited and translated by Ph. Boehner. London, Nelson, 1957. 147, 154 pp.

A selection of Latin texts with facing English translations.

5. MODERN PHILOSOPHY

The period of philosophy covered here goes roughly from the end of the Renaissance through the Nineteenth Century.

Section 5.2 includes the philosophers generally recognized to be the major philosophers of the period. Some lesser figures are also included. The list of philosophers could have been expanded considerably. I have included only those philosophers who are reasonably well known and either whose works have been collected or about whose works a substantial bibliography has been published. For the philosophers included I have gathered together information about their collected works, bibliographies, biographies, societies, and so on. In general I have not listed individual works, except for a few of the major figures.

Bibliographical and other information on philosophers not listed can be obtained by consulting the *Encyclopedia of Philosophy* (1.4.1), the histories listed in 5.1, or the bibliographies and biographical sources listed in other chapters of this book.

5.1 GENERAL: HISTORIES, BIBLIOGRAPHIES, DICTIONARIES

Histories

5.1.1 **Beck, Lewis White**. Early German philosophy: Kant and his predecessors. Cambridge, Mass., Harvard University Press, 1969. 556 pp.

5.1.2 **Cassirer, Ernst**. The philosophy of the enlightenment. Trans. by Fritz C. A. Koelln and James P. Pettegrove. Princeton, Princeton University Press, 1951. 366 pp.

A translation of *Die Philosophie der Aufklarung*, 1932.

An excellent study of 18th century thought, with bibliographical footnotes.

5.1.3 **Collins, James**. A history of modern European philosophy. Milwaukee, Bruce, 1954. 854 pp.

Annotated bibliographies of sources and secondary works.

Objective and reliable. Criticism from Thomistic point of view.

Parts of this work have been published separately in paperbound editions.

5.1.4 **Gilson, Etienne**, and **Thomas Langan**. Modern philosophy; Descartes to Kant. New York, Random House, 1963. 570 pp.

Notes and bibliography: pp. 457-560.

5.1.5 **Hazard, Paul**. European thought in the 18th century from Montesquieu to Lessing. Trans. by J. Lewis May. Cleveland, World, 1963. 477 pp.

Translation of *La pensée européenne au XVIIIème siècle: De Montesquieu à Lessing*, 1963.

Bibliographical footnotes.

5.1.6 **Höffding, Harald**. A history of modern philosophy. Trans. by B. E. Meyer. New York, Humanities Press, 1950. 2v.

Reissue: New York, Dover, 1955. 2v.

A translation of *Geschichte der neueren Philosophie*, Leipzig, Reisland, 1895-96, 2v.

5.1.7 Lévy-Bruhl, Lucien. A history of modern philosophy in France. Trans. by G. Coblence. Chicago, Open Court, 1899. 500 pp.

Bibliography: pp. 483-94.

5.1.8 Lowith, Karl. From Hegel to Nietzsche; the revolution in nineteenth-century thought. Trans. by David E. Green from 3d German ed. New York, Holt, Rinehart, and Winston, 1964. 464 pp.

A translation of *Von Hegel zu Nietzsche: Der revolutionäre Bruch im Denken des neunzehnten Jahrhunderts.* Zürich, Europa Verlag, 1941.
Bibliography: pp. 389-95; and extensive bibliographical information in the notes.

5.1.9 Merz, John Theodore. A history of European thought in the nineteenth century. New York, Dover, 1965. 4v.

1st ed., Edinburgh, W. Blackwood, 1904-12, 4v.
Treats topics, not individuals.
Bibliography in the footnotes.

5.1.10 Stephen, Sir Leslie. History of English thought in the eighteenth contury. 3d ed. New York, P. Smith, 1949. 2v.

1st ed. 1876.
A standard work. Includes bibliographies.

See also: 1.1.1-1.1.3, 1.1.7, 1.1.11, 10.5.48.

French

5.1.11 Maréchal, Joseph, S. J. Précis d'histoire de la philosophie moderne, de la Renaissance à Kant. 2. éd. Paris, Desclée de Brouwer, 1951. 355 pp.

1st ed. 1933.
The second edition contains a bibliographical supplement from 1933-49.

5.1.12 Sortais, Gaston. La philosophie moderne depuis Bacon jusqu'à Leibniz. Paris, P. Lethielleux, 1920-22. 2v.

Includes bibliographies.

See also: 1.1.13-1.1.17.

German

5.1.13 Brockdorff, Cay von. Die deutsche Aufklärungsphilosophie. München, E. Reinhardt, 1926. 180 pp.

5.1.14 Erdmann, Johann Eduard. Grundriss der Geschichte der Philosophie. 4. Aufl. Berlin, W. Hertz, 1896. 3v.

I. Philosophie der Altertums und des Mittelalters.
II. Philosophie der Neuzeit.
III. Die deutsche Philosophie seit Hegel's Tod.
Reprinted: Stuttgart, 1964.
English translation: *A History of Philosophy,* N. Y., Macmillan, 1915-22. 3v.

5.1.15 Kroner, Richard. Von Kant bis Hegel. Tubingen, Mohr, 1921-24. 2v.

Reprinted: 1961, 2v. in 1.

5.1.16 Zeller, Eduard. Geschichte der Deutschen Philosophie seit Leibniz. 2 Aufl. München, R. Oldenbourg, 1875. 774 pp.

Reprinted: N. Y., Johnson.

See also: 1.1.18, 1.1.19.

Bibliographies

5.1.17 Curley, E. "Recent work on 17th c. continental philosophy," American Philosophical Quarterly, XI (1974), 235-55.

5.1.18 Gumposch, Victor P. Die philosophischen Literatur der Deutschen von 1400 bis um 1850. Regensberg, G. J. Manz, 1851. 640 pp.

Reprinted: Düsseldorf, 1967.

5.1.19 **Sass, Hans-Martin**. Inedita philosophica; ein Verzeichnis von Nachlässen deutschsprachiger Philosophen Des 19. und 20. Jahrhunderts. Düsseldorf, Univ. Philosophisches Inst. Kleine philosophische Bibliographie, vol. 3, Philosophia Verlag, 1974. 86 pp.

Series

5.1.20 **Popkin, Richard H.**, and **Giorgio Tonelli**, *eds*. Historia Philosophiae (Series). New York, Olms Reprints.

Series: (1) First or best editions of famous philosophical texts; (2) Works and bibliographies on history of philosophy compiled primarily in the 18th or early 19th century.

5.1.21 **Wellek, René**, *ed*. British philosophers and theologians of the 17th and 18th centuries. New York, Garland. 101v.

See also: 10.2.41.

5.2 INDIVIDUAL PHILOSOPHERS, ALPHABETICALLY FROM BAKUNIN TO WOLFF (COLLECTED AND STANDARD WORKS, BIBLIOGRAPHIES, BIOGRAPHIES)

Bakunin, Michael
(1814-1876)

Works

5.2.1 **Bakunin, Mikkail Aleksandrovich**. Sobranie sochinenii i pisem, 1828-1876. Ed. by Iu. M. Steklov. Moskva, Politkatorzhan, 1934-35. (Klassiki revoliutsionnoi mysli domarksistskogo perioda, 1) 4v.

Ann Arbor, Mich., University Microfilms International, "Demand Reprints."

Biography

5.2.2 **Carr, E. H.** Michael Bakunin. London, Macmillan, 1937. 501 pp.

Bibliography: pp. 489-91.
Reprinted: N. Y., Octagon Books, 1975.

Archives

5.2.3 **Archives Bakounine/Bakunin Archiv**. Leiden, E. J. Brill (Publiées pour Internationaal Instituut voor Sociale Geschiedenis, Amsterdam par A. Lehning), 1961-1971. Leiden, E. J. Brill, 1961- .

In progress.
15v. projected. 4v. published by 1978.

Bauer, Bruno
(1809-1882)

Bibliography

5.2.4 **Sass, H. M.**, *ed*. Feld zuge der reinen Kritik. Frankfurt, Nachwort, 1968, pp. 269-78.

A primary bibliography 1838-45, and a secondary bibliography 1842-1967.

Bentham, Jeremy
(1748-1832)

Bibliography

5.2.5 **Halévy, Elie**. The growth of philosophic radicalism. Trans. by Mary Morris. London, Faber & Gwyer, 1928. 554 pp.

Contains a Bentham bibliography by Charles W. Everett: pp. 522-46.

5.2.6 **Milne, Alexander Taylor**. Catalogue of the manuscripts of Jeremy Bentham in the library of University College, London. 2d ed. London, University of London, Athlone Press, 1962. 104 pp.

Works

5.2.7 **The collected works of Jeremy Bentham**. General ed., J. H. Burns. London, Athlone Press, 1968- .

In progress.

38v. projected.

This will be a comprehensive, definitive edition. When completed it will replace *The Works of Jeremy Bentham*, ed. by J. Bowring, Edinburgh, William Tait, 1838-43, 11v. (reprinted: N. Y., Russell & Russell, 1962), which is an incomplete collection.

Biography

5.2.8 **Atkinson, Charles Milner.** Jeremy Bentham; his life and work. London, Methuen, 1905. 247 pp.

5.2.9 **Everett, C. W.** The education of Jeremy Bentham. New York, Columbia University Press, 1931. 216 pp.

5.2.10 **Stephen, Leslie.** The English utilitarians, Vol. 1. London, Duckworth; and New York, Putnam's, 1900.

Berkeley, George
(1685-1753)

Bibliography

5.2.11 **Jessop, T. E.** A bibliography of George Berkeley . . . . With an inventory of Berkeley's manuscript remains by A. Luce. 2nd ed. (rev. and enl.). The Hague, Nijhoff, 1973. 135 pp.

1st ed. Oxford, 1934.
Continued by 5.2.14.

5.2.12 **Keynes, Geoffrey.** A bibliography of George Berkeley, Bishop of Cloyne: his works and his critics in the eighteenth century. Pittsburgh, Pa., University of Pittsburgh Press, 1976. 285 pp.

" . . . a bibliographical study . . . . Historical preface for each major work . . . . This bibliography belongs alongside the Luce-Jessop edition of Berkeley's Works" (Js. Collins in *Cross Currents*, Spr., 1977).

5.2.13 **Turbayne, C. M.,** and **Robert X. Ware.** "A bibliography of George Berkeley, 1933-1962," Journal of philosophy, LX (1963), 93-112.

A continuation of the 1st ed. of 5.2.11.

5.2.14 **Turbayne, C. M.,** and **Robert Appelbaum.** "Bibliography of George Berkeley, 1963-1974," Journal of the History of Philosophy, XV (1977), 83-95.

A continuation of 5.2.11.

This bibliography is being continued in the *Berkeley Newsletter*, issued annually since 1977, by E. J. Furlong and David Berman, Trinity College, Dublin.

Works

5.2.15 **The works of George Berkeley,** Bishop of Cloyne. Ed. by A. A. Luce and T. E. Jessop. London, T. Nelson, 1948-57. 9v.

Reprinted: Nelson, 1964.
A critical edition. Also has a useful introduction and notes.

Biography

5.2.16 **Luce, Arthur A.** The life of George Berkeley, Bishop of Cloyne. London and New York, T. Nelson, 1949. 260 pp.

Society

5.2.17 **International Berkeley Society.** Founded in 1977. Prof. Raymond W. Houghton, President. International Berkeley Society; P. O. Box 359; Newport, R. I. 02840.

See also: 10.5.48.

Brentano, Franz
(1838-1917)

Bibliography

5.2.18 **Gilson, Lucie.** Méthode et métaphysique selon F. Brentano. Paris, Vrin, 1955.

Bibliography: pp. 16-23.

5.2.19 **Mayer-Hillebrand, Franziska.** "Rückblick auf die bisherigen Bestrebungen zur Erhaltung und Verbreiturn von Fr. Brentanos philosophischen Lehren und kurze Darstellung dieser Lehren," Zeitschrift für Philosophische Forschung, XVII (1963), 146-69.

Covers works on and reviews of Brentano's writings.

See also: 8.6.2.

Works

5.2.20 **Gesammelte philosophische Schriften.** Hrsg. von O. Kraus und A. Kastil. Leipzig, Meiner, 1922-30. 10v.

,

5.2.21 **Works.** Individually issued English translations. Editors vary. Atlantic Highlands, N. J., Humanities Press, 1969- .

Butler, Joseph
(1692-1752)

Works

5.2.22 **The works of Joseph Butler.** Ed. by The Rt. Hon. W. E. Gladstone. 2d ed. Oxford, Clarendon Press, 1910. 2v.

1st ed. 1897.

Comte, Auguste
(1798-1857)

Bibliography

5.2.23 **Ducasse, Pierre.** La méthode positive et l'intuition comtienne; bibliographie. Paris, Alcan, 1939. 172 pp.

Reprinted: N. Y., Burt Franklin.
A bibliography on Comte and on the Positivist School.

Works

5.2.24 **Oeuvres.** Paris, Editions Anthropos, 1968-72. 12v.

A reprinted collection of Comte's works as

published in various editions from 1844-95.

An English condensation, *The Positive Philosophy of Auguste Comte*, trans. by H. Martineau, London, Bohn, 1853, 2v., was repudiated by some positivists.

Biography

5.2.25 **Gouhier, Henri.** La vie d'Auguste Comte. Paris, Gallimard, 1931. 300 pp.

". . . the best biography" (Bruce Mazlish in 1.4.1).

Descartes, René
(1596-1650)

Bibliography and Index

5.2.26 **Sebba, Gregor.** Bibliographia Cartesiana; a critical guide to the Descartes literature, 1800-1960. The Hague, Nijhoff, 1964. 510 pp.

The standard bibliography for the dates indicated.

5.2.27 **Doney, Willis.** "Some recent work on Descartes: a bibliography," Philosophy Research Archives, Vol. II (1976), No. 1134.

5.2.28 **L'Equipe Descartes** (C. N. R. S.) "Bibliographie critique des études cartésiennes."

Annually in *Archives de Philosophie* (10.3.2), Vol. 35 (1972)- .

5.2.29 **Guibert, A. J.** Bibliographie des oeuvres de René Descartes publiées au XVIIe siècle. Paris, C. N. R. S., 1977. 276 pp.

5.2.30 **Gilson, Etienne.** Index scolastico-cartésien. Paris, Alcan, 1913. 354 pp.

Reprinted: N. Y., Burt Franklin.
Indicates how Descartes uses scholastic terms.

See also: 1.2.5, pp. 46-49.

Works

5.2.31 Oeuvres de Descartes. Publiées par C. Adam et P. Tannery. Paris, Cerf, 1896-1913. 12v. and supplement.

The collected, critical, standard edition. The supplement is a general index.
The edition has been re-edited and published in a 7v. edition by the Centre national de la recherche scientifique, Paris, Vrin, 1964.

5.2.32 Correspondance. Ed. by C. Adam and G. Milhaud. Paris, 1936-1963. 8v.

Reprinted: N. Y., Kraus Reprints.

5.2.33 The philosophical works of Descartes. Trans. by E. S. Haldane and G. T. R. Ross. Cambridge, The University Press, 1968. 2v.

A reprint of the corrected 1934 edition. 1st ed. 1911-12.
The most complete of the English editions.

Dictionary

5.2.34 Morris, John. Descartes Dictionary. New York, Philosophical Library, 1971, 247 pp.

Biography

5.2.35 Alquié, Ferdinand. Descartes: l'homme et l'oeuvre. Paris, Hatier-Boivin, 1956. 174 pp.

"An excellent recent work" (Tobey in 1.2.11).

5.2.36 Haldane, Elizabeth S. Descartes, his life and times. New York, Collier, 1962. 398 pp.

Journal

5.2.37 Studia Cartesiana. 1978- . Annual. Sec.: P. M. Miny Chustka, c/o Quadratures, Postbus 6463, 1005 EL, Amsterdam, Netherlands.

A multidisciplinary journal devoted to Descartes and Cartesianism.
Also publishes: *Cartesian Newsletter/Nouvelles Cartésiennes.*

See also: 10.5.48.

Diderot, Denis
(1713-1784)

Bibliography

5.2.38 Cabeen, D. C., *ed.* A critical bibliography of French literature. Syracuse, N. Y., Syracuse University Press, 1947-61. 4v.

See vol. IV, pp. 165-94, for a Diderot bibliography.
Supplement to vol. IV, 1968.

Works

5.2.39 Oeuvres complètes. Notices, notes . . . par J. Assezat et M. Tourneux. Paris, Garnier, 1875-77. 20v.

Reprinted: N. Y., Kraus Reprints.

5.2.40 Oeuvres complètes. Edition chronologique. Introductions de Roger Lewinter. Paris, le Club Français du Livre, 1969- .

In progress.

5.2.41 Diderot's early philosophical works, trans. and edited by Margaret Jourdain. London and Chicago, Open Court, 1916. 246 pp.

Reprinted: N. Y., Burt Franklin.

5.2.42 Diderot's thoughts on art and style, with some of his shorter essays, selected and translated by Beatrix L. Tollemache. London, 1893. 291 pp.

Reprinted: N. Y., Burt Franklin.

Biography

5.2.43 Wilson, Arthur M. Diderot: the testing years (1713-1759). New York, Oxford, 1957. 417 pp.

"Best biography to date and best critical studies of early works. The first of two volumes" (Norman L. Torrey in 1.4.1).

Dilthey, Wilhelm
(1833-1911)

Bibliography

5.2.44 **Diaz de Cerio, Franco, S. J.** "Bibliografia de W. Dilthey," *Pensamiento,* XXIV (1968), 195-258.

Lists editions of Dilthey's writings and works about them.

5.2.45 **Hermann, Ulrich.** Bibliographie Wilhelm Dilthey. Quellen und Literatur. (Pädagogische Bibliographien, Reihe A., Bd. 1). Berlin; Basel, Beltz, 1969. 237 pp.

5.2.46 **Zeeck, Hans.** "Im Druck erschienene Schriften von Wilhelm Dilthey," *Archiv für Geschichte der Philosophie,* XXV (1912), 154-60.

Works

5.2.47 **Gesammelte Schriften.** 2. Aufl. Stuttgart, Teubner, Göttingen/Zürich, Vandenhoeck & Ruprecht, 1961- .

In progress. 19v. projected.
1st ed. 1914-36, 12v., was not complete.

5.2.48 **Dilthey, Wilhelm.** Selected writings. Ed., trans. and introduced by H. P. Rickman. Cambridge, N. Y., Cambridge University Press, 1976. 268 pp.

Bibliography: pp. 264-68.

Feuerbach, Ludwig Andreas
(1804-1872)

Bibliography

5.2.49 **Ludwig Feuerbach.** Jugendschriften. Hrsg. von H.-M. Sass. Stuttgart, Frommann, 1962.

The appendix contains a primary and secondary bibliography, 1830-1960.
This is vol. 11 of 5.2.53. Continued by 5.2.50.

5.2.50 **Luebbe, H. und H.-M. Sass,** *eds.* Atheismus in der Diskussion. Mainz, Grünewald, 1975. 280 pp.

Bibliography, 1960-73: pp. 263-80.

5.2.51 **Sass, H.-M.** Ludwig Feuerbach. Hamburg, Rowohlt, 1978.

Contains a very full primary and secondary bibliography.

Works

5.2.52 **Gesammelte Werke.** Hrsg. von W. Schuffenhauer. Berlin, Akademie Verlag, 1967- .

In progress.
20v. projected. 11v. published by 1978.

5.2.53 **Sämtliche Werke.** Neu. hrsg. von Wilhelm Bolin und Friedrich Jodl. 2. Aufl. Stuttgart, Frommann, 1959. 13v.

Includes critical apparatus and bibliographies of works by and about him.

5.2.54 **Ausgewählte Briefe von und an Ludwig Feuerbach.** Hrsg. von W. Bolin. Leipzig, O. Wigand, 1904. 2v.

See also: 5.2.51.

Biography

5.2.55 **Wartofsky, Marx W.** Feuerbach. Cambridge and New York, Cambridge University Press, 1977. 460 pp.

Bibliography: pp. 453-55.

Fichte, Johann Gottlieb
(1762-1814)

Bibliography

5.2.56 **J. G. Fichte-Bibliographie.** Hrsg. von Hans Michael Baumgartner und Wilhelm Jacobs. Stuttgart, Frommann, 1968. 346 pp.

Published in conjunction with 5.2.57.

Works

5.2.57 **Gesamtausgabe der Bayerischen Akademie der Wissenschaften.** Hrsg. von Reinhard Lauth und Hans Jacob. Stuttgart, Frommann, 1964- .

In progress.
26v. projected. 15v. published by 1978. The complete works, which will supersede all other editions.

5.2.58 **Johann Gottlieb Fichtes Nachgelassene Werke.** Hrsg. von I. H. Fichte. Bonn, A. Marcus, 1834-35. 3v.

Reprinted: Berlin, de Gruyter, 1962.

5.2.59 **Johann Gottlieb Fichtes Sämmtliche Werke.** Hrsg. von J. H. Fichte. Berlin, Veit, 1845-46. 8v.

Reprinted: Berlin, de Gruyter, 1964-65.

5.2.60 **Werke.** Hrsg. von F. Medicus. Leipzig, Meiner, 1908-12. 6v.

Reprinted: Darmstadt, Wissenschaftliche Buchgesellschaft, 1954-1967.
Not complete, but better than the J. H. Fichte edition (5.2.59).

5.2.61 **Fichtes Briefwechsel,** kritische gesamtausgabe gesammelt und hrsg. von Hans Schultz. 2. Aufl. Leipzig, H. Haessel, 1930. 2v.

Reprinted: Hildesheim, Olms, 1967.

5.2.62 **Fichte, J. G.** Attempt at a critique of all revelation. Trans. by G. D. Green, New York, Cambridge University Press, 1978. 186 pp.

A translation from the German of Fichte's first published work.

Biography

5.2.63 **Adamson, Robert.** Fichte. Edinburgh and London, Blackwood, 1881. 222 pp.

Reprinted: Freeport, N. Y., Books for Libraries, 222 pp.

5.2.64 **Léon, Xavier.** Fichte et son temps. Paris, Colin, 1922-27. 2v. bound in 3.

5.2.65 **Wundt, Max.** Johann Gottlieb Fichte. Stuttgart, Frommann, 1927. 317 pp.

Reprinted: Stuttgart-Bad Cannstatt, Frommann-Holzboog, 1976.

Frege, Gottlob
(1848-1925)

Bibliography

5.2.66 **Stroll, Avrum.** "On the first flowering of Frege's reputation," Journal of the history of philosophy, IV (1966), 72-81.

Lists articles on Frege, 1950-65, pp. 79-81. For a list of works by and on Frege, see *Encyclopedia of Philosophy* (1.4.1), p. 237.

Works

5.2.67 **[Works.]** Editors vary. Individually issued. Hildesheim, Olms, 1961-64.

Begriffsschrift und andere Aufsatze, 1964.
Grundgesetze der Arithmetik, 1962.
Die Grundlagen der Arithmetik, 1961.
Kleine Schriften, 1967.

Green, Thomas Hill
(1836-1882)

Works

5.2.68 **The works of Thomas Hill Green.** Ed. by R. L. Nettleship. 2d ed. London, Longmans, Green, 1889-90.

Reprinted: N. Y., Kraus Reprints. 1st ed. 1885-88.

Contains all his works except his introduction to Hume's Works and his *Prolegomena to Ethics*, ed. by A. C. Bradley, 5th ed., Oxford, Clarendon Press, 1929. Also contains a memoir.

Biography

5.2.69 **Richter, Melvin**. The politics of conscience: T. H. Green and his age. London, Weidenfeld & Nicolson; and Cambridge, Mass., Harvard University Press, 1964. 415 pp.

Supplements the memoir in 5.2.68.

Hegel, Georg Wilhelm Friedrich
(1770-1831)

Bibliography

5.2.70 **Hegel-Studien**. *See* 10.3.29.

5.2.71 **Leipner, K.**, *ed.* Hegel 1770-1970. Leben-Werk-Wirkung. (Katalog von F. Nicolin.) Stuttgart, E. Klett, 1970. 262 pp.

5.2.72 **Steinhauer, S. J. Kurt**. Hegel, an international bibliography. München, Verlag Documentation, 1978. 1,200 pp.

Contains 13,400 entries, covering editions of Hegel's work plus publications on Hegel, from Hegel's first work to publications of 1973.

See also: 1.2.5, pp. 70-73.

Works

5.2.73 **Gesammelte Werke**. Herausgegeben im Auftrag der deutschen Forschungsgemeinschaft. Hamburg, Meiner, 1968- .

1st complete critical edition.
In progress. 40v. projected.

5.2.74 **Sämtliche Werke**. Jubiläumsausgabe. Neu. hrsg. von Hermann Glockner. Stuttgart, Frommann, 1927-40. 26v.

Based on the 1832-45 ed. 19v. in 22.
Vols. 23-26 are a *Hegel-Lexikon*; also separately reprinted in a 2d ed. in 2v., 1957.

5.2.75 **Sämtliche Werke**: neue kritische Ausgabe. Hrsg. von Johannes Hoffmeister. Hamburg, F. Meiner, 1952-60. 30v.

A critical edition, originally planned by G. Lasson in 1907, and replanned by Hoffmeister.

5.2.76 **[Selected Works.]** New York, Oxford University Press.

Phenomenology of spirit;
Hegel's aesthetics: lectures on fine art;
Hegel's logic: being part I of the encyclopaedia of the philosophical sciences. 1830, 3d ed.;
Hegel's philosophy of mind (Part III of the Encyclopaedia);
Hegel's philosophy of right.

Biography

5.2.77 **Rosenkranz, Karl**. Georg Wilhelm Friedrich Hegels Leben. Berlin, Duncker and Humblot, 1844. 566 pp.

5.2.78 **Harris, H. S.** Hegel's development: toward the sunlight 1770-1801. New York, Oxford University Press, 1972. 600 pp.

An intellectual biography of Hegel.

Journals

5.2.79 **Owl of Minerva**. 1969-to date. Quarterly. Ed. Frederick G. Weiss, Department of Philosophy, Florida State University.

A newsletter of Hegel studies. Published by the Hegel Society of America (12.1.36).

See also: 10.3.29.

Center

5.2.80 **Hegel Research Center**. Seilergraben 27, Ch-8001 Zürich. Founded 1974.

Research on the sources of Hegel's philosophy and of the evolution of his philosophical system.

See also: 12.1.36, 10.5.48.

Hobbes, Thomas
(1588-1679)

Bibliography

5.2.81 **Jessop, Thomas Edmund**. Thomas Hobbes. (Bibliographical Series of Supplements to British Book News on Writers and Their Work, no. 130.) Harlow, Eng., published for the British Council and the National Book League, by Longmans, Green, 1968. 40 pp.

5.2.82 **Macdonald, Hugh**, and **Mary Hargreaves**. Thomas Hobbes; a bibliography. London, The Bibliographical Society, 1952. 83 pp.

5.2.83 **Pacchi, A.** "Bibliografia Hobbesiana dal 1840 a oggi," Rivista Critica di Storia della Filosofia, XVII (1962), 528-47.

Includes editions of and works on Hobbes, 1840-1962.

5.2.84 **Valls, Francisco Javier**. "Bibliografía sobre Hobbes, 1960-1974," *in* H. C. W. Sigwart,ed., Vergleichung der Rechts—und Staats—theorien des B. Spinoza und des Th. Hobbes, Aalen, Scientia, 1974, pp. 187-203.

Works

5.2.85 **The English works of Thomas Hobbes**. Ed. by Sir William Molesworth. London, J. Bohn, 1830. 11v.

Reprinted: Oxford, 1962.
The standard edition, together with 5.2.86; contains an index.

5.2.86 **Thomae Hobbes Malmesburiensis opera philosophica** quae Latine scripsit omnia . . . collecta studio et labore Gu. Molesworth. London, J. Bohn, 1839-45. 5v.

Reprinted: Oxford, 1961.
The standard edition, together with 5.2.85.

Biography

5.2.87 **Laird, John**. Hobbes. New York and London, E. Benn, 1934. 324 pp.

5.2.88 **Peters, Richard S.** Hobbes. Harmondsworth, England, Penguin, 1956. 271 pp.

5.2.89 **Stephen, Leslie**. Hobbes. London and New York, Macmillan, 1904. 243 pp.

Hume, David
(1711-1776)

Bibliography

5.2.90 **Hall, Roland**. A Hume bibliography from 1930. York, England, Ronald Hall, 1971. 80 pp.

About 800 items. Subject index. Completes Jessop (5.2.92) since 1930. Continued in the *Philosophical Quarterly* (Edinburgh), XXVI (1976), 92-101. Superseded by 5.2.91.

5.2.91 **Hall, Roland**. Fifty years of Hume Scholarship; a bibliographical guide. Edinburgh, University Press, 1978. 150 pp.

5.2.92 **Jessop, Thomas Edmund**. A bibliography of David Hume and of Scottish philosophy from Francis Hutcheson to Lord Balfour. London, A. Brown, Hull, 1938. 201 pp.

Reprinted: N. Y., Russell and Russell, 1966.
Continued by 5.2.90.

5.2.93 **Ronchetti, Emanuele**. "Bibliografia humiana dal 1937 al 1966," Revista critica di storia della filosofia," XXII (1967), 495-520.

Works

5.2.94 **Philosophical works**. Ed. by T. H. Green and T. H. Grose. London, Longmans, Green, 1874-75. 4v.

Reprint of 1886 ed., Aalen, Scientia, 1964.
Superseded by 5.2.95 and 5.2.96 for those works; the standard edition for other works.

5.2.95 Enquiries concerning the human understanding and concerning the principles of morals. Ed. by L. A. Selby-Bigge. 3d ed. with text revised and notes by P. H. Nidditch. Oxford, Clarendon Press, 1975. 417 pp.

1st ed. 1894.
Standard edition; includes index.

5.2.96 A treatise of human nature. Ed. by L. A. Selby-Bigge. Oxford, Clarendon Press, 1888. 709 pp.

Reprinted: 1955.
The standard edition; includes index.

5.2.97 The natural history of religion, ed. by A. W. Colver; and Dialogues concerning natural religion, ed. by J. V. Price. New York, Oxford University Press, 1976. 299 pp.

Biography

5.2.98 Burton, John H. Life and correspondence of David Hume (from the papers bequeathed by his nephew to the Royal Society of Edinburgh and other original sources). Edinburgh, W. Tait, 1846. 2v.

Reprinted: N. Y., Burt Franklin.

5.2.99 Mossner, Ernest Campbell. The life of David Hume. Oxford, Clarendon Press, 1970. 683 pp.

Bibliography: pp. 625-40.
Also contains *The life of David Hume, Esq.,* written by himself, Adam Smith, ed.

Journal

5.2.100 Hume Studies. See 10.2.37.

See also: 10.5.48, 12.1.37.

Husserl, Edmund
(1859-1938)

Bibliography

5.2.101 Allen, J. "Husserl bibliography of English translations," The monist, LIX (1975), 133-37.

5.2.102 Patocka, Jan. "Husserl-Bibliographie," Revue internationale de philosophie, I (1939), 374-97.

Continued by: Raes, Jean, "Supplément à la bibliographie de Husserl," ibid., IV (1950), 469-75; G. Maschke and I. Kern, ibid., XIX (1965), 153-202; and H. L. van Breda, "Bibliographie der bis zum 30. Juni 1959 veröffentlichten Schriften Edmund Husserls," Edmund Husserl 1859-1959, The Hague, Nijhoff, 1959, pp. 289-306.

See also: 1.2.5, pp. 78-79.

Works

5.2.103 Husserliana. The Hague, Nijhoff.

This series includes:
I. Edmund Husserl, Gesammelte Werke. Hrsg. von H. L. van Breda. The Hague, Nijhoff, 1950- .
In progress. 18v. projected.
Based on the collection of the Husserl-Archiv (5.2.107), divided into: Textkritische Neuausgaben and Nachlassbande.
II. Dokumente, 1977- .
III. Studienausgabe, 1977- .
IV. Nijhoff translations of Husserl classics (See 5.2.104).

5.2.104 [Works.] Atlantic Highlands, N. J., Humanities Press. Issued separately.

The series includes:
Cartesian meditations: an introduction to phenomenology, 1960;
Formal and transcendental logic, 1969;
The idea of phenomenology, 1964;
Ideas: General introduction to phenomenology, 1931, 1958;
Logical investigations, 1970, 2v.;
The Paris lectures, 2d. ed., 1975;
Phenomenological psychology, 1977.
This series is the American equivalent of

5.2.103, IV.

Translation Guide

5.2.105 **Cairns, Dorion**. Guide for translating Husserl. The Hague, Nijhoff (Phaenomenologica 55), 1973. 145 pp.

Journal

5.2.106 **Analecta Husserliana**. 1971-to date. Annual. Editor: Anna-Teresa Tymieniecka. Published by Dordrecht, Holland, D. Reidel.

Focuses on the phenomenology of man and the human condition. Some volumes are proceedings of conferences on phenomenology.

See also: 12.2.14.

Archives

5.2.107 **Husserl-Archiv**. Kardinal Mercier-plein 2, B-3000, Leuven, Belgium.

Contains Husserl's inedita.
See 5.2.103.

5.2.108 **Husserl Archiv**. The New School. Established in the memory of Alfred Schutz. Contains a complete set of Husserl's inedita photo-copied from the original transcriptions held in the Husserl Archiv at Louvain. The New School for Social Research, 65 Fifth Avenue, New York, N. Y. 10003.

Society

5.2.109 **International Husserl and Phenomenological Research Society**. Secretary-General, Anna-Teresa Tymieniecka, 348 Payson Road, Belmont, Mass., 02178.

"Created to promote communication among those specializing in Husserlian phenomenology."

Hutcheson, Francis
(1694-1746)

Works

5.2.110 **Hutcheson, Francis**. Collected Works. Facsimile editions prepared by Bernard Fabian. Münster and Hildesheim, Olms, 1969-71. 7v.

Reprints of original individual works. Original publishers vary.

James, William
(1842-1910)

Bibliography

5.2.111 **McDermott, John J.** The writings of William James; a comprehensive edition. New York, Modern Library, 1967. 858 pp.

Annotated bibliography of the writings of William James, pp. 811-58.

5.2.112 **Perry, Ralph Barton**. Annotated bibliography of the writings of William James. New York, Longmans, Green, 1920. 69 pp.

Reprinted: Wm. C. Brown.
Annotated.

Works

5.2.113 **The works of William James**. Frederick Burkhardt, General Editor. Cambridge, Mass., Harvard University Press, 1975- .

In progress. 16v. projected.

See also: 5.2.111.

Biography

5.2.114 **The letters of Henry James**, selected and edited by Percy Lubbock. New York, Scribner's, 1920. 2v.

"Charming letters, primarily of biographical and historical significance, edited by James's son" (William James Earle in 1.4.1).

See also: 10.5.36.

Kant, Immanuel
(1724-1804)

Bibliography

5.2.115 **Adickes, Erich.** "Bibliography of writings by and on Kant which have appeared in Germany up to the end of 1887," The philosophical review, II-IV (1893-95).

Published separately as *German Kantian Bibliography.* Boston, Ginn and Ginn, 1895-96. 623 pp.
Reprinted: N. Y., Burt Franklin, 1970.

5.2.116 **Malter, Rudolf.** "Bibliographie der deutschsprachigen Kant-Literatur,' 1957-1967," Kant-Studien, LX (1969), 234-64.

Continued in vols. LXII, LXIV, LXV. See *Kant-Studien* (10.3.30) for periodic bibliographies.

5.2.117 **Scott-Taggart, M. J.** "Recent work in the philosophy of Kant," American philosophical quarterly, III (1966), 171-209.

Reprinted and enlarged in *Kant Studies Today*, L. W. Beck, ed., La Salle, Ill., Open Court, 1969, pp. 1-71.

See also: 1.2.5, pp. 84-86.

Works

5.2.118 **Kants gesammelte Schriften.** Herausgegeben von der Preussischen Akademie der Wissenschaften zu Berlin. Berlin, de Gruyter, 1902-56. 23v.

The standard critical edition.
Supplemented by: *Vorlesungen*, vols. 24-28, 1966- ; and *Allgemeiner Kantindex zu Kants gesammelten Schriften*, 1967- .
When completed, this index will supplement Rudolf Eisler, *Kant-lexikon* (5.2.120); and Heinrich Ratke, *Systematisches Handlexikon zu Kants Kritik der reinen Vernunft*, Leipzig, Meiner, 1929, 330 pp. Vols. 1-15 will be an index of the text location of every word in the above 23 volumes; vols. 16-19 will be an index of word frequencies; vol. 20 is an index of persons and sources.

5.2.119 **Werke.** In Gemeinschaft mit H. Cohen, A. Buchenaw, O. Buek, [u. A.], hrsg. von E. Cassirer. Berlin, B. Cassirer, 1922-23. 11v.

Lexicon

5.2.120 **Eisler, Rudolf.** Kant-Lexikon; Nachschlagewerk zu Kants sämtlichen Schriften, Briefen und handschriftlichen Nachlass; hrsg. unter Mitwirkung der Kantgesellschaft. Berlin, Mittler, 1930. 642 pp.

Reprinted: N.Y., Burt Franklin; Hildesheim, Olms.
See 5.2.118.

Biography

5.2.121 **Cassirer, Ernst.** Kants Leben und Lehre. Berlin, Cassirer, 1921. 448 pp.

Collections

5.2.122 **Aetas Kantiana.** Brussels. Editions Culture et Civilisation, 1973- .

Reprints of works of Kant's disciples, critics, colleagues. 265 volumes published through 1978. A total of 314 volumes announced.

5.2.123 **Beck, Lewis White,** *ed.* The philosophy of Immanuel Kant. New York, Garland.

Eleven of the most important books on Kant's philosophy, reprinted in 14v.

Journal

5.2.124 **Kant-Studien.** *See* 10.3.30.

See also: 5.2.125.

Congress

5.2.125 **International Kant Congress.**

3rd: University of Rochester, 1970. Pro-

ceedings, Atlantic Highlands, N. J., Humanities Press, 1972;
4th: Mainz, 1974. Proceedings, Dordrecht, Holland, Reidel, 1974.

See also: 10.5.48.

Kierkegaard, Søren Aabye
(1813-1855)

Bibliography

5.2.126 **Himmelstrup, Jens.** Søren Kierkegaard; international bibliografi. København, Nyt Nordisk Forlag, Arnold Busck, 1962. 216 pp.

Includes works by and about Kierkegaard, 1835-55. Continued for 1956-62 by M. Allessandro Cortese, "Una nuova bibliografia Kierkegaardiana," *Revista di filosofia neoscolastica,* LV (1963), 98-108.

5.2.127 **Jorgensen, Aage,** *comp.* Søren Kierkegaard-litteratur 1961-1970: En forelobig bibliografi. Maarslet, Denmark, Aage Jorgensen, 1971. 99 pp.

5.2.128 **Nielsen, Edith Ortmann.** Søren Kierkegaard; bidrag til en bibliografi. Contributions towards a bibliography. København, Munksgaard, 1951. 96 pp.

See also: 1.2.16 (No. 4) and 1.2.5, pp. 87-89.

Works

5.2.129 **Søren Kierkegaards samlede vaerker:** ungivne af A. B. Drachmann, J. L. Heiberg og H. O. Lange. 3. udgeve. København, Gyldendal, 1962-64. 20v.

1st ed. 1901-06. 14v.

5.2.130 **Søren Kierkegaards Papirer.** Udgivne of P. A. Heiberg. V. Kuhr, og S. Torsting. København, Gyldendal, 1909-48. 11v. in 20.

A 2d ed. is in progress, 1968- .

5.2.131 **Gesammelte Werke.** Hrsg. von H. Gottsched und C. Schrempf. Jena, Diederichs, 1903-25. 12v.

A German translation.

5.2.132 **Kierkegaard's Writings.** Gen. Ed. Howard V. Hong. Princeton, Princeton University Press, 1978- .

25v. of text projected, and a separate cumulative index. Each volume of translation includes a historical introduction, selections from Kierkegaard's journals, and provisional manuscripts, notes, and an index.

5.2.133 **Søren Kierkegaard's Journals and Papers.** Ed. and trans. by Howard V. and Edna H. Hong. Bloomington, Ind., Indiana University Press, 1967-75. 7v.

Contains translations of portions of 5.2.129.
V. 5-6, Autobiographical; v. 7, Index and composite collation.
Entries arranged chronologically and according to theme.

5.2.134 **Søren Kierkegaard.** [Selected Works.]

Individual titles published separately. Most are translated by Walter Lowrie. Princeton, Princeton University Press. Includes:

Either/Or;
Training in Christianity and the edifying discourses which accompanied it;
The sickness unto death;
Christian discourses;
Attack upon Christendom;
For self-examination and *Judge for yourselves;*
Fear and trembling and *The sickness unto death;*
The concept of dread.

Indices

5.2.135 **McKinnon, Alastair,** *comp.* The Kierkegaard Indices. Leiden, E. J. Brill.

I. Kierkegaard in translation/en traduction/in Ubersetzung, 1970. 133 pp.
Provides page and line correlations among

the second and third Danish editions of Kierkegaard's *Samlede Vaerker* and the standard English, French and German translations. Designed to assist the scholar using any of the three translations to move to the corresponding section of text in either of the Danish originals.

II. Fundamental polyglot konkordans til Kierkegaards Samlede Vaerker, 1971. 1137 pp.

III. Index verborum til Kierkegaards Samlede Vaerker, 1973. 1322 pp.

IV. A computational analysis of Kierkegaards Samlede Vaerker, 1975. 1088 pp.

Biography

5.2.136 **The journals of Søren Kierkegaard**: a selection. Ed. and trans. by Alexander Dru. Oxford, The University Press, 1938. 603 pp.

Autobiography.

5.2.137 **Hohlenberg, J. E.** Søren Kierkegaard. London, Routledge & Kegan Paul, 1954. 321 pp.

5.2.138 **Lowrie, W.** A short life of Kierkegaard. Princeton, Princeton University Press, 1942. 271 pp.

Series

5.2.139 **Kierkegaardiana.** 1955-to date. Pub., Copenhagen, Rosenkilde and Bagger.

The annual publication of The Kierkegaard Society. Articles in English, German, and Danish.

La Mettrie, Julien Offray de
(1709-1751)

Works

5.2.140 **Oeuvres philosophiques de La Mettrie.** Paris, C. Tutot, 1796. 3v.

Reprinted: Hildesheim, Olms, 1970.

Leibniz, Gottfried Wilhelm
(1646-1716)

Bibliography

5.2.141 **Leibniz-Bibliographie.** Ein Verzeichnis der Literatur über Leibniz. Bearb. von K. Müller. Hrsg. von der Niedersächsischen Landesbibliothek, 1966. 480 pp.

5.2.142 **Ravier, Emile.** Bibliographie des oeuvres de Leibniz. Paris, Alcan, 1937. 703 pp.

Reprinted: Hildesheim, Olms, 1965.

5.2.143 **"Leibnitz-Bibliographie,"** Studia Leibnitiana. A continuing bibliography since 1969. See 5.2.153.

See also: 1.2.5, pp. 93-96.

Works

5.2.144 **Sämtliche Schriften und Briefe.** Hrsg. von der Akademie der Wissenschaften der DDR. Darmstadt, O. Reichl, 1923- .

A critical edition, but still incomplete; includes bibliographies.

80v. projected in seven series: I. Allgemeiner, politischer und historischer Briefwechsel. II. Philosophischer Briefwechsel. III. Mathematischer, naturwissenschaftlicher und technischer Briefwechsel. IV. Politische Schriften. V. Historische Schriften. VI. Philosophische Schriften. VII. Mathematische, naturwissenschaftliche und technische Schriften.

5.2.145 **Sämtliche Schriften und Briefe.** Hrsg. von der Deutschen Akademie der Wissenschaft zu Berlin unter Leitung von Kurt Müller. Hildesheim, Olms, 1970- .

5.2.146 **Die mathematischen Schriften** von G. W. Leibniz. Hrsg. von C. I. Gerhardt. Berlin, Ascher, 1849-63. 7v.

Reprinted: Hildesheim, Olms.

5.2.147 **Die philosophischen Schriften** von G. W. Leibniz. Hrsg. von C. I. Gerhardt. Berlin, Weidmann, 1875-90. 7v.

Reprinted: Hildesheim, Olms.

5.2.148 **Philosophical papers and letters**: a selection translated and edited, with an introduction by Leroy E. Loemker. 2d ed. Dordrecht, Holland, D. Reidel, 1976. 736 pp.

1st ed., 1956.
Standard English edition; bibliography.

Biography

5.2.149 **Guhrauer, Gottschalk E.** Gottfried Wilhelm, Freiherr von Leibniz. Breslau, F. Hirt 1842. 2v.

Reprinted: Hildesheim, Olms.
The most complete of the biographies.

5.2.150 **Fischer, Kuno.** Gottfried Wilhelm Leibniz; leben, werke und lehre. 5th ed. Willy Kabitz, ed. Heidelberg, C. Winter, 1920. 797 pp.

"Of great value, with appendix containing many new details and corrections" (L. J. Russell in 1.4.1).

5.2.151 **Merz, J. T.** Leibniz. Edinburgh and London, Blackwood, 1884. 4v.

Reprinted: New York, 1948.
"Still useful" (L. J. Russell in 1.4.1).

5.2.152 **Müller, Kurt** und **Gisela Kronert.** Leben und Werk von G. W. Leibniz: eine chronik. Frankfurt, Klostermann, 1969. 331 pp.

Journal

5.2.153 **Studia Leibnitiana.** Sponsored by the Gottfried-Wilhelm-Leibniz-Gessellschaft. Directed by Kurt Müller, Heinrich Schepers, and Wilhelm Totok. Founded 1969. Twice yearly. Wiesbaden, Steiner.

Focuses upon Leibnizian research as a philosophical mathematical, and historical basis. Publishes a Leibniz bibliography on a regular basis.

Society and Congress

5.2.154 **Leibniz Society.** Contact Laurence B. McCollough. Dept. of Philosophy and Humanities, Texas A&M Univ., College Station, Tex. 77843.

5.2.155 **International Leibniz Congress.**

Sponsored by the Leibniz Gesellschaft, Niedersachsische Landesbibliothek, D 3000 Hannover 1, Waterloostr. 8, Federal Republic of Germany.
Held every five years. Latest was in 1977.

See also: 10.5.48.

Lessing, Gotthold Ephraim
(1729-1781)

Bibliography

5.2.156 **Seifert, Siegfried.** Lessing-bibliographie. Berlin, Aufbau, 1973. 857 pp.

Works

5.2.157 **Gesammelte Werke.** Hrsg. von P. Rilla. Berlin, Aufbau, 1954-58. 10v.

Locke, John
(1632-1704)

Bibliography

5.2.158 **Christophersen, H. O.** A bibliographical introduction to the study of John Locke. Skrifter utgitt av det Norske videnskapsakademi: Historisk-filosofisk klasse (1930, no. 8). Oslo, I Kommisjon hos J. Dybwad., 1930. 134 pp.

Reprinted: N. Y., Burt Franklin, 1968.
Continued by Roland Hall and Roger Woolhouse, "Forty years of work on John Locke (1929-1969), a bibliography," *The Philosophical Quarterly*, XX (1970), 258-68.
Addenda: XX (1970), 394-96; *Locke Newsletter*, 1970, 5-11.

5.2.159 **Cranston, Maurice.** Locke. London, Longmans, Green, 1961. 38 pp.

Published for the British Council; British book news bibliographical series of supplements no. 135.

5.2.160 **Hall, Roland.** "Omissions from Christophersen," Locke Newsletter (1974), 18-23.

Supplemented: summer, 1975, 23-25.

5.2.161 **Long, Philip.** A summary catalogue of the Lovelace collection of papers of John Locke in the Bodleian Library. Oxford bibliographical society. Publications (n.s., vol. VIII). Oxford, printed for the society at the University Press, 1959. 64 pp.

A catalogue of the writings, many of which are still unpublished, of John Locke in the Lovelace Collection of the Bodleian Library, Oxford

See also: 5.2.169 and 1.2.5, pp. 99-101.

Works

5.2.162 **Works.** Clarendon edition. Oxford, Clarendon Press, 1975- .

In progress.
A critical edition.
1st vol. is 5.2.165.
Will include 8v. of the correspondence of John Locke.

5.2.163 **The works of John Locke.** 12th ed. London, C. and J. Rivington, 1824. 9v.

Reprinted in 10v., Aalen, Scientia, 1963.
1st ed. London, 1714. 3v.
One of the most complete collections; but 5.2.164 is the standard edition of the *Essay*.

5.2.164 **Essay concerning human understanding.** Ed. with a critical introduction and notes by A. C. Fraser. Oxford, Clarendon Press, 1894. 2v.

Reprinted: N. Y., Dover, 1959.

5.2.165 **An essay concerning human understanding.** Ed. with an intro., critical apparatus, glossary by Peter H. Nidditch. Oxford, Clarendon Press, 1975. 867 pp.

This is the 4th ed. of the *Essay* but it includes material of the 5th and variants.

5.2.166 **An essay concerning human understanding.** Ed. with an introduction by John W. Yolton. Rev. ed. New York, Dutton (Everyman's Library), 1965. 2v.

". . . the full text of the Fifth Edition, that edition willed by Locke to Bodleian with his final approval" (p. xiv).

5.2.167 **The correspondence of John Locke.** Ed. by E. S. DeBeer. Oxford, Clarendon Press, 1976.

Bibliography: I, lxxx-xcv.
In progress. 8v. projected.

Biography

5.2.168 **Cranston, Maurice.** John Locke, a biography. London, Longmans, Green, 1957. 496 pp.

"A thorough study of the life of Locke, using all materials available at present" (James Gordon Clapp in 1.4.1).

Newsletter

5.2.169 **The Locke Newsletter.** Ed. by Roland Hall. University of York, England. 1970- Annual.

Carries bibliography and information on works dealing with Locke.

See also: 10.5.48.

Lotze, Rudolf Hermann
(1817-1881)

Bibliography

5.2.170 **Santayana, George.** Lotze's system of philosophy. Ed. by Paul Kuntz. Bloomington,

Ind., Indiana University Press, 1971. 274 pp.

Lists all the works of Lotze and catalogs Lotze's influence, especially on Anglo-American philosophy.

Biography

5.2.171 Wentscher, Max. Hermann Lotze. Lotzes Leben und Werke. Vol. I. Heidelberg, C. Winter, 1913. 376 pp.

Maine de Biran
(1766-1824)

Bibliography

5.2.172 Ghio, M. Michelangelo. "Essai de bibliographie raisonée de Maine de Biran (1766-1824)," *in* Maine de Biran e la tradizione biraniana in Francia, Turin, Ed. di "Filosofia," 1962, pp. 181-99.

5.2.173 Mayjonade, J. B. Maine de Biran, étude biographique et bibliographique. Lille, Taffin-Lefort, 1895. 32 pp.

Works

5.2.174 Oeuvres de Maine de Biran. Publiées par Pierre Tisserand et Henri Gouhier. Paris, Alcan, 1922-49. 14v.

Definitive and standard edition.

Biography

5.2.175 Hallie, Philip Paul. Maine de Biran; reformer of empiricism. Cambridge, Mass., Harvard University Press, 1959. 217 pp.

Malebranche, Nicholas
(1638-1715)

Bibliography

5.2.176 Rome, Beatrice K. The philosophy of Malebranche. Chicago, Regnery, 1963. 448 pp.

Bibliography: pp. 331-362.

5.2.177 Robinet, André. Malebranche vivant. Documents biographiques et bibliographiques. Vol. 20 of 5.2.178. 489 pp.

See also: 1.2.5, pp. 107-08.

Works

5.2.178 Oeuvres complètes de Malebranche. Direction: André Robinet. Paris, Vrin, 1958-67. 20v.

A definitive, critical edition.

Vol. 20, 1967, includes a biography and a bibliography. *See* 5.2.177.

Added to this collection is: *Index des citations bibliques, patristiques, philosophiques et scientifiques.* Paris, Vrin, 1970, 400 pp. An index to the *Oeuvres complètes.*

Biography

5.2.179 André, Y. M. La vie du R. P. Malebranche. Paris, Poussielque, 1886. 430 pp.

See also: 5.2.178, vol. 20.

Marx, Karl
(1818-1883)

Bibliography and Dictionary

5.2.180 Eubanks, Cecil L. Karl Marx and Friedrich Engels; an analytical bibliography. (Vol. XXIII of Garland Reference Library of Social Science.) New York and London, Garland, 1977. 163 pp.

Bibliography of books, articles, dissertations and biographies in English by and about Marx and Engels (through 1976). Includes a general overview of trends in Marxian scholarship and a comparative essay on Marx and Engels.

5.2.181 Lachs, John. Marxist philosophy; a bibliographical guide. *See* 8.5.6.

5.2.182 **Rubel, Maximilien.** Bibliographie des oeuvres de Karl Marx. Avec en appendice un répertoire des oeuvres de Friedrich Engels. Paris, Marcel Rivière, 1956. 273 pp.

——Supplement, 1960. 79 pp.

5.2.183 **Stockhammer, Morris.** Karl Marx dictionary. New York, Philosophical Library, 1965. 273 pp.

See also: 8.5.1-8.5.6 and 1.2.5, pp. 110-15.

Works

5.2.184 **Karl Marx, Friedrich Engels.** Historisch-kritische Gesamtausgabe; Werke, Schriften, Briefe. Hrsg. von D. Ryazanov and V. Adoratsky. Frankfurt, Marx-Engels Institute, 1927-36.

Commonly referred to as MEGA.

A critical edition, but never completed. Of the 42v. projected only 7v. of works by Marx and Engels, a commemorative volume on Engels, and 4v. of correspondence were published.

5.2.185 **Karl Marx, Friedrich Engels.** Gesamtausgabe (MEGA) Hrsg. vom Institut für Marxismus-Leninismus beim Zentralkomitee der Kommunistischen Partei der Sowjetunion und vom Institut für Marxismus-Leninismus beim Zentralkomitee der Sozialistischen Einheitspartei Deutschlands. Berlin, Dietz, 1972- .

In progress.

100v. projected in 4 sections.

When finished, this will be a complete, critical edition.

5.2.186 **Karl Marx, Friedrich Engels.** Werke. Berlin, Dietz, 1956- .

In progress. 44v. projected.

Commonly referred to as MEW.

5.2.187 **Karl Marx, Frederick Engels.** Collected Works. New York, International Publishers; London, Lawrence & Wishart; Moscow, Progress Publishers, 1975- .

In progress.

50v. projected.

"Will include all the works of Marx and Engels published in their lifetimes or since, their complete correspondence, a considerable part of their unpublished handwritten manuscripts, and newly discovered works and letters."

Biography

5.2.188 **Berlin, Isaiah.** Karl Marx, his life and environment, London, Butterworth, 1939. 256 pp.

5.2.189 **Mehring, Franz.** Karl Marx: the story of his life. 4th ed. Trans. by E. Fitzgerald. Leipzig and Atlantic Highlands, N. J., Humanities Press, 1936. 575 pp.

5.2.190 **McLellan, David.** Karl Marx; his life and thought. London, Macmillan, 1973. 498 pp.

Bibliography: pp. 469-89.

5.2.191 **Rubel, Maximilien.** Karl Marx; essai de biographie intellectuelle. Paris, M. Rivière, 1957. 463 pp.

5.2.192 **Meyer, Gustav.** Friedrich Engels. The Hague, Nijhoff, 1934, 2v.

An abridged English edition, London, Chapman & Hall, 1936, 323 pp.

See also: the biographies of Karl Marx.

Center

5.2.193 **Hegel and Marx Center.** *See* 5.2.80.

Meinong, Alexius
(1853-1920)

Works

5.2.194 **Gesamtausgabe.** Hrsg. von R. Haller und R. Kindinger. Graz, Akademische Druck-u. Verlagsanstalt, 1968- .

In progress.
7v. projected.
The 1st 2v. are reprints of *Gesammelte Abhandlungen*, Leipzig, 1913-14.

Mill, John Stuart
(1806-1873)

Bibliography

5.2.195 **Cranston, Maurice**. John Stuart Mill. London, Longmans, Green, 1958. 34 pp.

Published for the British Council; British book news bibliographical series of supplements no. 99.

5.2.196 **MacMinn, N., J. R. Hainds**, and **J. M. McCrimmon**. Bibliography of the published writings of John Stuart Mill. Edited from his manuscript with corrections and notes. (Northwestern University Studies in the Humanities, 12.) Evanston, Ill., Northwestern University Press, 1945. 101 pp.

5.2.197 **The Mill newsletter**. Ed. by John M. Robson and Michael Lane, 1965- . Semi-annual.

Published by Unversity of Toronto Press, in association with Victoria College, University of Toronto. Carries a continuing bibliography on Mill.

5.2.198 "**John Stuart Mill** [a bibliography]," *in* George Watson, ed., The new Cambridge bibliography of English literature. Cambridge, Cambridge University Press, 1969, vol. 3, cols. 1551-1756.

Works

5.2.199 **The collected works of John Stuart Mill**. Toronto, University of Toronto Press, 1963- .

In progress.
20v. projected.
A critical edition.

Biography

5.2.200 **Mill, J. S.** Autobiography. Indianapolis and New York, Bobbs-Merrill, 1957. 201 pp.

1st ed., 1873.

5.2.201 **Packe, M. St. John**. The life of John Stuart Mill. London, Secker & Warburg, 1954. 567 pp.

See also: 10.5.48.

Montaigne, Michel de
(1533-1592)

Bibliography

5.2.202 **Tannenbaun, Samuel Aaron**. . . . Michel Eyquem de Montaigne (a concise bibliography). Elizabethan Bibliographies, no. 24. New York, S. A. Tannenbaum, 1942. 137 pp.

5.2.203 **Richou, Gabriel Charles Marie**. Inventaire de la collection des ouvrages et documents, réunis par J.-F. Payen et J.-B. Bastide sur Michel de Montaigne. Paris, L. Techener, 1878. 396 pp.

Reprinted: N. Y., Burt Franklin, 1970.

Works

5.2.204 **Oeuvres complètes**. Paris, Seuil, 1967. 624 pp.

Contains notes by Robert Barral with Pierre Michel and the works: *Essais, Journal du voyage en Italie, Lettres, Ephémérides de Beuther*, and *Sentences de la Librairie*.

Montesquieu
(1689-1755)

Bibliography

5.2.205 **Cabeen, David Clark**. Montesquieu: a bibliography. New York, New York Public Library, 1947. 87 pp.

Also found in *New York public library bulletin*, vol. LI (1947), 359-83, 423-30, 513-25, 545-65, 593-616.

Works

5.2.206 Oeuvres. Paris, J. F. Bastien, 1788. 5v.

5.2.207 Oeuvres complètes. Paris, 1875-79. 7v.

Contains variants of the first editions, a choice of the best commentaries, and of the new notes by Edouard Laboulaye. Reprinted: Hildesheim, Olms.

Newman, John Henry
(1801-1890)

Works

5.2.208 Newman, John Henry. The complete works of Cardinal Newman. Westminster, Md., Christian Classics, 1966- .

A reprint of the entire uniform edition. In progress. 42v. projected.

Nietzsche, Friedrich
(1844-1900)

Bibliography

5.2.209 Reichert, Herbert W., and **Karl Schlechta.** International Nietzsche bibliography. Chapel Hill, University of North Carolina Press, 1960. 133 pp.

Partially annotated; full, but not exhaustive.
Rev. and expanded: University of North Carolina Studies in Comparative Literature, No. 45, 1968. 162 pp.

5.2.210 Reichert, Hubert W. "International Nietzsche Bibliography 1968 through 1971," Nietzsche-Studien (Berlin, New York), vol. 2 (1973), 320-39.

Nietzsche-Studien (5.2.220) carries a continuing Nietzsche bibliography.

Works

5.2.211 Werke. Kritische Gesamtausgabe. Hrsg. von Georgio Colli und Mazzino Montinari. Berlin, de Gruyter, 1967- .

In progress.
30v. in eight sections projected.
A critical edition which, when completed, will supersede all other editions.

5.2.212 Gesammelte Werke. Grossoktav Ausgabe. 2. Aufl. Leipzig, Kroner, 1901-13. 19v.

Not complete.
Supplemented by Richard Oehler, *Nietzsche Register*, 1926, considered vol. XX. Also separately published, Stuttgart, Kroner, 1965.

5.2.213 Gesammelte Werke. Musarionausgabe. München, Musarion, 1920-29. 23v.

The most complete edition presently available.

5.2.214 Werke in drei Bänden. Hrsg. von Karl Schlechta. 2. Aufl. München, C. Hanser, 1960. 3v.

1st. ed. 1954-56. Not complete, though it contains all of Nietzsche's books. It is supplemented by *Nietzsche-Index zu den Werken in drei Bänden*, 1965. 517 pp.

5.2.215 Werke und Briefe. Historisch-kritische Gesamtausgabe. München, C. H. Beck, 1934-52. 9v.

5.2.216 The complete works of Friedrich Nietzsche. Ed. by Oscar Levy. Edinburgh and London, T. N. Foulis, 1909-13. 18v.

Reprinted: N. Y., Russell & Russell, 1964.
The most complete collection in English but defective in various ways and not entirely reliable.

Biography

5.2.217 Hollingdale, R. G. Nietzsche: the man and his philosophy. Baton Rouge, La. and

London, Routledge & Kegan Paul, 1965. 326 pp.

"By far the best biography in English . . . in which Nietzsche's ideas are discussed in the context of his life" (Walter Kaufmann in 1.4.1).

5.2.218 **Bernoulli, E. A.** Franz Overbeck und Friedrich Nietzsche. Jena, 1908. 2v.

"Important for its biographical material, takes issue with the version of Nietzsche's life presented by his sister" (Walter Kaufmann in 1.4.1).

Society, Journal, Series

5.2.219 **Société Nietzsche.** Formed in Paris on the occasion of the 125th anniversary of his birth. 1969- . Address: 27 Rue Lacépède, Paris 5e, France.

5.2.220 **Nietzsche Studien.** Internationales Jahrbuch für die Nietzsche-forschung. Hrsg. von Mazzino Montinari, Wolfgang Müller-Lauter, Heinz Wenzel. 1972-to date. Annual. Pub. by Berlin, de Gruyter.

5.2.221 **Monographien und texte zur Nietzsche-Forschung.** Ed. by Mazzino Montinari, Wolfgang Müller-Lauter, Heinz Wenzel. Berlin and New York, de Gruyter, 1972-to date.

Irregular.

Pascal, Blaise
(1623-1662)

Bibliography

5.2.222 **Maire, Albert.** Bibliographie générale des oeuvres de Blaise Pascal. Paris, L. Giraud-Badin, 1925-27. 5v.

5.2.223 **Flasche, Hans.** "Stand, Methoden, und Aufgaben der Pascalforschung," Dichtung und Volkstum (Stuttgart), vol. 27 (1953), 611-35.

Useful for the period 1939-1952.

5.2.224 **Bishop, Morris,** and **Sister Marie Louise Hubert.** "Pascal [an annotated bibliography]," *in* D. C. Cabeen and J. Brody, gen. eds., A critical bibliography of French literature, Syracuse, N. Y., Syracuse University Press, 1961. Vol. III, pp. 417-56.

See also: 5.2.225 and 5.2.226.

Works

5.2.225 **Oeuvres complètes.** Ed. L. Brunschvicg, P. Boutroux, F. Gazier. Paris, Hachette, 1904-14. 14v.

Standard edition.
Reprinted: N. Y., Kraus Reprints.

5.2.226 **Oeuvres complètes.** Texte établi et annoté par Jacques Chevalier. Paris, Gallimard, 1954. 1529 pp.

Bibliography included in "Note bibliographique," pp. xxiii-xxvi.

5.2.227 **Oeuvres complètes.** Texte établi, présenté et annoté par Jean Mesnard. Paris, Desclée de Brouwer, 1964- .

In progress.
Includes bibliographies.

Biography

5.2.228 **Bishop, Morris.** Pascal: the life of genius. New York, Reynal & Hitchcock, 1936. 398 pp.

"Excellent intellectual biography" (Richard Popkin in 1.4.1).

5.2.229 **Mesnard, Jean.** Pascal, l'homme et l'oeuvre. Paris, Boivin, 1951. 192 pp.
Trans. by G. S. Fraser as *Pascal, his life and works.* London, Harvill, 1952. 211 pp.

"Excellent biography and introduction" (Richard Popkin in 1.4.1).

Peirce, Charles Sanders
(1839-1914)

Bibliography

5.2.230 **A comprehensive bibliography and index** of the published works of Charles Sanders Peirce with a bibliography of secondary studies. Ed. by Ketner, Kloesel, Ransdell, Fisch and Hardwick. Greenwich, Conn., Johnson Associates, 1977. 337 pp.

The first comprehensive primary and secondary bibliography of Peirce.
Supersedes the earlier bibliographies.

Works

5.2.231 **Charles Sanders Peirce**: complete published works including selected secondary material. Ed. by Ketner, Kloesel, Ransdell, Fisch and Hardwick. Greenwich, Conn., Johnson Associates, 1977.

Microfiche collection (includes comprehensive bibliography/index), 149 fiches of 14,000 pages of material; includes some 870 of Peirce's publications.

5.2.232 **Collected papers of Charles Sanders Peirce**. Cambridge, Mass., Harvard University Press, 1931-58. 8v.

Vols. 1-6, ed. by C. Hartshorne and P. Weiss, 1931-35;
vols. 7-8, ed. by A. W. Burks, 1958.

5.2.233 **Charles Sanders Peirce**: contributions to the nation. In 4 parts. Graduate Studies, Texas Tech University.

In progress.
Part I: 1869-93, 1975.

5.2.234 **The new elements of mathematics**. Ed. Carolyn Eisele. Atlantic Highlands, N. J., Humanities Press, 1976. 4v.

Vol. I, Arithmetic;
vol. II, Algebra and geometry;
vol. III, Mathematical miscellanea;
vol. IV, Mathematical philosophy.

5.2.235 **Semiotic and significs**: the correspondence between Charles S. Peirce and Victoria Lady Welby, ed. Charles S. Hardwick. Bloomington, Indiana University Press, 1977. 256 pp.

5.2.236 **Peirce edition project**.
A new edition of Peirce's works is in progress. Indiana University Press.

Biography

5.2.237 **Weiss, Paul.** "Charles Sanders Peirce," *in* Dictionary of American biography. New York, 1934. Vol. XIV.

Journal and Newsletter

5.2.238 **Transactions of the Charles S. Peirce Society.** *See* 10.2.135.

5.2.239 **The Charles S. Peirce newsletter.** Nov. 1973-to date. Semiannual. Institute for Studies in Pragmaticism, Texas Tech University, P. O. Box 4530, Lubbock, Tex. 79409.

Prepared by members of the Institute, it carries information on meetings, publications, and other activities related to Peirce studies.

Plekhanov, Georgii Valentinovich
(1856-1918)

Works

5.2.240 **Sochineniia**. Pod red. D. Ryazanova. Moskva, Gos. izd., 1923-27. 24v.

5.2.241 **Selected philosophical works**. Trans. by B. Trifonov. Moscow, Foreign Languages Publishing House, 1961- .

In progress.
5v. projected.

Biography

5.2.242 **Baron, Samuel H.** Plekhanov; the father of Russian Marxism. Stanford, Stanford University Press, 1963. 400 pp.

5.2.243 **Vol'Fson, S. Ja.** Plekhanov. Minsk, Beltrestpechat', 1924. 363 pp.

Reid, Thomas
(1710-1796)

Works

5.2.244 **Philosophical works.** 8th ed., Edinburgh, 1895. 2v.

Reprinted: Hildesheim, Olms, 1967.

Rousseau, Jean-Jacques
(1712-1778)

Bibliography

5.2.245 **Sénelier, Jean.** Bibliographie générale des oeuvres de J.-J. Rousseau. Paris, Encyclopédie française, 1949. 282 pp.

Reprinted: N. Y., Burt Franklin.
For a continuing bibliography see *Annales de la société Jean-Jacques Rousseau* (Geneva), 1905- .

5.2.246 **Dufour, Théophile.** Recherches bibliographiques sur les oeuvres imprimées de J.-J. Rousseau. Paris, L. Giraud-Badin, 1925. 2v.

Reprinted: N. Y., Burt Franklin.

See also: 1.2.5, pp. 143-44.

Works

5.2.247 **Oeuvres complètes.** Mises dans un nouvel ordre, avec des notes historiques et des éclaircissements, par V.-D. Musset-Pathay. Paris, P. Dupont, 1823-26. 25v.

5.2.248 **Oeuvres complètes de Jean-Jacques Rousseau.** Ed. publiée sous la direction de Bernard Gagnebin et Marcel Raymond. Paris, Bibliothèque de la Pléiade, 1959- .

In progress.
5v. projected.

5.2.249 **Correspondance complète de Jean-Jacques Rousseau.** Ed. critique établie et annotée par R. A. Leigh. Genève, Institut et Musée Voltaire, 1965- .

In progress.
Until completed, see *Correspondance générale*, éd. par P.-P. Plan et Th. Dufour, Paris, Colin, 1924-34, 20v.

5.2.250 **Oeuvres complètes.** Paris, Seuil, 1967- .

In progress.
The first volume, annotated by Michel Launay, contains the autobiographical works and an index of names cited.

5.2.251 **The miscellaneous works.** Trans. into English. London, T. Becket and P. A. De Hondt, 1767. 5v.

24 titles.
Reprinted: N. Y., Burt Franklin.

5.2.252 **The political writings of Jean Jacques Rousseau.** Ed. from the original manuscripts and authentic editions, with intro. and notes by C. E. Vaughan. Cambridge, The University Press; and New York, Wiley, 1915. 2v.

Reprinted: N. Y., Burt Franklin.

Biography

5.2.253 **Green, F. C.** Jean-Jacques Rousseau: a critical study of his life and writings. Cambridge, University Press, 1955. 376 pp.

5.2.254 **Guéhenno, Jean.** Jean-Jacques. Paris, B. Grasset, 1948-52. 3v.

A new edition, *Jean-Jacques, histoire d'une conscience*, was published in 1962: Paris, Gallimard. 2v.

Royce, Josiah
(1855-1916)

Bibliography

5.2.255 **Cotton, James Harry.** Royce on the

human self. Cambridge, Mass., Harvard University Press, 1954. 347 pp.

Bibliography: pp. 305-311.

5.2.256 **Loewenberg, Jacob.** "A bibliography of the unpublished writings of Josiah Royce," The philosophical review, XXVI (1917), 578-82.

5.2.257 **Oppenheim, F. M.** "Bibliography of the published works of J. Royce," and A. A. Devaux, "Bibliographie des traductions d'ouvrages de Royce et des études sur l'oeuvre de Royce," Revue internationale de philosophie, XXI (1967), 138-58, 159-82.

5.2.258 **Rand, Benjamin.** "A bibliography of the writings of Josiah Royce," The philosophical review, XXV (1916), 515-22.

5.2.259 **Smith, John Edwin.** Royce's social infinite. New York, Liberal Arts Press, 1950. 176 pp.

Bibliography: pp. 171-73.

Works

5.2.260 **The basic writings of Josiah Royce.** Ed. with an introduction by John J. McDermott. Chicago, Chicago University Press, 1969. 2v.

Vol. II also contains "Annotated Bibliography of the Published Works of Josiah Royce," by Ignas Skrupskelis.

Schelling, Friedrich Wilhelm Joseph von
(1775-1854)

Bibliography

5.2.261 **Schneeberger, Guida.** Friedrich Wilhelm Joseph von Schelling. Eine Bibliographie. Bern, Francke, 1954. 190 pp.

Works

5.2.262 **Werke.** Nach der Originalausgabe in neuer Anordnung hrsg. von Manfred Schröter. München, C. H. Beck and R. Oldenbourg, 1927-56. 10v.

5.2.263 **Friedrich Wilhelm Joseph von Schellings sämmtliche Werke.** Stuttgart und Augsburg, J. G. Cotta, 1856-61. 14v. in 13.

5.2.264 **Schelling-Akademieausgabe.** The Hague, Nijhoff, 1975- .

In progress. 80v. projected in 4 sections: I. Werke; II. Nachlass; III. Briefe von und an Schelling; IV. Kollegnachschriften.

Biography

5.2.265 **Fischer, Kuno.** Geschichte der neueren Philosophie. Vol. VII. 3rd ed. Heidelberg, C. Winter, 1902.

Contains the best study of Schelling's life and works.

Exchange

5.2.266 **Schelling Exchange.**

Formed to circulate information about current research and publication and to provide an organ of communication among Schelling scholars. A mimeographed newsletter will be circulated periodically. Contact: Victor L. Nuevo, Dept. of Religion, Middlebury College, Middlebury, Vt. 05753.

Schopenhauer, Arthur
(1788-1860)

Bibliography

5.2.267 **Grisebach, Eduard.** Edita und Inedita. Schopenhaueriana: Eine Schopenhauer-Bibliographie, sowie Randschriften und Briefe Arthur Schopenhauers mit Porträt, Wappen und Facsimile der Handschrift des Meisters. Hrsg. zu seinem hundertjährigen Geburtstage. Leipzig, F. J. Brockhaus, 1888. 221 pp.

5.2.268 **Stäglich, Hans.** Johann Wolfgang von Goethe und Arthur Schopenhauer. Eine . . .

Bibliographie einschlägiger Literatur. 3. Aufl. Bonn, Rhein, 1960. 64 pp.

1st ed. 1932.

5.2.269 Hübscher, Arthur. "Schopenhauer-Bibliographie. Nachtrage 1959-1968," Schopenhauer-Jahrbuch, 51 (1970), 165-81.

Schopenhauer-Jahrbuch (5.2.275) carries regular Schopenhauer bibliographies.

See also: 1.2.5, pp. 151-53.

Works

5.2.270 Sämtliche Werke. Nach der I., von Julius Frauenstädt besorgten Gesamtaug. Neu bearb. und hrsg. von Arthur Hübscher. 2. Aufl. Wiesbaden, E. Brockhaus, 1946-50. 7v.

The Frauenstädt edition first appeared in 1873-74.

See also his *Schopenhauer-Register,* 2. Aufl., Stuttgart, Frommann, 1960, 530 pp., based on this edition.

5.2.271 The works of Schopenhauer, abridged. Ed. by Will Durant. Garden City, N. Y., Garden City Pub. Co., 1928. 539 pp.

An English translation of some of Schopenhauer's works.

Index

5.2.272 Hertslet, William. Schopenhauer register: ein hilfswörterbuch zur schnellen auffindung aller stellen, betreffend gegenstaende, personen und begriffe sowie der citate vergleiche und unterscheidungen welche in A. Schopenhauer's werken, ferner in seinen briefen, enthalten sind. Leipzig, Brockhaus, 1890. 261 pp.

Reprinted: N. Y., Burt Franklin.

Biography

5.2.273 Schneider, Walther. Schopenhauer, eine Biographie. Vienna, Bermann-Fischer, 1937. 422 pp.

"The most complete life of Schopenhauer" (Patrick Gardiner in 1.4.1).

5.2.274 Wallace, William. Life of Schopenhauer. London, W. Scott, 1890. 217 pp.

Society and Journal

5.2.275 Schopenhauer-Gesellschaft. Founded 1911. Pres., Arthur Hübscher, Beethovenstrasse 48, D-6000 Frankfurt am Main 1. Publishes a Jahrbuch, 1912- .

The yearbook contains an excellent running bibliography.

Vols. 1-50 (1912-69) reprinted: N. Y., Kraus Reprints.

Sidgwick, Henry
(1838-1900)

Biography

5.2.276 Sidgwick, A., and **E. M. Sidgwick.** Henry Sidgwick: a memoir. London and New York, Macmillan, 1906. 633 pp.

"The standard biography, written by his brother and his widow. It contains letters, unpublished papers, and a complete bibliography of his writings" (J. B. Schneewind in 1.4.1).

Solovyov, Vladimir Sergeyevich
(1853-1900)

Works

5.2.277 Sobranie sochinenii Vladmira Sergievicha Solov'eva. 2. izd. St. Petersburg, Knigoizdatel'skoe tovarishchestvo "Proveschenie," 1911-14. 10v.

1st ed. 1901-07. 9v.

Spencer, Herbert
(1820-1903)

Bibliography

5.2.278 Watson, George, *ed.* "Herbert

Spencer (a bibliography)," *in* The new Cambridge bibliography of English literature. Cambridge, Cambridge University Press, 1969, vol. 3, cols. 1583-1592.

Works

5.2.279 **The works of Herbert Spencer.** Osnabruck, Zeller, 1966. 21v.

A reprint of the 1880-1907 ed.

Biography

5.2.280 **Duncan, David.** Life and letters of Herbert Spencer. New York, Appleton, 1908. 2v.

Spinoza, Benedict (Baruch)
(1632-1677)

Bibliography

5.2.281 **Oko, Adolph S.** The Spinoza bibliography. Boston, G. K. Hall, 1964. 602 pp.

Published under the auspices of the Columbia University Libraries.
Contains reproductions of 7000 cards.
See also *Chronicon Spinozanum* (The Hague), 1921- ; and *Bibliotheca Spinozana* (Amsterdam), 1922- .

5.2.282 **Wetlesen, Jon** [in loose-leaf]. Spinoza-Bibliografi. Oslo, 1967. 3v. [in loose-leaf].

Part I, Primarily 19th and early 20th centuries;
Part II, An expansion of Part I;
Part III, Influence of Spinoza on others and influences on Spinoza.
Supplements 5.2.281.
Also published as: A Spinoza bibliography 1940-1970. Oslo, Universitetsforlaget, 1968; New York, Humanities Press, 1970. 88 pp.

5.2.283 **Freeman, Eugene** and **Maurice Mandelbaum**, eds. Spinoza: essays in interpretation. La Salle, Ill., Open Court, 1973. 323 pp.

Bibliography by E. M. Curley, pp. 265-316.
Covers major European languages 1960-72.

See also: 1.2.5, pp. 158-59.

Dictionaries

5.2.284 **Richter, Gustav Theodor.** Spinozas philosophische Terminologie; historisch und immanent kritisch untersucht. Leipzig, J. A. Barth, 1913. 170 pp.

I. Abt. Grundbegriffe der Metaphysik. No more published.

5.2.285 **Spinoza dictionary.** Ed. by Dagobert D. Runes, with a foreword by Albert Einstein. New York, Philosophical Library, 1951. 309 pp.

Works

5.2.286 **Spinoza opera.** Hrsg. von C. Gebhardt. Heidelberg, C. Winter, 1925. 4v.

Standard, critical edition.

5.2.287 **The chief works of Spinoza.** Trans. by R. H. M. Elwes. New York, Dover, 1955. 2v.

Reprint of the 1883-84 edition.

5.2.288 **Correspondence of Spinoza.** Ed. by A. Wolf. London, Allen & Unwin, 1928. 502 pp.

Includes the biographies by Colerus and Lucas.

5.2.289 **Earlier philosophical writings.** Trans. by F. A. Hayes. Indianapolis, Bobbs-Merrill, 1963. 161 pp.

5.2.290 **Oeuvres complètes de Spinoza.** Texte nouvellement traduit ou revu, présenté et annoté par R. Caillois, Madeleine Frances, et P. Misrahi. Paris, Gallimard, 1954. 1604 pp.

A French translation with annotations,

indices, and the biographies of Colerus and Lucas.

Lexicon

5.2.291 **Lexicon Spinozanum**. Giancotti Boscherini, Emilia, *comp*. La Haye, Nijhoff, 1970. 2v.

Index to the works of Spinoza.

Biography

5.2.292 **Pollock, F.** Spinoza: his life and philosophy. London, C. K. Paul, 1880. 467 pp.

An excellent study.

5.2.293 **Colerus, Johannes.** Das Leben des Benedict von Spinoza. Ed. by Carl Gephardt. Heidelberg, Weissbach, 1952. 126 pp.

Also in 5.2.290.

See also: 10.5.48.

Vico, Giambattista
(1668-1744)

Bibliography

5.2.294 **Croce, Benedetto.** Bibliografia vichiana. Accrescuita e rielaborata da F. Nicolini. Napoli, Ricciardi, 1947-48. 2v.

5.2.295 **Donzelli, Maria.** Contributo alla bibliografia vichiana (1948-1970) (Studi vichiani, 9). Napoli, Guida, 1973. 110 pp.

Works

5.2.296 **Opere complete**. A cura di Benedetto Croce, Giovanni Gentile, e Fausto Nicolini. Bari, Laterza, 1911-14. 8v. in 11.

Standard edition.

Biography

5.2.297 **The autobiography of Giambattista**

Vico. Trans. by T. G. Bergin and M. H. Fisch. Ithaca, N. Y., Cornell University Press, 1944. 240 pp.

Voltaire, François Marie Arouet de
(1694-1778)

Bibliography

5.2.298 **Bengesco, Georges.** Voltaire: bibliographie de ses oeuvres. Paris, Emile Perrin, 1882-85. 5v.

5.2.299 **Malcolm, Jean.** Table de la bibliographie de Voltaire par Bengesco. (Publications de l'Institut et Musée Voltaire, Série d'études, 1). Genève, Institut et Musée Voltaire, 1953. 127 pp.

Supplements 5.2.298.

5.2.300 Barr, Mary Margaret Harrison. A century of Voltaire study; a bibliography of writings on Voltaire, 1825-1925. Institute of French Studies, 1929.

Reprinted: N. Y., Burt Franklin, 1972. 123 pp.

Supplemented by her *Quarante années d'études voltairiennes*. Bibliographie analytique des livres et articles sur Voltaire, 1925-1965. Paris, Armand Colin, 1968. 212 pp.

Works

5.2.301 **Oeuvres complètes**. L. Moland, éd. Paris, Garnier, 1877-85. 52v.

The standard edition.
Reprinted: N. Y., Kraus Reprints.

5.2.302 **Oeuvres inédites**. Ed. Fernand Caussy. Paris, E. Champion, 1914.

Vol. 1, Mélanges historiques.
Reprinted: N. Y., Kraus Reprints.

5.2.303 **Correspondence**. Ed. by Theodore Besterman. Genève, Institut et Musée Voltaire, Les Délices, 1953- .

In progress.
French text with notes in English.

5.2.304 **Philosophical dictionary**. Trans. Theodore Besterman. Baltimore, Penguin, 1972. 400 pp.

Biography

5.2.305 **Brailsford, Henry N.** Voltaire. New York, H. Holt; and London, T. Butterworth, 1935. 256 pp.

"Vivid view of Voltaire as reformer" (Norman L. Torrey in 1.4.1).

5.2.306 **Torrey, Norman L.** The spirit of Voltaire. New York, Columbia University Press, 1938. 314 pp.

Reprinted: Oxford, 1962.
"A character study" (Torrey in 1.4.1).

Wolff, Christian
(1679-1754)

Works

5.2.307 **Gesammelte Werke**. Hrsg. von J. Ecole (et al). Hildesheim, Olms, 1962- .

In progress.
In part, photographic reproductions of earlier editions, with added new editorial material.

Lexicon

5.2.308 **Meissner, H. A.** Philosophisches Lexicon aus Christian Wolffs sämmtlichen deutschen Schriften. 1737.

Reprinted: Düsseldorf, Stern, 1970.

Biography

5.2.309 **Campo, Mariano.** Christian Wolff e il razionalismo precritico. Milano, Società Editrice "Vita e Pensiero," 1939. 2v.

6. CONTEMPORARY PHILOSOPHY

This section contains information on philosophers of the Twentieth Century. The number of such philosophers is extremely large. I have tried to include at least some of the important philosophers of this period. A number of important authors have not been listed simply because no significant bibliography of their works is available and their works have yet to appear in a collected edition. These are clearly bibliographical and not philosophical criteria for exclusion, and the omission of any particular name does not necessarily indicate a value judgment about his or her philosophical contribution or about his or her importance in the history of philosophy. In some cases the absence of a name is an indication of a gap in the philosophical literature and of the need for the development of a bibliography, biography, or a set of collected works.

For recent authors the bibliographies listed in 1.2 can usually be used to develop a fairly comprehensive primary and secondary bibliography.

6.1 GENERAL: HISTORIES AND COLLECTIONS

Histories

6.1.1 **Bochenski, I. M.** Contemporary European philosophy. Trans. by D. Nicholl and K. Aschenbrenner. Berkeley, University of California Press, 1956. 326 pp.

Translation of *Europäische Philosophie der Gegenwart*, 2. Aufl., Bern, Francke, 1951. Bibliography: pp. 267-321.

6.1.2 **Gilson, Etienne, Thomas Langan,** and **Armand Maurer.** Recent philosophy; Hegel to the present. New York, Random House, 1966. 876 pp.

The notes, pp. 671-864, contain a wealth of bibliographical material.

6.1.3 **Klibansky, Raymond,** *ed.* Philosophy in mid-century; a survey. Firenze, La Nuova Italia, 1958. 4v.

Surveys the period from 1949 to the end of 1955.

Includes bibliographies.
Continued by 6.1.4.
Reprinted: N. Y., Kraus Reprints.

6.1.4 **Klibansky, Raymond,** *ed.* Contemporary philosophy; a survey. Firenze, La Nuova Italia, 1968-69. 4v.

Follows and complements 6.1.3.
Includes bibliographies.
Vol. I, Logic and foundations of mathematics;
vol. II, Philosophy of science;
vol. III, Metaphysics, ontology, existence, mind and body, language and structure;
vol. IV, Ethics, aesthetics, law, religion, social philosophy, dialectical and historical materialism, contemporary philosophy in Asia.

6.1.5 **Passmore, John A.** A hundred years of philosophy. New York, Macmillan, 1957. 523 pp.

Bibliography: pp. 479-502.
Rev. ed. 1966, 574 pp., contains only an abbreviated bibliography, pp. 547-49.

6.1.6 **Schmidt, Raymund.** Philosophie der Gegenwart in Selbstdarstellungen. Leipzig, Meiner, 1923-29. 7v.

6.1.7 **Sciacca, Michele Federico.** Philosophical trends in the contemporary world. Trans. by Attilio Salerno. Notre Dame, University of Notre Dame Press, 1964. 656 pp.

Bibliographical footnotes.
A translation of La filosofia, oggi, dalle origini romantiche della filosofia contemporaneo ai problemi attuali, Milano, Mondadori, 1945.

6.1.8 **Sciacca, Michele Federico.** Les grands courants de la pensée mondiale contemporaine. Publié sous la direction de M. F. Sciacca. Milan, Marzorati, 1958-61. 4v.

Pt. I, a survey by countries; Pt. II, a survey by movements.
By various authors. Includes bibliographies.

6.1.9 **Spiegelberg, Herbert.** The phenomenological movement; a historical introduction. 2d ed. The Hague, Nijhoff, 1965. 2v.

Contains good bibliographies on individual philosophers in the movement.

6.1.10 **Stegmüller, W.** Main currents in contemporary German, British and American philosophy. See 9.3.13.

6.1.11 **Urmson, James O.** Philosophical analysis; its development between the two World Wars. Oxford, Clarendon Press, 1956. 202 pp.

See also: 1.1.1-1.1.3, 1.1.7, 1.1.11, 1.1.13- 1.1.17, 1.1.19, 1.1.20.

Collections

6.1.12 **Alston, William P.** and **George Nakhnikian,** eds. Readings in twentieth century philosophy. Glencoe, Free Press, 1963. 782 pp.

An anthology of writings by W. James, H. Bergson, J. Maritain, A. N. Whitehead, J. Dewey, G. E. Moore, B. Russell, E. Husserl, M. Heidegger, P. Tillich, J.-P. Sartre, and on logical positivism and on ordinary language philosophy.

6.1.13 **Barrett, William** and **Henry D. Aiken,** eds. Philosophy in the twentieth centruy. New York, Random House, 1962. 4v.

An anthology of original writings, with introductions.
Vol. 1, Royce, Peirce, James, Dewey, Santayana;
vol. 2, Bradley, Moore, Russell, Wittgenstein, Austin, Whitehead;
vol. 3, Schlich, Ayer, Quine, Husserl, Heidegger, Bergson, Marcel, Sartre, Camus;
vol. 4, Croce, Lenin, Jaspers, Gilson, Tillich, Buber.

6.1.14 **Hartman, James B.,** ed. Philosophy of recent times. New York, McGraw Hill, 1967. 2v.

Vol. 1, Readings in nineteenth-century philosophy;
vol. 2, Readings in twentieth-century philosophy.

See also: 2.2.7.

Series

6.1.15 **Library of Living Philosophers.** See 10.5.47.

6.2 INDIVIDUAL PHILOSOPHERS, ALPHABETICALLY FROM ADORNO TO WITTGENSTEIN (COLLECTED AND STANDARD WORKS, BIBLIOGRAPHIES, BIOGRAPHIES)

Adorno, Theodor W.
(1903-1969)

Works

6.2.1 **Gesammelte Schriften.** Hrsg. von Rolf Tiedemann. Frankfurt, Suhrkamp, 1970- . 23v. projected.

Ayer, Alfred J.
(1910-)

Biography

6.2.2 **Ayer, A. J.** Part of my life. London, Collins, 1977. 318 pp.

Bergson, Henri
(1859-1941)

Bibliography

6.2.3 **Gunter, P. A. Y.** Henri Bergson: a bibliography. Bowling Green, Philosophy Documentation Center, 1974. 457 pp.

Contains 470 entries by Bergson, 4000 entries about Bergson; annotated; through 1973; indexed.
Supersedes earlier bibliographies.

Works

6.2.4 **Oeuvres.** Textes annotés par André Robinet. 3. éd. Paris, Presses Universitaires de France, 1971. 1632 pp.

Bibliographical references in "Notes."

Biography

6.2.5 **Chevalier, Jacques.** Henri Bergson. Trans., Lilian A. Clare. New York, Macmillan, 1928. 351 pp.

Journal

6.2.6 **Etudes Bergsoniennes.** Vol. 1 (1961)- .

Broad, Charlie Dunbar
(1887-1971)

Bibliography and Biography

6.2.7 **Lewy, C.** "Bibliography of the writings of C. D. Broad to the end of July 1959," *in* P. A. Schilpp, ed., The philosophy of C. D. Broad, New York, Tudor, 1959, pp. 831-52.

This same volume contains Broad's autobiography.

Buber, Martin
(1878-1965)

Bibliography

6.2.8 **Catanne, Moshe.** A bibliography of Martin Buber's works (1897-1957). Jerusalem, Bialik Institute, 1958. 142 pp.

6.2.9 **Friedman, Maurice S.** Martin Buber, the life of dialogue. 3d ed. Chicago, University of Chicago Press, 1976. 322 pp.

Contains a bibliography of works by and about Buber, pp. 283-309.

6.2.10 **Friedman, Maurice.** "Bibliography of the writings of Martin Buber," *in* P. A. Schilpp and Maurice Friedman, eds., Martin Buber, La Salle, Ill., Open Court, 1967, pp. 745-86.

Works

6.2.11 **Werke.** München, Kösel, 1962- .

In progress.
Also includes bibliographies.

6.2.12 **[Selected Works.]** Heidelberg, Lambert Schneider.

Individually issued works, including letters, philosophical works, works on the Old Testament, and "Kleinere Schriften." Most were published or reissued in 1978.

Autobiography

6.2.13 **The philosophy of Martin Buber.** Ed

P. A. Schilpp and Maurice Friedman. La Salle, Ill., Open Court, 1967.

Contains autobiographical writings.

Camus, Albert
(1913-1960)

Bibliography

6.2.14 **Fitch, Brian T.** Albert Camus; essai de bibliographie des études en langue française consacrées à Albert Camus (1937-1962). Paris, Minard, 1965. 231 pp.

6.2.15 **Roeming, Robert F.** Camus: a bibliography. Madison, Milwaukee, and London, University of Wisconsin Press, 1968. 298 pp.

The 2nd ed. is being published on six 4x6 inch microfiches and is now maintained by a computerized system. This edition includes almost 4000 entries. Center for Twentieth Century Studies, University of Wisconsin, Milwaukee.

Carnap, Rudolf
(1891-1970)

Bibliography

6.2.16 **Benson, Arthur L.** "Bibliography of the writings of Rudolf Carnap," *in* P. A. Schilpp, ed., The philosophy of Rudolf Carnap, La Salle, Ill., Open Court, 1963, pp. 1015-70.

Cassirer, Ernst
(1874-1945)

Bibliography

6.2.17 **Hamburg, Carl H.** and **W. M. Solmitz.** "Bibliography of the writings of Ernst Cassirer to 1946," *in* P. A. Schilpp, ed., The philosophy of Ernst Cassirer, Evanston, Ill., Library of Living Philosophers, 1949, pp. 881-910.

For bibliography to 1964, *see* H. J. Paton and Raymond Klibansky, eds., *Philosophy and History: Essays Presented to Ernst Cas-*

sirer, New York, Harper & Row, 1963, pp. 338-53.

See also: 10.5.29.

Collingwood, Robin George
(1889-1943)

Bibliography

6.2.18 **"Collingwood Bibliography,"** *in* Critical essays on the philosophy of R. G. Collingwood. Ed. by Michael Krauz. Oxford, Clarendon Press, 1972, pp. 327-48.

6.2.19 **Collingwood, R. B.** The idea of history. Ed. by T. M. Knox. Oxford, Clarendon Press, 1946. 339 pp.

See the "preface" for a Collingwood bibliography.
See also the obituary essays by R. B. McCallum, T. M. Knox, and I. A. Richmond in *Proceedings of the British Academy,* XXIX (1943), pp. 463-80.

Croce, Benedetto
(1866-1952)

Bibliography

6.2.20 **Borsari, Silvano.** L'opera di Benedetto Croce. (Istituto italiano per gli studi storici). Napoli, "Nella sede dell'istituto," 1964. 619 pp.

6.2.21 **Cione, Edmondo.** Bibliografia Crociana. Roma, Bocca, 1965. 481 pp.

Works by and about Croce.
For a continuing bibliography see *Revista di studi Crociani* (10.3.51).

6.2.22 **Stella, Vittorio.** "Il giudizio su Croce; consuntivo di un centenario," Giornale di metafisica, XXII (1967), 643-711.

Includes a bibliography of works published since 1962.

See also: 1.2.5, pp. 42-43.

Works

6.2.23 **Opere complete**. Bari, Laterza, 1965- . 75v.

Biography

6.2.24 **Croce, Benedetto**. An autobiography. Trans. from the Italian by R. G. Collingwood. Freeport, N. Y., Books for Libraries Press, 1970. 116 pp.

Journal

6.2.25 **Revista di studi Crociani**. *See 10.3.51.*

Dewey, John
(1859-1952)

Bibliography

6.2.26 **Boydston, Jo Ann**. Guide to the works of John Dewey. Carbondale, Ill., Southern Illinois University Press, 1970. 416 pp.

Contains essays by Dewey scholars on nearly 1,000 issues treated in Dewey's writings.

6.2.27 **Boydston, Jo Ann**, and **Kathleen Poulos**, eds. Checklist of writings about John Dewey, 1887-1977. 2d ed. Carbondale, Ill., Southern Illinois University Press, 1978. 476 pp.

6.2.28 **Boydston, Jo Ann**, and **Robert L. Andersen**, *eds.* John Dewey: a checklist of translations, 1900-1967. Carbondale, Ill., Southern Illinois University Press, 1969. 123 pp.

6.2.29 **Thomas, Milton Halsey**. John Dewey; a centennial bibliography. Chicago, University of Chicago Press, 1962. 370 pp.

The third edition of a bibliography of John Dewey by M. H. Thomas and H. W. Schneider, 1st published in 1929. Supplemented by *The Dewey Newsletter*,

Dewey Project, Southern Illinois University, 1967-78.

6.2.30 **"Bibliography of the writings of John Dewey,"** *in* P. A. Schilpp, ed. The philosophy of John Dewey, 2d ed., La Salle, Ill., Open Court, 1951, pp. 609-86.

About 800 works chronologically arranged.

Works

6.2.31 **Works of John Dewey**. Carbondale, Ill., Southern Illinois University Press, 1967- .

In progress.

Three series are projected: The early works of John Dewey, 1882-1898 (15v.); The middle works of John Dewey, 1899-1924 (15v.); The later works of John Dewey, 1925-1952 (25v.); plus several volumes of miscellaneous material and an index.

This will be a definitive, critical edition of the works of Dewey.

Biography

6.2.32 **Dykhuizen, George**. The life and mind of John Dewey. Carbondale, Ill., Southern Illinois University Press, 1973. 429 pp.

6.2.33 **Hook, Sidney**. John Dewey: an intellectual portrait. New York, John Day, 1939. 242 pp.

Society and Newsletter

6.2.34 **The John Dewey Society for the Study of Education and Culture**. Founded, Feb., 1935. Sec.-treas.: Robert R. Sherman, 314 Norman Hall, Univ. of Florida, Gainesville, Florida 32611.

Sponsors meetings, lectures, and publications. Annual meeting with the American Association of Colleges for Teacher Education.

6.2.35 **The Dewey newsletter**. Jo Ann Boydston, *ed.* Center for Dewey Studies. Southern Illinois University, 1967-78.

Carried miscellaneous information on Dewey and Dewey scholarship. stopped publication with Vol. VII, No. 2 (Oct., 1978).

See also: 10.5.28.

Gadamer, Hans Georg
(1900-)

Works

6.2.36 **Kleine Schriften**. Tübingen, J. C. B. Mohr, 1967-77. 4v.

Vol. 1, Philosophie-Hermeneutik. 2d ed. 1976;
vol. 2, Interpretationen. 1967;
vol. 3, Idee und Sprache. Platon, Husserl, Heidegger. 1972;
vol. 4, Variationen. 1977.

Gentile, Giovanni
(1875-1944)

Bibliography

6.2.37 **Bellezza, Vita A**. Bibliographia degli scritti di Giovanni Gentile. Firenze, Sansoni, 1950. 141 pp.

Also issued as vol. III of 6.2.38.

Works

6.2.38 **Opere complete di Giovanni Gentile**. A cura della Fondazione G. Gentile per gli studi filosofici. Firenze, Sansoni, 1935- .

In progress.
At least 59v. projected.

Gilson, Etienne
(1884-1978)

Bibliography

6.2.39 **Edie, Callistus James**. "The writings of Etienne Gilson chronologically arranged," in Mélanges offerts à Etienne Gilson de l'Académie française. Toronto, Pontifical Institute of Medieval Studies, 1959, pp. 15-58.

Hartmann, Nicolai
(1882-1950)

Bibliography

6.2.40 **Heimsoeth, Heinz, und Robert Heiss**. Nicolai Hartmann. Der Denker und sein werk. Gâttingen, Vandenhoeck & Ruprecht, 1952. 312 pp.

Contains a bibliography by Theodor Balluf, pp. 286-308.

Works

6.2.41 **Kleinere Schriften**. Berlin, de Gruyter, 1955-58. 3v.

His major works are also individually published by de Gruyter, though not in a particular edition.

See also: 8.6.2.

Hartshorne, Charles
(1897-)

Bibliography

6.2.42 **Hartshorne, Mrs. Charles**. "Published writings of Charles Hartshorne," in William L. Reise and Eugene Freeman, eds., Process and divinity; the Hartshorne Festschrift. La Salle, Ill., Open Court, 1964, p. 579-91.

6.2.43 **Hartshorne, Dorothy C**. "Charles Hartshorne: a secondary bibliography," Process studies 3 (1973), 179-227.

6.2.44 **Fowler, Dean R**. "Bibliography of dissertations and theses on Charles Hartshorne," Process studies 3 (1973), 304-7.

Heidegger, Martin
(1889-1976)

Bibliography

6.2.45 **Hoeller, Keith**. "Heidegger bibliography of English translations," Journal of the

British Society of Phenomenology, VI (1975), 206-8.

6.2.46 Materialien zur Heidegger-Bibliographie 1917-1972, unter Mitarbeit von T. S. Grigoljuk, E. Landolt, T. Kakihara und T. Kozuma, hrsg. von H.-M.Sass. Meisenheim am Glan, Anton Hain, 1975. 225 pp.

Supplements 6.2.47.

6.2.47 Sass, Hans-Martin. Heidegger-Bibliographie. Meisenheim am Glan, Anton Hain, 1968. 181 pp.

Supplemented by 6.2.46.

See also: 1.2.5, p. 73.

Works

6.2.48 Martin Heidegger Gesamtausgabe. Frankfurt, Klostermann, 1975- .

In progress.
70v. planned.

6.2.49 Martin Heidegger. Works. Co-ed., J. Glenn Gray and Joan Stambauge. New York, Harper & Row.

Volumes issued separately. The following had appeared by 1978: *Basic Writings; Being and Time; Discourse on Thinking; Early Greek Thinking; The End of Philosophy; Hegel's Concept of Experience; Identity and Difference; On the Way to Language; On Time and Being; Poetry, Language, Thought; The Question Concerning Technology and Other Essays; What is Called Thinking?*

Index

6.2.50 Feick, Hildegard. Index zu Heideggers "Sein und Zeit." 2., neubearb. Aufl., Tübingen, Niemeyer, 1968. 132 pp.

Jaspers, Karl
(1883-1969)

Bibliography and Biography

6.2.51 Bentz, Hans Walther. Karl Jaspers in Ubersetzungen. Karl Jaspers translated. Karl Jaspers traduit. Frankfurt am Main, Bentz, 1961. 31 pp.

6.2.52 Rossmann, Kurt. "Bibliography of the writings of Karl Jaspers to spring, 1957," *in* P. A. Schilpp, ed., The philosophy of Karl Jaspers. New York, Tudor, 1957, pp. 871-87.

This volume also contains Jaspers' autobiography.

Lewis, Clarence Irving
(1883-1964)

Bibliography and Biography

6.2.53 Adams, E. M. "The writings of C. I. Lewis," *in* P. A. Schilpp, ed., The philosophy of C. I. Lewis. La Salle, Ill., Open Court, 1968, pp. 677-89.

This volume also contains Lewis' autobiography.

6.2.54 Parrill, W. T. "Bibliography of C. I. Lewis," *in* Notre-Dame journal of formal logic, XI (1970), 136-40.

Works

6.2.55 Goheen, John D., and **John L. Mothershead, Jr.,** *eds.* Collected papers of Clarence Irving Lewis. Stanford, Calif., Stanford University Press, 1970. 444 pp.

Marcel, Gabriel
(1889-1973)

Bibliography

6.2.56 Lapointe, François H. and **Claire C. Lapointe.** Gabriel Marcel and his critics: an international bibliography (1935-1976). New York, Garland, 1976.

Contains 3,000 entries on the philosophical, literary, and psychological aspects of

Marcel's thought. The bibliography of his own writings is complete and includes translations into major European languages.

Biography

6.2.57 **Cain, Seymour.** Gabriel Marcel. London, Bowes & Bowes, 1963. 128 pp.

Society

6.2.58 **"Présence de Gabriel Marcel,"** Siège Social, 85 boulevard de Port Royal, 75013 Paris, France.

An international association. Its membership is open to those who have known Gabriel Marcel personally or through his work. The association's activities include: sponsorship of an annual meeting in Paris, an annual publication, gathering of memorabilia and information on current activities, coordination of projects affecting classification of the Gabriel Marcel archives, compilation of updated bibliographies, edition of unpublished manuscripts, re-edition of works out of print, and promotion of activities and publications that contribute further to the understanding and appreciation of Gabriel Marcel's work.

Maritain, Jacques
(1882-1973)

Bibliography

6.2.59 **Gallagher, Donald A.,** and **Idella Gallagher.** The achievement of Jacques and Raïssa Maritain; a bibliography, 1906-1961. Garden City, N. Y., Doubleday, 1962. 256 pp.

An annotated list, including varying editions and translations.

6.2.60 **Evans, Joseph W.** "A Maritain Bibliography," The new scholasticism, XLVI (1972), 118-28.

Biography

6.2.61 **Bars, Henry.** Maritain en notre temps. Paris, Grasset, 1959. 397 pp.

6.2.62 **Evans, Joseph W.,** ed. Jacques Maritain: the man and his achievement. New York, Sheed and Ward, 1965. 258 pp.

Society and Newsletter

6.2.63 **American Maritain Association.** Founded, 1977. Secretary: Anthony O. Simon, 1373 Squire Drive, South Bend, Ind. 46637.

Publishes 6.2.64.

6.2.64 **American Maritain Association Newsletter.** Vol. 1 (1977)- . Editor: Ralph J. Masiello, Department of Philosophy, Niagara University, Niagara, N. Y. 14109.

Mead, George Herbert
(1863-1931)

Bibliography

6.2.65 **Natanson, Maurice.** The social dynamics of George Herbert Mead. Washington, Public Affairs Press, 1956. 102 pp.

Bibliography: pp. 96-102.

6.2.66 **Reck, Andrew.** "The writings of George Herbert Mead," in George Herbert Mead, Selected writings, ed. by Andrew J. Reck, Indianapolis, Bobbs-Merrill, 1964, pp. lxiii-lxix.

See also: 9.1.23.

Merleau-Ponty, Maurice
(1908-1961)

Bibliography

6.2.67 **Lapointe, François H.** and **Claire C. Lapointe.** Maurice Merleau-Ponty and his critics: an international bibliography (1942-1976). New York, Garland, 1976. 169 pp.

Contains over 1,200 entries on all aspects of Merleau-Ponty's thought, a complete bibliography of all of Merleau-Ponty's own writings and their translations into the major European languages.

Works

6.2.68 Fischer, Alden L. The essential writings of Merleau-Ponty. New York, Harcourt, Brace & World, 1969. 383 pp.

Bibliography: pp. 379-83.

Moore, George Edward
(1873-1958)

Bibliography and Biography

6.2.69 Buchanan, Emerson, and G. E. Moore. "Bibliography of the writings of G. E. Moore (to July, 1952)," *in* P. A. Schilpp, ed., The philosophy of G. E. Moore, 2d ed., La Salle, Ill., Open Court, 1952, pp. 689-99.

This volume also contains Moore's autobiography.

6.2.70 Klemke, E. D., Dennis A. Robatyn, and Michael Rothschild. "Bibliography of G. E. Moore scholarship, 1903-present" The southwestern journal of philosophy, VII (1966), 149-78.

6.2.71 Malcolm, Norman. "George Edward Moore" *in* Knowledge and certainty, Englewood Cliffs, N. J., Prentice Hall, 1963, 244 pp.

Ortega y Gasset, Jose
(1883-1955)

Bibliography

6.2.72 Rukser, Udo. Bibliografía de Ortega. Madrid, Estudios orteguianos, Editiones de la Revista de occidente, 1971. 420 pp.

Works

6.2.73 Obras completas. Madrid, Revista de occidente, 1962- .

In progress.
11v. by 1978.
1st ed. 1946-47. 6v.

Biography

6.2.74 Márias, Julián. Ortega y tres antípodas. Buenos Aires, Revista de Occidente, 1950. 218 pp.

Popper, Karl
(1902-)

Bibliography and Biography

6.2.75 Hansen, Troels Eggers. "Bibliography of the writings of Karl Popper," *in* P. A. Schilpp, ed., The philosophy of Karl Popper, La Salle, Ill., Open Court, 1974, pp. 1199-1287.

This volume also contains Popper's philosophical autobiography.

Rawls, John
(1921-)

Bibliography

6.2.76 Wellbank, J. H. "A bibliography of Rawlsian justice: 1951-1975," Philosophy research archives, II (1976).

255 entries, 18 by Rawls.

Ricoeur, Paul
(1913-)

Bibliography

6.2.77 Vansina, Dirk F. "Bibliographie de Paul Ricoeur," Revue philosophique de Louvain, LXXII (1974), 156-81.

Bibliography of the writings of Ricoeur through 1973.

Russell, Bertrand Arthur William
(1872-1970)

PHILOSOPHY

Bibliography and Dictionary

6.2.78 **Dennon, L. E.** "Bibliography of the writings of Bertrand Russell to 1951," *in* P. A. Schilpp, ed., The philosophy of Bertrand Russell, 2d ed., New York, Tudor, 1952, pp. 743-804.

6.2.79 **Dennon, Lester E.,** *ed.* Bertrand Russell's dictionary of mind, matter and morals. New York, Philosophical Library, 1952. 209 pp.

6.2.80 **Feinberg, Barry,** [et al.]. A detailed catalogue of the archives of Bertrand Russell. London, Continuum 1, 1967. 341 pp.

Includes material by and about Russell: books, articles, letters, name index, Russell and Stanley family trees, autobiography, legal actions.

Biography

6.2.81 **The autobiography of Bertrand Russell.** Boston, London and Toronto, Allen and Unwin, 1967-69. 3v.

There are other publishers.

6.2.82 **Clark, Ronald W.** The life of Bertrand Russell: life and times. London, J. Cape; and New York, Knopf, 1975. 766 pp.

An excellent biography.

Journal and Society

6.2.83 **Russell:** the journal of the Bertrand Russell archives (2.2.6). Vol, I 1971- .

Published quarterly by the McMaster University Press, McMaster University, Hamilton, Ontario. Address communications to the Editor, c/o the Bertrand Russell Archives, McMaster University Library.
Editors' notes, articles, recent acquisitions, recent literature.

6.2.84 **The Bertrand Russell Society.** Founded, 1974. 2108½ Walton Way, Augusta, Ga., 30904.

Santayana, George
(1863-1952)

Bibliography and Biography

6.2.85 **Santos Escudero, Ceferino.** "Bibliografia general de Jorge Santayana," Miscelanea Comillas, XLIV (1965), 155-310.

Also published separately: Comiolas, Pontificia Universitas Comillensis, 1965. 158 pp.

6.2.86 **Terzian, Shonig.** "Bibliography of the writings of G. Santayana to Oct. 1940," *in* P. A. Schilpp, ed., The philosophy of George Santayana, Evanston and Chicago, Northwestern University, 1940, pp. 607-68.

This volume also contains Santayana's autobiography.
2d ed., 1951.

Works

6.2.87 **The works of George Santayana.** New York, Scribner's, 1936-40. 15v.

This collection is not complete.
Reprinted: Hildesheim, Olms.

Sartre, Jean-Paul
(1905-)

Bibliography

6.2.88 **Belkind, Allen.** Jean-Paul Sartre: Sartre and existentialism in English, a bibliographical guide. Kent, Ohio, Kent State University Press, 1970. 234 pp.

6.2.89 **Contat, Michel** and **Michel Rybalka.** The writings of Jean-Paul Sartre. Trans. Richard C. McCleary. Evanston, Northwestern University Press, 1973. 2v.

Vol. 1, A bibliographical life;
vol. 2, Selected prose.

6.2.90 **Lapointe, François H.** and **Claire Lapointe.** Jean-Paul Sartre and his critics: an international bibliography (1938-1975). Bowling Green, Philosophy Documentation Center, 1975. 447 pp.

Over 5,000 entries.

6.2.91 **Lapointe, François.** "Sartre's Marxism: a bibliographical essay," Journal of British Society for Phenomenology, V (1974), 184-92.

Biography

6.2.92 **Murdoch, Iris.** Sartre: romantic rationalist. London, Bowes & Bowes; and New Haven, Yale University Press, 1953. 78 pp.

6.2.93 **Sartre, J.-P.** The words. Trans. from the French by Bernard Frechtman. New York, George Braziller, 1964. 255 pp.

A brief autobiography, written when Sartre was 59.

Scheler, Max
(1874-1928)

Bibliography

6.2.94 **Hartmann, Wilfried.** Max Scheler; bibliographie. Stuttgart, Frommann, 1963. 128 pp.

6.2.95 **"M. Scheler: bibliography** (1963-1974) of primary (English translations) and secondary literature," in M. S. Frings, ed., Max Scheler. Centennial essays. The Hague, Nijhoff, 1974, pp. 492-510.

See also: 8.6.2.

Works

6.2.96 **Gesammelte Werke.** Hrsg. von Maria Scheler. Bern, Francke, 1953- .

In progress.
13v. projected.

Schutz, Alfred
(1899-1959)

Works

6.2.97 **Gesammelte aufsätze.** The Hague, Nijhoff, 1971- .

In progress.

6.2.98 **Collected papers.** Atlantic Highlands, N. J., Humanities Press, 1962-66. 3v.

Teilhard de Chardin, Pierre
(1881-1955)

Bibliography

6.2.99 **Baudry, Gérard Henry.** Pierre Teilhard de Chardin; bibliographie (1881-1972). Lille, Facultés catholiques, 1972. 116 pp.

6.2.100 **Cuénot, Claude, et Yves Vade.** "Oeuvres, livres et principaux articles consacrés à Teilhard de Chardin," in Essais sur Teilhard de Chardin, éd. F. Russo, et al., Paris, Fayard, 1962, pp. 97-148.

See also *Archivum historicum Societas Iesu*, which annually carries a list of works about Teilhard de Chardin.

6.2.101 **Jarque i Jutglar, Joan E.** Bibliographie générale des oeuvres et articles sur Pierre Teilhard de Chardin parus jusqu'à fin décembre 1969. Fribourg, Editions Universitaires, 1970. 206 pp.

6.2.102 **Polgar, Laszlo.** Internationale Teilhard bibliographie 1955-65. Freiburg, Alber, 1965. 93 pp.

See also: 6.2.104 and 1.2.5, pp. 163-64.

Works

6.2.103 **Oeuvres.** Paris, Seuil. 13v.

Each volume issued separately under its own title.
The series began in 1955.

PHILOSOPHY

Biography

6.2.104 Cuénot, Claude. Pierre Teilhard de Chardin, les grandes étapes de son évolution. Paris, Plon, 1958. 489 pp.

Trans. by Vincent Colimore and ed. by René Hague as *Teilhard de Chardin: a biographical study*, London, Burns and Oates, 1965, 492 pp.
Bibliography of Chardin's works: pp. 409-82.

Index and Lexicon

6.2.105 Cuénot, Claude. Nouveau lexique, Teilhard de Chardin. Paris, Seuil, 1968. 224 pp.

6.2.106 Archévèque, P. Teilhard de Chardin: nouvel index analytique. Québec, Les Presses de l'Université Laval, 1972. 289 pp.

Center and Journal

6.2.107 Teilhard Center for the Future of Man. Founded 1966. 81 Cromwell Road, London, SW 7 5BW.

Publishes *The Teilhard Review* (6.2.109).
Critical study and development of Teilhard's thought and its application to the problem of human development.
The American Teilhard de Chardin Association Library, founded in 1968, 157 E. 72nd St., N.Y., N.Y., contains manuscripts of Teilhard's letters, dissertations on him, and other material.

6.6.108 Revue Teilhard de Chardin. 1960 to date. Quarterly. Organ of the Société Teilhard de Chardin. Editor, Dominique De Wespin, 42 Rue des Champs Elysées, 1050 Bruxelles, Belgium.

No. 1/2-12, June 1960-Sept. 1962; V. 4, No. 14, Mar. 1963- .

6.2.109 The Teilhard Review. 1966-to date. Semi-annual. Editor, John Newson. Published by the Center for the Future of Man (6.2.107).

Unamuno y Jugo, Miguel de
(1864-1936)

Bibliography

6.2.110 Onís, F. de. "Homenaje a Miguel de Unamuno," La torre (San Juan de Puerto Rico) IX (1961), nos. 35-36, 636 pp.

A full bibliography.

Works

6.2.111 Obras completas. Dirigada por Manuel Garcia Blaco. Madrid, Aguado, 1950-64. 16v.

6.2.112 Obras completas. Ed. with introduction, bibliography and notes by M. G. Blanco. Madrid, Escelier, 1968. 2v.

"Edición definitiva."

Weiss, Paul
(1901-)

Bibliography

6.2.113 Getrich, Richard J. "Bibliography of Paul Weiss's publications," The review of metaphysics, XXV (1972), 166-77.

Works

6.2.114 [Works.] Carbondale, Southern Illinois University Press.

The published books of Paul Weiss together with 7v. of his *Philosophy in process.* Issued individually by title.

Whitehead, Alfred North
(1861-1947)

Bibliography and Biography

6.2.115 Lowe, Victor, and **R. C. Baldwin.** "Bibliography of writings of Alfred North Whitehead to Jan. 3, 1951 (with selected reviews)," *in* P. A. Schilpp, ed., The philosophy of Alfred North Whitehead. 2d ed. New York, Open Court, 1951, pp. 745-78.

This volume also contains Whitehead's autobiography.

6.2.116 Woodbridge, Barry A., *ed.* Alfred North Whitehead: a primary-secondary bibliography. Bowling Green, Philosophy Documentation Center, 1977. 405 pp.

1,870 entries. Comprehensive listing of articles, books, and dissertations published prior to 1976. Annotated.

Center

6.2.117 Center for Process Studies. Founded, 1973. 1325 North College, Claremont, Calif. 91711 John B. Cobb, Jr., Director, and David R. Griffin, Exec. Director.

Services provided to visiting scholars, whether working on dissertations or more advanced projects, will include consultations, a complete-as-possible library of materials related to Whitehead's thought, and occasionally, limited financial aid. The Center organizes conferences on the relation of Whitehead's thought to various subjects and sponsors some publications.

6.2.118 Newsletter of the Center for Process Studies. *See* 10.5.4.

6.2.119 Process studies. *See* 10.2.111.

Wittgenstein, Ludwig Josef Johann
(1889-1951)

Bibliography

6.2.120 Fann, K. T. A Wittgenstein bibliography. Berkeley, University of California Press, 1977. 200 pp.

A bibliography of works by Wittgenstein and of writings on Wittgenstein.

Also contains a catalog of the Wittgenstein manuscripts, a chronology of his life, a list of his Cambridge lectures and the names of students who attended.

6.2.121 Wright, Georg Henrik von. "The Wittgenstein papers," Philosophical review, LXXVII (1969), 483-503.

An annotated list of the manuscripts and typescripts of Wittgenstein's philosophical works.

Works

6.2.122 Schriften. Hrsg. von Friedrich Waismann. Frankfurt am Main, Suhrkamp, 1960- .

In progress. 7v. published by 1978.

A proposed complete edition under the direction of Michael Nedo, London, Blackwell, and Frankfurt, Suhrkamp, has been announced. 14v. projected.

Index and Concordance

6.2.123 Index zu Wittgensteins Tractatus logico-philosophicus und Wittgenstein-Bibliographie. Freiburg i. Br., Karl Alber, 1969. 113 pp.

6.2.124 Kaal, H. and **A. McKinnon,** *eds.* Concordance to Wittgenstein's Philosophische Untersuchungen. Leiden, E. J. Brill, 1975. 596 pp.

Biography

6.2.125 Malcolm, Norman. Ludwig Wittgenstein: a memoir. London, New York, Oxford University Press, 1958. 100 pp.

See also: 10.5.48.

III
Systematic Philosophy: Branches, Movements and Regions

7. BRANCHES

The branches of philosophy listed here are admittedly somewhat arbitrary. Philosophy forms a whole and divisions within it are often artificial. Sometimes a certain set of divisions represents a particular philosophical point of view. The divisions listed here are some of those generally agreed upon in the philosophical community in the United States. The list is not exhaustive.

I have grouped together dictionaries, bibliographies, histories, journals, societies, newsletters, and so on, dealing with a particular branch of philosophy. In some instances, as with ethics, I have subdivided the branch because of a significant interest in and body of literature dealing with the subdivisions.

Bibliographies for branches not listed can be generated by using the items listed in 1.2.

7.1 AESTHETICS

Dictionaries

7.1.1 **Caillois, Roger**. Vocabulaire esthétique. Paris, Editions de la Revue Fontaine, 1946. 141 pp.

Essays on a variety of topics connected with art and aesthetics.

7.1.2 **Mantegazza, Paolo**. Dizionario delle cose belle. Milano, Fratelli Treves, 1891. 346 pp.

Contains articles on terms and on "beautiful things."

7.1.3 **Ovsiannikov, Mikhail Fedorovich, i V. A. Razumnii**. Kratkii slovar' po estetike. Moskva, Izd. politicheskoi literatury, 1936. 542 pp.

Covers about 250 terms and concepts of Marxist-Leninist aesthetics.

7.1.4 **Saisselin, Rémy**. The rule of reason and the ruses of the heart. A philosophical dictionary of classical French criticism, critics, and aesthetic ideas. Cleveland, Case Western Reserve University Press, 1970. 308 pp.

See also: 19.1.9-19.1.11.

Bibliographies

7.1.5 **Albert, Ethel M.**, and **Clyde Kluckhorn**. A selected bibliography on values, ethics and aesthetics in the behavioral sciences and philosophy, 1920-1958. Glencoe, Ill., Free Press, 1959. 342 pp.

An annotated list of books and articles.

7.1.6 **Baxandall, Lee**, *comp*. Marxism and aesthetics; a selective annotated bibliography; books and articles in the English language. Atlantic Highlands, N. J., Humanities Press, 1968. 261 pp.

Reprinted: 1973.

7.1.7 **Bibliographie d'esthétique** (1950). Revue esthétique, V (1952), 71-110, 177-206.

7.1.8 Beardsley, Monroe C. Aesthetics. New York, Harcourt, Brace, 1958. 614 pp.

Copious bibliographies follow each section.

7.1.9 Chandler, Albert Richard, and **Edward N. Barnhart.** A bibliography of psychological and experimental aesthetics, 1864-1937. London, Cambridge University Press, 1938. 190 pp.

7.1.10 Draper, J. W. Eighteenth century English aesthetics; a bibliography. Heidelberg, Winter, 1931. 140 pp.

Supplemented by: W. D. Tempelman, "Contributions to the bibliography of eighteenth-century aesthetics," *Modern philology*, XXX (1932-33), 309-16.

7.1.11 Gayley, Charles Mills, and **F. N. Scott.** A guide to the literature of aesthetics. Berkeley, 1890. 116 pp.

Univ. of Calif., library bulletin, no. 4. Reprinted: N. Y., Burt Franklin.

7.1.12 Hammond, W. A. A bibliography of aesthetics and of the philosophy of the fine arts from 1900 to 1932. Rev. ed. New York, Longmans, Green, 1934. 205 pp.

Originally published as a supplement to the May, 1933 issue of the *Philosophical Review*.
Covers 1900-32 and continues Rand (1.2.18). Continued by "Selective current bibliography for aesthetics and related fields," in the June issue of *Journal of Aesthetics and Art Criticism*, from 1941.
Reprinted: N. Y., Russell & Russell, 1966.

7.1.13 Pinilla, Norberto. Bibliografía de estética. Santiago de Chile, M. Barros Borgoño, 1939. 64 pp.

7.1.14 Shields, Allan. A bibliography of bibliographies in aesthetics. San Diego, San Diego State University Press, 1974. 79 pp.

7.1.15 Wollheim, Richard. Art and its objects; an introduction to aesthetics. New York, Harper, 1968. 152 pp.

Bibliography: pp. 135-52.

7.1.16 Journal of aesthetics and art criticism. See 10.2.49.

Carries annual bibliographies.

See also: 1.2.5, pp. 179-84; and 19.1.1-19.1.8.

Histories

7.1.17 Beardsley, Monroe C. Aesthetics from classical Greece to the present. New York, Macmillan, 1966. 414 pp.

Reprinted: University of Alabama Press, 1975.

7.1.18 Bosanquet, B., *ed.* A history of aesthetics. 2d ed. London, Allen and Unwin, 1904.

Reprinted: N. Y., Meridian, 1957.
Includes bibliography.

7.1.19 Gilbert, Katharine E., and **Helmut Kuhn.** A history of esthetics. Rev. ed. Bloomington, Ind., Indiana University Press, 1953. 613 pp.

Includes bibliographies.

7.1.20 Tatarkiewicz, Wladyslaw. History of aesthetics. Trans. from the Polish by Adam and Ann Czerniawski, et al. The Hague, Mouton, 1971-74. 3v.

Vol. I, Ancient aesthetics;
vol. II, Medieval aesthetics;
vol. III, Modern aesthetics: 1400-1700.

See also: 19.1.12.

Journals and Series

7.1.21 The British journal of aesthetics. *See* 10.2.16.

7.1.22 **Journal of aesthetics and art criticism.** *See* 10.2.49.

7.1.23 **Revue d'esthétique.** *See* 10.3.10.

See also: 12.1.8, 12.1.24, 12.1.58.

7.2 ETHICS

Dictionaries

7.2.1 **Ferm, Vergilius Ture Anselm,** *ed.* Encyclopedia of morals. New York, Philosophical Library, 1956. 682 pp.

Articles were contributed by a number of contemporary philosophers, including L. W. Beck, W. Frankena, and W. Kaufmann. Contains bibliographies.

7.2.2 **Kratkii slovar' po etike.** Pod. red. O. G. Drobnitskogo, I. S. Kona. Moskva, Izd. politicheskoi literatury, 1965. 543 pp.

Contains more than 270 terms and concepts of Marxist-Leninist ethics and communist morality.

7.2.3 **Macquarrie, John.** Dictionary of Christian ethics. Philadelphia, Westminster, 1967. 366 pp.

Articles by many different contributors including Harvey Cox, Joseph Fletcher, and D. M. MacKinnon.

7.2.4 **Mathews, Shailer,** and **Gerald Birney Smith,** *eds.* A dictionary of religion and ethics. New York, Macmillan, 1921. 513 pp.

Contributors include F. Boas, G. H. Mead, and J. H. Tufts. Bibliographies.

See also: 1.4.2.

Bibliographies

7.2.5 **Bastide, Georges.** Ethics and political philosophy. French bibliographical digest,

No. 34. New York, Cultural Center of the French Embassy, 1961. 96 pp.

Also published as: *Morale et philosophie politique,* Paris, Assoc. pour la diffusion de la pensée française, 1961. 91 pp.

7.2.6 **Blanpied, William.** "Selected bibliography of recent works on the ethical and human value implications of science and technology," Harvard newsletter on the public conceptions of science, no. 8, June, 1974, 71-130.

7.2.7 **Brock, D. W.** "Recent work in utilitarianism," American philosophical quarterly, X (1973), 241-76.

Critical review of literature from 1961-71 with bibliography.

7.2.8 **Gothie, Daniel L.** A selected bibliography of applied ethics in the professions, 1950-1970; a working sourcebook with annotations and indexes. Charlottesville, Va., University Press of Virginia, 1973. 176 pp.

7.2.9 **Lineback, Richard H.** Ethics: a bibliography. New York, Garland, 1976. 265 pp.

Lists some 2,000 articles and 500 books published in English. Annotated.

7.2.10 **Matczak, Sebastian A.** Philosophy: a select classified bibliography of ethics, economics, law, politics and sociology. (Philosophical questions series, no. 3). Louvain, Editions Nauwelaerts; Paris, Béatrice-Nauwelaerts; New York, Humanities Press, 1970. 308 pp.

7.2.11 **Rescher, Nicholas.** Introduction to value theory. Englewood Cliffs, N. J., Prentice-Hall, 1969. 199 pp.

"Bibliography on the theory of value," pp. 149-86.

7.2.12 **Sellars, Wilfrid,** and **John Hospers.** Readings in ethical theory. New York, Appleton-Century-Crofts, 1952. 707 pp.

Bibliography: pp. 701-7.

See also: 7.1.5 and 1.2.5, pp. 210-14.

Histories

7.2.13 **Bourke, Vernon J.** History of ethics; a comprehensive survey of the history of ethics from the early Greeks to the present time. Garden City, N. Y., Doubleday, 1968. 432 pp.

Bibliography: pp. 353-417.

7.2.14 **Brinton, Clarence Crane.** A history of Western morals. New York, Harcourt Brace, 1959. 502 pp.

7.2.15 **Dittrich, Ottmar.** Geschichte der Ethik. Die Systeme der Moral vom Altertum bis zum Gegenwart. Leipzig, Meiner, 1926-32. 4v.

Good and quite complete up to its time. Bibliographies.

7.2.16 **Mac Intyre, Alasdair C.** A short history of ethics. New York, Macmillan, 1966. 280 pp.

Treats about 30 major figures from the Sophists to Sartre.

7.2.17 **Sidgwick, Henry.** Outlines of the history of ethics. With an additional chapter by A. G. Widgery. 6th ed. London, Macmillan, 1931. 342 pp.

Reprinted: Boston, Beacon, 1964. 1st ed. 1886.

Journals

7.2.18 **Ethica.** See 10.3.42.

7.2.19 **Ethics.** See 10.2.27.

7.2.20 **The journal of religious ethics.** 1973 to date. Semi-annual. Ed. Charles Reynolds. Pub., Scholons Press, Univ. of Montana, Missoula, Mont. 59812.

7.2.21 **Man and medicine.** See 10.2.70.

7.2.22 **Revue de métaphysique et de morale.** See 10.3.11.

See also: 7.6.6.

Ethics in Medicine and Science

7.2.23 **Bibliography of bioethics.** Ed. by LeRoy Walters. Detroit, Gale Research, 1976- .

V. 1 covers 1973; v. 2, 1973 and 1974; v. 3, 1973-76. Annual thereafter.

Each volume contains Introduction, List of Journals Cited, Bioethics Thesaurus, Subject Entry Section, Title Index, Author Index.

7.2.24 **The bioethics digest.** Monthly. Published by: Information Planning Associates, Inc., P. O. Box 1523, Rockville, Md., 20850.

A journal of abstracts.
Summaries of current books and articles in the area of medical ethics.

7.2.25 **Ethics in science and medicine.** [Formerly: Science, medicine and man]. Vol. I (1973)- .

7.2.26 **Bibliography of society, ethics and the life sciences.** Hastings Center. Hastings-on-Hudson, N. Y.

The 1976-77 edition was also separately published by Garland.

7.2.27 **Encyclopedia of bioethics.** Kennedy Institute. New York, Free Press, 1978. 4v.

315 articles. Basic educational tool and standard reference work of traditional and contemporary positions taken on the principles and problems of medical ethics and to point to new directions in the ethics of biomedicine.

7.2.28 **Hastings Center report.** Feb., 1975- . (6 issues per year, and annual bibliography, and annual reviews.) Hastings Center Institute of Society, Ethics and the Life Sciences, Hastings-on-Hudson, N. Y.

Combines Hastings Center studies (1973-75) and Hastings Center report.
The Hastings Center also publishes a *Bib-*

liography of Society, Ethics and the Life Sciences. 1973- . Annual.

7.2.29 **New titles in bioethics.** Kennedy Institute. Monthly newsletter. Washington, D. C., Georgetown University.

List of books, government documents, pamphlets, serial titles, and audiovisual aids acquired during the previous 4 weeks by the Center for Bioethics Library of the Kennedy Institute (for the Study of Human Reproduction and Bioethics).

7.2.30 **Journal of medical ethics.** Society for the Study of Medical Ethics (1972-). Dr. A. V. Campbell, Ed., University of Edinburgh, New College, The Mound, Edinburgh, England, EH1 2LX.

" . . . a multi-disciplinary journal devoted to issues raised by practice of medicine. It is addressed primarily to physicians and members of the health professions."

7.2.31 **The journal of medicine and philosophy.** Society for Health and Human Values. Edmund D. Pellegrino, Ed. University of Chicago Press. Vol. I (1976)- .

Each issue focuses on a particular theme.

7.2.32 **Newsletter of the committee on philosophy and medicine.** *See* 10.5.5.

7.2.33 **Walters, Le Roy.** Bibliography of bioethics. Detroit, Gale Research. Vol. 1 (1975)- . Annual.

Entries arranged by topic indexes.
Sponsored by the Center for Bioethics, Kennedy Institute, Georgetown University.

See also: 7.11.24, 10.2.70, 22.3.1-22.3.3.

Business and Professional Ethics

7.2.34 **Business and professional ethics**: a quarterly newsletter/report. Center for the Study of the Human Dimensions of Science and Technology. Robert J. Baum, Dir. Rens-

selaer Polytechnic Institute. Troy, N. Y., 12181.

7.2.35 **Gothie, Daniel L.** A selected bibliography of applied ethics in the professions, 1950-70. *See* 7.2.8.

7.2.36 **Jones, Donald G.** Business ethics bibliography, 1971-75. Charlottesville, University Press of Virginia.

Selective annotation. A continuation of 7.2.35.

See also: 12.2.5, 20.3.1-20.3.8.

Social Ethics

7.2.37 **Matczak, Sebastian A.** Philosophy: a select classified bibliography of ethics, economics, law, politics, sociology. *See* 7.2.10.

7.2.38 **Utz, Arthur.** Bibliographie der Sozialethik. Grundsatsfragen des öffentlichen Lebens. Freiburg i. Br., Herder. Vol. I (1960)-.

A continuing bibliography.

7.2.39 **Utz, Arthur.** Bases for social living. A critical bibliography embracing law, society, economics, and politics. New York, Herder, 1961. 446 pp.

Also published in German.

7.3 LOGIC

Dictionaries

7.3.1 **Dictionary of symbols of mathematical logic.** Ed. by R. Feys and F. B. Fitch. Amsterdam, North-Holland, 1969. 171 pp.

"The purpose of the present 'Dictionary' is to enable the reader to find with some ease the meaning and interpretation of symbols currently used in mathematical logic (symbolic logic)."

7.3.2 **Diez y Lozano, Baldomero.** Vocabulario

de lógica. 2. ed. Murcia, Spain, Imp. Lourdes, 1928. 198 pp.

1st ed. 1925.

7.3.3 **Kondakov, N. I.** Logicheskii slovar'. M., "Nauka," 1971. 656 pp.

Bibliographies

7.3.4 **Ainvelle, Varin d'.** Logic and the philosophy of science. French bibliographical digest, No. 29. New York, Cultural Center of the French Embassy, 1959. 60 pp.

7.3.5 **Cheng, Chung-ying.** "Selected bibliography with annotations and comments," in his "Inquiries into classical Chinese logic," Philosophy East and West, XV (1965), 204-15.

7.3.6 **Church, Alonzo.** "A bibliography of symbolic logic," Journal of symbolic logic, I (1936), 121-218.

Covers the years 1666-1935. Additions and corrections: *Journal of Symbolic Logic,* III (1938), pp. 178-212.

7.3.7 **Church Alonzo.** "Brief bibliography of formal logic," Proceedings of the American Academy of Arts and Sciences, LXXX (1952), 155-72.

7.3.8 **Moss, M.,** and **D. Scott.** A bibliography of books on symbolic logic. New York, Oxford University Press, 1977. 250 pp.

Also includes books on foundations of mathematics, philosophy of logic and mathematics, and history of logic.

7.3.9 **Risse, Wilhelm.** Bibliographia logica. Hildesheim, Olms, 1965- .

Vol. 1 includes separately printed works on logic from 1472-1800, 293 pp.;
vol. 2 covers 1801-1969;
vol. 3 will review articles, and vol. 4, manuscripts.

7.3.10 **Ashworth, E. J.** "Some additions to

Risse's 'Bibliographia Logica,'" Journal of the history of philosophy, XII (1974), 361-65.

Lists works published during the period 1472-1800 that do not appear in Risse.

See also: 1.2.16 (No. 3); and 1.2.5, pp. 258-62; 9.4.8.

Histories

7.3.11 **Bochenski, I. M.** A history of formal logic. Trans. and ed. by Ivo Thomas. Notre Dame, Notre Dame University Press, 1961. 567 pp.

A translation of *Formale Logik,* Freiburg and Munich, 1956.
Good bibliographies.

7.3.12 **Dumitriu, Anton.** History of logic. Tunbridge Wells, Abacus Press, 1978. 4v.

Vol. I, (I) Logic in non-European cultures, (II) Logic in ancient Greece, (III) Rhetors and commentators;
vol. II, (IV) Scholastic logic, (V) Renaissance logic;
vol. III, (VI) Methodological logic;
vol. IV, (VII) Mathematical logic.
An extensive and comprehensive reference work. Includes extensive quotations from original works. Bibliographies for each book. The most comprehensive of the histories of logic.

7.3.13 **Kneale, William,** and **Martha Kneale.** The development of logic. Oxford, Oxford University Press, 1962. 761 pp.

7.3.14 **Prantl, Carl.** Geschichte der Logik im Abendlande. Leipzig, 1866. 4v.

Reprinted: 1927.

7.3.15 **Rescher, Nicholas.** The development of Arabic logic. Pittsburgh, University of Pittsburgh Press, 1964. 262 pp.

Complete bibliography.

7.3.16 **Risse, Wilhelm**. Die Logik der Neuzeit. Stuttgart, 1964- .

2v. to date.

Journals

7.3.17 **Annals of mathematical logic**. *See* 10.2.8.

7.3.18 **Informal logic newsletter**. 1978-to present. Three nos. yearly. Eds. Ralph H. Johnson and J. Anthony Blair, Dept. of Philosophy, Univ. of Windsor, Ontario N9B 3P4 Canada.

Serves as a clearinghouse for the exchange of ideas and information about the theory, practice, and pedagogy of informal logic.

7.3.19 **International logic review**. *See* 10.2.43.

7.3.20 **Journal of philosophical logic**. *See* 10.2.55.

7.3.21 **The journal of symbolic logic**. *See* 10.2.61.

7.3.22 **Notre Dame journal of formal logic**. *See* 10.2.81.

7.3.23 **Rassegna internazionale de logica**. *See* 10.2.43.

7.3.24 **Relevance logic newsletter**. *See* 10.5.9.

See also: 10.5.56, 12.1.19, 12.1.30.

7.4 METAPHYSICS

Bibliographies

7.4.1 **Campbell, Keith**. Metaphysics; an introduction. Dickenson, 1976. 248 pp.

Bibliography: pp. 235-42.

7.4.2 **De George, Richard T.**, *ed.* Classical and contemporary metaphysics; a source book. New York, Holt, Rinehart and Winston, 1962. 323 pp.

Bibliographies at the end of each Part.

7.4.3 **Drennen, D. A.**, *ed.* Modern introduction to metaphysics, readings from classical and contemporary sources. Glencoe, Ill., Free Press, 1962. 738 pp.

Bibliographies at the end of each Part.

Histories

7.4.4 **Heimsoeth, Heinz**. Die sechs grossen Themen der abendlandischen Metaphysik und der Ausgang des Mittelalters. 3 Aufl. Stuttgart, W. Kohlhammer, 1954. 255 pp.

1st ed., 1922.

7.4.5 **Lange, Friedrich Albert**. History of materialism and criticism of its present importance. 3d ed. New York, Humanities Press, 1950. 3v.

1st English edition, 1877.

7.4.6 **Lovejoy, Arthur Oncken**. The great chain of being; a study in the history of an idea. Cambridge, Mass., Harvard University Press, 1936. 382 pp.

Reprinted: Harper, 1960.

See also: 7.12.11.

Journals

7.4.7 **Giornale de metafisica**. *See* 10.3.45.

7.4.8 **Review of metaphysics**. *See* 10.2.114.

7.4.9 **Revue de métaphysique et de morale**. *See* 10.3.11.

See also: 12.1.4, 12.1.38.

7.5 PHILOSOPHICAL ANTHROPOLOGY

Bibliography

7.5.1 **Landmann, Michael**, [u.a.]. De homine, der Mensch, im Spiegel seines Gedankens. München, Alber, 1962. 620 pp.

Bibliography: pp. 543-614.

7.6 PHILOSOPHY OF EDUCATION

7.6.1 **Broudy, Harry S.** [et al.]. Philosophy of education; an organization of topics and selected sources. Urbana, University of Illinois Press, 1967. 287 pp.

An annotated bibliography relating philosophy and education.

7.6.2 **Powell, John P.** Philosophy of education: a select bibliography. 2d ed. Manchester, England, Manchester University Press; distr. New York, Humanities Press, 1970. 51 pp.

Listing of articles from 74 journals from 1950 to 1970. Cross referenced. Listings under 26 subjects. Author index.

7.6.3 **Brumbaugh, Robert S.,** and **N. W. Lawrence**. Philosophers on education. New York, Houghton, 1963. 211 pp.

7.6.4 **Park, Joe,** ed. Selected readings in the philosophy of education. 3d ed. New York, Macmillan, 1968. 433 pp.

7.6.5 **Scheffler, Israel,** ed. Philosophy and education. 2d ed. Boston, Allyn & Bacon, 1966. 387 pp.

See also: 22.1.1-22.1.10.

Journals

7.6.6 **Journal of moral education**. 1971-to present. 3 issues a year. Ed. Monica Taylor. National Foundation for Educational Research in England and Wales, the Mere.

Organ of the Social Morality Council.

NFER Publishing Co., Ltd., 2 Jennings Bldg., Thames Ave., Windsor, Berkshire SL4 1Q5 England.

7.6.7 **Studies in philosophy and education.** See 10.2.124.

See also: 10.5.22, 12.1.41, 12.1.60.

7.7 PHILOSOPHY OF HISTORY

Bibliographies

7.7.1 **Danto, Arthur**. Analytical philosophy of history. Cambridge, University Press, 1965. 318 pp.

Bibliographical references in "Notes," pp. 285-313.

7.7.2 **Nadel, George H.,** ed. Studies in the philosophy of history; selected essays from History and theory (10.2.34). New York, Harper and Row, 1965. 220 pp.

Bibliographical footnotes.

7.7.3 **Nowicki, M.** "Bibliography of works in the philosophy of history 1958-1961," History and theory, 1964. 25 pp.

Beiheft 3 to 10.2.34. A continuation of 7.7.4.

7.7.4 **Rule, John C.** "Bibliography of works in the philosophy of history 1945-1957," History and theory, 1961. 87 pp.

Beiheft 1 to 10.2.34. 87 pp.

7.7.5 **Walton, Craig**. Bibliography of the historiography and philosophy of the history of philosophy. Torino, Filosofia, 1977. 34 pp.

7.7.6 **Wurgaft, Lewis D.** "Bibliography of works in the philosophy of history 1962-1965," History and theory, 1967.

Beiheft 7 to 10.2.34, pp. 1-45. A continuation of 7.7.3.

Continued thereafter every three years.

7.7.7 Witschi-Bernz, Astrid. "Bibliography of works in the philosophy of history, 1500-1800," History and theory, vol. 12 (1972), pp. 3-50.

Journal

7.7.8 History and theory. See 10.2.34.

See also: 10.4.2, and section 18.4.

7.8 PHILOSOPHY OF MATHEMATICS

Bibliography

7.8.1 Mostowski, Andrzej. Thirty years of foundational studies; lectures on the development of mathematical logic and the study of the foundations of mathematics in 1930-1964. (Acta philosophica Fennica, no. 17.) New York, Barnes & Noble, 1966. 180 pp.

Bibliography: pp. 157-71.

See also: 21.1.5, 21.1.7.

History

7.8.2 Brunschvicg, L. Les étapes de la philosophie mathématique. 2. éd. Paris, Alcan, 1922. 591 pp.

Journal

7.8.3 Philosophia mathematica. See 10.2.87.

7.9 PHILOSOPHY OF RELIGION

Bibliographies

7.9.1 Berkowitz, Morris I., and **J. Edmund Johnson.** Social scientific studies of religion; a bibliography. Pittsburgh, Pittsburgh University Press, 1967. 258 pp.

7.9.2 Galama, I. J. K., and **A. F. Sanders.** Logic, epistemology and analysis of religious language, a selected bibliography. Groningen Theologisch Instituit van de Rijk-universitet, 1974. 64 pp.

7.9.3 Wainwright, William J. Philosophy of religion; an annotated bibliography of twentieth-century writings in English. New York, Garland, 1978. 790 pp.

Covers the divine attributes, arguments for the existence of God, the problem of evil, mysticism and religious experience, faith and revelation, miracles, religious language, and justification of systems of religious belief.

See also: 1.4.2.

Journal

7.9.4 International journal for philosophy of religion. See 10.2.41.

See also: 10.2.48, 10.3.8, 10.3.13, 10.3.16, 10.3.27, 10.3.36, 10.3.52, 12.1.48, 12.1.52, and section 17.

7.10 PHILOSOPHY OF SCIENCE AND OF THE SOCIAL SCIENCES

Bibliographies

7.10.1 "Critical bibliography of the history of science and its cultural influences." Isis, 1913-to date.
The title varies.
Isis carries a continuing bibliography in the philosophy of science. See 10.2.47.

7.10.2 Danto, Arthur, and **Sidney Morgenbesser,** eds. Philosophy of science. New York, Meridian, 1960. 477 pp.

Selected bibliography: pp. 471-77.

7.10.3 Feigl, Herbert, and **May Brodbeck,** eds. Readings in the philosophy of science. New York, Appleton-Century-Crofts, 1953. 811 pp.

Bibliography: pp. 783-99.

7.10.4 Grünbaum, Adolf. Philosophical problems of space and time. 2d, enl. ed. Dordrecht, Reidel, 1973. 884 pp.

Bibliographies throughout.

7.10.5 International encyclopedia of unified science. Foundations of the unity of science. Chicago, 1938-69.

Bibliography and Index by Herbert Feigl and Charles Morris. Constitutes Vol. II, monograph no. 10.

Each of the 2 vols. includes 10 monographs, including those by Bohr, Carnap, and Dewey, among others. The volumes are not an encyclopedia in the ordinary sense, and were intended as an introduction to an encyclopedia which has been discontinued.

7.10.6 Logic and the philosophy of science: with an introduction by Robert Blanché. French bibliographical digest, No. 30. New York, Cultural Center of the French Embassy, 1959. 60 pp.

Annotated.

7.10.7 Mitcham, Carl, and **Robert Mackey.** Bibliography of the philosophy of technology. Chicago, University of Chicago Press, 1973. 205 pp.

7.10.8 Robert, Jean-Dominique. Philosophie et science. Philosophy and science. Eléments de bibliographie. Elements of bibliography. Paris, Beauchesne, 1968. 384 pp.

Supplement for 1968 and 1969: *Archives de philosophie* (Paris), vol. 33 (1970), pp. 110-12, 295-324.

7.10.9 Sarton, George H. A guide to the history of science. New York, Ronald Press, 1952. 316 pp.

See pp. 86-93 for scientific methods and the philosophy of science; pp. 194-248 for journals and serials concerning the history and philosophy of science.

7.10.10 Sarton, George H. Introduction to the history of science. Washington, D. C., Carnegie Institute, 1927-48. 3v. in 5.

Copious bibliographies throughout. "General bibliography," vol. 3, 1872-1911.

7.10.11 Wartofsky, Marx W. Conceptual foundations of scientific thought; an introduction to the philosophy of science. New York, Macmillan, 1968. 560 pp.

Bibliography: pp. 489-548.

See also: 21.1.1-21.1.14.

Journals and Series

7.10.12 Boston studies in the philosophy of science series. *See* 10.5.39.

7.10.13 The British journal for the philosophy of science. *See* 10.2.15.

7.10.14 Isis. *See* 10.2.47.

7.10.15 Methodos. *See* 10.2.74.

7.10.16 Philosophy and medicine series. *See* 10.5.52.

7.10.17 Philosophy and technology newsletter. *See* 10.5.8.

7.10.18 Philosophy of science. *See* 10.2.103.

7.10.19 Scientia. *See* 10.2.116.

7.10.20 Studies in history and philosophy of science. *See* 10.2.123.

7.10.21 Studies in the foundations, methodology and philosophy of science series. *See* 10.5.60.

7.10.22 Theory and decision. *See* 10.2.131.

7.10.23 Zeitschrift für Allgemeine Wissenschaftstheorie. *See* 10.3.37.

See also: 10.2.103, 10.2.104, 10.2.117, 10.2.126, 10.2.127, 10.3.32, 10.3.41, 10.4.14, 10.4.16, 10.5.7, 10.5.61, 10.5.62.

Society

7.10.24 **American Association for the Advancement of Science.** Section L. *See* 12.1.21.

7.10.25 **Philosophy of Science Association.** *See* 12.1.42.

See also: 12.1.19, 12.1.57.

7.11 POLITICAL, SOCIAL AND LEGAL PHILOSOPHY

Bibliographies

7.11.1 **Benn, Stanley I.,** and **R. S. Peters.** Principles of political thought. New York, Collier, 1964. 478 pp.

First published as *Social Principles and the Democratic State,* 1959.
Bibliography in the "Notes," pp. 441-62.

7.11.2 **Brodbeck, May.** Readings in the philosophy of the social sciences. New York, Macmillan, 1968. 789 pp.

Bibliography: pp. 737-68.

7.11.3 **Connolly, William E.** Political science and ideology. New York, Atherton, 1967. 179 pp.

Bibliography: pp. 169-74.

7.11.4 **Conte, Amedeo G.** "Bibliografia de logica giuridica (1936-1960)," Revista internazionale di filosofia del diritto, XXXVIII (1961), 120-44.

Addenda, XXXIX (1962), 45-46.

7.11.5 **Freiburg, Schweiz.** Internationalen Institut fur Sozialwissenschaft und Politik. Bibliographie der Sozialethik. Freiburg, Schweiz, Heider, 1961-63. 530 pp.

7.11.6 **Friedmann, Wolfgang Gaston.** Legal theory. 5th ed. New York, Columbia University Press, 1967. 607 pp.

Bibliography: pp. 581-92.

7.11.7 **Friedrich, Carl Joachim.** Man and his government; an empirical theory of politics. New York, McGraw-Hill, 1963. 737 pp.

Bibliography: pp. 677-715.

7.11.8 **Friedrich, C. J.** Philosophy of law in historical perspective. 2d ed. Chicago, University of Chicago Press, 1963. 296 pp.

Bibliography: pp. 277-84.

7.11.9 **Golding, M. P.** The nature of law; readings in legal philosophy. New York, Random House, 1966. 276 pp.

Bibliography: pp. 275-78.

7.11.10 **Kent, Edward Allen.** Law and philosophy: readings in legal philosophy. New York, Appleton-Century-Crofts, 1970.

Bibliography: pp. 599-622.

7.11.11 **Krimerman, Leonard I.** The nature and scope of social science; a critical anthology. New York, Appleton-Century-Crofts, 1969. 796 pp.

Bibliography: pp. 759-75.

7.11.12 **Martin, Rex,** and **James W. Nickel,** "A bibliography on the nature and foundations of rights, 1947-1977," Political theory, VI (1978), 395-413.

7.11.13 **Natanson, Maurice.** Philosophy of the social sciences; a reader. New York, Random House, 1963. 560 pp.

Bibliography: pp. 509-41.

7.11.14 **Negley, Glenn.** Utopian literature: a bibliography with a supplementary listing of works influential in utopian thought. Lawrence, Kans., The Regents Press of Kansas, 1977. 228 pp.

7.11.15 **Nettlau, Max.** Bibliographie de l'anarchie (préf. d'Elisée Reclus). Bibliothéque des temps nouveaux, no. 8. Paris, 1897. 294 pp.

"Remains the basic bibliography of the early material on the various radical movements of the 19th century, covering some 25 countries including the U. S. Comprises some 5,000 items conveniently classified and annotated, including a listing of anarchist journals and newspapers."
Reprinted: N. Y., Burt Franklin.

7.11.16 **Pound, Roscoe.** An introduction to the philosophy of law. Rev. ed. New Haven, Yale University Press, 1954. 201 pp.

1st ed. 1922. 307 pp.
Bibliography: pp. 285-307.

See also: 7.2.5, 20.1.1-20.1.9, 22.2.1-22.2.11.

Histories

7.11.17 **Cairns, Huntington.** Legal philosophy from Plato to Hegel. Baltimore, Johns Hopkins Press, 1949. 583 pp.

7.11.18 **Cook, Thomas Ira.** A history of political philosophy from Plato to Burke. New York, Prentice-Hall, 1936. 725 pp.

Includes bibliographies.

7.11.19 **Friedrich, Carl Joachim.** The philosophy of law in historical perspective. 2d ed. Chicago, University of Chicago Press, 1963. 296 pp.

1st ed. 1958.
Bibliography: pp. 277-84.
An English version of *Die Philosophie des Rechts in historischer Perspektive*, Berlin, Springer, 1955, 153 pp.

7.11.20 **Plamenatz, John Petrov.** Man and society; political and social theory. New York, McGraw-Hill, 1963. 2v.

Vol. 1, Political and social theory: Machiavelli through Rousseau;

vol. 2, Political and social theory: Bentham through Marx.

7.11.21 **Popper, Karl Raimund.** The open society and its enemies. 5th ed. rev. London, Routledge and Kegan Paul, 1966. 2v.

1st ed. 1945.
Bibliography in "Notes" at the end of each volume.

7.11.22 **Sabine, George Holland.** A history of political theory. 4th ed. rev. by Thomas Landon Thorson. Hinsdale, Dryden, 1973. 871 pp.

Bibliographies at the end of each chapter.

7.11.23 **Vecchio, Giorgio del.** Philosophy of law. Trans. by Thomas Owen Martin from the 8th ed., 1952. Washington, D. C., Catholic University of America Press, 1953. 474 pp.

"History of Philosophy of Law," pp. 23-243, contains abundant bibliographical references. This section, which is part of del Vecchio's *Lezioni di filosofia del diritto*, was published separately as *Storia della filosofia del diritto*, 2. ed., Milano, Guiffre, 1958, 200 pp.

Journals

7.11.24 **American journal of law and medicine.** 1975- . Quarterly. MIT Press, Journals Dept., 28 Carleton St., Cambridge, Mass. 02142.

". . . often publishes articles combining topics in ethics and philosophy of law, especially those about issues in health care." (11.2.16.)

7.11.25 **Archiv für Rechts-und Sozialphilosophie.** *See* 10.3.25.

7.11.26 **Journal of legal philosophy.** *See* 10.2.54.

7.11.27 **Journal of social philosophy.** *See* 10.2.60.

7.11.28 **Philosophy and public affairs.** *See* 10.2.97.

7.11.29 **Philosophy of the social sciences.** *See* 10.2.104.

7.11.30 **Social theory and practice.** *See* 10.2.118.

7.11.31 **Twentieth century legal philosophy** series. Cambridge, Mass., Harvard University Press, 1970- .

Irregular.

See also: 10.2.46, 10.2.132, 12.1.6, 12.1.25, 12.1.26.

7.12 THEORY OF KNOWLEDGE AND PHILOSOPHY OF MIND

Bibliographies

7.12.1 **Canfield, John V.,** and **Franklin H. Donnell,** *eds.* Readings in the theory of knowledge. New York, Appleton-Century-Crofts, 1964. 520 pp.

Bibliographies at the end of each Part.

7.12.2 **Chappell, Vere Claiborne,** *ed.* The philosophy of mind. Englewood Cliffs, N. J., Prentice-Hall, 1962. 178 pp.

Bibliography: pp. 173-78.

7.12.3 **Edwards, Paul,** and **Arthur Pap,** *eds.* A modern introduction to philosophy; readings from classical and contemporary sources. Rev. ed. New York, Free Press, 1965. 797 pp.

Excellent annotated bibliographies after each section.

7.12.4 **Emmett, Kathleen,** and **Peter Machamer.** Perception: an annotated bibliography. New York and London, Garland Reference Library of the Humanities, Vol. 39, 1976. 177 pp.

7.12.5 **Minnesota studies in the philosophy of science,** vol. II: Concepts, theories, and the mind-body problem. Ed. by Herbert Feigl, Michael Scriven, and Grover Maxwell for the Minnesota Center for Philosophy of Science. Minneapolis, University of Minnesota Press, 1958. 553 pp.

Bibliographies throughout; see especially pp. 484-97.

7.12.6 **Nagel, Ernest,** and **Richard Brandt,** *eds.* Meaning and knowledge; systematic readings in epistemology. New York, Harcourt, Brace & World, 1965. 668 pp.

Bibliographies at the end of each chapter.

7.12.7 **Robert, Jean Dominique.** Philosophies, épistémologies, sciences de l'homme: leurs rapports; éléments de bibliographie. (Namur, Belgium. Facultés univs. Notre-Dame de la Paix. Faculté de philosophie et lettres. Bibliothèque fasc. 54) Presses univs. de Namur, 1974. 534 pp.

Histories

7.12.8 **Aster, Ernst von.** Geschichte der neueren Erkenntnistheorie (von Descartes bis Hegel). Berlin und Leipzig, de Gruyter, 1921. 638 pp.

7.12.9 **Bayer, R.** Epistémologie et logique depuis Kant jusqu'à nos jours. Paris, Presses Universitaires de France, 1954. 369 pp.

Bibliographical footnotes.

7.12.10 **Cassirer, Ernst.** Das Erkenntnisproblem in der Philosophie u. Wissenschaft der neueren Zeit. 3. Aufl. Berlin, Bruno Cassirer, 1922-57. 4v.

1st ed. 1907-21. 3v.
Vol. 4 appeared first in English translation: *The Problem of Knowledge; Philosophy, Science, and History Since Hegel,* New Haven, Yale University Press, 1950, 334 pp.

7.12.11 **Maréchal, Joseph.** Le point de départ de la métaphysique; leçons sur le développement historique et théorique du problème de la connaissance. Paris, Desclée de Brouwer, 1926-49. 5v.

Editions of individual volumes vary.

7.12.12 **Popkin, Richard H.** The history of scepticism from Erasmus to Descartes. New York, Harper Torchbooks, 1968. 242 pp.

Bibliography: pp. 219-34.

Newsletter

7.12.13 **Newsletter for Society for the Study of Mind/Brain/Machine.** Thomas W. Simon, Ed., Department of Philosophy, University of Florida, Gainesville, Fla. 32611.

See also: 10.2.22.

8. SELECTED SCHOOLS AND MOVEMENTS

The schools and movements listed in this chapter represent some of the principal ones of interest to members of the American philosophical community today. Not all schools or movements are listed. There is frequently some dispute about whether a certain philosopher belongs in a certain school or movement, just as there is not always agreement about what constitutes a school or movement. Frequently the designation of the characteristics of a school or movement is made by those outside of it.

The designation "analytic philosophy" (8.1) is especially troublesome, since most philosophers have in one way or another done analysis. For some this designation would include most of the philosophy done in the English-speaking world for decades, if not for most of the century. The references under each section are admittedly somewhat arbitrary and are intended as preliminary starting points for research and not as definitive lists.

8.1 ANALYTIC PHILOSOPHY

Bibliographies and Collections

8.1.1 **Ayer, A. J.**, *ed.* Logical positivism. Glencoe, Ill., Free Press, 1959. 455 pp.

Bibliography: pp. 381-446. An excellent bibliography of the philosophical literature in the analytic tradition. The best bibliography available on this topic.

8.1.2 **Black, Max**, *ed.* Philosophical analysis; a collection of essays. Ithaca, Cornell University Press, 1950. 429 pp.

Bibliography: pp. 421-26.

8.1.3 **Feigl, H.**, and **W. Sellars**, *eds.* Readings in philosophical analysis. New York, Appleton-Century-Crofts, 1949. 626 pp.

Bibliography: pp. 617-26.

8.1.4 **Neu, J.**, and **R. Rorty**. "Bibliography of writings in English on linguistic method in philosophy and related issues, 1930-1965," *in* Richard Rorty, ed., Linguistic turn, recent essays in philosophical method, Chicago, University of Chicago Press, 1967, pp. 361-93.

8.1.5 **Williams, Bernard**, and **Alan Montefiore**, *eds.* British analytical philosophy. New York, Humanities Press, 1966. 346 pp.

Bibliography: pp. 335-43.

See also: 10.2.7, 10.2.51, 10.2.76, 10.2.86, 10.2.130, 10.3.28, 10.3.32.

8.2 BUDDHISM

Dictionaries

8.2.1 **Humphreys, Christmas**. A popular dictionary of Buddhism. London, Arco, 1962. 233 pp.

8.2.2 **Soothill, William Edward**, and **Lewis**

Hodous. A dictionary of Chinese Buddhist terms. Rev. by Shih Sheng-kang et al., with Sanskrit and English equivalents and a Sanskrit-Pali index. Taipei, Buddhist Cultural Service, 1962. 510 pp.

Bibliographies

8.2.3 Beautrix, Pierre. Bibliographie du bouddhisme Zen. (Publications de l'Institut belge des hautes études bouddhiques. Série bibliographique, 1.) Bruxelles, Institut belge des hautes études bouddhiques, 1969. 114 pp.

8.2.4 Bibliographie bouddhique. Paris, Maisonneuve, 1928-to date.

An international periodical with résumés.

8.2.5 Hanayama, S. Bibliography on Buddhism. Tokyo, Hokuseido Press, 1961; New York, Perkins Oriental Book, 1962. 869 pp.

8.2.6 Regamey, C. Buddhistische philosophie. *See* 1.2.16, nos. 20/21.

8.2.7 Yoo, Yushin. Books on Buddhism; an annotated subject guide; with a foreword by Edwin C. Strohecker. Metuchen, N. J., Scarecrow Press, 1976. 251 pp.

Lists works in English, grouped by topic, through 1973.

See also: 1.2.16 (No. 20/21).

History

8.2.8 Kalupahana, David J. Buddhist philosophy: a historical analysis. Honolulu, University Press of Hawaii, 1976. 189 pp.

Includes bibliographies.

Journal

8.2.9 The Eastern Buddhist. New Series, 1965- . 2 issues yearly. The Eastern Buddhist Society, Otani University, Kita-Ku, Kyoto, Japan.

A nonsectarian journal devoted to an open and critical study of Mahayana Buddhism.

8.3 EXISTENTIALISM

Dictionary

8.3.1 Winn, Ralph Bubrich. A concise dictionary of existentialism. New York, Philosophical Library, 1960. 122 pp.

Quotations from Kierkegaard, Heidegger, Jaspers, Marcel, Sartre, and de Beauvoir.

Bibliographies

8.3.2 Bollnow, Otto Friedrich. Deutsche existenzphilosophie. *See* 1.2.16, no. 23.

8.3.3 Douglas, Kenneth. "A Critical bibliography of existentialism (The Paris School)," Yale French Studies, special monograph No. 1 (1950).

Reprinted: N. Y., Kraus Reprints.

8.3.4 Valentini, Francesco. "Esistenzialismo e marxismo; rassegna di scritti francesi," Giornale critico della filosofia italiana, XXXI (1952), 78-96.

8.3.5 Yanitelli, Victor R. "A bibliographical introduction to existentialism," Modern schoolman, XXVI (1949), 345-63.

See also: 1.2.16 (Nos. 9 and 23), and 6.1.9.

Journal

8.3.6 Journal of existentialism. *See* 10.2.52.

See also: 6.2.4-6.2.5, 6.2.45-6.2.50, 6.2.51-6.2.52, 6.2.56-6.2.58, 10.5.57, 12.1.46.

8.4 IDEALISM

Bibliography

8.4.1 Ewing, A. C., *ed.* The idealist tradition;

from Berkeley to Blanshard. Glencoe, Ill., Free Press, 1957. 369 pp.

Bibliography: pp. 347-62.

See also: 9.2.6, 9.3.13.

Journal

8.4.2 **Idealistic studies.** *See* 10.2.38.

8.5 MARXISM

Bibliographies

8.5.1 **The American bibliography of Russian and East European studies.** Bloomington, Ind., Indiana University Press, 1958-66. Vols. 1-11.

An annual bibliography of works in the Slavic and Soviet area, including Marxist philosophy; 1947-57 in one volume (1958). Continued by 8.5.2.

8.5.2 **The American bibliography of Slavic and East European studies.** Vol. 12 (1967)- . Columbus, Ohio, American Association for the Advancement of Slavic Studies.

Continues 8.5.1.

8.5.3 **Baxandall, Lee,** *comp.* Marxism and aesthetics. *See* 7.1.6.

8.5.4 **Bochenski, J. M.** et al., *eds.* Guide to Marxist philosophy: an introductory bibliography. Chicago, Swallow Press, 1972. 81 pp.

8.5.5 **Kolarz, Walter.** Books on Communism; a bibliography. 2d ed. New York, Oxford University Press, 1964. 568 pp.

1st ed. 1959, by R. N. C. Hunt.

8.5.6 **Lachs, John.** Marxist philosophy; a bibliographical guide. Chapel Hill, University of North Carolina Press, 1967. 166 pp.

A partially annotated list of articles and books in English, German, and French on various aspects of Marxist philosophy. A useful guide to the literature.

See also: 5.2.80-5.2.83, 8.5.8.

Encyclopedia and Journals

8.5.7 **Marxism, Communism and Western society;** a comparative encyclopedia. Ed. by C. D. Kernig. New York, Herder & Herder, 1972-73. 8v.

Includes bibliographies. Contains comparative articles written respectively from the Marxist and from non-Marxist perspectives on a wide range of topics, including philosophical ones.

8.5.8 **The American Institute for Marxist Studies Newsletter.** 20 E. 30th St., New York, N. Y. 10016. 1964- . Bi-monthly.

Reprinted: vols. 1-13 (1964-76), N. Y., Kraus Reprints.
Carries running bibliography of books and articles on Marxism.

8.5.9 **Praxis.** *See* 10.2.109.

8.5.10 **Science and society.** *See* 10.2.115.

See also: 10.2.23, 10.2.121, 10.2.125, 10.5.55, 12.1.50.

8.6 PHENOMENOLOGY

Bibliographies

8.6.1 **Colette, J.** "Chronique de phénoménologie," Revue des sciences philosophiques et théologiques, LIX (1975), 613-44.

8.6.2 **Spiegelberg, Herbert.** The phenomenological movement; a historical introduction. *See* 6.1.9.

Bibliographies of Franz Brentano, Edmund Husserl, Max Scheler, Martin Heidegger, Nicolai Hartmann, Gabriel Marcel, J.-P.

Sartre, Maurice Merleau-Ponty, as well as of general works.

Journals and Series

8.6.3 **The journal of the British Society for Phenomenology.** *See* 10.2.62.

8.6.4 **Phenomenology information bulletin.** Organ of the World Phenomenological Institute. 1976- . Editors: Veda A. Cobb and A.-T. Tymieniecka, 348 Payson Road, Belmont, Mass. 02178.

8.6.5 **Philosophy and phenomenological research.** *See* 10.2.96.

8.6.6 **Research in phenomenology.** *See* 10.2.113.

8.6.7 **Duquesne studies.** Series. *See* 10.5.42.

8.6.8 **Phaenomenologica.** Series. *See* 10.5.50.

8.6.9 **Research in phenomenology.** Series. *See* 10.5.54.

See also: 10.2.4, 10.2.6, 10.2.71, 10.5.4, 10.5.50, 10.5.57.

Centers

8.6.10 **Center for the Study of Phenomenology.** University of Oklahoma. Founded 1978.

Develops and maintains an archives and research collection of significant phenomenological materials, facilitates and promotes participation in the University instructional program, and sponsors an annual conference.

Has the Alfred Schutz Nachlass, the Franz Brentano papers, and the Dorian Cairns papers on microfilm.

Publishes *Phenomenological Sociology Newsletter.*

8.6.11 **Phenomenological Study Centers.** Founded 1972.

I. Bayerische Staatsbibliothek, Munich.

II. The Center for Advanced Research in Phenomenology. Dept. of Philosophy, Univ. of Waterloo, Ontario, Canada.

Salvaged papers and libraries of noted phenomenologists and encourages the wider dissemination of work by younger scholars in the field. Contains manuscripts and/or papers (in original, xerox, or microform) of Felix Kaufmann, Winthrop Bell, Franz Brentano, and others.

See also: 5.2.107, 5.2.108, 12.1.11, 12.1.46, 12.1.56, 12.2.14.

8.7 POSITIVISM

Bibliographies

8.7.1 **Ayer, A. J.** "Bibliography of logical positivism," *in his* Logical positivism (8.1.1).

8.7.2 **Ducasse, Pierre.** La méthode positive et l'intuition comtienne; bibliographie. Paris, Alcan, 1939. 172 pp.

See also: 1.2.16 (No. 11), 10.5.46, 10.5.64.

8.8 THOMISM AND SCHOLASTIC PHILOSOPHY

Dictionaries

8.8.1 **Signoriello, Nuntius.** Lexicon peripateticum philosophico-theologicum in quo Scholasticorum distinctiones et effata praecipua explicantur. 5. ed. Roma, Pustet, 1931. 470 pp.

1st ed. 1854.

A dictionary of scholastic distinctions and principles.

8.8.2 **Wuellner, Bernard, S. J.** Dictionary of scholastic philosophy. 2d ed. Milwaukee, Bruce, 1966. 339 pp.

Includes more than 37,000 words and phrases.

A reference work primarily for the undergraduate student.

Bibliographies

8.8.3 **Mandonnet, Pierre Felix, et J. Destrez.** Bibliographie thomiste. La Saulchoir, Kain (Belgique), Revue des sciences philosophiques et théologiques, 1921. 116 pp.

Includes works pertaining to the study of the life, work, and thought of St. Thomas Aquinas, 1800-1920.

Continued by 8.8.4.

8.8.4 **Bourke, Vernon J.** "Thomistic bibliography, 1920-1940," The modern schoolman. Suppl. to vol. XXI. St. Louis, 1945. 312 pp.

A continuation of 8.8.3. It lists both books and articles and covers theological as well as philosophical topics.

8.8.5 **Bulletin thomiste,** 1924- . See 10.3.5.

Carries critical bibliographical information concerning Thomism, often with résumés or critical analyses, as a continuation of 8.8.3.

See also: 1.1.17, 1.2.16 (No. 15/16).

Journals

8.8.6 **Bulletin thomiste.** See 10.3.5.

8.8.7 **The modern schoolman.** See 10.2.77.

8.8.8 **The new scholasticism.** See 10.2.80.

8.8.9 **Rassegna di letteratura tomistica.** Pontifical University of St. Thomas, Rome. 1971- to date.

8.8.10 **Revue thomiste.** See 10.3.20.

8.8.11 **Rivista di filosofia neoscolastica.** See 10.3.50.

8.8.12 **The thomist.** See 10.3.133.

See also: 10.3.46, 10.5.25.

9. NATIONS AND REGIONS

Some countries have taken great pride in cataloguing the work of their philosophers; others have done nothing along these lines.

I have collected in this chapter those national and regional bibliographies, histories, and so on, which are available and which might be of use to someone interested in them. In some cases the bibliographies listed are the most complete available. In other cases the general philosophical bibliographies listed in 1.2 are more useful for a given country. The section dealing with American philosophy is obviously limited in its scope. Additional information on American (as well as other national) associations, journals, and the like is listed under chapters dealing with those topics.

9.1 AMERICAN

Bibliographies

9.1.1 **Bibliografia Argentina de filosofia.** La Plata, Inst. Bibliográfico, 1960- .

Irregular, but attempts to issue one volume a year.

9.1.2 **Bibliografia filosòfica mexicana,** 1968- . (México, D. F.), Universidad Nacional Autónoma de México, 1970- .

Divided by topics. Index (Mexico).

9.1.3 **Kurtz, Paul,** ed. The American philosophers. New York, Macmillan, 1965-66. 2v.

Vol. I, American thought before 1900; a sourcebook, from puritanism to Darwinism, 448 pp.;
vol. II, American philosophy in the twentieth century; a sourcebook, from pragmatism to philosophical analysis, 573 pp.
Bibliographies throughout and at the end of each volume.

9.1.4 **Rorty, Amelie,** ed. Pragmatic philoso-

phy; anthology. New York, Doubleday, 1966. 548 pp.

Bibliography: pp. 523-48.

9.1.5 **La Salle, Edmundo.** Philosophic thought in Latin America; a partial bibliography. Washington, D. C., Division of Intellectual Cooperation, Pan American Union, 1941. 17 pp.

9.1.6 **Valverde Téllez, Emeterio.** Bibliografía filosófica méxicana. 2d ed. Léon, Imprenta de J. Rodríguez, 1913. 2v.

See also: 1.2.16 (No. 2).

Dictionary

9.1.7 **Nauman, St. Elmo, Jr.** Dictionary of American philosophy. Totowa, N. J., Littlefield, Adams, 1974. 273 pp.

147 contributors to American thought.

Histories

9.1.8 **American philosophic addresses 1700-**

109

1900. Ed. by Joseph L. Blau. New York, Columbia University Press, 1946. 762 pp.

Contains a biobibliography at the beginning of each address.

9.1.9 Ayer, A. J. The origins of pragmatism: studies in the philosophy of C. S. Peirce and William James. San Francisco, Freeman, Cooper, 1968. 336 pp.

9.1.10 Blau, Joseph Leon. Men and movements in American philosophy. Englewood Cliffs, N. J., Prentice-Hall, 1958. 403 pp.

1st published 1952.
Covers American philosophy from its Puritan background through John Dewey.
Bibliographical references are included in "Footnotes and suggested reading": pp. 357-83.

9.1.11 Chisholm, Roderick M. and others. Philosophy. (The Princeton studies: humanistic scholarship in America.) Englewood Cliffs, N. J., Prentice-Hall, 1964. 560 pp.

9.1.12 Cohen, Morris Raphael. American thought; a critical sketch. Ed. with a foreword by Felix S. Cohen. Glencoe, Ill., Free Press, 1954, 360 pp.

9.1.13 Contemporary American philosophy. 34 personal statements. Edited by G. P. Adams and W. P. Montague. New York, Macmillan, 1930. 2v.

Biobibliographical information on the authors is included.

9.1.14 Contemporary American philosophy: second series. Ed. by John E. Smith. (Muirhead series.) London, Allen & Unwin; New York, Humanities Press, 1970. 351 pp.

9.1.15 Estudios de historia de la filosofía en México. México, Universidad Nacional Autónoma de México, 1963. 322 pp.

9.1.16 Flower, Elizabeth, and **Murray G. Murphey.** A history of philosophy in America. New York, Putnam, 1977. 2v.

Examines American thought from its 17th century European sources to the work of C. I. Lewis in the 20th century.

9.1.17 Frankel, Charles. The golden age of American philosophy. New York, G. Braziller, 1960. 543 pp.

9.1.18 Kuklick, Bruce. The rise of American philosophy. New Haven, Yale University Press, 1977. 674 pp.

9.1.19 May, Henry F. The enlightenment in America. New York, Oxford University Press, 1976. 419 pp.

Covers 1688 to 1815.

9.1.20 Reck, Andrew. Recent American philosophy; studies of ten representative thinkers. New York, Pantheon Books, 1964. 343 pp.

Contains studies of the philosophy of R. B. Perry, W. E. Hocking, G. H. Mead, J. E. Boodin, W. M. Urban, D. H. Parker, R. W. Sellars, A. O. Lovejoy, E. Jordan, and E. S. Brightman.
Includes bibliographical references.

9.1.21 Reck, Andrew. The new American philosophers; an exploration of thought since World War II. Baton Rouge, Louisiana State University Press, 1968. 362 pp.

A sequel to 9.1.20. Contains studies of the philosophy of C. I. Lewis, S. C. Pepper, B. Blanshard, E. Nagel, J. H. Randall, J. Buchler, S. Hook, F. S. C. Northrop, J. K. Feibleman, J. Wild, C. Hartshorne, and P. Weiss.
Biobibliographical material throughout.

9.1.22 Schneider, Herbert. A history of American philosophy. 2d rev. ed. New York, Columbia University Press, 1963. 523 pp.

1st ed. 1946.
A standard work with excellent bibliographies.

9.1.23 **Scheffler, Israel**. Four pragmatists: a critical introduction to Peirce, James, Mead and Dewey. (International Library of Philosophy and Scientific Method) Atlantic Highlands, N. J., Humanities Press, 1974. 269 pp.

9.1.24 **Smith, John E.** The spirit of American philosophy. New York, Oxford University Press, 1963. 219 pp.

9.1.25 **Smith, John E.** Themes in American philosophy: purpose, experience and community. New York, Harper & Row, 1970. 248 pp.

9.1.26 **Werkmeister, William Henry**. A history of philosophical ideas in America. New York, Ronald Press, 1949. 599 pp.

9.1.27 **White, Morton G.**, ed. Documents in the history of American philosophy from Jonathan Edwards to John Dewey. New York, Oxford University Press, 1972. 479 pp.

9.1.28 **White, Morton G.** Science and sentiment in America: philosophical thought from Jonathan Edwards to John Dewey. New York, Oxford University Press, 1972. 358 pp.

See also: 9.3.14.

Association

9.1.29 **Society for the Advancement of American Philosophy**. *See* 12.1.49.

9.2 BRITISH

9.2.1 **Albee, Ernest**. History of English Utilitarianism. New York, Macmillan, 1957. 427 pp.

9.2.2 **Contemporary British philosophy**. New York, Macmillan, 1924-76. 4v.

First series, 1924, ed. by J. H. Muirhead. Second series, 1925, ed. by J. H. Muirhead, reprinted: 1953. Third series, 1956, ed. by H.

D. Lewis. Fourth series, 1976, ed. by H. D. Lewis.

Statements of their philosophy by British philosophers. The first two volumes included such figures as Broad, Bosanquet, and Russell. All volumes include bibliographies.

9.2.3 **Mace, C. A.**, ed. British philosophy in the mid-century. Atlantic Highlands, N. J., Humanities Press, 1957. 396 pp. 1966, 406 pp.

9.2.4 **Metz, Rudolf**. A hundred years of British philosophy. Trans. by J. W. Harvey et al. Ed. by J. H. Muirhead. London, Allen and Unwin, 1938. 828 pp.

2d impression: New York, Macmillan, 1951.

A translation of *Die philosophischen Stromungen der Gegenwart in Grossbritannien*, Leipzig, Meiner, 1935, 2v.

Includes bibliographies.

9.2.5 **Paul, Leslie**. The English philosophers. London, Faber & Faber, 1953. 380 pp.

Bibliography: pp. 353-66.

9.2.6 **Pucelle, J.** L'idéalisme en Angleterre de Coleridge à Bradley. Neuchâtel, La Baconnière, 1955. 295 pp.

Includes bibliographical references.

9.2.7 **Sorley, W. R.** A history of British philosophy to 1900. Cambridge, The University Press, 1956. 386 pp.

Bibliography: pp. 323-79.
Reprinted: Westport, Conn., Greenwood Press, 1973.
First published as *A History of English Philosophy*, 1920.
Covers the period from John Scotus Erigena to the end of the Victorian era. Includes biographical material and treats "early and now almost forgotten philosophers" as well as the great writers, e.g., it treats the critics and contemporaries of Locke as well as Locke himself.
Very full bibliography. Comparative

chronological table of the chief works in English philosophy along with the dates of some other writings, English and foreign, and of some leading events, pp. 303-21.

9.2.8 Warnock, Geoffrey James. English philosophy since 1900. Oxford, Oxford University Press, 1958. 180 pp.

Includes bibliography.

See also: 9.3.14.

9.3 WEST EUROPEAN

France

9.3.1 "Bibliographie philosophique française de l'année," L'année philosophique, vols. 1-24, 1890-1913. See 10.3.1.

An annual bibliography of philosophical books in French which appeared during the years of its publication.

9.3.2 Union française des organismes de documentation (Paris). Manuel de la recherche documentaire en France. Philosophie. Pub. sous la direction de Raymond Bayer. Bayeux, Colas, 1950. 421 pp.

9.3.3 Belin, Jean Paul. Le mouvement philosophique en France de 1748 à 1789. Paris, Belin, 1913. 381 pp.

Bibliography: pp. 5-10.
Reprinted: N. Y., Burt Franklin.

9.3.4 Benrubi, Isaak. Les sources et les courants de la philosophie contemporaine en France. Paris, Alcan, 1933. 2v.

9.3.5 Farber, Marvin, *ed.* Philosophic thought in France and the United States; essays representing major trends in contemporary French and American philosophy. Buffalo, University of Buffalo Press, 1950. 775 pp.

Bibliographies throughout.

9.3.6 Bulletin de la société française de philosophie. *See* 10.3.4.

See also: 1.1.17, 1.2.16 (No. 9).

Germany

9.3.7 Baumgartner, Hans Michael, und **Hans-Martin Sass**. Philosophie in Deutschland, 1945-1975; Standpunkte, Entwicklungen, Literatur. Meisenheim, Anton Hain, 1978. 58 pp.

Covers philosophy in both West and East Germany.

9.3.8 Die deutschen Universitätsschriften zur Philosophie und ihre Grenzgebieten. Erfurt, 1924-30. Annual.

Ed. Kurt Gassen.

9.3.9 Koehler & Volckmar-Fachbibliographien: Philosophie und Grenzgebiete 1945-1964. Stuttgart, Koehler & Volckmar, 1965. 434 pp.

Bibliography of all philosophical works in the German language, 1945-1964, with a list of periodicals.

9.3.10 Literarische Berichte aus dem Gebiete der Philosophie. Erfurt, 1-26, 1923-32. Semi-annual.

Bibliography of German periodicals, together with bibliographies of individual philosophers.

9.3.11 Philosophischer Literaturanzeiger. *See* 1.2.44.

9.3.12 Sass, Hans-Martin. Inedita Philosophica. Ein Verzeichnis von nachlassen deutschsprachinger Philosophen des 19. und 20. jahrhunderts. Düsseldorf, Philosophia, 1974. 86 pp.

Name and subject indexes. Arranged by author's name. About 1,000 entries.

9.3.13 Hartmann, Nicolai. Die Philosophie

des deutschen Idealismus. Berlin und Leipzig, de Gruyter, 1923-29. 2v.

9.3.14 **Stegmüller, W.** Main currents in contemporary German, British and American philosophy. Trans. from the 4th German edition, rev. and enl. by Albert E. Blumberg. Bloomington, Indiana University Press, 1970. 567 pp.

9.3.15 **Wundt, Max.** Die deutsche Schulmetaphysik im 17. Jahrhundert. Tübingen, J. C. B. Mohr, 1939. 288 pp.

9.3.16 **Wundt, Max.** Die deutsche Schulphilosophie im Zeitalter der Aufklarung. Tübingen, J. C. B. Mohr, 1945. 346 pp.

Reprinted: Hildesheim, Olms, 1964.

See also: 1.1.17, 1.2.16 (No. 23), 5.1.16.

Greece

9.3.17 **Voumvlinopoulous, Georges E.** Bibliographie critique de la philosophie grecque depuis la chute de Constantinople à nos jours, 1453-1953. Athènes, Institut français d'Athènes, 1966. 236 pp.

Italy

9.3.18 **Bibliografia filosofica italiana** dal 1900 al 1950. Roma, Delfino, 1950-56. 4v.

Continued by 9.3.19.

9.3.19 **Bibliografia filosofica italiana.** Milano, Marzorati, 1951- . Annual.

Continues 9.3.18 in periodical form.

9.3.20 **Sciacca, Michele Federico,** ed. Storia della filosofia italiana. Milano, Bocca, 1941- .

In progress.
Multivolume, each with bibliographies.
Alliney, G. I pensatori della seconda meta del s. XIX, 1942. Bibliography: pp. 341-423.
Sciacca, M. F. Il secolo XX. 2. ed., 1947. 2v. At end of 2d vol., bibliography of Italian philosophy since 1894, pp. 705-900.

9.3.21 **Zampetti, Enrico.** Bibliografia ragionata delle riviste filosofiche italiane dal 1900 al 1955. (Istituto di Studi Filosofici, Roma) Roma, Università, 1956. 136 pp.

Reprinted from vol. 4 of 9.3.18.
Describes Italian philosophical periodicals of the period covered.

9.3.22 **Giornale critico della filosofia italiana.** See 10.3.44.

See also: 1.2.16 (No. 7), and 1.2.5, pp. 251-53.

Scandinavia

9.3.23 **Hintikka, J.,** ed. Bibliography of philosophy in Finland, 1828-1975. Amsterdam, Elsevier, North Holland.

In preparation.

9.3.24 **"Scandinavian bibliography,"** Theoria (10.2.130).

Philosophical works published in Denmark, Finland, Norway, and Sweden are listed once a year.

Spain

9.3.25 **Carreras y Artau, Tomás.** Historia de la filosofía española; filosofía cristiana de los siglos XIII al XV. Madrid, Real academia de ciencias exactas, físicas y naturales, 1939-43. 2v.

Includes bibliographies.

9.3.26 **Guy, Alain.** Los filósofos españoles de ayer y de hoy. (Artes Gráficos Bartolomé U. Chiesino) Buenos Aires, Edit. Losada, 1966. 344 pp.

Biobibliographical descriptions of 51 Spanish philosophers.

9.3.27 **Martinez Gómez, Luis.** Bibliografía filosófica española e hispanoamericana. Barcelona, Flors, 1961. 500 pp.

Covers the period from 1940-1958.

9.4 EAST EUROPEAN

9.4.1 Dossick, Jesse. Doctoral research on Russia and the Soviet Union. New York, Garland. 2v.

V. 1 up to 1959; v. 2, 1960-1975.

Lists American, Canadian, and British dissertations. Includes dissertations on philosophical topics. Non-Soviet Eastern Europe also covered.

Poland

9.4.2 Grzegorczyk, Andrzeij, and **Ludwik Kasinski.** Bibliografia filozofii w Polsce 1945-1946. Krakow, Duk. narodowa, 1947.

9.4.3 Polska Akademia Nauk. Komitet Filozoficzny. Bibliografia filozofii polskiej . . . . Warszawa, Panstwowe Wydawnictwo Naukowe, 1955-71.

Contents: 1750-1830; 1831-1864; 1865-1895.
Editors vary.

9.4.4 Jordan, Z. A. Philosophy and ideology: the development of philosophy and Marxism-Leninism since the second world war. Dordrecht, Holland, D. Reidel, 1963. 600 pp.

Part I deals with "Philosophy between the two wars."

Russia

9.4.5 Akademiia Nauk SSSR. Fundamental'naia Biblioteka Obshchestvennykh Nauk. Novaia sovetskaia literatura po filosofii. 1954- .

In progress.

9.4.6 Bibliographie der sowjetischen Philosophie. Dordrecht, Holland, D. Reidel, 1959-68. 7v.

Lists Soviet philosophical books and articles, 1947-66. Continued by bibliographies in *Studies in Soviet Thought* (10.2.125).

9.4.7 Bochenski, J. M. Soviet Russian dialectical materialism. Dordrecht, Holland, D. Reidel, 1963. 173 pp.

9.4.8 Küng, Guido. "Bibliography of Soviet work in the field of mathematical logic and the foundations of mathematics, from 1917-1957," Notre Dame journal of formal logic, III (1962), 1-40.

9.4.9 Novaia sovetskaia literatura po filosofii. Moskva, 1965- .

9.4.10 Edie, James M., James P. Scanlan, & **Mary-Barbara Zeldin**; with the collaboration of George L. Kline. Russian philosophy. Chicago, Quadrangle Books, 1965. 3v.

An anthology of Russian philosophy with bibliographies throughout of primary and secondary sources.

9.4.11 Masaryk, Thomas Garrigue. The spirit of Russia; studies in history, literature and philosophy. Trans. from the German original by Eden and Cedar Paul with additional chapter and bibliographies by Jan Slavik, the former translated and the latter condensed and translated by W. R. and Z. Lee. New York, Macmillan, 1919. 2v.

3d impression, 1961.
Bibliography: pp. 627-53.

9.4.12 Shein, Louis J., *ed.* Readings in Russian philosophical thought. Edited and translated (from the Russian) with preface and introductory chapter and notes by L. J. Shein. The Hague, Paris, Mouton, 1968-77. 3v.

9.4.13 Wetter, Gustav. Dialectical materialism: a historical and systematic survey of philosophy in the Soviet Union. New York, Praeger, 1963. 609 pp.

9.4.14 Zenkovsky, Vasilii Vasilevich. A history of Russian philosophy. Trans. by George L. Kline. London, Routledge and Kegan Paul, 1953. 2v.

A basic work.

9.4.15 **Studies in Soviet thought.** *See* 10.2.125.

9.4.16 **Soviet studies in philosophy.** *See* 10.2.121.

See also: 10.5.55, 14.3.1.

9.5 NEAR EASTERN

Islam

9.5.1 **Calverley, E.** "A brief bibliography of Arabic philosophy," The Moslem world, XXXII (1942), 60-68.

9.5.2 **Chauvin, Victor Charles.** Bibliographie des ouvrages arabes ou relatifs aux Arabes publiées dans l'Europe chrétienne de 1810 à 1885. Liége, H. Vaillant-Carmanne, 1892-1922. 12v.

9.5.3 **"Histoire de la pensée musulmane,"** Revue thomiste, LXXV(1975), 655-72.

9.5.4 **Pearson, J.** Index Islamicus 1906-55. *See* 17.2.24.

9.5.5 **Pfannmüller, P. G.** Handbuch der Islam-Literatur. Berlin, de Gruyter, 1923. 436 pp.

9.5.6 **Sarton, Georges.** Introduction to the history of science. *See* 7.10.10.

A rich source of bibliography for Arabic, as well as Western, philosophy and science.

9.5.7 **Sauvaget, J.** Introduction to the history of the Muslim East: a bibliographical guide. Berkeley, University of California Press, 1965. 252 pp.

Based on the 2d edition of J. Sauvaget, *Introduction à l'histoire de l'orient musulman; éléments de bibliographie,* refondue et complétée par Claude Cahen, Paris, Adrien-Maisonneuve, 1961, 252 pp.

9.5.8 **Corbin, Henry.** Histoire de la philosophie. Paris, Gallimard, 1964- .

In progress.
Vol. 1, Des origines jusqu'à la mort d'Averroës.

9.5.9 **De Boer, T. J.** The history of philosophy in Islam. Trans. by E. Jones. 2d ed. New York, Dover, 1933. 229 pp.

Reissue, 1961.
Translated from *Geschichte der Philosophie im Islam,* Stuttgart, Frommann, 1901.

9.5.10 **Fakhry, Majid.** A history of Islamic philosophy. New York, Columbia University Press, 1970. 427 pp.

See also: 1.2.16 (No. 6), 9.2.7.

Jewish

9.5.11 **Kirjath Sepher.** Jerusalem, Jewish National and University Library, 1924- .

Useful for recent bibliographies.
Index: vols. 1-15, 1923-39; vols. 16-25, 1940-50.
A quarterly bibliographical review.

9.5.12 **Shunami, S.** Bibliography of Jewish bibliographies. 2d ed. Jerusalem, University Press, 1965. 992 pp.

Supplement, 1965-75, Leiden, E. J. Brill, 1977. 500 pp.

9.5.13 **Cahn, Zvi.** The philosophy of Judaism; the development of Jewish thought throughout the ages, the Bible, the Talmud, the Jewish philosophers, and the Cabala, until the present time. New York. Macmillan, 1962. 524 pp.

Bibliography: pp. 507-11.

9.5.14 **Guttmann, Julius.** Philosophies of Judaism; the history of Jewish philosophy from Biblical times to Franz Rosenzweig. Trans. by D. Silverman. New York, Holt, Rinehart and Winston, 1964. 464 pp.

Bibliography: pp. 399-411.

9.5.15 **Spiegler, Julius S.** Geschichte der Philosophie des Judentums. Leipzig, W. Friedrich, 1890. 369 pp.

Reprinted: Leipzig, Zentralantiquariat der Deutschen Demokratischen Republik, 1971.

9.5.16 **Vajda, G.** Jüdische Philosophie. *See* 1.2.16, No. 19.

See also: 4.1.3, 10.3.15.

9.6 FAR EASTERN

China

9.6.1 **Chan, Wing-tsit.** Chinese philosophy, 1949-1963; an annotated bibliography of mainland China publications. Honolulu, East-West Center Press, 1967. 290 pp.

9.6.2 **Chan, Wing-tsit.** An outline and annotated bibliography of Chinese philosophy. Rev. ed. New Haven, Yale Far Eastern Publications, 1969. 220 pp.

9.6.3 **Creel, Herlee Glessner.** Chinese thought, from Confucius to Mao Tsê-tung. Chicago, University of Chicago Press, 1953. 292 pp.

Bibliography: pp. 266-71.

9.6.4 **Forke, Alfred.** Geschichte der alten chinesischen Philosophie. 2., unveränderte Aufl., Hamburg, Cram, de Gruyter, 1964. 594 pp.

1st ed. 1927.

9.6.5 **Forke, Alfred.** Geschichte der mittelalterlichen chinesischen Philosophie. 2., unveränderte Aufl., Hamburg, Cram, de Gruyter, 1964. 410 pp.

1st ed. 1934.

9.6.6 **Forke, Alfred.** Geschichte der neueren chinesischen Philosophie. 2., unveränderte

Aufl. Hamburg, Cram, de Gruyter, 1964. 693 pp.

1st ed. 1938.

9.6.7 **Fung-Yu-lan.** A history of Chinese philosophy. Trans. by Derk Bodde. 2d ed. Princeton, Princeton University Press, 1952-53. 2v.

Vol. 1, 1st ed., London, Allen & Unwin, 1937.
A basic work. Bibliographies: vol. 1, pp. 410-22; vol. 2, pp. 726-54.
Abridged version: *A Short History of Chinese Philosophy*, New York, Macmillan, 1948, 368 pp.

9.6.8 **Chinese studies in philosophy.** *See* 10.2.18.

9.6.9 **Journal of Chinese philosophy.** *See* 10.2.50.

See also: 1.2.5, pp. 195-97; 1.2.20; 9.6.24-9.6.26, 12.1.13.

India

9.6.10 **C. P. Ramaswami Aiyar Research Endowment Committee.** A bibliography of Indian philosophy. Madras, 1963. 2v.

9.6.11 **Dandekar, R. N.** Vedic bibliography; an up-to-date comprehensive and analytically arranged register of all important work done since 1930 in the field of the Veda and allied antiquities. Bombay, Karnatak, "New Indiana Antiquary," 1946-61. 2v.

Supplements.

9.6.12 **Hall, Fitzedward.** A contribution towards an index to the bibliography of the Indian philosophical systems. Calcutta, Baptist Mission Press, 1859. 236 pp.

9.6.13 **Potter, Karl H.,** *comp.* Bibliography of Indian philosophies. Delhi, Motilal Banarsidoss, 1970. 811 pp.

Vol. I of a proposed Encyclopedia of Indian philosophies.

For supplements, see *Journal of Indian Philosophy* (10.2.53).

9.6.14 **Renou, L.** Bibliographie védique. Paris, Maisonneuve, 1931. 339 pp.

Covers the history of Hinduism. Supplemented by 9.6.10.

9.6.15 **Renou, L.** "Travaux récents sur la philosophie indienne," Diogène, 1954, 133-41.

9.6.16 **Riepe, Dale.** "Recent Indian philosophical literature," Philosophy and phenomenological research, XV (1955), 563-70.

9.6.17 **Riepe, Dale.** "Indian philosophical literature 1955-1957," Philosophy and phenomenological research, XVIII (1957-58), 384-87.

9.6.18 **Dasgupta, Surendra Nath.** A history of Indian philosophy. Cambridge, The University Press, 1922-55. 5v.

A basic work.

9.6.19 **Frauwallner, E.** Geschichte der Indischen Philosophie. Salsburg, Müller, 1953- .

10v. projected.

9.6.20 **Radhakrishnan, Sir Sarvepalli.** Indian philosophy. 2d ed. New York, Macmillan, 1951. 2v.

9.6.21 **Radhakrishnan, Sir S.,** and **H. H. Muirhead,** *eds.* Contemporary Indian philosophy. 2d ed. New York, Humanities Press, 1952. 649 pp.

9.6.22 **Radhakrishnan, Sarvepalli,** and **C. S. Moore,** *eds.* A source book in Indian philosophy. Princeton, N. J., Princeton University Press, 1957. 683 pp.

Bibliography: pp. 643-69.

9.6.23 **Journal of Indian philosophy.** *See* 10.2.53.

See also: 1.2.20, 10.2.39.

Oriental

9.6.24 **Moore, Russell Franklin.** Bibliography for Oriental philosophies. New York, R. F. Moore, 1951. 11 pp.

Reprinted from W. D. Gould, G. B. Arbaugh, R. F. Moore, *Oriental Philosophies*, 3d ed., New York, R. F. Moore Co., 1951, 220 pp.

9.6.25 **Müller, August, E. Kuhn, L. Scherman.** Orientalische Bibliographie 1887-1911. Berlin, Reuther, 1888-1922. 24v.

The best bibliography for the period covered.

9.6.26 **Senny, I.** Traductions françaises de littératures orientales. Bruxelles, Commission Belge de bibliographie, 1958. 299 pp.

See also: 1.1.13, 1.1.16, 8.2.1-8.2.9, 9.6.1-9.6.9, 10.2.100, 12.1.44.

9.7 AFRICAN

9.7.1 **Cahiers philosophiques Africains/African philosophical journal.** Publ. by: Department of Philosophy of the National University of Zaïre. Mss. and subscr. to: Prof. Paulin Hountondji, B. P. 1. 825, Lubumbashi, Zaïre.

9.7.2 **Second order:** an African journal of philosophy. Ed. Prof. J. O. Sodipo, Department of Religions and Philosophy, University of Ife, Ile-Ife, Nigeria.

IV
Serials, Publishing, and Professional Life

10. PHILOSOPHICAL SERIALS

Periodicals are the lifeblood of contemporary philosophy, and provide a ready outlet for the writings of philosophers. Articles are an ideal medium in which to develop or approach a single problem, present a new insight, or analyze a particular argument. Being relatively short they usually require less time to write and can be published more quickly than a book. They also offer the possibility of philosophical discussion in print. Consequently philosophical journals can be used to keep up with current philosophical developments, philosophical problems, and continuing discussions and debates.

Many philosophical journals list new books in philosophy as they appear, often giving brief summaries of them and carrying review articles of the more important and significant ones. By following the journals one can keep abreast of new books and can often decide from the summaries and reviews which to read, buy, or recommend to a university or public library.

Some journals also list philosophical meetings, appointments, and other news of interest to the philosophical community. They are thus useful for keeping up with news of the profession.

The items in 10.1 are either guides or can be used to obtain information on journals in related areas or on philosophical journals not included in the following lists, which do, however, contain the most important philosophical journals in English (10.2) and in the major European languages (10.3). If foreign journals publish articles in English, this is indicated.

The data on journals is very volatile. New journals are constantly appearing, editors change, publishers vary, and so on. Whenever the current address or other such information is required it is safest to consult the most recent issue of the journal in question.

The multidisciplinary journals listed in 10.4 all carry articles on philosophy or philosophical articles. The other philosophical serials listed in 10.5 include newsletters, proceedings and annuals, lecture series, and some selected book series in philosophy.

10.1 PHILOSOPHICAL PERIODICAL DIRECTORIES AND GUIDES

10.1.1 **Gerber, William.** "Philosophical Journals," Encyclopedia of philosophy (1.4.1) vol. VI, pp. 199-216.

Contains a discussion of philosophical journals, treated chronologically.

10.1.2 **Hogrebe, Wolfram, Rudolf Kamp,** and **Gert König.** Periodica philosophica; eine internationale Bibliographie philosophischer Zeitschriften von den Anfangen bis zur Gegenwart. Düsseldorf, Philosophia, 1972. 728 col.

An international list of philosophy journals.

10.1.3 International directory of philosophy and philosophers. *See* 2.1.3.

10.1.4 Irregular serials and annuals: an international directory. A classified guide to current foreign and domestic serials, excepting periodicals issued more frequently than once a year. First edition, edited by Emery Koltay. 5th ed. 1978-79. New York & London, Bowker, 1978.

Covers 50,000 publications in the bibliographically confused area between books and periodicals, including "serials and continuations, such as proceedings, transactions, progresses, advances, reports, yearbooks, annual reviews, handbooks, periodical supplements, etc."
Separate listing of 1,450 serials which have ceased publication.
A companion volume to Ulrich (10.1.8).

10.1.5 Moulton, Janice M. Guidebook for publishing philosophy. *See* 11.2.16.

10.1.6 New York Public Library. A check list of cumulative indexes to individual periodicals in the New York Public Library, compiled by Daniel C. Haskell. New York, Library, 1942. 370 pp.

10.1.7 The standard periodical directory. 2d ed. New York, Oxbridge, 5th ed., 1977. 1,715 pp.

1st ed. 1964. Irregular.
Lists U. S. and Canadian periodicals.

10.1.8 Ulrich's international periodicals directory. New York, Bowker, 1932- .

A classified guide to a selected list of current periodicals, American and foreign. Lists periodicals by subject. Issued biennially.
A companion publication to 10.1.4 issued in alternate years.

10.1.9 U. S. Library of Congress. Reference Department. Philosophical periodicals; an annotated world list by David Baumgardt. Washington, D. C., Government Printing Office, 1952. 89 pp.

Contains 489 entries.

10.1.10 World list of specialized periodicals in philosophy; Liste mondiale des périodiques spécialisés en philosophie. Paris, Mouton, 1967. 124 pp.

10.2 SELECTED PHILOSOPHICAL JOURNALS: ENGLISH LANGUAGE

10.2.1 Acta philosophica Fennica. 1935-to date. Annual in four issues. Ed., Jaakko Hintikka. Dept. of Philosophy, Univ. of Helsinki, Unioninkatu 40B, 00170 He. Published by North-Holland Publishing Co. for the Philosophical Society of Finland.

1935-75, v. 1-28, published as a book-series.

10.2.2 Aitia: philosophy humanities magazine. 1975-to date. Three nos. yearly. Eds., James P. Friel and Louise Horowitz. Knapp Hall 22, SUNY, Farmingdale, N. Y. 11735.

Devoted to philosophy and the humanities in 2 year colleges and high schools.

10.2.3 Ajatus. 1926-to date. Ed., Juha Manninen. University of Helsinki, 00103 Helsinki, Porthaniz, Finland. Yearbook of the Philosophical Society of Finland.

10.2.4 Aletheia. An international journal of philosophy. 1977-to date. Annual. Box 477, University of Dallas, Irving, Tex. 75061.

Phenomenological orientation.

10.2.5 American philosophical quarterly. Jan. 1964-to date. Quarterly (Jan., Apr., July, Oct.). Ed., Nicholas Rescher, Dept. of Philosophy, University of Pittsburgh, Pittsburgh, Pa. 15260.

Publishes only self-sufficient articles (no book reviews, critical studies, etc.), varying in length from 2,000-25,000 words on any aspect of philosophy, substantive or historical. Primarily analytically inclined. Also irregularly publishes a supplementary monograph series since 1968.

10.2.6 **Analecta Husserliana**, the yearbook for phenomenological research. 1971-to date. Annual. Published by Humanities Press for the World Institute for Advanced Phenomenological Research and Learning. Ed. by A.-T. Tymieniecka.

Aim is to facilitate collaboration among scholars toward the advance of original work in phenomenology.

10.2.7 **Analysis**. 1933-40 (vols. 1-7); 1947-to date. Quarterly, plus a supplement for longer papers. Ed., Christopher Kirwan, Exeter College, Oxford, OX1 3DP, England.

Suspended Nov. 1940-Sept. 1947; vol. 1, No. 1 (Oct. '47) also called NS. no. 1.
Articles and discussion papers of 3,000 words or less on metaphysics, logic, ethics, and aesthetics; index. Oriented towards analytic philosophy and logic.
Vols. 21-30 reprinted; available from Harper & Row.

10.2.8 **Annals of mathematical logic**. 1970-to date. Quarterly. North-Holland Publishing Co., Amsterdam. Eds., C. C. Chang (UCLA), A. Mostowski (Warsaw), M. O. Rabin (Hebrew Univ.), and H. Rogers, Jr. (MIT).

Publishes longer papers and short monographs not exceeding 100 printed pages on topics of current interest in mathematical logic and the foundations of mathematics. Papers devoted to topics in related fields—such as, e.g., the automata theory—are also accepted, provided that they contain material relevant to mathematical logic and foundations of mathematics.

10.2.9 **Apeiron**. 1969-to date. Semiannual. Eds., P. J. Bicknell and H. D. Rankin, Monash University, Clayton, Victoria, Australia 3168, and R. W. Hall, University of Vermont, Burlington, Vt. 05401.

Deals with ancient philosophy and science.

10.2.10 **Artificial intelligence**. 1970-to date. Quarterly. Eds., B. Meltzey (Univ. of Edinburgh), B. Raphael (Stanford Research Institute). Pub., Elsevier-North Holland, 52 Vanderbilt Ave., New York, N. Y. 10017.

Interdisciplinary. Papers "dealing with the theory and practice of computer programmes and other artifacts that manifest intelligent behavior."

10.2.11 **Auslegung**: a journal of philosophy. 1973-to date. Three nos. yearly (Nov., Feb., May). Dept. of Philosophy, Univ. of Kansas, Lawrence, Ks. 66045.

"Outstanding essays on any philosophical topic by new Ph.D.'s and by graduate students pursuing a Ph.D. in philosophy."

10.2.12 **Australasian journal of philosophy**. 1947 (vol. 25)-to date. Three nos. yearly (May, Aug., Dec.). Pub. by Australasian Assoc. of Philosophy. Ed., Brian Ellis, Dept. of Philosophy, La Trobe Univ., Bundoota, Melbourne, VIC 3083.

Articles, critical notices, reviews, books received, notes and news, index. A continuation of 10.2.13.
Reprinted: (up to vol. 52), New York, Kraus Reprints.

10.2.13 **Australasian journal of philosophy and psychology**. 1923-46 (vols. 1-24).

Cum. index: 1-24 (1923-46).
Continued as 10.2.12.

10.2.14 **Blackfriars** (Oxford). 1920-to date. Monthly. Ed. by English Dominicans, Blackfriars Publications, 2 Sergeants' Inn, Fleet St., London, E. C. 4.

Articles, book reviews, index. A learned Catholic journal of theology, philosophy, sociology, art, literature and contemporary affairs.
Supplement: *Life of the spirit*, 1-3 (nos. 1-28), Feb. 1944-June 1948; continued as separate publication under the same name.

10.2.15 The British journal for the philosophy of science. May 1950-to date. Quarterly (May, Aug., Nov., Feb.). Organ of the British Society for the Philosophy of Science. Eds., John Worrall and J. W. N. Watkins, Dept. of Philosophy, London School of Economics, Haughton St., Aldwych, London WC2A 2AE, England.

Articles (not exceeding 5,000 words), discussions, reviews, recent publications, lists of articles in the philosophy of science, and abstracts of articles published in *Dialectica, Methodos,* and *Philosophy of Science.*
Reprinted: vols. 1-27 (1950/51-1976), N. Y., Kraus Reprints.

10.2.16 The British journal of aesthetics; a journal for the understanding of the principles of criticism and appreciation. 1960-to date. Quarterly (Jan., Apr., July, Oct.). Official organ of the British Society of Aesthetics. Ed., Harold Osborne, 90A St. John's Wood, High St., London, NW8.

Articles, book reviews, books received, correspondence.
Reprinted: vols. 1-14 (1961-74), N. Y., Kraus Reprints.

10.2.17 Canadian journal of philosophy. 1971-to date. Quarterly. Ed., Brian Chellas et al. Published by the Canadian Association for Publishing in Philosophy.

Review for the publication of philosophical work in Canada's two official languages. Executive editors: John King-Farlow, et al.
"The *Canadian Journal of Philosophy* is published by the Canadian Association for Publishing in Philosophy. Its purpose is the publication in Canada of philosophical work of high quality, in English or in French, without restriction to any field of philosophy or to any philosophical school. Book reviews will not be included; but the journal will include article-length critical notices of important books, and discussions, complete in themselves, of previous articles."
Mss. should be sent to the Exec. Secretary, Roger A. Shiner, 4-108 Humanities Center, University of Alberta, Edmonton, Alberta, Canada T6G 2E5.

10.2.18 Chinese studies in philosophy. 1967-to date. Quarterly. International Arts & Sciences Press, Inc., 901 North Broadway, White Plains, N. Y. 10603.

Translations of material from mainland China. Ed., Chung-ying Cheng, Dept. of Philosophy, University of Hawaii, Honolulu, Hawaii 96822.

10.2.19 Cross currents. 1950-to date. Quarterly (Winter, Spring, Summer, Fall). Ed., Joseph E. Cunneen, 103 Van Houten Fields, West Nyack, N. Y. 10994.

Original articles, translations from European journals, notes, reviews, plus an Annual Review of Philosophy by James Collins. Concerned with exploring "the implications of Christianity for our times."
Reprinted: vols. 1-13 (1950-63), N. Y., Kraus Reprints.

10.2.20 Cultural hermeneutics. 1973-78. Quarterly. *Continued as* Philosophy and social criticism (10.2.99).

10.2.21 Darshana international; an international quarterly of philosophy, psychology, psychical research, religion, mysticism, and sociology. 1961-to date. Ed., J. P. Atreya, Darshana International, Moradabad, India.

Title varies (vols. 1-2, 1961-62, *Darshana*). Articles, book reviews, index.

10.2.22 Dialectica; international review of philosophy of knowledge. 1947-to date. Quarterly. Ed., Henri Lauener, Langfeldstrasse 5 8, 3063 Ittigen/Bern, Switzerland.

Text and subtitle in English, French, and German.
Articles (with some emphasis on philosophy of science), books received, book reviews, abstracts from *Philosophy of Science* and *The British Journal of the Philosophy of Science,* index. Cumulative index (subject, 1966; authors, 1967).
Partially reprinted: Johnson Reprint Corp.

10.2.23 Dialectics and humanism. 1974-to

date. Chief ed. is Janusy Kuczynski, Nowy Swiat 49, 00-042, Warsaw, Poland. Published by the Institute of Philosophy and Sociology of the Polish Academy of Sciences.

Available in English. Marxist in orientation.

10.2.24 Dialogue; Canadian philosophical review/Revue canadienne de philosophie. 1962-to date. Quarterly (June, Sept., Dec., Mar.). Organ of the Canadian Philosophical Association. Ed., John Woods, Dept. of Philosophy, Univ. of Calgary, Alberta T2N 1N4 Canada.

Text in English and French. Largely but not exclusively analytic in orientation. Articles, notes, discussions, critical notices, many book reviews, books received, announcements, index.

10.2.25 Diogenes; an international review of philosophy and humanistic studies. 1953-to date. Quarterly (Dec., Mar., June, Sept.). Publication of the International Council for Philosophy and Humanistic Studies. Ed., Roger Caillois, 1 Rue Miollis, 75732 Paris, France.

English, French, Spanish, Arabian parallel editions. Articles, notes and discussion. Often has an issue devoted to a single general topic, e.g., No. 39, "Esthetic Problems: Past and Present." Articles of a technically philosophical nature are not usually carried.

10.2.26 Erkenntnis. See Journal of unified science (10.2.66).

10.2.27 Ethics; an international journal of social, political and legal philosophy. 1937/38 (vol. 48)-to date. Quarterly (Oct., Jan., Apr., July). Ed., Warner A. Wick, The University of Chicago Press, 5811 Ellis Avenue, Chicago, Ill. 60637.

Articles, discussions, book reviews, shorter notices, books received, index. "Devoted to study of the ideas and principles which form the basis for individual and social action. It publishes articles in ethical theory, social science, and jurisprudence contribut-

ing to an understanding of the basic structure of civilization and society. It is not the organ of any group and is not committed to any policy or program." A continuation of 10.2.42. Cum. index: 1890-1965.

Reprinted: vols. 1-25 (1891-1915), Johnson Reprint Corp.

10.2.28 Foundations of language; international journal of language and philosophy. 1965-to date. Quarterly (Feb., Aug., May, Nov.). Ed., W. Abraham et al. Published by D. Reidel, Dordrecht, Holland.

Articles, short notices, reviews, and publications received for review. Deals with language and the foundations of its study, including the impact of language on various disciplines.

10.2.29 Franciscan studies. 1924-to date. Annual. Ed., Conrad L. Harkins, Franciscan Education Conference, St. Bonaventure University, St. Bonaventure, N. Y. 14778.

Vol. 22, 1941- also as NS. vol. 1- . Formerly quarterly; annual as of 1963. Articles on topics related to Franciscan philosophy or theology, published in English, Latin, French, German, or Italian.

10.2.30 Graduate faculty philosophy journal. 1977-to date. New School for Social Research. The Editor, Graduate Faculty Philosophy Journal, Dept. of Philosophy, New School for Social Research, 65 Fifth Ave., New York, N. Y. 10003.

10.2.31 The Harvard theological review. 1908-to date. Quarterly (Jan., Apr., July, Oct.). Issued by the Faculty of Divinity in Harvard University. Ed., Helmut Koester, The Divinity School, Harvard University, Cambridge, Mass. 02138.

Articles, notes and observations, books received. Includes theology, ethics, the history and philosophy of religion, and cognate subjects.

10.2.32 The Heythrop journal; a review of philosophy and theology. 1960-to date. Quarterly. Ed., Robert Murray, Heythrop College, Univ. of London, 11-13 Cavendish Square, London W1M 0AN, England.

Articles, bibliographies, book reviews, index.

10.2.33 **Hibbert journal**. 1902-1968 (vols. 1-66, no. 262/3). Quarterly (Winter, Spring, Autumn, Summer).

A review of religion, theology, and philosophy, containing articles, book reviews, index.

Cum. index: vols. 1-10 (1902-11).

10.2.34 **History and theory**: studies in the philosophy of history. 1960-to date. Quarterly and 1 Beiheft. Ed., Richard T. Vann, Wesleyan Station, Middletown, Conn. 06457.

Monographs, reviews, essays, exchanges, comments, and bibliographies. Devoted to theory of history, historiography, method of history, and the relation of historical theory and method of the social sciences.

Index to vols 1-5 (1960-66) contains an annotated list of articles, a list of review articles, and titles of the Beihefte.

10.2.35 **The human context**. 1968-1975. A multilingual quarterly. Pub. by Martinus Nijhoff. Ed., Paul A. Senft, 17 Platt's Lane, London NW3 7NP, England.

Subtitle also in French, German, Spanish, and Italian.

"Based on the conviction that the human sciences need to be linked in a trans-disciplinary approach."

Ceased publication Aut., 1975.

10.2.36 **The humanist**. 1941-to date. Six nos. yearly (Jan., Mar., May, July, Sept., Nov.). Published by the American Humanist Association and the American Ethical Union. Ed., Paul Kurtz, SUNY at Buffalo, Baldy Hall, Amherst, N. Y. 14260.

Editorials, articles, film, drama, book reviews, news, index. Attempts to bridge theoretical philosophical discussion and practical applications of humanism.

10.2.37 **Hume studies**. 1975-to date. Semiannual (Apr., Nov.). Ed., John W. Davis, Dept. of Philosophy, Talbot College, Univ. of Western Ontario, London, Ontario, N6A 3K7, Canada.

Short articles, notes, and discusions on David Hume. Hume bibliography is up to date, information on work in progress, symposia, congresses and translations.

Material in English, French, German and Italian.

10.2.38 **Idealistic studies**, an international journal of philosophy published by Clark University Press. 1971-to date. Three nos. yearly. Ed., Robert N. Beck, Dept. of Philosophy, Clark University, Worcester, Mass. 01610.

Welcomes historical and contemporary statements of idealism, critical studies of idealistic themes, and articles relating idealism to other philosophic movements including current analytic trends.

10.2.39 **Indian philosophy quarterly**. 1975-to date. Ed., S. S. Barlingay. Published by the University of Poona, Poona 7, India.

A revival of one of the oldest Indian philosophical journals, the *Philosophical Quarterly*.

10.2.40 **Inquiry**; an interdisciplinary journal of philosophy and the social sciences. 1958-to date. Quarterly (Spring, Summer, Autumn, Winter). Ed., Alastair Hannay, Dept. of Philosophy, College of Arts and Sciences, Univ. of Trondheim, 7000 Trondheim, Norway.

Articles, reviews, discussion, books received, abstracts of articles from *Philosophy of Science*. Orientation is somewhat analytic, but not entirely so. Some issues devoted to special topics.

10.2.41 **International journal for philosophy of religion**. 1970-to date. Quarterly. Published by Martinus Nijhoff. Ed., Bowman L. Clarke, Dept. of Philosophy and Religion, Univ. of Georgia, Athens, Ga. 30602.

An organ of the Society for the Philosophy of Religion.

10.2.42 **International journal of ethics.** 1890/91-1936/37 (vols. 1-47).

Continued as 10.2.27. Index, vols. 1-41 (Oct. 1890-July 1931).

Reprinted: vols. 1-25 (1891-1915), Johnson Reprint Corp.

10.2.43 **International logic review**; rassegna internazionale di logica. 1970-to date. Semiannual (Mar., Dec.). Ed., F. Spisani, Via Belmeloro 3, 40126 Bologna, Italy.

Articles and discussions in Italian, French, English, and German.

10.2.44 **International philosophical quarterly.** 1961-to date. Quarterly. Ed., W. Norris Clarke, Fordham University, Bronx, N. Y. 10458.

Articles, critical discussion, feature review, briefer book notices, contemporary currents, books received, index. "IPQ has been founded to provide an international forum in English for the interchange of basic philosophical ideas between the Americas and Europe and between East and West. Its primary orientation is to encourage vital contemporary expression—creative, critical and historical—in the intercultural tradition of theistic, spiritualist, and personalist humanism, but without further restriction of school within these broad perspectives."

10.2.45 **International studies in philosophy.** 1970-to date. Annual. Ed., Giorgio Tonelli, State Univ. of New York, Binghamton, N. Y. 13901.

Publishes historical and systematic articles in all areas of philosophy, reviews. Articles in English, Italian, French, and German.

10.2.46 **Interpretation**; a journal of political philosophy. 1969-to date. Three nos. yearly. Ed., Hilail Gildin, G101, Queens College, CUNY, Flushing, N. Y. 11367.

Welcomes contributions from those interested in political philosophy regardless of orientation.

10.2.47 **Isis**; an international quarterly review devoted to the history of science and its cultural influences. 1913-to date. Quarterly (Mar., June, Sept., Dec.) with a special critical bibliography, issued annually in May by Univ. of California Press. Official journal of the History of Science Society. Ed., Robert P. Multauf, Smithsonian Institution, Washington, D. C. 20560.

Subtitle varies. Suspended July 1914-Aug. 1919. Articles, notes and correspondence, news.

Cum. Index: vols. 1-3 in vol. 3; vols. 1-20 (1913-33) in vol. 21.

10.2.48 **Journal for the scientific study of religion.** 1961-to date. Semiannnual (Fall and Spring). Official journal of the Society for the Scientific Study of Religion. Ed., Richard L. Gorsach, Graduate School of Social Work, Univ. of Texas, Arlington, Tex. 76010.

Articles, reviews, notes, index.

10.2.49 **Journal of aesthetics and art criticism.** 1941-to date. Quarterly (Fall, Winter, Spring, Summer). Published by the American Society for Aesthetics. Ed., John Fisher, Dept. of Philosophy, Temple Univ., Philadelphia, Pa. 19122.

Studies of visual arts, literature, music, theatre arts from a philosophic or other theoretical point of view; book reviews, index.

Cum. index: vols 1-20 (1941-1963), N. Y., AMS Reprint Co.

10.2.50 **Journal of Chinese philosophy.** 1973-to date. Quarterly. Ed., Chung-ying Chen, Univ. of Hawaii, Honolulu, Hawaii 96822. Published by Reidel.

Devoted to the study of Chinese philosophy and Chinese thought in all their phases and stages of articulation and development.

10.2.51 **The journal of critical analysis.** 1969-

to date. Quarterly. Ed., P. S. Schievella, Dept. of Philosophy, 2039 Kennedy Blvd., Jersey City State College, Jersey City, N. J. 07305.

A journal of applied philosophy devoted to discussion of the relation between teaching of basic techniques and philosophical analysis in various academic disciplines.

10.2.52 **Journal of existentialism**; the international quarterly of existential thought. 1960-67.

Title varies: vols. 1-4, *Journal of Existential Psychiatry*. Associated with the Association for Phenomenology and Existential Philosophy. Articles on philosophy, psychology, psychiatry, social sciences, and literature; bibliography, book reviews, index.
Reprinted: vols. 1-3 (1960-63), Johnson Reprint Corp.

10.2.53 **The journal of Indian philosophy**. 1970-to date. Quarterly. Ed., B. K. Matilal, All Souls College, Oxford, U. K.

10.2.54 **Journal of legal philosophy**. 1976-to date. Ed., George Schedler, Philosophy Dept., Southern Illinois Univ., Carbondale, Ill. 62901.

Articles dealing with topics in jurisprudence and philosophy of law. English only.

10.2.55 **Journal of philosophical logic**. 1972-to date. Quarterly. Eds., Bas C. van Fraassen, Dept. of Philosophy, Univ. of Toronto, Toronto, Ont. Canada, and R. M. Thomason, Dept. of Philosophy, Univ. of Pittsburgh, Pittsburgh, Pa. 15260. Published by D. Reidel, Dordrecht, Holland. Sponsored by the Association for Symbolic Logic.

The journal is concerned with philosophical studies utilizing formal methods or dealing with topics in logical theory.

10.2.56 **Journal of philosophical studies**. 1926-1930. (vols. 1-5).

Continued as 10.2.95.

10.2.57 **Journal of philosophy**. 1921 (vol. 18)-

to date. 22 nos. yearly. (A monthly as of 1977.) Managing Ed., Leigh S. Cauman, 720 Philosophy Hall, Columbia Univ., New York, N. Y. 10027.

Articles, reviews, new books, notes, and news of the profession; index; carries major papers of the American Philosophical Association Eastern Division Meetings prior to the meetings. A continuation of 10.2.58.
50-yr. Index: 1904-1953; 10-yr. supplement, 1954-1963.

10.2.58 **Journal of philosophy, psychology and scientific methods**. 1904-1920 (vols. 1-17).

Continued as 10.2.57.

10.2.59 **Journal of pre-college philosophy**. 1975-to date. Quarterly. Ed., P. S. Schievella, Jersey City State College, 2039 Kennedy Boulevard, Jersey City, N.J. 07305.

Journal of the National Council for Critical Analysis: The Institute for Philosophy on the Pre-College Level.
Articles, news and announcements. Provides a forum for pre-college teachers of philosophy and institutions to exchange ideas.

10.2.60 **Journal of social philosophy**. 1970-to date. Three nos. yearly. Ed., W. Creighton Peden, Augusta College, Augusta, Ga. 30904.

10.2.61 **The journal of symbolic logic**. 1936-to date. Quarterly (Mar., June, Sept., Dec.). Official organ of the Association for Symbolic Logic. Eds., Yiannis Moschovakis, Dept. of Mathematics, UCLA, Los Angeles, Calif. 90024, and others.

Articles (sometimes in French and German), reviews, bibliographies, news of the Association, abstracts of papers delivered at meetings of the Association, offices and members of the Association, official notices of the Division of Logic, Methodology and Philosophy of Science of the international Union of the History and Philosophy of Science, index. Technical papers in logic, the history of logic and the philosophy of logic.
Vol. 26 is an index for vols. 1-25.

10.2.62 **The journal of the British Society for Phenomenology**. 1969-to date. Three nos. yearly. Ed., D. W. Mays, Dept. of Philosophy, Univ. of Manchester, Manchester MI3 9PL England.

Articles on phenomenology and related topics in the humanities, discussion notes, book reviews, bibliography, reports of the Society, correspondence.

10.2.63 **Journal of the history of ideas**; a quarterly devoted to cultural and intellectual history. 1940-to date. Quarterly (Jan./Mar., Apr./June, July/Sept., Oct./Dec.). Ed., Philip Wiener, Humanities 749, Temple Univ., Philadelphia, Pa. 19122.

An organ of the International Society for the History of Ideas.
Articles, discussion, notes, reviews, index. Fosters studies which emphasize the interrelations of several fields of historical study.
Cum. index: vols. 1-25 (1940-1964).
Partially reprinted: Johnson Reprint Corp.

10.2.64 **Journal of the history of philosophy**. 1963-to date. Quarterly (Jan., Apr., July, Oct.). Ed., Richard Popkin, Dept. of Philosophy, Washington Univ., St. Louis, Mo. 63130.

Articles on the history of Western philosophy broadly conceived, in English, French, and German, notes and discussions, book reviews, book notes, books received.

10.2.65 **Journal of the philosophy of sport**. 1974-to date. Annual. Ed., Robert G. Osterhoudt, Dept. of Physical Education, 217 Cooke Hall, Univ. of Minnesota, Minneapolis, Minn. 55455.

Published by the Philosophic Society for the Study of Sport.

10.2.66 **The journal of unified science** (Erkenntnis). 1930-40 (vols. 1-8, no. 5/6). Eds., Rudolf Carnap and Hans Reichenbach.

Superseded *Annalen der Philosophie und philosophischen Kritik*. Vols. 1-7 (1930-39) as *Erkenntnis*.
Articles and reviews in English and German. Carried discussions of the Vienna Circle.

10.2.67 **The journal of value inquiry**. 1967-to date. Quarterly (somewhat irregular). Eds., James Wilbur and others, Dept. of Philosophy, SUNY, Geneseo, N. Y. 14454.

Articles on any aspect of value theory without restriction of method, scope, or orientation, discussion, book reviews, books received. One issue per year contains the proceedings of the Conference on Value Inquiry.

10.2.68 **Kinesis**: graduate journal in philosophy. 1968-to date. Twice a year. Editors change annually. Dept. of Philosophy, Southern Illinois Univ., Carbondale, Ill. 62901.

10.2.69 **Main currents in modern thought**; journal of the foundation of integrative education. 1940-43. Five nos. yearly (Sept., Nov., Jan., Mar., May). Ed., F. L. Kunz, 12 Church St., New Rochelle, N. Y. 10805.

Suspended Apr.-Dec. 1943.
Articles, news and views, reviews. Promotes the integration of all knowledge.

10.2.70 **Man and medicine**: the journal of values and ethics in health care. 1976-to date. Ed., Arthur Carr, 630 W. 169th St., New York, N. Y. 10032.

10.2.71 **Man and world**; an international philosophical review. 1968-to date. Quarterly (Feb., May, Aug., Nov.). Eds., John Anderson and Joseph Kockelmans, 246 Sparks Bldg., University Park, Pa. 16802, and Calvin Schrag, Recitation Bldg., Purdue Univ., West Lafayette, Ind. 47907.

Articles in English, French, German, and Spanish (with short summaries in English of articles not written in English), reviews, critical discussions, chronicles. Aims at increasing contact among countries of North, Central, South America, and Europe by discussing philosophical issues of mutual interest; not explicitly related to any one trend or school.

10.2.72 Mediaeval studies. 1939-to date. Annual. Ed., Virginia Brown, Pontifical Institute of Mediaeval Studies, 59 Queens Park Crescent East, Toronto, Ont. M5S 2C4. Sponsored by the Institute.

10.2.73 Metaphilosophy. 1969-to date. Quarterly (Jan., Apr., July, Oct.). Ed., T. W. Bynum, Dept. of Philosophy, SUNY, 1400 Washington Ave., Albany, N. Y. 12222.

Articles and reviews of books about philosophy or some particular school, method, or field of philosophy.

10.2.74 Methodos; language and cybernetics; linguaggio e cibernetica. 1949-to date. Quarterly. Pub. under the auspices of the Center of Cybernetics and Linguistic Activities of the University of Milan and of CNR. Ed., Marsilio Editori, via S. Eufemia, 5, Padova.

Subtitle varies: Quarterly review of methodology and symbolic logic until 1954.

Articles (in original language often followed by complete English translation [after 1954 there are more articles in English but articles in other languages are not always translated into English]), book reviews, books received, news, notes, index. Publishes unconventional essays on language, cybernetics, and applications to the design of intelligent machines of the results obtained by the Italian Operation School.

10.2.75 Midwest studies in philosophy. 1976-to date. Annual. University of Minnesota-Morris, Morris, Minn. 56267.

10.2.76 Mind; a quarterly review of psychology and philosophy. 1876-1891 (vols. 1-16); 1892 (ns. vol. 1)-to date. Quarterly (Jan., Apr., July, Oct.). Publication of the Mind Association. Ed., D. W. Hamlyn, Dept. of Philosophy, Birkbeck College, Univ of London, Malet St., London.

Articles, critical notices, book reviews, new books, notes (primarily British) list of officers and members of Mind Association. Analytic in orientation. 1896-1900 contain papers of the Aristotelian Society.

Cum. index: vols. 1-16 (1876-91) in vol. 16; ns. vols. 1-75 (1892-1903); ns. vols. 13-32 (1904-23); ns. vols. 33-42 (1924-33).

Reprinted: os. vols. 1-16 (1876-1891); ns. vols. 1-75 (1892-1966), Kraus Reprints.

10.2.77 The modern schoolman; a quarterly journal of philosophy. 1925-to date. Quarterly (Nov., Jan., Mar., May). Ed., John L. Treloar, 3700 West Pine Blvd., St. Louis, Mo. 63108.

Articles, notes and discussions, book reviews, book notes, books received, index. "Dedicated to furthering the work begun by the great Schoolmen of the Middle Ages."

10.2.78 The monist; an international quarterly journal of general philosophical inquiry. 1890-1936 (vols. 1-46); 1962 (vol. 47)-to date. Quarterly (Jan., Apr., July, Oct.). Ed., Eugene Freeman, Philosophy Division, The Hegeler Institute, Box 1908, Los Gatos, Calif. 95030.

Subtitle varies.

Articles, books received, authors' abstracts of recent books, index. Each issue devoted to a particular topic, announced in advance (e.g., Winter 1963, "Metaphysics Today"; Summer, 1963, "Ethics and Anthropology"; Apr., 1978, "The Philosophy of Thomas Reid").

Reprinted: vols. 1-49 (1891-1965), Kraus Reprints.

10.2.79 Natural law forum. Quarterly. 1956-1968. V. 1-13.

Continued, v. 14 (1969-) as *American Journal of Jurisprudence.* Law School, University of Notre Dame, Notre Dame, Ind.

10.2.80 The new scholasticism; a quarterly of philosophy. 1927-to date. Quarterly (Jan., Apr., July, Oct.). Journal of the American Catholic Philosophical Association. Ed., Ralph M. McInerny, University of Notre Dame, Notre Dame, Ind. 46556.

Articles, discussion, book reviews, chronicle, index. The Secretary's notes are extremely full as of Oct. 1963, and include news of the Association, other meetings, special studies, collections, lecture programs, news of other societies, periodicals and series, research instruments, classical works, translations, and appointments.

Cum. index, vols. 1-40 (1927-1966). Reprinted: vols. 1-10 (1927-1936), Johnson Reprint Corp.

10.2.81 Notre Dame journal of formal logic. 1960-to date. Quarterly (Jan., Apr., July, Oct.). Ed., Boleslaw Sobocinski, Box 28, Notre Dame, Ind. 46556.

Articles on symbolic logic, foundations of mathematics, history of logic, metalogic, semantics, and the fields immediately related to logic.

10-yr. index in last issue of vol. 10.

10.2.82 Noûs. 1967-to date. Quarterly (Feb., May, Sept., Nov.). Ed., Hector-Neri Castaneda, Dept. of Philosophy, Indiana University, Bloomington, Ind. 47401.

Articles, critical studies, symposia, publications received, index. Emphasis on articles which apply the techniques of formal logic to philosophical questions.

10.2.83 Pacific philosophy forum. *See* Philosophy forum (10.2.101).

10.2.84 Personalist; an international review of philosophy. 1920-to date. Quarterly (Jan., Apr., July, Oct.). Ed., John Hospers, for the School of Philosophy, University of Southern California, 3518 University Park, Los Angeles, Calif. 90007.

Subtitle varies.
Articles, book reviews, notices, index. Previously included articles on religion and literature; now devoted exclusively to philosophy.
Reprinted: vols. 1-50 (1920-69), N. Y., Kraus Reprints.

10.2.85 The philosopher's index; an international index to philosophical periodicals. Quarterly. *See* 1.2.28.

10.2.86 Philosophia; philosophical quarterly of Israel. 1971-to date. Eds., Alex Blum and Asa Kosher. Pub. by Israel Universities Press, P. O. Box 7145, Jerusalem.

Publishes contributions (articles, discussion notes, reviews, etc.) in analytic philosophy from all parts of the world, and is especially interested in the applications of formal logic and linguistics to philosophy. Articles in English or Hebrew.

10.2.87 Philosophia mathematica. 1964-to date. Annual. Official journal of the Association for Philosophy of Mathematics. Ed., J. Fang, Old Dominion University, Norfolk, Va. 23518.

Devoted to the philosophy of mathematics. Articles, discussion, reviews, recent publications.
Frequency varies.

10.2.88 Philosophical books. 1960-to date. Three nos. yearly (Jan., May, Oct.). Ed., M. A. Stewart, Dept. of Philosophy, Univ. of Lancaster, Bowland College, Lancaster L., England.

Frequency varies.
Reviews of philosophical books, primarily from an analytic point of view.

10.2.89 The philosophical forum. 1943-to date. Quarterly (Fall, Winter, Spring, Summer). Ed., Marx Wartofsky, Box 247 Boston Univ. Station, Boston, Mass. 02215.

Annual until Sept. 1968.
Articles, replies, critical studies, translations.
"Open to contributions of all types and schools."

10.2.90 Philosophical journal; transactions of the Royal Philosophical Society of Glasgow. 1964-to date. Semiannually (Jan., July). Ed., Ro. O. Mackenna, 2 Turnberry Ave., Glasgow G11, Scotland.

Articles, book reviews, index. "Publishes not only papers given before the Society but also outside contributions on topics within the general aims of the Society."

10.2.91 The philosophical quarterly. 1950-to date. Quarterly (Jan., Apr., July, Oct.). Publication of the Scots Philosophical Club of the University of St. Andrews. Ed., Bernard Mayo, Dept. of Moral Philosophy, The University, St. Andrews, Fife, KY16 9AL Scotland.

Articles, discussions, critical studies, book reviews, books received. Primarily analytic in orientation, it publishes works from philosophers in any part of the world and gives "special attention to surveys of philosophical literature and to book reviews."

10.2.92 Philosophical review. 1892-to date. Quarterly (Jan., Apr., July, Oct.). Ed. by Faculty of the Sage School of Philosophy, 218 Goldwin Smith Hall, Cornell University, Ithaca, N. Y. 14853.

Articles, discussions, many book reviews, books received, notes, index. Orientation is analytic.
Cum. index: vols. 1-3 (1892-1926).
Reprinted: vols. 1-77 (1892-1968), AMS Reprint Co.

10.2.93 Philosophical studies (Maynooth). 1951-to date. Annual. Ed., James D. Bastable, Room D 502, Arts Bldg., Univ. College, Belfield, Dublin 4, Ireland.

Articles, critical notices, and a large number of book reviews. Aims at the development and diffusion of Christian philosophy by way of exact analysis and specialized study with emphasis on contemporary problems and movements.

10.2.94 Philosophical studies: an international journal for philosophy in the analytic tradition. 1950-to date. 8 nos. yearly. Ed., Keith Lehrer, Dept. of Philosophy, Univ. of Arizona, Tucson, Ariz. 85721.

Analytic in orientation. Articles (of less than 3,000 words), books received, index. A book series edited by Wilfrid Sellars and Keith Lehrer accompanies the journal to accommodate larger manuscripts.
Frequency varies.

Reprinted: Vols. 1-17 (1950-1966), Johnson Reprint Corp.

10.2.95 Philosophy. 1931 (vol. 6)-to date. Quarterly (Jan., Apr., July, Oct.). The journal of the Royal Institute of Philosophy. Ed., Renford Bambrough, Univ. of Cambridge, Cambridge, England.

Articles, discussions, book reviews, books received, Institute news and notes, index.
A continuation of 10.2.56.
Reprinted: vols. 1-11 (1926-1945), Johnson Reprint Corp.

10.2.96 Philosophy and phenomenological research. 1940-to date. Quarterly (Sept., Dec., Mar., June). Organ of the International Phenomenological Society (12.1.11). Ed., Marvin Farber, Dept. of Philosophy, SUNY, Buffalo, N. Y. 14260.

Articles, discussions, reviews, notes and news, recent publications, index. In addition to papers on phenomenology it publishes articles in most of the branches of philosophy.
Partially reprinted: vols. 1-21 (1940/41-1960/61), Kraus Reprints.

10.2.97 Philosophy and public affairs. 1971-to date. Quarterly. Ed., Marshall Cohen. Mss., communications and inquiries to Managing Editor, Princeton Univ. Press, Princeton, N. J. 08540.

The journal welcomes philosophic discussions of substantive legal, social, and political problems, as well as discussions of the more abstract questions to which they give rise. In addition, it intends to publish studies of the moral and intellectual history of such problems.

10.2.98 Philosophy and rhetoric. 1968-to date. Quarterly (Winter, Spring, Summer, Fall). Ed., Donald Verene, Dept. of Philosophy, Pennsylvania State Univ., University Park, Pa. 16802.

Concerned primarily with rhetoric as a philosophical concept, the role of rhetoric, and the relation of rhetoric and other human activities.

10.2.99 **Philosophy and social criticism**; an international journal for the philosophical interpretation of the special languages of the human sciences. 1978-to date. Quarterly. Ed., David M. Rasmussen, Dept. of Philosophy, Boston College, Chestnut Hill, Mass. 02167.

A continuation of *Cultural hermeneutics* (10.2.20).
Begins with v.5 (1978).

10.2.100 **Philosophy east and west**; a quarterly journal of oriental and comparative thought. 1951-to date. Quarterly (Jan., Apr., July, Oct.). Ed., Eliot Deutsch, 2530 Dole St., The University of Hawaii, Honolulu, Hawaii 96822.

Articles on Oriental and comparative philosophy and culture, book reviews, current periodicals (i.e., a listing of articles in Oriental and comparative philosophy appearing in other journals), news and notes pertaining to Oriental and comparative philosophy.
Reprinted: vols. 1-14 (1951-1964), Johnson Reprint Corp.

10.2.101 **The philosophy forum**. 1962-to date. Quarterly (Sept., Dec., Feb., May). Ed., Ervin Laszlo, SUNY College of Arts and Sciences, Geneseo, N. Y. 14454.

Called *The Pacific Philosophy Forum*, vols. 1-6 (1962-68). Each volume has a common theme (e.g., vol. 2, 1963-64, "The Democratic Idea"). Each number contains a longer essay developing a philosophical thesis on that theme, two shorter articles developing a counter-thesis, and an article examining the thesis and counter-theses. Beginning with vol. IX each issue also includes uncommissioned articles dealing with topics associated with the sub-theme of a given issue, and reviews of recent works.

10.2.102 **Philosophy in context**. 1972-to date. Annual. Eds., Joseph P. DeMarco and Leslie Armour, Dept. of Philosophy, Cleveland State Univ., Cleveland, Ohio 44115.

Frequency varies.
Each year a series of articles on various philosophical issues appears. After discussion, a supplementary number is published answering questions about the previous articles.

10.2.103 **Philosophy of science**. 1934-to date. Quarterly (Mar., June, Sept., Dec.). Official journal of the Philosophy of Science Association. Ed., Kenneth F. Schaffner, Dept. of History and Philosophy of Science, Univ. of Pittsburgh, Pittsburgh, Pa. 15260.

Co-sponsored by the Institute for the Unity of Science and by Section L of the American Association for the Advancement of Science.
Articles on the philosophy of science, book reviews, membership list of the Association, abstracts of articles from *Inquiry, Dialectica*, and *The British Journal for the Philosophy of Science*, index.
Reprinted: vols. 1-25 (1934-58), Johnson Reprint Corp.

10.2.104 **Philosophy of the social sciences**. 1971 to date. Quarterly. Pub. by Aberdeen University Press for York University of Toronto, Canada. Ed., I. C. Jarvis, Dept. of Philosophy, York Univ., 4700 Keele St., Downside, Ontario, M3J 1P3 Canada.

10.2.105 **Philosophy research archives**: a bilingual microfiche journal of philosophy. 1975-to date. Ed., A. I. Melden, Dept. of Philosophy, Univ. of Calif., Irvine, Calif. 92664.

Publishes articles, translations, monographs and bibliographies on microfiche; page prints available on demand. Published by the Philosophy Documentation Center, Bowling Green State Univ., Bowling Green, Ohio 43403.

10.2.106 **Philosophy today**. 1957-to date. Quarterly (Spring, Summer, Fall, Winter). Ed., Robert F. Lechner, Carthegena Station, Celina, Ohio 45822.

Loosely affiliated with DePaul Univ.
Articles, index. Frequently contains reprints or translations of articles which have appeared elsewhere.

10.2.107 **Phronesis**; a journal for ancient philosophy. 1955-to date. Three times a year. Ed., G. B. Kerferd, School of Classical Studies, Univ. of Manchester M13 9PL England.

Text in English, French, German, Latin. Articles only, index.

10.2.108 **Political theory**: an international journal of political philosophy. 1973-to date. Quarterly (Feb., May, Aug., Nov.). Ed., Benjamin R. Barber, Rutgers Univ. Pub. by Columbia Univ., Dept. of Political Science, 420 W. 118th St., New York, N. Y. 10027.

10.2.109 **Praxis**; international edition. 1965-1974. Quarterly. Eds., Gajo Petrović and Rudi Supek, Filosofski Fakultet, Zagreb, Dure Salaja 3, Yugoslavia.

Text in English, French, German. Articles, "Portraits and situations," "Thought and reality," discussion, reviews, notes, philosophical life. Marxist in orientation. Issues frequently focus on some theme or problem. Suspended publication with No. 1/2, 1974.

10.2.110 **Premise**: undergraduate philosophy journal. General publication issued twice yearly. Mss. to Editor, Premise, Dept. of Philosophy, 3052 Wescoe Hall, Univ. of Kansas Lawrence, Ks. 66045.

10.2.111 **Process studies**. 1971-to date. Quarterly. Ed., Lewis S. Ford, 3157 Trumpet Road, Chesapeake, Va. 23321.

Focuses on the thought of A. N. Whitehead, related philosophers, and other process thinkers.

10.2.112 **Ratio**. 1957-to date. Semiannual. (June, Dec.). Official organ of the Society for the Furtherance of Critical Philosophy. Ed., Stephen Korner, Dept. of Philosophy, Univ. of Bristol, Bristol BS8 1RJ England.

Published in an English and a German edition.
Articles, book reviews, books received, announcements, index. Deals with all branches of philosophy; is opposed to irra-

tionalism and scepticism.

10.2.113 **Research in phenomenology**. 1971-to date. Annual. Pub. by Duquesne Univ. Press. Ed., John Sallis.

Articles, review articles. Devoted exclusively to publications in phenomenological philosophy. Dedicated to encouraging original creative phenomenological research in all problem areas and to furthering the interpretive and critical study of the writings of the great phenomenological thinkers. Provides a survey of the most important current work in phenomenology.

10.2.114 **Review of metaphysics**. 1947-to date. Quarterly (Sept., Dec., Mar., June). Ed., Jude P. Dougherty, Dept. of Philosophy, Catholic Univ. of America, Washington, D. C. 20064.

Articles in all branches of philosophy, critical studies, problems and perplexities, exploration, discussion, summaries and comments of books received, announcements, abstracts of articles from other leading philosophical journals, annual list of doctoral dissertations (since 1958; listing is incomplete), emeriti professors, visiting philosophers from abroad, index. No special orientation. Annually publishes the presidential address of the Metaphysical Society of America.
Cum. index: vols. 1-20 (1947-67).
Reprinted: vols. 1-21 (1947-68), AMS Reprint Co.

10.2.115 **Science and society**; an independent journal of Marxism. Quarterly (Winter, Spring, Summer, Fall). Ed., David Goldway, Room 4331, John Jay College, CUNY, 445 W. 59th St., New York, N. Y. 10019.

Articles, communications, book reviews, index. Marxist in orientation; sometimes carries articles in philosophy.

10.2.116 **Scientia**; international review of scientific synthesis. 1907-to date. Three times yearly. Eds., Nora Bonetti and Angela de Murtas, Via Vivaio 16, 20122, Milano, Italy.

Frequency varies.

Articles in English, Italian, French, Spanish, German (supplement with a French translation of non-French articles), book reviews, analysis, chronicle. Multidisciplinary, with emphasis on the convergence of the various branches of knowledge.

10.2.117 **Social praxis**: international and interdisciplinary quarterly of social sciences. 1973-to date. Quarterly. Ed., K. T. Fann, 65 Astley Ave., Toronto, Ontario, M4W 3B5 Canada. Pub. by Mouton, P. O. Box 1132, The Hague, Netherlands.

Articles, book reviews. "For ideas in social philosophy."

10.2.118 **Social theory and practice**; an international and interdisciplinary journal of social philosophy. 1970-to date. Semiannual. Ed., Alan R. Mabe, Dept. of Philosophy, The Florida State Univ., Tallahassee, Fla. 32306.

Frequency varies.

Part of each issue is devoted to a specific theme. Concerned with the relevance of philosophical criticism to the solution of pressing social problems.

10.2.119 **The southern journal of philosophy**. 1963-to date. Quarterly (Spring, Summer, Autumn, Winter). Ed., Nancy D. Simco, Dept. of Philosophy, Memphis State University, Memphis, Tenn. 38152.

Articles, book reviews, news, index. "The journal does not confine itself to any particular set of issues or problems, nor to any particular orientation, regional or other."

Reprinted: vols 1-3 (1963-65), N. Y., Kraus Reprints.

10.2.120 **The southwestern journal of philosophy**. 1970-to date. Three times annually. Eds., Robert W. Shahan, Dept. of Philosophy, and A. E. Keaton, Dept. of Information Sciences, 605 Dale Hall Tower, 455 West Lindsey, The Univ. of Oklahoma, Norman, Okla. 73019.

Articles concern the various facets of phi-

losophy or philosophical problems which arise in conjunction with the analysis of the content and methods of other disciplines. One issue each year includes the proceedings of the annual meeting of the Southwestern Philosophical Society. Beginning 1978, 4 issues per volume.

10.2.121 **Soviet studies in philosophy**; selected articles from Soviet journals in English translation. 1962-to date. Quarterly (Summer, Fall, Winter, Spring). Ed., John Sommerville, 1426 Merritt Dr., E. Cajon, Calif. 92020.

Publishes translations of Russian articles in philosophy.

10.2.122 **Speculum**; a journal of mediaeval studies. 1926-to date. Quarterly (Jan., Apr., July, Oct.). Published by the Mediaeval Academy of America. Cambridge, Mass. Ed., Paul J. Meyvaert, 1430 Mass. Ave., Cambridge, Mass. 02138.

Articles, book reviews, bibliography, index. An important journal in its field.

10.2.123 **Studies in history and philosophy of science**. May, 1970-to date. Quarterly. Eds., Gerd Buchdahl, Free School Lane, Univ. of Cambridge, CB2 3RH England, and L. L. Laudan, Univ. of Pittsburgh, Pittsburgh, Pa. Pub. Pergamon Press Ltd., Headington Hall, Oxford, OX3 OBW England.

10.2.124 **Studies in philosophy and education**. 1960-to date. Quarterly (Winter, Spring, Summer, Autumn). Ed., Francis T. Villemain, Southern Illinois Univ., Edwardsville, Ill. 62025.

Essays, articles, reviews and rejoinders, book reviews, bibliographies. Once a year an issue is devoted to the literature in and related to the philosophy of education.

10.2.125 **Studies in Soviet thought**. 1961-to date. Quarterly (Mar., June, Sept., Dec.). Ed., T. J. Blakeley, Dept. of Philosophy, Boston College, Chestnut Hill, Mass. 02167.

Vol. 1 published in one bound issue.

Text in English, French, German.

Articles, notes and comments, bibliography, chronology, book reviews, report from the Institute of East European Studies, Fribourg, Switzerland, index. Concerned with all aspects of Soviet and East European philosophy from both a descriptive and a critical point of view.

10.2.126 Synthese; an international journal for epistemology, methodology and philosophy of science. 1936-1963 (vols. 1-15); 1966 (vol. 16)-to date. Quarterly (Mar., June, Sept., Dec.). Ed., Jaakko Hintikka, Univ. of Helsinki and Dept. of Philosophy, Florida State University.

Suspended 1940-Apr., 1946; 1964-65. Subtitle varies. Text in English, French, and German.

Articles, reviews, abstracts, books received, index. Also publishes selected papers read at the Boston Colloquium for the Philosophy of Science, and minutes and announcements of the Division of Logic, Methodology and Philosophy of Science, International Union of History and Philosophy of Science. Most issues are partially devoted to symposia on a prescribed theme.

Cum. index: vols. 1-17 (1936-67).

10.2.127 Systematics; the journal of the Institute for the Comparative Study of History, Philosophy and the Sciences. 1963-to date, Quarterly (Mar., June, Sept., Dec.). Eds., John G. Bennett and Karl S. Schaffer, Academy for Continuous Education, Sherborne House, NR Cheltenham, Glos.

Articles, reviews, review discussions. Interdisciplinary, with emphasis on "the field of structural thinking and organization."

10.2.128 Teaching philosophy. 1975-to date. Semi-annual. Ed., Arnold Wilson, Dept. of Philosophy 206, Univ. of Cincinnati, Cincinnati, Ohio 45221.

1979, will become a quarterly.

Papers concerned with teaching philosophy, planning philosophy courses, training teachers, assessing impact of new teaching ideas. Notes, news items, book reviews. Reviews textbooks.

10.2.129 Theological studies. 1940-to date. Quarterly (Mar., June, Sept., Dec.). Publication of the Theological Faculties of the Society of Jesus in the U. S. Ed., Walter J. Burghardt, S. J., 3520 Prospect St. N. W., Room 401, Washington, D. C. 20007.

Articles, notes, book reviews, books recieved, index.

10.2.130 Theoria; a Swedish journal of philosophy. 1935-to date. 2-3 nos. yearly. Ed., Krister Segerberg, Abo Akademi, SF-20500 Abo 50, Finland.

Subtitle varies. Text primarily in English, also in French and German.

Articles, discussions, annual bibliography of Scandinavian literature and of articles in philosophy and related fields, index. Emphasis on analytic philosophy and articles employing symbolic logic.

10.2.131 Theory and decision: an international journal for philosophy and methodology of the social sciences. 1970 to date. Quarterly. Ed., G. L. Eberlein, Technical Univ. of Munich, Munich, West Germany. Pub., D. Reidel Publishing Co., Dordrecht, Holland, and Boston.

Concentrates on: application of the advanced methodology of philosophy of science, logic, and mathematics; discussion of empirical models in terms of formal structures; intensification of interdisciplinary communication.

Connected with 10.5.60.

10.2.132 Theory and society: renewal and critique in social theory. 1974-to date. Quarterly. Pub., American Elsevier Publishing Co., Inc., 52 Vanderbilt Ave., New York, N. Y. 10017.

10.2.133 The thomist; a speculative quarterly of theology and philosophy. 1939-to date. Quarterly (Jan., Apr., July, Oct.). Ed., William

J. Hill, 487 Michigan Ave., N. E., Washington, D. C. 20017.

Articles, book reviews, books received, index.
Cum. index: vols. 1-15 (1939-52).
Reprinted: vols. 1-30 (1939-67), Kraus Reprints.

10.2.134 **Traditio**; studies in ancient and medieval history, thought, and religion. 1943-to date. Annual. Eds., Edwin A. Quain, Charles H. Lohr, Bernard M. Peebles, and Richard E. Doyle, Fordham Univ., Bronx, N. Y. 10458.

Articles, miscellany, bibliography, Institute of Medieval Canon Law Bulletin. Carries some articles on philosophy.

10.2.135 **Transactions of the Charles S. Peirce Society**; a quarterly journal in American philosophy. 1965-to date. Eds., Richard Robin, Dept. of Philosophy, Mount Holyoke College, South Hadley, Mass. 01075, and Peter Hare, Dept. of Philosophy, SUNY, Buffalo, 4244 Ridge Lea Road, Buffalo, N. Y. 14226.

Articles on American philosophy and source materials on American pragmatism and Peirce in particular, proceedings and members of the Society, books received, book reviews, news and notes.

10.2.136 **Vivarium**; a journal for mediaeval philosophy and the intellectual life of the Middle Ages. 1963-to date. Semiannual (May, Nov.). Ed., L. M. de Rijk, Witte Singel 71, Leyden, The Netherlands.

Articles in English, French, German; reviews, books recieved, index.
Concerned with medieval philosophy in relation to the field of liberal arts.

10.2.137 **Zygon**; journal of religion and science. 1966-to date. Quarterly (Mar., June, Sept., Dec.). Published by the Institute on Religion in an Age of Science and Meadville Theological School of Lombard College. Ed., Ralph W. Burhoe, 1524 E. 59th St., Chicago, Ill. 60637.

Editorial, articles, book reviews, a survey of periodicals, announcements. Seeks to bridge the gap between science and religion.

See also: 7.2.30, 7.2.31, 7.9.4, 7.11.24, 8.2.9, 9.7.1, 9.7.2, 12.1.40.

10.3 SELECTED JOURNALS: OTHER LANGUAGES

French

10.3.1 **L'année philosophique.** 1890-1913 (vols. 1-24). Paris. Annual.

Superseded *Critique philosophique.* Paris, no. 1-26, 1872-85; ns. vols. 1-10, 1885-89.
Articles, bibliography of French philosophy for the year.
Reprinted: vols. 1-24 (1890-1913), N. Y., Kraus Reprints.

10.3.2 **Archives de philosophie**; recherches et documentation. 1923-to date. Quarterly. Ed., M. Régnier, Les Fontaines, F60500 Chantilly.

Suspended between vol. 18, no. 2 (1952) and vol. 19, no. 1 (1955). Vol. 18- , called "nouvelle série."
Articles, book reviews, bibliographies, index. Each issue devoted to a particular topic.
Cum. index: vols. 1-12 (1923-34).

10.3.3 **Archives internationales d'histoire des sciences.** 1947-to date. Semiannual. Published by Académie Internationale d'Histoire des Sciences. Ed., John D. North, 28 Chalfont Road, Oxford, England.

Text in French and English. N. S., 1972. Articles, reviews, bibliographies, news.

10.3.4 **Bulletin de la société française de philosophie.** 1901-to date. Quarterly. Organ of the Société. Ed., Suzanne Delorme, Société Française de Philosophie, Librairie Colin, 12 Rue Colbert, F 75002 Paris, France.

Suspended 1915-16, 1918-20. Numbering irregular. Vols. 20-24 omitted in numbering; vol. 26, no. 5 (Dec. 1936) never published.

Texts and communications of the society, followed by the complete discussion.
Also contains *Bibliographie de la philosophie française*, nos. 1-4 for 1909-12, appended to years 1910-13. Year 1928 contains a "sommaire des séances" for 1901-27.

10.3.5 **Bulletin thomiste.** 1924-to date. Quarterly. Organ of the Société Thomiste. Ed., Università S. Tommaso, Largo Angelicum 1, I-00184 Roma, Italy.

Vols. 1-7 (1924-30) in *Revue thomiste*; vol. 8 (1931) published separately. Vol. 12 (years 1940-42, 1963-65), the last of the old series contains book reviews and a Thomistic bibliography through 1965 (pp. 209-435). See 8.8.5.
Cum index: 1924-33.

10.3.6 **Etudes franciscaines.** 1899-1936; ns. 1950-to date. Semiannual. Ed., Bibliothèque Franciscaine Provinciale, Couvent des Capucins, 26 Rue Boissonade, Paris, France.

Subtitle varies. Articles and bibliographies connected with the Franciscans.
Cum. index: vols. 1-20 (1899-1928).

10.3.7 **Les études philosophiques.** 1926-1945 (vols. 1-20); 1946 (ns. vol. 1)-to date. Quarterly. Ed., Pierre Aubenque, 5 Rue Berteaux-Dumas, F 92200, Neuilly S/Seine, France. Published by the Presses Universitaires de France.

Articles, critical studies, book reviews (which encompass about half of each issue), philosophical life (international), news (international), doctoral defenses, index. Each issue is devoted to a particular theme.
Reprinted: vols. 1-20 (1926-45); ns. vols. 1-14 (1946-59), N. Y., Kraus Reprints.

10.3.8 **Laval théologique et philosophique.** 1945-to date. Three times a year. Ed., Emmanuel Trépanier, Faculté de philosophie, Pavillon des Arts, Cité Universitaire, Québec G1K 7P4 Canada.

1928-45, published irregularly as *Bulletin Laval des sciences philosophiques et théologiques.*

Articles, theses extracts, bibliography.

10.3.9 **Recherches de philosophie.** 1955-to date. Annual. Publication of the Association des Professeurs de Philosophie des Facultés Catholiques de France. Ed., Pierre Colin, 21 Rue d'Assas, 75006 Paris, France.

Articles, confrontations, notes, chronicle. Each volume dedicated to a particular theme; some issues of book length.
A continuation of *Revue de philosophie* (10.3.12).

10.3.10 **Revue d'esthétique.** 1948-to date. Three nos. yearly. Organ of the Société Française d'Esthétique. Eds., E. Souriau et al. , 162 Rue St. Charles, 75740 Paris Cedex 15, France.

Articles, chronicle, book reviews, news of the society, index.

10.3.11 **Revue de métaphysique et de morale.** 1893-1941 (vols. 1-48); 1944 (vol. 49)-to date. Quarterly. Ed., Paul Ricoeur, Librairie Armand Colin, 103 Boulevard St. Michel, Paris 75505.

Suspended Jan.-Dec. 1915; 1942-44; 1944 replaced by *Etudes de métaphysique et de morale,* later considered vol. 49 of the *Revue.*
Articles, critical studies, book reviews, critical notes, index. Publishes articles on topics other than metaphysics and ethics. The major French philosophical journal.
Cum. index: vols. 1-30 (1893-1923).
Reprinted: vols. 1-17 (1893-1909), Johnson Reprint Corp.

10.3.12 **Revue de philosophie.** 1900-1939 (vols. 1-39).

Suspended 1915-18. 1931-39 also called ns. vols. 1-8. Some irregularity in numbering.
Cum. index: vols. 1-23 (1900-13).
1902-03 published *Index philosophique,* vols. 1-2.
Continued as 10.3.9.

10.3.13 **Revue de théologie et de philosophie.** 1868-1911 (vols. 1-44); 1913-50 (ns.

vols. 1-38); 1951 (s3, vol. 1)-to date. 6 nos. yearly. Eds., G. A. Boss et al., 7 Chemin des Cèdres, 1004, Lausanne, Switzerland.

Vols. 1-5 (1868-72), as *Théologie et philosophie.*
Articles, discussion, reviews.
Reprinted: vols. 1-44 (1868-1911), Johnson Reprint Corp.

10.3.14 Revue des études augustiniennes. 1955-to date. Quarterly. Ed., 8 Rue François Ier, 75008 Paris, France.

Continues *Année théologique augustinienne*, vols. 1-14 (1940-54).
Publishes articles related to the work and thought of St. Augustine; reviews of related books, index.

10.3.15 Revue des études juives; historia judaica. 1880-to date. Three nos yearly. Publication of Ecole Pratique des Hautes-Etudes (6e section) and Société des Etudes Juives. Ed., Georges Vajda, 17 Rue St Georges 75009 Paris, France.

N. 101, 1937 also as ns. vol. 1.
Articles, notes, reviews.
Cum. index: vols. 1-50 (1880-1905); vols. 51-100 bis.

10.3.16 Revue des sciences philosophiques et théologiques. 1907-41 (vols. 1-30); 1947 (vol. 31)-to date. Quarterly. Published by the Professeurs aux Facultés de Philosophie et de Théologie, O. P., Le Saulchoir. Ed., Père Quelquejeu, Facultés Dominicaines du Saulchoir, 43 Bis, Rue de la Glacière, 75016-Paris, France.

Suspended 1941-46.
Articles, notes, bulletins, reviews (sometimes two-thirds of an issue), contents of articles from many journals (with one-sentence summaries of some), bibliographies, index.

10.3.17 Revue internationale de philosophie. 1938-to date. Quarterly. Ed., Michel Meyer, 145 Avenue Adolphe Buyl, 1050 Bruxelles, Belgium.

Suspended after vol. 2, no. 5, Oct. 1939; resumed with special no. vol. 2, no. 6, pub. Aug. 1948, which completes vol. 2.
Articles (in French, English, German, Italian, Spanish), notes and discussions, book reviews, books received, contents of a number of journals, philosophical life, index. Each number dedicated to a study of a philosopher, movement, or a problem of philosophy, often with an extensive bibliography on the topic.
Reprinted: Johnson Reprint Corp.

10.3.18 Revue philosophique de la France et de l'étranger. 1876-to date. Three nos yearly. Ed., Jean Leroy, Ecole de Théologie, 1, Avenue Lacordaire, F-31078 Toulouse Cedex, France. Published by the Presses Universitaires de France.

Articles, critical reviews, notes, information, news, correspondence, index.
Reprinted: vols. 1-150 (1876-1960), N. Y., Kraus Reprints.

10.3.19 Revue philosophique de Louvain. 1894-to date. Quarterly. Published by the Société Philosophique de Louvain. Ed., Georges Van Riet, Kardinaal Mercierplein 2, B-3000 Louvain, Belgium.

1894-1909 as *Revue néo-scolastique*; 1910-45 as *Revue néo-scolastique de philosophie.* Vols. 1-25 also called no. 1-100; 26-43 also called s2, no. 1-67/68; vol. 44- , also called s3. Suspended Aug. 1914-Nov. 1919 (vol. 21, no. 84 called Nov. 1914-1919): May 1940-Aug. 1945 (vol. 43, no. 3 dated Aug. 1940-Aug. 1945).
Articles (some in English, some in French with English summary), book reviews, index.
Supplement: *Répertoire bibliographique de la philosophie* (1.2.23).
Cum. index: vols. 1-20 (1894-1913).

10.3.20 Revue thomiste. 1893-to date. Quarterly. Ed., M. V. Jean Leroy, Ecole de Théologie, 1 Ave. Lacordaire, F-31078 Toulouse Cedex, France.

Suspended Oct./Dec. 1939-Jan./Mar. 1946.
Articles, reviews of books, reviews of reviews, summaries of articles, index.

Reprinted: vols. 1-74 (1893-1974), N. Y., Kraus Reprints.

10.3.21 Les temps modernes. 1945-to date. Monthly. Ed., Jean-Paul Sartre, 26 Rue de Condé, Paris 75006 France.

Supersedes *Nouvelle revue française*.
Articles, debates, chronicles. An outlet for articles by Sartre and members of the Paris existentialist school, and their debates with others.
Reprinted: vols. 1-15 (1945/46-1959/60), N. Y., Kraus Reprints.

German

10.3.22 Archiv für Begriffsgeschichte. 1955-to date. Ed., Karlfried Gruender. Pub. by Bouvier Verlag, Herbert Grundmann, Am Hof 32, Post Fach 1268, 5300 Bonn 1, West Germany (B. R. D.).

Each issue contains excellent bibliographical notes and reviews in the field of history of technological terms in humanities.

10.3.23 Archiv für Geschichte der Philosophie. 1888-1932; 1959-to date. Quarterly. Ed., Dr. Hans Wagner, Philosophisches Seminar A der Universität, Bonn, Am Hof E 1 Germany. American co-ed., Charles H. Kahn, Dept. of Philosophy, Univ. of Pennsylvania, 305 Logan Hall, Philadelphia, Pa. 19174; Bonn office: Redaktion, Archiv für Geschichte der Philosophie, Philosophisches Seminar A, Universität, 53 Bonn, Am Hof, Germany.

Suspended 1933-59.
Vols. 37-39, 1925-30 as *Archiv für Geschichte der Philosophie und Soziologie*; vols. 8-39 (1895-1930) as vols. 1-32; vols. 8-33 (1895-1924) as *Archiv für Philosophie,* Abteilung 1.
Articles (in English, French, German), critical reviews.

10.3.24 Archiv für Philosophie. 1947-63. Quarterly.

Articles, book reviews, index.
Ceased publication with v.13, no. 1-2.

Reprinted: vols. 1-13 (1947-63), N. Y., Kraus Reprints.

10.3.25 Archiv für Rechts-und Sozialphilosophie. Archives for Philosophy of Law and Social Philosophy. 1907-to date. Quarterly. Ed., Alwin Diemer, Philosophisches Institut der Universtät, Düsseldorf, D-4000 Germany. Pub.: Wiesbaden, Franz Steiner Verlag.

Reprinted: v.1-36, N. Y., Johnson Reprint Corp.; v.37-40, Wurzburg, Liebing.
Organ of the International Association for Philosophy of Law and Social Philosophy.
Articles in German, English and French. Summaries in the three languages for each article. Also publishes periodical supplementary issues.

10.3.26 Deutsche Zeitschrift für Philosophie. 1953-to date. Monthly. Ed., Frank Rupprecht, DDR, 104 Berlin, Marienstrasse 19120, Germany.

Frequency varies.
Table of contents also in Russian, English, French, Spanish.
Articles, remarks and discussion, book reviews, notes, index.
Marxist in orientation; emphasis on Eastern European philosophy and dialectical materialism.

10.3.27 Freiburger Zeitschrift für Philosophie und Theologie. 1954-to date. Semiannual. Ed., Editions Saint-Paul, Pérolles 36, CH 1700 Fribourg, Switzerland.

Frequency varies.
Superseded *Divus Thomas*, 1887-1953; also numbered *Jahrbuch für Philosophie und speculative Theologie*, ser. 4.
Texts in French and German. Articles, book reviews, bibliography, index.

10.3.28 Grazer Philosophische Studien. Internationale Zeitschrift für analytische Philosophie. 1975-to date. Ed., Rudolf Haller, Philosophisches Institut, Universität Graz, Heinrichstrasse 26, A-8010 Graz, Austria.

10.3.29 Hegel-Studien. 1961-to date. Annual.

Eds., F. Nicolin and O. Pöggeler, Hegel-Archiv der Ruhr-Universität, 463 Bochum, Germany.

Published in connection with the Hegel-Kommission der Deutschen Forschungsgemeinschaft and the International Hegel Association.
Articles on Hegel, Hegel texts, reviews of Hegel literature.

10.3.30 Kant-Studien; philosophische Zeitschrift der Kant-Gesellschaft. 1897-to date. Quarterly. Eds., Gerhard Funke and Joachim Kopper. Mss. to Manfred Kleinschneider, Philosophisches Seminar der Universität, Saarstrasse 21; 25 Mainz, W. Ger.

Suspended 1937-41, 1945-52.
Articles (in German, English, French, Italian), discussions, book reviews, bibliography, information, index. Not exclusively on Kant.
Reprinted: Wurzburg, Leibing.
Diemer, Alwin (ed.) *Gesamtregister der Kant-Studien*, Meisenheim/Glan, Anton Hain Verlag, 1970. 2v.

10.3.31 Neue Hefte für Philosophie. 1973-to date. Semiannual. Eds., Rüdiger Bubner, Konrad Cramer, Reiner Wiehl, 69 Heidelberg, Marsiliusplatz 1, W. Germ. Pub. Vandenhoeck and Rupprecht, Göttingen.

Devoted to single themes: No. 1, Phänomenologie und Sprachanalyse; no. 2/3 Dialog als Methode.

10.3.32 Philosophia naturalis; Archiv für Naturphilosophie und die philosophischen Grenzgebiete der exakten Wissenschaftsgeschichte. 1953-to date. Quarterly. Ed., Joseph Meurers, Direktor der Universitätssternwarte, Türkenschanzstr 17, A-1180 Wien, Austria.

Articles, book reviews, index. Emphasis on analytic philosophy, logic and philosophy of science. Also publishes special issues.

10.3.33 Philosophische Rundschau. 1957-to date. Quarterly. Eds., R. Bubner and B. Waldenfels, POB 2040, 7400 Tübingen, Germany.

Articles, book reviews, bibliography, index.

10.3.34 Philosophisches Jahrbuch im Auftrag der Görres-Gesellschaft. 1893-to date. Semiannual. Ed., Hermann Krings, Institut für Philosophie, Universität München, Geschw Schollplatz, D8000 München, Germany.

Frequency varies.
Articles, reviews, reports.
Reprinted: vols. 1-60 (1888-1950), N. Y., Kraus Reprints.

10.3.35 Studium Generale; Zeitschrift für interdisziplinäre Studien; Journal for interdisciplinary studies. 1947-to date. Monthly. Ed., G. H. Muller, 6900 Heidelberg 1, Postfach 1780, Germany.

Subtitle and frequency vary.
Articles (in German and English), short summaries of journal articles (but no book reviews). Emphasis on philosophy of science and analytic philosophy.

10.3.36 Theologie und Philosophie. 1926-to date. Quarterly. Ed., Alois Grillmeier, Offenbacher Landstrasse D-6000 224, Frankfurt am Main, W.Germany (B. R. D.). Pub. by Verlag Herder, Hermann-Herder Str. 4, 7800 Freiburg, W. Germany (B. R. D.).

Supersedes *Scholastic*, 1926-65. Published by the Jesuit Faculty of Theology and Philosophy of St. Georgen in Frankfurt.

10.3.37 Zeitschrift für Allgemeine Wissenschaftstheorie; Journal for general philosophy of science. Founded 1970. Semiannual. Eds., Alwin Diemer, Lutz Geldsetzer, and Gert Konig, Institute of Philosophy of the University of Düsseldorf. Pub. Franz Steiner Verlag, Wiesbaden.

10.3.38 Die Zeitschrift für philosophische Forschung. 1946-to date. Quarterly. Ed., Otfried Höffe, Keferloher Str 6, D8000 München 40, Germany.

Articles, discussion, book reviews, contents of other journals, reports and information.

Cum. index every 10 years. *Gesamtregister der Zeitschrift für philosophische Forschung*, Bde. 1-21. Gleisenheim, Anton Hain, 1968.

Italian

10.3.39 Archivio di filosofia. 1931-to date. Three nos. yearly. Organ of the Istituto di Studi Filosofici dell'Università di Roma. Ed., Enrico Castelli, Gattinara, Via La Grange 1, Roma, Italy.

Suspended 1943-45.
Articles (in Italian, English, French, German), bibliography, information on activities of the Institute.

10.3.40 Aut aut; rivista di filosofia e di cultura, 1951-to date. Bi-monthly. Eds., Enzo Paci and Pier Aldo Rovatti, Via Curti 8, 20136 Milano, Italy.

10.3.41 Epistemologia; an Italian journal for the philosophy of science. 1978-to date. Ed., Evandro Agazzi. Pub., Genova, Tilgher.

Bilingual. A journal for the philosophy of science in a broad sense. Monographical issues appear occasionally, containing proceedings of significant conferences. Articles in Italian carry a long English summary.

10.3.42 Ethica; rassegna di filosofia morale. 1962-to date. Quarterly. Ed., M. Gianfranco Morra, Via Albonetti 21, 47100, Forli, Italy.

Articles, book reviews, notes.

10.3.43 Filosofia. 1950-to date. Three nos. yearly. Ed., Augusto Guzzo, 25 Piazza Statuto, 10144 Turino, Italy.

Frequency varies. Usually three nos. in Italian, one international number in English, French, German, or Spanish.
Articles on all branches of philosophy, book reviews, index.
Cum. index every 10 years.
Also publishes an annual: *Studi Internazionali de Filosofia.*

10.3.44 Giornale critico della filosofia italiana. 1920-32 (vols. 1-13); 1933 (s2 vol. 1)-to date. Quarterly. Ed., Ugo Spirito, Piazza del Collegio Romano 2, Roma, Italy.

Suspended 1946-53. s2 vol. 1 (1933) also vol. 14. Text in Italian, English, French. Founded by G. Gentile.
Articles, discussion, book reviews, notes, bibliography, index.

10.3.45 Giornale di metafisica. 1946-to date. Bimonthly. Ed., Michele Federico, Istituto di Filosofia, Facolta di Magistero, Università di Genova, Via Privata Lungoparco Gropallo 3-6, 16122 Genova, Italy.

Studies, notes, book reviews, chronicle, index.

10.3.46 Gregorianum; periodicum trimestre a Pontifica Universitate Gregoriana edita. 1920-to date. Quarterly. Ed., Karl Becker, Piazza della Pilotta 4, 00187 Rome, Vatican, Italy.

Subtitle varies.
Articles (in English, French, German, Italian, Latin, Spanish), notes, reviews, bibliography. Thomistic in orientation.

10.3.47 Rassegna bibliografica di storia della filosofia—ricavata dalle riviste; Bibliographic review of the history of philosophy—extracted from magazines. 1966-to date. Annual. Published by L'Istituto di Filosofia dell'Università de Parma. Eds., D. Pesce, Mario Micheletti.

Aims to provide researchers with information on what has been published every year in the major journals concerning the history of philosophy by way of articles, notes, and reviews.
Vol. I (1968) covered 1966; vol. II (1969) covered 1967; etc.

10.3.48 Rivista critica di storia della filosofia. 1946-to date. Quarterly. Organ of the Ist. di Storia della Filosofia dell'Università di Milano. Ed., Mario Dal Pra (et al.), Via Emilio de Marchi, 8, Milano, Italy.

Text in Italian, French, Greek, Latin. Articles on historical studies broadly conceived, documents, notes, discussion, book reviews, information, index. Some numbers dedicated to an author or subject, with exhaustive bibliographies.

10.3.49 Rivista di filosofia. 1919-to date. Three nos. yearly. Ed., Nicola Abbagnano, Via Morosini 22, 20135 Milano, Italy.

Suspended 1922. Supersedes *Rivista filosofica*, 1899-1908.
Articles on all aspects of philosophy, discussion, book reviews, chronicle, index.

10.3.50 Rivista di filosofia neoscolastica. 1909-to date. Three nos. yearly. Published by Università Cattolica del Sacro Cuore, Facoltà di Filosofia, Adriano Bausola, Via S Calocero 9-20123, Milano, Italy.

Articles, notes and discussions, announcements, bibliographies, book reviews, index.

10.3.51 Rivista di studi Crociani. 1964-to date. Three nos. yearly. Ed., Alfredo Parente, Società Napoletana di Storia Patria, Via Luca Giordano 7, 80127, Napoli, Italy.

Dedicated to the study and continuation of Croce's thought.

10.3.52 Sapienza; rivista internationale di filosofia e di teologia. Edited by the Dominicans of Italy. 1948-to date. Quarterly. Ed., Benedetto d'Amore, Vicoletto S. Pietro a Maiella, 4, 80134 Napoli, Italy.

Subtitle varies.
Articles, discussions, critical notes, book reviews, books received.

10.3.53 Sistematica, Rivista di filosofia. Vol. 1 (1968)-to date. Quarterly. Pub. Pergamena Editrice. Milano, Italy 20169.

10.3.54 Sophia; rassegna critica di filosofia e storia della filosofia. 1933-to date. Quarterly. Ed., Carmelo Ottaviano, Via Mesopotamia 21, 00179 Roma, Italy.

Subtitle varies.
Articles (in English, French, German, Italian), book reviews, index. Emphasis on the history of philosophy, with an annual bibliography of new works.

Russian

10.3.55 Nauchnye doklady vysshei shkoly; filosofskie nauki. 1958-to date. Bimonthly. Ed., M. T. Iovchuk, Moskva, K-19, prospekt Marksa 18, Korpus 5, U. S. S. R.

Articles, book reviews, discussions and debates, new books in philosophy. Table of contents also in English, French, German. Exclusively Marxist-Leninist in orientation.

10.3.56 Voprosy filosofii. 1947-to date. Monthly. Published by Akademiia Nauk SSSR. Institut Filosofii. Ed., I. T. Frolov, Moskva, B. Bronnaja 2/6, apt. 34, U. S. S. R.

Summaries in English of the major articles. Table of contents also in English, French, German, Spanish.
Articles, consultation, notes, discussion, book reviews, bibliography, index. Exclusively Marxist-Leninist. The major Soviet philosophical journal.

Spanish

10.3.57 Augustinus. 1956-to date. Quarterly. Published by Orden de Padres Agustinos Recoletos, General Dá ila 5, Madrid-3, Spain. Ed., José Oroz.

Articles, book reviews, news, index. Dedicated to all aspects of the writings of St. Augustine; devotes much space to bibliography.

10.3.58 Critica; revista hispanoamericana de filosofia. 1967-to date. Three nos. yearly. Ed., Editorial Board, Apartado 27-414, México 7, DF.

Articles (in Spanish and English with summaries in the other language), discussions, bibliographical notes. Represents the various philosophical tendencies in Latin

America, with some emphasis on analytic philosophy.

Not published in 1973-74; vol. VII, 1975- .

10.3.59 Estudios filosóficos. 1952-to date. Three nos. yearly. Published by the Dominicos de la Provincia de España, Apartado 586, Valladolid, Spain. Ed., P. Teofilo Urdanoz, O. P.

Articles, notes, commentaries, chronicles, bibliography, book reviews. Thomistic in orientation.

10.3.60 Pensamiento; revista de investigación e información filosófica. 1945-to date. Quarterly. Published by the Facultades de Filosofia de la Compañía de Jesús en España. Ed., Juan Roig Gironella, Pablo Aranda 3, Madrid-6, Spain.

Articles, notes, commentaries, reviews of books, extracts of articles, chronicle, annual bibliography of Spanish and hispanoamerican philosophy.

10.3.61 Revista de filosofia. 1942-to date. Quarterly. Pub. by Instituto "Luis Vives" de Filosofia. Ed., Sergio Rabade Romeo, Serrano 127, Madrid-6, Spain.

Also called *Revista Española de filosofia*. Articles, notes, texts, book reviews, chronicle, and acts of the Soc. Esp. de Fil., bibliography, notices. Primarily scholastic in orientation.

10.3.62 Revista Latinoamericana de Filosofia. 1975-to date. Quarterly. Eds., Rafael Braun et al. CP 5379, 1000 Correo Central, Buenos Aires, Argentina.

Spanish and Portugese.

10.3.63 Sapientia. 1946-to date. Quarterly. Published by the Facultad de Filosofía, Universidad Católica Argentina. La Plata, Argentina. Ed., O. N. Derisi, Calle 24 entre 65 y 66, La Plata.

Articles, notes, bibliography. Thomistic in orientation.

Cum. index: 1946-55.

10.4 SELECTED PHILOSOPHICALLY ORIENTED JOURNALS: MULTIDISCIPLINARY

10.4.1 Abraxas. 1970-to date. Eds., M. J. García-Gomez (et al.), Humanities Division, Southampton College, Southampton, N. Y. 11968.

Interdisciplinary journal devoted to the theoretical study of philosophy and the humanities.

10.4.2 Clio: an interdisciplinary journal of literature, history and the philosophy of history. 1971-to date. 3 nos. yearly. Eds., Robert H. Canary and Henry Kozicki, Univ. of Wisconsin, Parkside, and Clark Butler, Indiana Univ.-Purdue Univ.

Concentrates on philosophy of history, history-related literary criticism and historiography.

10.4.3 Consciousness and culture. Ed., J. R. Staude, Box 345, Orinda, Calif. 94563.

Interdisciplinary journal.

10.4.4 Dionysius, a new journal for the philosophical study of classical antiquity and Christianity. 1977-to date. Mss. to Secretary, Dept. of Classics, Dalhousie University, Halifax, Nova Scotia, B3H 315, Canada.

Articles about the reception and place of philosophy in Judaism and Islam fall within the interest of the journal.

10.4.5 ETC; a review of general semantics. Journal of the International Society for General Semantics. 1943-to date. Quarterly. Ed., Neil Postman, Box 2469, San Francisco, Calif. 94126.

10.4.6 Humanitas. Journal of the Institute of Man. 1965-to date. Three nos. yearly. Ed., Adrian van Kaam, Center for the Study of Human Development, Duquesne Univ., Pittsburgh, Pa. 15219.

10.4.7 **Ideologie**, Quaderni de storia contemporanea. 1969-to date. Three nos. yearly. Eds., Ferruccio Rossi-Landi and Mario Sabbatini under the direction of Francesco Tolin, 35100 Padova, via Mancinelli, 6, Padua, Italy.

The review focuses upon philosophy and contemporary political and economic theories.

10.4.8 **Journal of pragmatics**. An interdisciplinary quarterly of language studies. 1977-to date. Ed., Jacob L. Mey, Odense Univ., Niels Bohrs Alle 25, DK-5000, Odense, Denmark. Pub. North-Holland, P. O. Box 211, Amsterdam, The Netherlands.

10.4.9 **Linguistics and philosophy**. An international journal. 1976-to date. 6 nos. yearly. Mng. Ed., Robert Wall, Dept. of Linguistics, Univ. of Texas, Austin, Tex. 78712. Pub., D. Reidel, P. O. Box 17, Dordrecht, Holland.

The journal focuses on studies in natural language which are of interest to both disciplines mentioned in the title. The following list of topics partially describes its range: meaning and truth, reference, description, entailment, speech acts, syntax, semantics, modal logic, tense logic, linguistic methodology, the nature of linguistic universals, language acquisition, and language as a social convention. Articles, review articles, notes, discussions, or remarks and replies. Two volumes published yearly.

10.4.10 **Philosophy and literature**. A new interdisciplinary journal of literary and philosophical studies. 1976-to date. Semiannual. Ed., Denis Dutton, Univ. of Michigan-Dearborn, College of Arts, Sciences and Letters, 4901 Evergreen Road, Dearborn, Mich. 48128.

10.4.11 **Praxis**. A journal of radical perspectives on the arts. 2125 Hearst Ave., Berkeley, Calif. 94709.

10.4.12 **Reason papers**. A journal of interdisciplinary normative studies. 1974-to date. Ed., Tibor R. Mochan, Dept. of Philosophy, SUNY College, Fredonia, N. Y. 14063.

10.4.13 **Sistm quarterly**: communications of the Society for the Interdisciplinary Study of the Mind. Vol. I, No. 1 (Sept. 1977)- to date. Ed., Martin Ringle. Pub., Philosophy Dept. ASB, Univ. of Florida, Gainesville, Fla. 32611.

10.4.14 **Social sciences**. Quarterly. Editorial office: 33/12, Arbat, Moscow, U. S. S. R.

English, French, and Spanish, with articles in history, philosophy, law, economics, sociology, and linguistics.

10.4.15 **Studia Cartesiana**. *See* 5.2.37.

10.4.16 **Theoria to theory**: an international journal of science, philosophy and contemplative religion. 1966-to date. Quarterly. Pub., Gordon & Breach, 42, William IV St., London WC2 or One Park Ave., New York, N. Y. 10016.

10.4.17 **Thought**; a review of culture and ideas. 1926-to date. Quarterly (Spring, Summer, Autumn, Winter). Published by Fordham Univ. Ed., Joseph E. Grennen, Fordham Univ., Bronx, N. Y. 10458.

Subtitle varies.
Articles and book reviews, some of them in or on philosophy, index.

10.5 OTHER PHILOSOPHICAL SERIALS

Newsletters

10.5.1 **Le bulletin de philosophie médiévale**. 1954-to date. Annual. Pub. by Société Internationale pour l'Etude de la Philosophie Médiévale. Kardinaal Mercierplein 2, B-3000, Louvain, Belgique.

Carries information on contemporary work and activities concerned with medieval philosophy.

10.5.2 **Business and professional ethics**; a quarterly newsletter/report. Center for the Study of the Human Dimensions of Science

& Technology, Rensselaer Polytechnic Institute, Troy, N. Y. 12181.

Announcements, surveys of the literature, bibliographies, discussions, short articles.

10.5.3 Cartesian Newsletter. *See* 5.2.37.

10.5.4 Newsletter of the Center for Process Studies (12.2.4). 1975-to date. Quarterly. Center for Process Studies at the School of Theology at Claremont, 1325 N. College, Claremont, Calif. 91711.

10.5.5 Newsletter of the American Philosophical Association Committee on Philosophy and Medicine. John Ladd, Chm., Dept. of Philosophy, Brown Univ., Providence, RI 02912.

Calendar, announcements, reports, bibliography.

10.5.6 Newsletter of the International Society for Neoplatonic Studies. No. 1, Feb. 1976-to date. Ed., R. Baine Harris, Old Dominion Univ., Norfolk, Va. 23508.

10.5.7 Newsletter on science, technology, and human values. Quarterly (Oct., Jan., April, June). Aiken Computation Laboratory 231, Harvard Univ., Cambridge, Mass. 02138.

News items, calendar, legislative report, bibliography, short articles.
Formerly: *Newsletter of the Program on Public Conceptions of Science.*

10.5.8 Philosophy and technology. A newsletter published by the Univ. of Delaware. October, 1975-to date. Ed., Paul T. Durbin, Dept. of Philosophy, Univ. of Delaware, Newark, Del. 19711.

10.5.9 The Price-Priestley newsletter. Eds., Martin Fitzpatrick, Dept. of History, and D. O. Thomas, Dept. of Philosophy, The University College of Wales, Aberystwyth, Wales, U. K.

Designed for scholars interested in the lives, thought, and work of Richard Price

(1723-91) and Joseph Priestley (1733-1804).

10.5.10 Relevance logic newsletter. Jan. 1976-to date. At least 3 times yearly. Eds., Kenneth W. Collier and Robert G. Wolf, Dept. of Philosophical Studies, Southern Illinois Univ., Edwardsville, Ill. 62026.

Abstracts, short papers, reviews, work in progress.

See also: 5.2.14, 5.2.79, 5.2.197, 5.2.239, 5.2.266, 6.2.35, 6.2.64, 7.2.34, 7.3.18, 7.12.13, 8.5.8, 8.6.4, 8.6.10, 10.4.13, 12.1.27

Proceedings and Annuals

10.5.11 American Catholic philosophical association. Proceedings. 1926-to date. Annual. Ed., George F. McLean.

1944 not published.
Contains all papers presented at annual meetings; Association reports; list of members. Each annual meeting is devoted to a particular problem.
Issued by the Office of the National Secretary of the Association, The Catholic University of America, Washington, D. C. 20064.
Cum. index: vols. 1-39 (1926-65).
Partially reprinted: Johnson Reprint Corp.

10.5.12 American philosophical association (12.1.23). Proceedings and addresses. Ed., John O'Connor. 1926-to date. 6 nos. yearly.

Frequency varies. Annual to v.49 (1975-76).
Presidential addresses, proceedings, officers, Association reports, list of members, grants and fellowships, teaching, announcements.
Proceedings 1902-26 were printed in the *Philosophical Review* (10.2.92). Now published by the Association, Univ. of Delaware, Newark, Delaware 19711.
Cum. index: vols. 1-39 (1926-65).

10.5.13 American philosophical society. Proceedings. 1838-to date. Early proceedings . . . from the manuscript of its meetings from 1744 to 1838 in vol. 22, pt. 3.

Cum. index: vols. 1-100 (1838-1957). 3v.
——-. *Transactions*. 1769-1809 (vols. 1-6); 1818 (ns. vol. 1)-to date. Bi-monthly.

Though not concerned only with philosophy, papers and monographs on philosophy are included.

Published by the Society, 104 S. Fifth St., Philadelphia, Pa. 19106.

10.5.14 Annales de l'Institut de Philosophie. 1969-to date. Annual. Ed., Ch. Perelman. Editions de l'Université de Bruxelles. Institut de Philosophie, Avenue AD Buyl 145, B1050, Bruxelles, Belgium.

Publishes 8-10 articles per year in all areas of philosophy. Also book reviews.

10.5.15 Aristotelian society for the systematic study of philosophy. Proceedings. 1887-96 (vols. 1-3); 1900 (ns. vol. 1)-to date. Annual. Ed., A. A. Kassman, 31 West Heath Drive, London NW11 7GQ, England.

1897-1900 published in *Mind* (10.2.76), vols. 5-9.
Contains papers read before the Society. Supplementary volumes of symposia, 1918-to date.
Reprinted: Johnson Reprint Corp. Os. vols. 1-3 (1887/8-1896); ns. vols. 1-61 (1900-1960/61); supplements, vols. 1-34 (1918-60).

10.5.16 Center for Philosophic Exchange. Annual proceedings. State University of New York at Brockport, N. Y. 14420. Director: Joseph Gilbert. 1969-to date.

Publishes papers presented at the Center.

10.5.17 Danish year-book of philosophy. Organ of the Danish Society for Philosophy and Psychology. 1964-to date. Annual. Eds., Mogens Blegvad (et al.), Univ. of Copenhagen, Dept. of Philosophy, Kobmagergade 50, DK-1150, Copenhagen, Denmark.

English, occasionally French or German, papers of varying length on philosophical topics, preferably written by Danish philosophers.

10.5.18 International Congress of Philosophy: Proceedings. *See* 12.1.9.

Reprinted: vols. 5-17, 10-11, N. Y., Kraus Reprints.

10.5.19 Nomos. Yearbook of the American society for political and legal philosophy. 1958-to date. Annual.

Each volume contains papers on a particular theme or topic (e.g., vol. 1, Authority).
Publisher varies. Recent volumes have been published by The Atherton Press (New York).

10.5.20 The philosopher's annual. 1978-to date. Eds., David L. Boyer, Patrick Grim, and John T. Sanders. Totowa, N. J., Rowman and Littlefield, Publishers.

Reprints the ten outstanding articles (as chosen by the journal's board) published in philosophical journals each year.

10.5.21 Philosophic exchange (12.2.22); the annual proceedings of the Center for Philosophic Exchange. 1971-to date. State Univ. of New York, College of Arts & Sciences at Brockport, N. Y. 14420.

10.5.22 Philosophy of education society. Proceedings of the annual meeting. 1958 (vol. 14)-to date. Annual.

Vols. 1-13 not published.

10.5.23 Proceedings of the International Congress of Medieval Philosophy. *See* 12.1.18.

10.5.24 Studia philosophica; Jahrbuch der schweizerischen philosophischen Gesellschaft; annuaire de la société suisse de philosophie. 1941-to date. Annual. Eds., Daniel Christoff and Hans Saner, 11, CH des Fleurettes, 1007 Lausanne. Basel, Verlag für Recht und Gesellschaft.

Also supplements, 1943-to date.
Contains articles, book reviews, critical studies.

Supplementary vol. II: *Bibliographie der philosophischen, psychologischen und pädagogischen Literatur in der deutschsprachigen Schweiz 1900-1940*. Continued in vol. 5 for 1941-44, and in later volumes.

See also: 13.2.15.

Lecture Series

10.5.25 Aquinas lecture. 1937-to date. Annual.

Sponsored by Marquette University and the Aristotelian Society of Milwaukee, Wis. Published by Marquette University Press. Lecturers have included M. Adler, J. Maritain, E. Gilson, J. Collins, and P. Weiss.

10.5.26 Paul Carus lectures. 1925-to date.

Sponsored by the American Philosophical Association (the lecturer is selected biannually by a special committee) and the Edward C. Hegeler Foundation. The lectures are delivered alternately at one of the divisional meetings of the American Philosophical Assn. (e.g., R. Chisholm presented the 16th annual lectures at the 1967 meetings of the Pacific Division; C. Hempel presented the 17th annual lectures at the 1970 meetings of the Western Division). Published by Open Court. Lecturers have included J. Dewey, G. H. Mead, C. I. Lewis, C. J. Ducasse, G. Boas, B. Blanshard, E. Nagel, and R. McKeon.

10.5.27 Deems lectures. 1895-to date. Irregular.

Sponsored by New York University; endowed by the American Institute of Christian Philosophy. Publisher varies, though recent lectures have been published by the New York University Press.
Lecturers have included F. S. C. Northrop and J. M. Bochenski.

10.5.28 Dewey lectures. 1968-to date.

Sponsored by Columbia University. The lectures are given once every two years.
The first lecturer was W. V. O. Quine.

10.5.29 Ernst Cassirer Lectures. Yale University Press.

Recent lectures include:
L. W. Beck, The actor and the spectator;
L. Kolakowski, Husserl and the search for certitude.

10.5.30 Gifford Lectures. Aberdeen University.

Publishers vary. The series has included: Josiah Royce, *The world and the individual*, 1899-1900;
John Dewey, *The quest for certainty*, 1929;
Etienne Gilson, *L'esprit de la philosophie médiévale*, 1939;
W. D. Ross, *Foundations of ethics*, 1939;
G. Marcel, *The mystery of being*, 1949/50.

10.5.31 Howison lecture. 1927-to date. Irregular.

Sponsored by California University, Berekley, published in 10.5.40.
Lecturers have included C. I. Lewis, W. H. Sheldon, G. Boas, and B. Blanshard.

10.5.32 John Locke Lectures. Oxford.

Published by the Clarendon Press. Irregular.

10.5.33 Lindley lecture. 1961-to date. Annual.

Sponsored by the Dept. of Philosophy, The Univ. of Kansas. Lectures on the theme "Values of Living," broadly conceived. Published by the Department.
Lecturers have included R. B. Brandt, R. M. Chisholm, S. Hampshire, W. K. Frankena, W. Sellars, P. Ricoeur, R. M. Hare, A. Gewirth and P. Foot.
Most of the lectures through 1975 have been issued in *Freedom and Morality*, ed., John Bricke, Univ. of Kansas Humanistic Studies, 46, 1976.

10.5.34 Terry lectures. 1925-to date. Irregular.

Sponsored by Yale University. Lectures on

Religion in the Light of Science and Philosophy. Published by Yale University Press.
Lecturers have included W. P. Montague, C. G. Jung, J. Dewey, W. E. Hocking, J. Maritain, C. Hartshorne, P. Tillich, and E. E. Harris.

10.5.35 The Thalheimer Lectures. 1968- . Biennial. Thalheimer Foundation and the Dept. of Philosophy, Johns Hopkins Univ.

10.5.36 William James lectures on philosophy. 1929-to date. Irregular.

Sponsored by Harvard University to honor the memory of William James.
Lecturers have included John Dewey (*Art as Experience*), A. O. Lovejoy (*The Great Chain of Being*), E. Gilson (*The Unity of Philosophical Experience*), and J. L. Austin (*How to Do Things with Words*).
Publisher varies.

10.5.37 Woodbridge lectures. 1943-to date. Irregular.

Sponsored by Columbia University and published by Columbia University Press.
Lecturers have included W. Sheldon, S. P. Lamprecht, C. I. Lewis, and I. Berlin.

Selected Series

10.5.38 Boston College studies in philosophy. The Hague, Nijhoff, 1966-to date. Annual.

Each volume contains a group of essays, usually on a common theme.

10.5.39 Boston studies in the philosophy of science.

Vol. I, Dordrecht, Holland, D. Reidel, 1963;
vols. II-VIII, irregular, Atlantic Highlands, N. J., Humanities Press;
vol. IX-to date, Dordrecht, Holland, D. Reidel.
Many volumes consist of the proceedings of the Boston Colloquium for the Philosophy of Science.

10.5.40 California University publications in philosophy. Berkeley, University of California Press, 1904-to date. Frequency varies.

Contains monographs and, since 1923, lectures delivered before the Philosophical Union.
Reprinted: vols. 1-25 (1904-50), Johnson Reprint Corp.

10.5.41 Catholic University of America. Philosophical studies. Catholic University of America Press. Irregular.

Vols. 1-33 issued without series title and numbering. Contains dissertations in philosophy accepted at Catholic University.

10.5.42 Catholic University of America. Studies in philosophy and the history of philosophy. Washington, D.C., Catholic University of America Press, 1961-to date. Irregular.

Each volume is a collection of essays, sometimes on a specific topic.

10.5.43 Duquesne studies. Philosophical series. Published by Duquesne Univ. 1952-to date. Irregular.

Contains primarily monographs, with some tendency towards phenomenology. Though irregular, volumes have appeared on the average of one a year.

10.5.44 History of ideas in ancient Greece. (49 books) Adv. Ed., Gregory Vlastos. New York, Arno Press.

A reprint series.

10.5.45 Iowa publications in philosophy. The Hague, Nijhoff, 1963-to date. Irregular.

Sponsored by the Dept. of Philosophy, Iowa Univ. "A series of analytical studies— essay collections, monographs, books—in ontology, the history of philosophy, the philosophy of science, and other branches of philosophy."

10.5.46 Library of exact philosophy. Ed., Mario Bunge. Wien and New York, Springer.

A series of volumes "to keep alive the spirit, if not the letter, of the Vienna Circle."

10.5.47 **Schilpp, Paul A.**, *ed.* The library of living philosophers. 1939- . Publishers vary. Most recent is La Salle, Ill., Open Court.

Individual volumes on: John Dewey (1939), George Santayana (1940), Alfred North Whitehead (1941), G. E. Moore (1942), Bertrand Russell (1944), Ernst Cassirer (1949), Albert Einstein (1949), Sarvepalli Radhakrishnan (1952), Karl Jaspers (1957), C. D. Broad (1959), Rudolf Carnap (1963), Martin Buber (1967), C. I. Lewis (1968), Karl Popper (1974). In preparation: Gabriel Marcel, Brand Blanshard, Georg Henrik von Wright, W. V. Quine, Jean-Paul Sartre.

Each volume contains essays appraising the philosopher's work, his reply to these essays, a bibliography of his work and his autobiography.

10.5.48 **Modern studies in philosophy.** Univ. of Notre Dame Press.

Collections of critical essays. Individual volumes on Aristotle, Descartes, Hegel, Hume, Kant, Leibniz, Mill, Locke and Berkeley, Plato, Spinoza, and Wittgenstein.

Most are reissues of Doubleday paperbacks.

10.5.49 **Muirhead library of philosophy.** Gen. ed., H. D. Lewis. 1890-to date. London, Allen & Unwin.

U. S. publisher varies. Irregular.

10.5.50 **Phaenomenologica.** A series sponsored by the Husserl Archives, Louvain. The Hague, Nijhoff, 1958- .

A collection founded by H. L. von Breda, devoted to works in phenomenology.

10.5.51 **Philosophical monographs.** 1976-to date. 4 monographs yearly. Ed., Joseph Margolis.

Publisher varies. 1978- , Temple University Press.

10.5.52 **Philosophy and medicine.** Eds., H. Tristram Engelhardt, Jr. and Stuart F. Spicker. Dordrecht, Holland, D. Reidel.

10.5.53 **The philosophy of Plato and Aristotle.** Ed., Gregory Vlastos. New York, Arno Press, 1973.

A collection of 26 books including Cataloging in Publication (CIP) data as provided by Library of Congress.

10.5.54 **Research in phenomenology.** 1971-to date. 1 vol. per year. Eds., John Sallis et al. Duquesne Univ., Pittsburgh, Pa. 15219. Atlantic Highlands, N. J., Humanities Press.

10.5.55 **Sovietica.** Publication and monographs of the Institute of East-European Studies, Univ. of Fribourg, Switzerland. Ed., Thomas J. Blakeley. Dordrecht, Holland, D. Reidel.

Publishes monographs on Soviet and East European philosophy.

10.5.56 **Studies in logic and the foundations of mathematics.** 1963-to date. Eds., A. Heyting et al. Atlantic Highlands, N. J., Humanities Press.

50 vols. of logical and mathematical theories and analyses. Irregular.

10.5.57 **Studies in phenomenology and existential philosophy.** General ed., James M. Edie. Bloomington, Indiana University Press.

Publishes translations of works in the area as well as original monographs.

10.5.58 **Studies in philosophy.** Vols. 1-26. The Hague, Mouton.

10.5.59 **Studies in philosophy and the history of philosophy.** 1960-to date. Ed., John K. Ryan, 300 Saint Bonaventure Hall, The Catholic Univ. of America, Washington, D. C. 20064.

Published at irregular intervals by Catholic Univ. of America and is bound in book form. The most recent volume was published in 1973. 50% of articles are invited.

10.5.60 Studies in the foundations, methodology and philosophy of science. 1967-to date. Ed., Mario Bunge, McGill Univ., in collaboration with P. G. Bergmann, S. Flugge, H. Margenau, P. Medawar, K. Popper, P. Suppes, and C. A. Truesdell. Berlin, Hendeberg, N. Y., Springer.

10.5.61 Synthese library. Eds., Donald Davidson et al. Dordrecht, Holland, D. Reidel.

Monographs on epistemology, logic, methodology, philosophy of science, sociology of science and of knowledge, and on the mathematical methods of social and behavioral sciences.

10.5.62 Theory and decision library; an international series in the philosophy and methodology of the social and behavioral sciences. 1974-to date. Eds., Gerald Eberlein and Werner Lein Fellner. Dordrecht, Holland, D. Reidel.

A series of monographs and symposia on the philosophy and methodology of the social and behavioral sciences.

Connected with the journal *Theory and decision* (10.2.131).

10.5.63 Tulane studies in philosophy. 1952-to date. Annual. Ed., Robert C. Whittemore, Dept. of Philosophy, Tulane Univ., New Orleans, La. 70118. The Hague, Nijhoff.

Vols. 1-19, New Orleans, Tulane University.

Each volume dedicated to a particular theme or topic.

10.5.64 Vienna Circle collection. About 30 vols, 1973-80. Eds., Robert S. Cohen et al. Dordrecht, Holland, D. Reidel.

Basically a series of anthologies translated into English of the most important work of single members, which contain, besides a detailed essay on the man, a complete bibliography of his work.

See also: 12.1.51.

11. PHILOSOPHICAL WRITING AND PUBLISHING

The results of research are frequently submitted by students in the form of papers, theses, and dissertations, and by scholars in book or article form. It is primarily by publication that knowledge is disseminated widely among specialists in any field, and that discoveries or insights can be shared with others, criticized, corrected, and used in turn to advance knowledge further. Form and style guides are listed in 11.1; books concerning the various facets of publishing (indexing, proofreading, etc.) are listed in 11.2.

11.1 THE PHILOSOPHICAL REPORT: FORM AND STYLE

11.1.1 **Albaugh, Ralph M.** Thesis writing; a guide to scholarly style. Paterson, N. J., Littlefield, Adams, 1960. 149 pp.

A short practical guide to the mechanical aspects of preparing a thesis in final form.

11.1.2 **Allen, George R.** The graduate students' guide to theses and dissertations; a practical manual for writing and research. San Francisco, Jossey-Bass, 1973. 108 pp.

A useful and informative guide.

11.1.3 **The Barnhart dictionary of new English since 1963.** Clarence L. Barnhart, Sol Steinmetz and Robert K. Barnhart, eds. Brownville, N. Y., Barnhart/Harper & Row, 1973. 512 pp.

11.1.4 **Bernstein, Theodore Menline.** The careful writer; a modern guide to English usage. New York, Atheneum, 1966. 487 pp.

Idioms, corrections, errors; alphabetical arrangement.

11.1.5 **Blanshard, Brand.** On philosophical style. Bloomington, Indiana University Press, 1954. 69 pp.

An urbane essay on clear writing as a vehicle of clear thought.

11.1.6 **Campbell, William Giles,** and **Stephen Vaughan Ballou.** Form and style: theses, reports, term papers. 4th ed. Boston, Houghton Mifflin, 1974. 177 pp.

11.1.7 **Chicago University Press.** A manual of style for authors, editors, and copywriters. 12th ed. Chicago, University of Chicago Press, 1969. 546 pp.

A basic manual used and recommended by many publishers. Contains information on manuscript preparation, copyright, obtaining permissions, matters of style, specimens of type, and production and printing.

11.1.8 **Copperud, Roy H.** Words on paper; a manual of prose style for professional writers, reporters, authors, editors, publishers, and teachers. New York, Hawthorn Books, 1960. 286 pp.

11.1.9 **Coyle, William.** Research papers. 2d ed. New York, Odyssey, 1965. 124 pp.

11.1.10 **Evans, Bergen,** and **Cornelia Evans.**

A dictionary of contemporary American usage. New York, Random House, 1957. 567 pp.

11.1.11 **Fowler, Henry Watson**. A dictionary of modern English usage. 2d ed., rev. by Sir Ernest Gowers. Oxford, Clarendon Press, 1965. 725 pp.

1st ed. 1926.

11.1.12 **Guitton, Jean**. A student's guide to intellectual work. Trans. by Adrienne Foulke. Notre Dame, Ind., University of Notre Dame Press, 1964. 155 pp.

A presentation of the author's view on how to study, think, and write.

11.1.13 **Gourmont, Robert de**. La dissertation philosophique; conseils pour préparer et rédiger la dissertation philosophique et méthode pour faire des progrès en cet exercice. 3. éd. Paris, O. R. A. C., 1966. 78 pp.

11.1.14 **Hook, Lucyle**, and **Mary Virginia Gaver**. The research paper. 2d ed. New York, Prentice-Hall, 1952. 85 pp.

11.1.15 **Hurt, Peyton**. Bibliography and footnotes; a style manual for students and writers. 3d ed., rev. and enl. by Mary L. Hurt Richmond. Berkeley and Los Angeles, University of California Press, 1968. 163 pp.

11.1.16 **Jordan, Lewis**, *ed.* The New York times manual of style and usage: a desk book of guidelines for writers and editors. New York, Quadrangle/N. Y. Times Book Co., 1976. 231 pp.

A guide for manuscript preparation.

11.1.17 **Kinney, Mary R.** Bibliographical style manuals; a guide to their use in documentation and research. Chicago, Association of College and Reference Libraries, 1953. 21 pp.

11.1.18 **Koefod, Paul E.** The writing requirements for graduate degrees. Englewood Cliffs, N. J., Prentice-Hall, 1964. 268 pp.

A discussion of thesis and dissertation writing and of graduate schools in general; an appendix reprints some pertinent articles by others, and lists model prospectuses of theses and dissertations.

11.1.19 **Koren, Henry J.** Research in philosophy; a bibliographical introduction to philosophy and a few suggestions for dissertations. Pittsburgh, Duquesne University Press, 1966. 203 pp.

Chapter 6: A few suggestions about dissertations.

11.1.20 **Matczak, Sebastian A.** Research and composition in philosophy. New York, Humanities Press, and Louvain, Nauwelaerts, 1968. 88 pp.

A guide for beginning undergraduate students.

11.1.21 **MLA handbook for writers of research papers, theses, and dissertations**. New York, Modern Language Association, 1977. 163 pp.

Based on MLA Style Sheet (1951), as revised in 1970.

11.1.22 **The MLA style sheet**. By William Riley Parker. 2d ed. 1970. 48 pp.

Obtainable from The Materials Center, Modern Language Association, 62 Fifth Ave., New York, N. Y. 10011.

A style sheet recommended by many philosophical journals. Contains information on preparing the manuscript, documentation, abbreviations, submitting the manuscript, proofreading, preparation of Masters' and Doctors' theses, and guidelines for abstracting scholarly articles.

11.1.23 **Morris, William**, and **Mary Morris**, *eds.* Harper dictionary of contemporary usage. New York, Harper & Row. 650 pp.

11.1.24 **Nicholson, Margaret**. A dictionary of American-English usage based on Fowler's

Modern English usage. New York, Oxford University Press, 1957. 671 pp.

11.1.25 **Nicholson, Margaret**. A practical style guide for authors and editors. New York, Holt, 1967. 143 pp.

Brief, clear instructions addressed to both the author and the copy editor. Indexed.

11.1.26 **Pugh, Griffith Thompson**. Guide to research writing. 2d ed. Boston, Houghton Mifflin, 1963. 56 pp.

11.1.27 **Richards, Paul I.**, and **Irving T. Richards**. Proper words in proper places; writing to inform. Boston, The Christopher Publishing House, 1964. 206 pp.

The strategy and mechanics of writing and proofreading.

11.1.28 **Strunk, William, Jr.**, and **Elwyn Brooks White**. The elements of style. 2d ed. New York, Macmillan, 1972. 78 pp.

A small, concise guide. One of the best.

11.1.29 **Seeber, Edward Derbyshire**. A style manual for authors. Bloomington, Indiana University Press, 1965. 96 pp.

Endeavors to clarify the author-printer relationship and publishers' requirements. Its procedures correspond to those of the MLA Style Sheet (11.1.22).

11.1.30 **Turabian, Kate L.** A manual for writers of term papers, theses, and dissertations. 4th ed. Chicago, University of Chicago Press, 1973. 216 pp.

A widely used guide for undergraduate and graduate students.

11.1.31 **U. S. Government Printing Office**. Style manual. Rev. ed. Washington, D. C., Government Printing Office, 1973. 548 pp.

Gives the practices of the Government Printing Office on preparing copy and rules of style. Frequently revised.

11.1.32 **U. S. Library of Congress. General reference and bibliography division**. Bibliographical procedures and style; a manual for bibliographers in the Library of Congress. By Blanche P. McCrum and Helen D. Jones. Washington, D. C., Government Printing Office, 1954; reprinted 1966 with list of abbreviations. 133 pp.

A guide to the forms of entry used by the Library of Congress.

11.1.33 **Van Steenberghen, Fernand**. Directives pour la confection d'une monographie scientifique avec applications concrètes aux recherches sur la philosophie médiévale. 2. éd. Louvain, Editions de l'Institut Supérieur de Philosophie, 1949. 86 pp.

11.2 SCHOLARLY PUBLISHING

11.2.1 **American book trade directory**; lists of publishers, booksellers, periodicals, trade organizations, wholesalers, etc. New York, Bowker, 1915- .

Title varies. Published about every two years. 22d ed. 1975-76.
Information about the American book market and markets abroad.

11.2.2 **Association of American University Presses**. Directory. New York, American University Press Service. 1947-to date.

Frequency varies; now issued every two years.
Available from the AAUP.
Lists addresses, officers, organizations, and publication interest of each university press.

11.2.3 **Association of American University Presses**. Scholarly books in America. 1959-to date. Quarterly. Published by the University of Chicago with the cooperation of the Association of American University Presses.

A quarterly bibliography sent free to scholars and libraries to keep them informed about scholarly publishing in North America. Contains brief articles and notes about university press publishing, and an annotated listing of publications issued by AAUP members.

11.2.4 **Balkin, Richard**. A writer's guide to book publishing. New York, Hawthorne Books, 1977. 236 pp.

A non-technical discussion of the steps of getting a manuscript published.

11.2.5 **Carey, G. V.** Making an index. 3d ed. New York, Cambridge University Press, 1963. 17 pp.

11.2.6 **Cargill, O.** [et al.]. The publication of academic writing. New York, Modern Language Association, 1966. 24 pp.

How to prepare a book for publication, how to choose a publisher, how to negotiate with him.

11.2.7 **Cassell's directory of publishing in Great Britain, the Commonwealth and Ireland**. London, Cassell, 1976-77. 581 pp.

1st ed. 1960-61.

11.2.8 **Collison, Robert**. Indexing books; a manual of basic principles. New York, John de Graff, 1962. 96 pp.

A succinct and useful guide.

11.2.9 **Dessauer, John P.** Book publishing: what it is, what it does. New York, Bowker, 1974. 231 pp.

11.2.10 **Directory of publishing opportunities**. 2d ed. Orange, N. J., Academic Media, 1973.

"A comprehensive guide to publishing opportunities in every major academic, research, scholarly and technical field."

11.2.11 **Gill, Robert S.** The author-publisher-printer complex. 3d ed. Baltimore, Williams & Wilkins, 1960. 138 pp.

A brief guide to terms, copy, proof, etc., including royalties.

11.2.12 **Hawes, Gene R.** To advance knowledge; a handbook on American university press publishing. New York, American University Press Service, 1967. 148 pp.

A discussion of scholarly publishing, with a chapter on "what the scholar and publisher expect of each other."

11.2.13 **International literary market place**. New York, Bowker, 1965- .

Biennial.
"A directory of publishers and book-trade organizations arranged by country."

11.2.14 **Lasky, Joseph.** Proofreading and copy-preparation; a textbook for the graphic arts industry. New York, Mentor Books, 1954. 656 pp.

1st ed. 1941.
A useful guide.

11.2.15 **Literary market place**; with names and numbers; the directory of American book publishing. New York, Bowker, 1940- . Annual.

Lists personnel and addresses of book publishers, advertising agencies, author's agents, associations, book manufacturers, and other aspects of commercial publishing.

11.2.16 **Moulton, Janice M.** Guidebook for publishing philosophy. Rev. and updated ed. Newark, Del., American Philosophical Association, 1977. 151 pp.

Descriptions of over 60 journals, 19 book publishers, and recent APA program committee evaluations.

11.2.17 **Nicholson, Margaret.** A manual of copyright practice for writers, publishers, and agents. 2d ed. New York, Oxford University Press, 1956. 273 pp.

A useful guide. The appendix reprints the text of the U. S. Copyright Law and of the Universal Copyright Convention.

11.2.18 **On the publication of research**;

essays by R. B. McKerrow and Henry M. Silver. New York, Modern Language Association, 1964. 20 pp.

"Trenchant advice on how to turn research into readable articles."

11.2.19 Scholarly publishing; a journal for authors and publishers. 1969-to date. Quarterly. Ed., Eleanor Harman, University of Toronto Press, Toronto, Canada M5S 1A6.

Articles, book reviews, correspondence, editorial positions available, index.

An international quarterly which aims to encourage scholarly publication by providing a forum for discussion and a source of current information and advice on developing manuscripts, editorial techniques, book production, sales and promotion, and related areas.

11.2.20 Skillin, Marjorie E. Words into type. Based on studies by Marjorie E. Skillin and Robert M. Gay, and other authorities. 3d ed., completely revised. Englewood Cliffs, N. J., Prentice-Hall, 1974. 585 pp.

Sections on manuscript preparation, copy and proof, typography and illustrations, printing, style, grammar, and use of words.

11.2.21 Smith, Datus Clifford, Jr. A guide to book publishing. New York, Bowker, 1966. 244 pp.

Explains the general principles of book publishing. Chapters include "The book-publishing process" and "Kinds of book-publishing."
Bibliography: pp. 229-33.

11.2.22 Spiker, Sina. Indexing your book; a practical guide for authors. 2d ed. Madison, University of Wisconsin Press, 1963. 40 pp.

11.2.23 Thomas, David St. John, and **Hubert Bermont**. Getting published: an author's

guide to book publishing. New York, Harper & Row, 1973. 188 pp.

11.2.24 Peters, Jean. The bookman's glossary. 5th ed. New York, Bowker, 1975. 169 pp.

11.2.25 Welter, Rush. Problems of scholarly publication in the humanities and social sciences; a report prepared for the Committee on Scholarly Publication of the American Council of Learned Societies. New York, American Council of Learned Societies, 1959. 81 pp.

An informative report on both book and scholarly journal publication.

11.2.26 Unwin, Stanley. The truth about publishing. 8th ed. rev. and partly rewritten. London, Allen & Unwin, 1976. 256 pp.

1st ed. 1926.
An informal discussion of book publishing written for authors by a distinguished publisher.

11.2.27 Wiles, Roy M. Scholarly reporting in the humanities. 4th ed. Toronto, University of Toronto Press, 1968. 58 pp.

A guide to format and style.

11.2.28 The writer's directory, 1971/73-. New York, St. Martin's Press.

Periodically revised.
Includes bibliographies, information on American authors, English authors, and publishers and publishing.

11.2.29 Writer's market. Cincinnati, Writer's Digest. 1931- . Annual.

25th ed. 1969. Frequency varied in the early years of its publication.
Contains lists of commercial book and journal publishers, but some of its notes on publishing apply equally well to scholarly publishing.

12. PHILOSOPHICAL PROFESSIONAL LIFE

Philosophical meetings serve a variety of purposes. They give philosophers a chance to meet one another so they can discuss, exchange ideas, compare views, and engage in dialogue both formally and informally. Some meetings bring together philosophers of similar interests; some, philosophers of diverse interests. Some meetings are centered on a particular topic for intensive discussion of it; others offer discussions of a variety of topics. Many offer philosophers the opportunity to overcome both geographic and intellectual provincialism; they give young philosophers a chance to hear known and established philosophers, as well as allowing the young themselves to be heard. They sometimes provide the possibility for those seeking teaching positions to meet those who have such positions available.

Philosophical meetings take place on many levels: local, regional, national, and international. Usually they are sponsored by philosophical societies or groups at appropriate levels. Some societies have as their sole function the calling of meetings, while others also publish a journal, represent the interests of philosophers on the regional or national scene, sponsor research by awarding or administering grants, and so on. Notices of meetings are frequently carried in journals. The *Philosophical Calendar* published by the Conference of Philosophical Societies (12.1.33) is the most complete list of forthcoming philosophical meetings.

There are a number of philosophical centers and institutes (12.2) at which specialized philosophical research is carried on. Information about other professional associations can be obtained from the *Encyclopedia of Associatons* (12.3.1).

The funding of scholarly research in philosophy comes largely from colleges and universities in the form of research grants and paid sabbatical leaves. Other sources of support include private foundations and government grants. Guides to research opportunities and a selected list of foundations can be found in 12.4.

Most professional philosophers in the United States are professors of philosophy at an educational institution. Information on teaching philosophy is not as well organized as information on research in philosophy. Some sources are listed in 12.5. In general information on teaching is best obtained from the department of philosophy in which one does his or her graduate work.

12.1 PHILOSOPHICAL ASSOCIATIONS AND MEETINGS

International Associations and Congresses

12.1.1 **International congress calendar;** 1960/61- . Brussels, Union of International Associations, 1961- . Annual.

Lists forthcoming international congresses projected as far ahead as five years.

12.1.2 **The Division of Logic, Methodology and Philosophy of Science,** of the International Union of the History and Philosophy of Science (IUHPS). Founded 1956.

Among its purposes, it organizes periodic

international congresses for logic, methodology, and the philosophy of science. The first general congress was held in Stanford in 1960. Other congresses have been held in Amsterdam, Oxford, Warsaw, and Helsinki, and some have been devoted to special topics.

12.1.3 Interamerican Congress of Philosophy.

Meets once every three years. The first Congress met in Port-au-Prince, 1944; II, New York, 1947; III, Mexico City, 1950; IV, Santiago de Chile, 1956; V, Washington, 1957; VI, Buenos Aires, 1959; VII, Quebec, 1967; VIII, Brazilia, 1972; IX, Caracas, 1977.

Secretary of the Interamerican Society of Philosophy: Prof. Julio C. Lizarraga, Apdo. 50371, Sabana Grande, Caracas, Venezuela.

12.1.4 Interamerican Society of Philosophy. Founded 1954. President: Ernesto Mayz Vallenilla (Venezuela).

Since 1956, meets with the Interamerican Congress of Philosophy. The IV Interamerican Congress of Philosophy is also called the first meeting of the Interamerican society.

12.1.5 International Association for Philosophy and Literature. Affiliated with World Institute for Advanced Phenomenological Research and Learning (12.2.14). Founded 1974.

12.1.6 International Association for Philosophy of Law and Social Philosophy. Founded 1959.

Gen.-sec.: Carl Wellman, Dept. of Philosophy, Washington Univ., St. Louis, Mo.

Sponsors international congresses every four years.

See 12.1.25.

12.1.7 International Berkeley Society. *See* 5.2.17.

12.1.8 International Executive Committee for International Congresses of Aesthetics.

President: Etienne Souriau, 3 Rue Michelet, Paris-Vle, France. Sponsors Congresses

every four years. The VIth Congress was held in Uppsala, 1968, the VIIth in Bucharest, 1973.

12.1.9 International Federation of Societies of Philosophy (IFSP). Founded 1948. Secretariat: Institut des Sciences Exactes, Sidlerstrasse 5, CH-3012 Berne, Switzerland.

Since its founding it has assumed the organization of the five-yearly International Congress of Philosophy. The first International Congress of Philosophy was held in 1900 in Paris; II, Geneva, 1904; III, Heidelberg, 1908; IV, Bologne, 1911; V, Naples, 1924; VI, Cambridge, Mass., 1926; VII, Oxford, 1930; VIII, Prague, 1934; IX, Paris, 1937; X, Amsterdam, 1948; XI, Brussels, 1953; XII, Venice, 1958; XIII, Mexico City, 1963; XIV, Vienna, 1968; XV, Varna, 1973; XVI, Düsseldorf, 1978.

The Proceedings are published.

Reprinted: I-II, N. Y., Kraus Reprints.

12.1.10 International Husserl and Phenomenological Research Society. *See* 5.2.109.

12.1.11 International Phenomenological Society. Founded 1939. Address: c/o Marvin Farber, State Univ. of New York at Buffalo, Buffalo, N. Y. 14260.

Its aim is to further the understanding, development and application of phenomenological inquiries as inaugurated by E. Husserl.

Publishes *Philosophy and Phenomenological Research* (10.2.96).

12.1.12 International Scotistic Society. Founded 1966. Segreteria della Società Internazionale Scotista, 00185 Roma, Via Merulana, 124B, Italia.

2nd Congress, 1966, Great Britain (Oxford-Edinburgh); 3rd Congress, 1970, Vienna.

12.1.13 International Society for Chinese Philosophy. Founded 1978. Annual meeting. Prof. Lik Kuen Tong, Dept. of Philosophy, Fairfield University, Fairfield, Conn. 06430.

12.1.14 International Society for Metaphysics. Founded 1973. Sec.-Treas., George F. McLean, Catholic Univ. of America, Washington, D. C. 20064.

I, 1973, Varna; II, 1976, Santiniketan; III, 1976 New York City; IV, 1977, Jerusalem; V, 1978, Düsseldorf.

12.1.15 International Society for Neoplatonic Studies. Founded 1973.

Information: R. Baine Harris, Dept. of Philosophy, Old Dominion Univ., Norfolk, Va. 23508.
Publishes a newsletter (10.5.6).

12.1.16 International Society for Phenomenology and the Sciences of Man. Founded July, 1976 in Arezzo-Sienna. Affiliated with World Phenomenology Institute (12.2.14).

12.1.17 International Society for the History of Ideas. Founded 1959.

Sec.: Dept. of Philosophy, Temple Univ., Philadelphia, Pa. 19122.
Publishes the *Journal of the History of Ideas* (10.2.63) and sponsors an international conference every three years.

12.1.18 International Society for the Study of Medieval Philosophy (ISSMP). Founded 1958.

Sec.: Kardinaal Mercierplein 2, B-300 Leuven, Belgium.
Membership is by nomination by a member. Publishes *Bulletin de philosophie médiévale*, which covers works in progress, national chronicles, and general information for those interested in medieval philosophy. Sponsors International Congresses of Medieval Philosophy: 1st Congress, Louvain, 1958; IId Congress, Cologne, 1961; IIId Congress, Bolzano, Italy, 1964; IVth Congress, Montreal, 1967; Vth Congress, Spain, 1972.

12.1.19 International Society of Logic and the Philosophy of Science.

Address: c/o F. Gonseth, Goldauerstrasse 60, Zürich, Switzerland.

12.1.20 World Union of Catholic Societies of Philosophy. Founded 1968.

Sec.-Gen.: P. Maximilian Roesle, Aignerstr. 25, Salzburg-Aigen, Austria.

U. S. Associations and Meetings

12.1.21 American Association for the Advancement of Science. Section L: The History and Philosophy of Science.

Holds annual meetings in December in alternate years with the Eastern Division of the APA and with the History of Science Society.

12.1.22 The American Catholic Philosophical Association (ACPA). Founded 1926.

Sec.: Catholic Univ. of America, Washington, D. C. 20064. The second largest U. S. philosophical association. Publishes the *Proceedings of the American Catholic Philosophical Association* (10.5.11), *The New Scholasticism* (10.2.80), and a Directory of Members.
Holds an annual meeting devoted to a single topic during the week after Easter. Also sponsors a Speakers' Bureau and a Personnel Placement Service.

12.1.23 American Philosophical Association (APA). Founded 1901.

United with the Western Philosophical Association and Philosophical Society of the Pacific Coast in 1926. National office: John O'Connor, Exec. Sec., Univ. of Delaware, Newark, Del. 19711.
The largest national association. Membership is open to those holding advanced degrees in philosophy, those engaged in careers of teaching philosophy, etc. Nomination for membership must be made by two members of the Association. Associate membership is available to students working toward the Ph.D.
The national organization consists of a board of officers and a number of committees.

Proceedings and Addresses of the American Philosophical Association (10.5.12) is published six times yearly. They contain the three Presidential Addresses and the programs for the annual meetings of the Association's three divisions: The Eastern Division, the Western Division, and the Pacific Division. They also contain committee and other reports and list of members. The association's standing committees are: The Committee on Lectures, Publications, and Research; The Committee on International Cooperation; The Committee on Career Opportunities; and The Committee on the Status and Future of the Profession.

The Association also publishes Jobs for Philosophers (six times yearly), which lists available positions.

See also: 10.5.5.

12.1.24 The American Society for Aesthetics. Founded 1942.

Address: Cleveland Museum of Art, 11150 East Blvd., Cleveland, Ohio 44106.

Publishes the *Journal of Aesthetics and Art Criticism* (10.2.49). Annual meetings in October.

12.1.25 American Section of the International Association for Philosophy of Law and Social Philosophy (AMINTAPHIL). Founded 1963.

Meets every two years.
Sec: Michael Bayles, Dept. of Philosophy, Univ. of Kentucky, Lexington, Ky.
See 12.1.6.

12.1.26 American Society for Political and Legal Philosophy. Founded 1955.

Address: c/o M. P. Golding, Dept. of Philosophy, Duke Univ., Durham, N. C. 27708. A candidate must be nominated by two members and elected to membership by the Membership Committee.

Its annual meetings follow (in rotation) the meetings of the American Philosophical Association, The American Political Science Association, and the Association of American Law Schools.

Publishes an annual volume devoted to

the topic of the meeting in *Nomos* (10.5.19).

12.1.27 American Society for Value Inquiry. Founded 1970.

Sec.: Stephan White, Dept. of Philosophy, East Tennessee State Univ., Johnson City, Tenn. 37601.

Annual meeting with the divisions of the American Philosophical Association.

12.1.28 Association for Philosophy of the Unconscious. Founded 1971. Dept. of Philosophy, Georgetown Univ., Washington, D. C. 20007.

"Forum for discussing the philosophical issues posed by psychoanalysis."

Pres.: Wilfried Ver Eecke.

Publishes a newsletter.

12.1.29 Association for Realistic Philosophy. Founded 1948.

Holds an annual meeting each fall and also meets in conjunction with the annual meetings of the Eastern Division of the APA.

12.1.30 Association for Symbolic Logic. Founded 1936.

Business office: P. O. Box 6248, Providence, R. I. 02940.

Membership is open to all persons interested in the work of the Association.

Publishes *The Journal of Symbolic Logic* (10.2.61).

Holds annual meetings, normally in conjunction with alternate annual meetings of the Eastern Division of the APA and of the American Mathematical Society.

12.1.31 Association of Philosophy Journal Editors. Founded 1971.

Sec.: Richard Lineback, Philosophy Documentation Center, Bowling Green State Univ., Bowling Green, Ohio 43403.

12.1.32 Charles S. Peirce Society. Founded 1946.

Publishes *Transactions of the Charles S.*

Peirce Society (10.2.135).
Holds an annual meeting with the Eastern Division of the APA.

12.1.33 Conference of Philosophical Societies. Founded 1977. Chm.: Richard De George, Dept. of Philosophy, Univ. of Kansas, Lawrence, Kans. 66045.

Annual meeting with the Eastern Division of the American Philosophical Association. Publishes *Philosophical Calendar.* Serves as a forum for common problems and joint activity by philosophical societies.

12.1.34 Division of Philosophical Psychology of the American Psychological Association. 1200 17th St. NW, Washington, D. C. 20036. Founded 1963.

Holds annual meetings together with the Association in September.

12.1.35 Duns Scotus Philosophical Association. Founded 1937.

Address: Our Lady of Angels Seminary, 3644 Rocky River Drive, Cleveland, Ohio. Holds an annual convention in April and other meetings twice a year.

12.1.36 Hegel Society of America. Founded 1969.

Treas.: Dept. of Philosophy, Marquette Univ., Milwaukee, Wis. 53233. Holds an annual meeting. Publishes a newsletter entitled *The Owl of Minerva* (5.2.79).

12.1.37 Hume Society. Founded 1974.

Dept. of Philosophy, Northern Illinois Univ., De Kalb, Ill. 60115. Annual meetings called "Hume Conferences." Publishes *Bulletin.*

12.1.38 The Metaphysical Society of America. Founded 1950.

Sec.: Eugene T. Long, Jr., Dept. of Philosophy, Univ. of South Carolina, Columbia, S. C. 29208.

Membership is open to those of demonstrated philosophical competence who are nominated by two members of the Society. Holds an annual meeting during the third weekend in March.

12.1.39 Personalist Discussion Group. Founded 1938.

Address: Philosophy Dept., 745 Commonwealth Ave., Boston Univ., Boston, Mass. 02215. Holds an annual meeting in conjunction with the Eastern Division of the APA.

12.1.40 Philosophic Society for the Study of Sport. Founded 1972.

R. Scott Kretchmar, Faculty of Physical Education, SUC Brockport, Brockport, N. Y. 14420. Annual meeting. Publishes *Journal of the Philosophy of Sport* (10.2.65).

12.1.41 Philosophy of Education Society. Founded 1941.

Address: Richard Pratte, 145 Ramseyer Hall, Ohio State Univ., 29 West Woodruff Ave., Columbus, Ohio 43210. Publishes the *Proceedings of the Philosophy of Education Society* (10.5.22) and *Educational Theory.* Holds an annual meeting during the week prior to Easter.

12.1.42 Philosophy of Science Association. Founded 1934.

Address: c/o Peter D. Asquith, 18 Morrill Hall, Dept. of Philosophy, Michigan State Univ., East Lansing, Mich. 48824. Publishes *Philosophy of Science* (10.2.103). Holds an annual meeting together with the American Association for the Advancement of Science.

12.1.43 Society for Ancient Greek Philosophy. Founded 1953.

Address: Dept. of Philosophy, Emory

158

Univ., Atlanta, Ga. 30322.

Meets with the Eastern Division of the APA and with the American Philological Association.

12.1.44 Society for Asian and Comparative Philosophy. Founded 1967.

Address: Univ. of Hawaii, 2530 Dole St., Honolulu, Hawaii 96822.

Annual meeting.

Sponsors a monograph series.

12.1.45 The Society for Exact Philosophy. Founded 1971.

c/o Nuel Belnap, Dept. of Philosophy, Univ. of Pittsburgh, Pittsburgh, Pa. 15260.

Annual meeting.

12.1.46 Society for Phenomenology and Existential Philosophy. Founded 1961.

Sec.: Ronald Bruzina, Univ. of Kentucky, Lexington, Ky. 40506.

Holds an annual meeting in October.

Publishes *The Selected Shades in Phenomenology and Existential Philosophy*, Nijhoff, 6v. to date.

12.1.47 Society for Philosophy and Public Affairs. Founded 1969.

Sec.: Thomas Nagel, Dept. of Philosophy, Princeton Univ., Princeton, N. J. 08540.

Membership is open to all teachers and graduate students of philosophy, and to others with the approval of the executive committee.

Annual national meeting with the Western Division of the APA; also regional and local meetings. The aim of the Society is to encourage and, if possible, extend concern with public issues among professional philosophers.

12.1.48 Society for Philosophy of Religion. Founded 1938.

c/o Frank Harrison, Dept. of Philosophy, Univ. of Georgia, Athens, Ga. 30602.

Annual meeting.

Publishes *The International Journal for Philosophy of Religion* (10.2.42).

12.1.49 Society for the Advancement of American Philosophy. Founded 1972.

Sec.: Joseph G. Grassi, Dept. of Philosophy, Fairfield Univ., Fairfield, Conn. 06430.

Annual meeting. Also meets in conjunction with APA meetings.

12.1.50 Society for the Philosophical Study of Marxism. Founded 1962.

1426 Merritt Drive, El Cajon, Calif. 92020.

Meets concurrently with each division of the APA. A national meeting every four years.

Publishes *SPSM Newsletter* and some monographs.

12.1.51 Society for the Philosophy of Creativity. Founded 1957.

Associated with The Foundation for Creative Philosophy, 303 S. Tower Road, Carbondale, Ill. 62901.

Meets with both the Western Division and the Eastern Division of the APA. The first National Conference for Philosophy of Creativity was held in 1969.

Publishes *Philosophy of Creativity Monograph Series*, vol. 1- , 1969- .

12.1.52 Society for the Scientific Study of Religion. Founded 1949.

Address: Box U68A, Univ. of Connecticut, Storrs, Conn. 06268.

Publishes the *Journal for the Scientific Study of Religion* (10.2.48).

Holds an annual meeting in October.

12.1.53 Society for the Study of Process Philosophies. Founded 1963.

Address: Dickinson College, Carlisle, Pa. 17013.

Holds an annual meeting with the Eastern Division of the APA.

12.1.54 Society for Women in Philosophy. Founded 1972.

Dept. of Philosophy, Western Illinois Univ., Macomb, Ill. 61455.

Meets concurrently with each division of the American Philosophical Association.

British Associations and Meetings

12.1.55 Aristotelian Society. Founded 1880.

Hon. Sec. and Ed.: A. A. Kassman, 31 West Heath Drive, London, NW11 7QG.

Publishes *Proceedings* and supplementary volumes (10.5.15).

Holds fortnightly meetings and annual joint sessions with The Mind Association.

12.1.56 The British Society for Phenomenology. Founded 1967.

Address: Extra-Mural Dept., Univ. of Manchester, Manchester, ML3 9PL.

Publishes *The Journal of the British Society for Phenomenology* (10.2.62).

Holds annual meetings at British universities.

12.1.57 British Society for the Philosophy of Science. Founded 1948.

Address: Hon. Sec., Philosophy Dept., London School of Economics, Houghton St., London, WC2A 2AE.

Publishes *The British Journal for the Philosophy of Science* (10.2.15).

Holds three meetings in each university term on Mondays at Univ. College, London, and an annual general conference.

12.1.58 British Society of Aesthetics. Founded 1960.

Address: Dept. of Philosophy, Birkbeck College, Malet St., London, WC1.

Publishes *The British Journal of Aesthetics* (10.2.16).

Holds monthly lecture meetings and an annual conference.

12.1.59 Mind Association. Founded 1900.

Dept. of Philosophy, The University, Southhampton.

Holds joint annual sessions with the Aristotelian Society.

Publishes *Mind* (10.2.76).

One can become a member by subscribing to *Mind.*

12.1.60 Philosophy of Education Society of Great Britain. Founded 1964.

Address: Univ. of Reading, School of Education, London Road, Reading, RGI 5AQ.

12.1.61 Royal Institute of Philosophy.

Sec., 14 Gordon Sq., London W. C. 1, England.

Publishes *Philosophy* (10.2.95).

12.1.62 Society of Philosophical Letter Writers. Founded 1967.

Address: E. H. Stubbes, Univ. of Aston in Birmingham, Gosta Green, Birmingham 4, England.

The aim of the society is to facilitate correspondence among philosophical writers of similar interests.

Membership is open to anyone, without charge.

12.2 PHILOSOPHICAL CENTERS AND INSTITUTES

12.2.1 Center for High School Philosophy. School of Education and Dept. of Philosophy, Univ. of Massachusetts, Amherst, Mass.

12.2.2 Center for Philosophic Exchange. Department of Philosophy, State University College, Brockport, N. Y. 14420.

Founded, 1969.

Sponsors public lectures and seminars. Produces and lends television tapes of its seminars and conferences.

Publishes: *Annual Proceedings of the Center for Philosophic Exchange* (10.5.16).

12.2.3 Center for Philosophy, Law, Citizenship, Inc.

Dir.: Jim Friel, 635 Washington Dr., Centerport, N. Y. 11721.

"Main goal, the recognition of the person as the focus of the community."

Publishes *Aitia* (10.2.2).

12.2.4 Center for Process Studies. 1325 North College, Claremont, Calif. 91711.

Founded, 1973.

Sponsors conferences, seminars, lectureships and publications on process philosophy, especially in the form articulated by A. N. Whitehead and C. Hartshorne. Publishes: *Process Studies* (quarterly since 1971); *Newsletter of the Center for Process Studies* (10.5.4).

12.2.5 Center for the Study of Ethics in the Professions. Project Mgr.: E. d'Anjou, 183 Life Sciences Bldg., Illinois Institute of Technology, Chicago, Ill. 60616.

Purpose—to encourage scholarship dealing with the moral and social issues involved in the practice of engineering, architecture, science, business, and other professions.

12.2.6 Council for Philosophical Studies. Exec. Sec.: Anita Silvers, Dept. of Philosophy, San Francisco State Univ., 1600 Holloway Ave., San Francisco, Calif. 94132.

Founded, 1965.

Sponsors summer institutes for teachers of philosophy, working conferences, and a visiting philosophers program. Established "to contribute to the advancement of teaching and scholarship in the field of philosophy," the Council sponsors both individual conferences concerned with scholarly problems and summer institutes for teachers of philosophy.

12.2.7 International Center for the Study of Arabian Philosophy.

Secretariat: c/o Institut Dominicain d'Etudes Orientales, 1 Rue Masna al-Tarabich, Abassiah-Le Caire, United Arab Republic.

Founded 1954.

Publishes *Mélanges de l'Institut Dominicain d'Etudes Orientales*. Biennial.

12.2.8 International Institute of Philosophy (IIP). Founded 1937.

Sec.: 173 Boulevard Saint-Germain, Paris VIe, France.

Composed of 100 elected members, representing 36 countries.

It helps organize international meetings and publishes the *Bibliography of Philosophy* (1.2.34) and *Chroniques de Philosophie* (1937- ; every 10 years), and occasional volumes.

12.2.9 The National Council for Critical Analysis. Founded 1968. Jersey City State College, Dept. of Philosophy, Jersey City, N. J. 07305.

Publishes *Journal of Critical Analysis* (10.2.51) and *Journal of Pre-College Philosophy* (10.2.59).

Encourages "philosophic dialogue and the introduction of philosophy on all levels of education, including pre-college.".

12.2.10 National Forum for Philosophical Reasoning in the Schools. Exec. Sec.: Darrell R. Shepard, Washburn Univ. of Topeka, Topeka, Kans. 66621. Founded 1975.

Publishes quarterly *Newsletter.*

12.2.11 National Translation Center. Dir.: Keith Botsford, 2621 Speedway, Austin, Tex. 78705.

News of translations in progress in humanities, including literature, the arts, philosophy, history, etc.

Publishes *Delos* (14.2.3). Consolidated index of translations into English. N. Y., Special Libraries Assoc., 1969. 948 pp.

See also: 12.2.13, 13.2.16.

12.2.12 Philosophy Documentation Center. Bowling Green State University, Bowling Green, Ohio. Dir.: Richard H. Lineback.

Founded, 1966.

Publishes *The Philosopher's Index*, the *Philosophy Research Archives*, the *Directory of American Philosophers*, the *International Directory of Philosophy and Philosophers*, the

Directory of Women in Philosophy, the publications of the National Information Center for the Teaching of Philosophy, and the series "Bibliographies of Famous Philosophers." It operates the Philosopher's Information Retrieval System, typesets journals, rents mailing lists of philosophers in the United States and Canada, and serves as the U. S. National Center for the Bibliography of Philosophy.

12.2.13 Translation Center. School of Humanities, Southern Illinois University, Edwardsville, Ill. 62025.

Founded, 1967.
Gathers information on philosophical translations in progress which is published in *The Philosopher's Index* (1.2.28). Also advises translators whether the work they intend to translate is already in progress elsewhere.
See also: 12.2.11, 13.2.16.

12.2.14 World Institute for Advanced Phenomenological Research and Learning. 348 Payson Rd., Belmont, Mass. 02178.

An international center of advanced phenomenological research and learning. The work of the Institute is conducted partly by the international Husserl and Phenomenological Research Society and the International Association for Philosophy and Literature, and partly by an academic establishment within the Institute. Two academic chairs, entitled respectively the "Edmund Husserl Chair" and the "Roman Ingarden Chair," were founded in order to promote advanced seminars and specialized research projects in relation to the programs of the Institute. Manuscripts resulting from the work of the Institute are published in the *Anelecta Husserliana*, The Yearbook for Phenomenological Research, and the series: The Phenomenology of Man and of the Human Condition, edited by Anna-Teresa Tymieniecka.
Also publishes *Phenomenology Information Bulletin* (8.6.4).
Affiliated societies: The International Husserl and Phenomenological Research Society; The International Association for Philosophy and Literature; The International

Society for Phenomenology and the Sciences of Man.
See also: 5.2.80.

12.3 OTHER PROFESSIONAL ORGANIZATIONS

12.3.1 Encyclopedia of associations. Detroit, Gale Research, 1956- .

12th ed., 1978. 3v. Revised about every two years.
Vol. 1, National associations of the United States;
vol. 2, Geographic and executive index;
vol. 3, New associations.
Gives addresses of national and international associations in each discipline and the publications they sponsor.

12.3.2 The American Association of University Professors. Founded 1915. 1785 Massachusetts Ave., N. W., Washington, D. C. 20036.

(Purpose is) "to advance the ideals and standards of the academic profession . . . . Vigorous in defense of academic standards and in the promotion of faculty welfare, the Association has come to be recognized as the authoritative voice of the profession."
Publishes *AAUP Bulletin.*

12.4 POSTDOCTORAL RESEARCH

12.4.1 American Council on Education. Fellowships in the Arts and Sciences. Washington, American Council of Education, 1957- . Annual.

Includes information on predoctoral and postdoctoral fellowships.

12.4.2 American foundations and their fields. 1931- . Irregular.

Published by American Foundations Information Service, 860 Broadway, N. Y. Supplemented until Sept. 1960 by American Foundation News.

The 7th ed., 1955, carried information on 4289 Foundations.
Largely superseded by 12.4.9.

12.4.3 Annual register of grant support, 1977-78. 11th ed. Chicago, Marquis Academic Media, Marquis Who's Who, Inc., 1977. 757 pp.

12.4.4 Council for Philosophical Studies. *See* 12.2.6.

12.4.5 David F. Swenson-Kierkegaard Memorial Fund.

Fellowship for study of writings of Kierkegaard. Write: Sec. of the Swenson-Kierkegaard Memorial Committee, 409 Prospect Street, New Haven, Conn.

12.4.6 Educational and Cultural Exchange Opportunities.

Published annually by the Dept. of State, Bureau of Educational and Cultural Affairs, Washington, D. C.

12.4.7 Feingold, S. Norman. Scholarships, fellowships and loans. Cambridge, Mass., Bellman, 1949-62. 4v.

12.4.8 Fellowships and Loans of the Organization of American States for Study Abroad.

Published by the Organization of American States, 17th & Constitution, N. W., Washington, D. C.

12.4.9 The foundation directory. Comp. by the Foundation Center, New York, distr. by Columbia University Press, 1960- .

6th ed., 1977. 2818 pp.
Contains information on 2,533 foundations.
Supplemented quarterly by the Foundation Library Center, 428 E. Preston St., Baltimore, Md.

12.4.10 Grants register, 1969/70- ; postgraduate awards in the English-speaking world. New York, St. Martin's Press.

3d. ed., 1977. Periodically revised.
A comprehensive and up-to-date source of information on postgraduate awards. International in scope.

12.4.11 Handbook on international study. New York, Institute of International Education, 1955- . Triennial.

Since 1961 it appears in 2v. Includes exchanges, fellowships, and government regulations.

12.4.12 Interuniversity Committee on Travel Grants. Indiana Univ., Bloomington, Ind.

Handles exchanges for study and research in the U. S. S. R., Bulgaria, Czechoslovakia, and Hungary.

12.4.13 National register of scholarships and fellowships. Ed., Juvenal L. Angel. 4th ed. New York, World Trade Academy Press, 1963-64. 2v.

Includes undergraduate, predoctoral, and postdoctoral opportunities.

12.4.14 Publications of the Modern Language Association (PMLA). 1952-to date.

Annually (in Sept.) publishes a list of fellowships and research programs, many of which apply to all areas of the humanities.

12.4.15 A selected list of major fellowship opportunities and aids to advanced education for United States citizens. Annual.

Published by The Fellowship Office, National Academy of Sciences—National Research Council, Washington, D. C.

12.4.16 Study abroad; international directory of fellowships, scholarships, and awards compiled by UNESCO. Paris, New York, 1948- . Annual.

See also: 10.5.12.

12.5 TEACHING

12.5.1 Jobs for philosophers. *See* 12.1.23.

12.5.2 **National Information and Resource Center for the Teaching of Philosophy** (NIRCTP). Box 32, Hyde Park, New York.

Gathers and disseminates ideas and curriculum materials for the teaching of philosophy and sponsors conferences and workshops. Materials disseminated by the Philosophy Documentation Center.

Its publications include *Teaching Philosophy Today* (12.5.4), and individual course material.

12.5.3 **Personnel Placement Service**. The American Catholic Philosophical Association, The Catholic Univ. of America, Washington, D. C. 20017. National Sec., George F. McLean, OMI.

Begins Oct. 1 each year; no charge to institutions of higher learning, additional fee to members.

12.5.4 **Teaching Philosophy Today**. Eds., Terrell Ward Bynum and Sidney Reisberg, Bowling Green, Philosophy Documentation Center, 1977-to date.

Contains critiques of contemporary philosophy teaching and descriptions of alternative teaching methods.

12.5.5 **Teaching philosophy**. *See* 10.2.128.

12.5.6 **United Nations Educational, Scientific and Cultural Organization**. The teaching of philosophy, an International enquiry of UNESCO. Paris, 1953. 232 pp. Ann Arbor, MI: Univ. Microfilms International, "Demand Reprints."

See also: 12.2.1, 12.2.10.

GENERAL RESEARCH TOOLS

13. BIBLIOGRAPHIES

The bibliographical tools in philosophy listed in earlier chapters are fairly well developed and are sufficient for most purposes. They are, however, not complete, and may well be supplemented at times by more general bibliographies.

The general bibliographical guides listed in 13.1 describe bibliographical tools in related disciplines, specialized national bibliographies, and a variety of other research tools. Especially comprehensive and useful is *Guide to Reference Books* (13.1.6). The general bibliographies listed in 13.2 can be used to supplement the specialized philosophical bibliographies. They are especially useful in tracking down items on the fringes of philosophy and in locating works written by a philosopher in non-philosophical journals.

Scholarly work on a particular author demands that the student or scholar ascertain as closely as possible what the philosopher in question really wrote. It is necessary both to identify a text as being from the author concerned and as being his latest thought on the matter (or as being from a certain period in his development). This always remains a difficulty, though it becomes less acute as one approaches nearer to the present time. The establishing of a text is not itself a philosophical task, but it may well be a necessary prelude to carrying out the philosophical task. Analytical (or critical) bibliography consists in the examination of books with respect to their physical characteristics and the details of their manufacture. It is divided into descriptive bibliography, which is concerned with establishing the physical form of a book for purposes of identification, and textual bibliography or criticism, which is concerned with coming as close as possible to the original or lost manuscript. Works dealing with analytical bibliography are listed in 13.3.

13.1 BIBLIOGRAPHICAL GUIDES

13.1.1 **Bulletin of bibliography.** 1897- . Quarterly. F. N. Faxon Co., Inc., 15 SW Park, Westwood, Mass. 02090.

Originally entitled *Bulletin of Bibliography and Magazine Notes.*

13.1.2 **Collison, Robert Lewis.** Bibliographies, subject and national; a guide to their contents, arrangement and use. 3d ed., rev. and enl. London, Crosby Lockwood, 1968. 203 pp.

13.1.3 **Gaskell, Philip.** A new introduction to bibliography. New York, Oxford University Press, 1972. 438 pp.

Deals with book production and bibliographic application.

13.1.4 **Marconi, Joseph V.** Indexed periodicals. Ann Arbor, Mich., Pierian Press, 1976. 416 pp.

A guide to 170 years of coverage in 33 indexing services.

13.1.5 **O'Brien, Robert,** and **Joanne Soder-**

167

man, *eds.* The basic guide to research sources. New York, New American Library, Mentor Books, 1975. 245 pp.

Research tools, general reference books, reference books in special subjects.

13.1.6 **Sheehy, Eugene P.** Guide to reference books. 9th ed. Chicago, American Library Association, 1976. 1015 pp.

An excellent annotated guide to general reference works in the humanities, social sciences, history and area studies, and the pure and applied sciences.

13.1.7 **Walford, A. J.** Guide to reference material. 3d ed. London, Library Association, 1973-77. 3v.

Annotated guide to a wide variety of reference books and bibliographies, with an emphasis on British material.
Vol. 1, Science and technology; vol. 2, Social and historical sciences, philosophy and religion; vol. 3, Generalities, languages, the arts and literature.

13.1.8 **Vitale, Philip H.** Bibliography, historical and bibliothecal; a handbook of terms and names. Chicago, Loyola University Press, 1971. 251 pp.

French

13.1.9 **Duprat, Gabrielle, Ksenia Liutova,** and **Marie-Louise Bossuat.** Bibliographie des répertoires nationaux de périodiques en cours. London and Paris, Fédération Internationale des Associations de Bibliothécaires and UNESCO, 1969. 141 pp.

Manuels bibliographiques de l'UNESCO, 12; IFLA/FIAB manuels internationaux, 3. "Identifies and describes on a country-by-country basis the directories and bibliographies of current periodicals available at the end of 1966."

13.1.10 **Malclès, Louise-Noëlle.** Les sources du travail bibliographique. Genève, Droz, 1950-58. 3v. in 4.

Reprinted: 1965.
Vol. I, Bibliographies générales; vol. II, Bibliographies spécialisées: 1. Sciences Humaines; vol. III, 2. Sciences exactes et techniques.
This supplements and replaces many older bibliographies. For general bibliographies and basic reference works, see vol. I. For philosophical bibliographies and basic reference works, see vol. II (2), pp. 633-83.

13.1.11 **Malclès, Louise-Noëlle.** Manuel de bibliographie. 2. éd. entièrement refondue et mise à jour. Paris, Presses Universitaires de France, 1969. 366 pp.

1st ed. 1963. " . . . serves as an abridgment of the author's *Les sources du travail bibliographique.*

German

13.1.12 **Totok, Wilhelm, Karl-Heinz Weimann,** und **Rolf Weitzel.** Handbuch der bibliographischen Nachschlagewerke. 4. Aufl. Frankfurt am Main, Klostermann, 1972. 367 pp.

An annotated guide of both general reference works and those specialized by discipline.

Spanish

13.1.13 **Zammarriego, Thomas.** Enciclopedia de orientación bibliográfica. Barcelona, Flors, 1964. 4v.

An annotated guide.
See vol. II, pp. 611-793 for philosophy.

13.2 GENERAL BIBLIOGRAPHIES

13.2.1 **Arnim, Max.** Internationale Personalbibliographie 1800-1943. 2 Aufl. Stuttgart, Hiersemann, 1944-52. 2v.

—— ——Bd. III, 1944-1959 und Nachtrage, von Gerhard Bock und Franz Hodes. 1963. 659 pp.
Useful for bibliographies of individual

philosophers, especially Germans. Includes bibliographies in books, periodicals, biographical dictionaries and other publications. Indexed. The first edition (1936) covered 1850-1935.

13.2.2 **Arts and humanities citation index.** Philadelphia, Pa., Institute for Scientific Information, 1977.

Multidisciplinary. Covers over 1000 of the world's most important journals in literature, history, language, religion, philosophy, drama/theater, art and other related fields; comprehensive indexing.

13.2.3 **Besterman, Theodore.** A world bibliography of bibliographies. 4th ed. Lausanne, Societas Bibliographica, 1965-66. 5v.

Vol. 5 is an index.
Contains bibliographies on individuals and general topics. For general bibliographies in philosophy, see "Philosophy," vol. III, cols. 4,809-4,827; but this section does not list bibliographies of individuals or of special subjects, which should be searched under the appropriate separate headings. Restricted to bibliographies which are published separately.

13.2.4 **Bibliographic index**; a cumulative bibliography of bibliographies, 1937- . New York, Wilson, 1938- .

Quarterly until mid-1951, then semiannually, with annual and more inclusive cumulations.
This is the best source for keeping up with new personal and subject bibliographies, published separately, as parts of books, or in periodicals.

13.2.5 **Bibliographische Berichte.** Frankfurt am Main, Klostermann. 1959-to date. Semi-annual.

Frequency varies. Lists bibliographies published in books, journals, and separately. Text in English and German. International in coverage, with emphasis on German. Cum. index: 1959-66; 1966-70.

13.2.6 **Bohatta, Hans,** und **Franz Hodes.** Internationale Bibliographie der Bibliographien. Ein Nachschlagewerk, unter Mitwerkung von Walther Funke. Frankfurt am Main, Klostermann, 1950. 652 pp.

Covers general, national, and subject bibliographies.

13.2.7 **Book review digest,** 1905- . New York, Wilson, 1905- .

Monthly, with annual cumulations and five-yearly cumulative subject and title indexes. Includes excerpts from 80 book-review periodicals, some of which review books in philosophy.

13.2.8 **British humanities index,** 1962- . London, Library Association, 1963- .

Quarterly, with annual cumulations.
A partial continuation of *Subject Index to Periodicals, 1915-61.* Indexes only British periodicals.

13.2.9 **Current contents/Arts and humanities.** Philadelphia, Institute for Scientific Information. Weekly.

Displays tables of contents from 950 journals in the arts and humanities. Subject index. *Current Book Contents* covers new books.

13.2.10 **General subject-indexes since 1548.** Ed., Archer Taylor. Philadelphia, Univ. of Pennsylvania Press, 1966. 336 pp.

Lists and describes the most notable attempts through the centuries to assemble and catalogue all available knowledge.

13.2.11 **Gray, Richard A.,** and **Dorothy Villmow.** Serial bibliographies in the humanities and social sciences. Ann Arbor, Pierian Press, 1969. 345 pp.

Author, title and subject indexes.

13.2.12 **Humanities index.** New York, Wilson, 1916- .

Quarterly with annual and larger cumulations. Supersedes with the *Social Sciences Index* (20.1.8), the *Social Sciences and Humanities Index* (1956-74); *International Index: a Guide to Periodical Literature in the Social Sciences and Humanities* (1955-66); and *International Index to Periodicals* (1907-1955).

Indexes scholarly journals, some of them in philosophy.

13.2.13 Index bibliographicus; directory of current periodical abstracts and bibliographies. Compiled by Theodore Besterman. 3d ed. Paris, UNESCO, 1952. 2v.

Lists periodicals with abstracts, reviews, and bibliographies. Vol. I, Science and technology; vol. II, Social sciences, education, humanistic studies.

A 4th ed. is in progress, 1959- .

13.2.14 Index to book reviews in the humanities. Detroit, Phillip Thomson, 1960- . Annual.

Indexes reviews which appear in about 700 journals.

13.2.15 Index to social sciences and humanities proceedings. Philadelphia, Institute for Scientific Information. Quarterly.

Covers 1000 proceedings to the level of individual papers. Six index sections.

13.2.16 Index translationum. Répertoire international des traductions. International bibliography of translations. Paris, International Institut of International Cooperation, 1932-40, nos. 1-31; n. s. v.1, 1948- . Paris, UNESCO, 1949-to date. Annual.

Lists words translated; arranged by country.

Cumulative index, 1948-68, pub. by Boston, G. K. Hall, 1973. 2v.

13.2.17 Internationale Bibliographie der Zeitschriftenliteratur aus allen Gebieten des Wissens (International bibliography of periodical literature covering all fields of knowledge). Osnabruck, Felix Dietrich, 1965- . Semiannual.

The most comprehensive of all indexes, covering more than 7,600 periodicals. Very useful, especially to fill in gaps in coverage supplied by the philosophical bibliographies. Previously published in three sections:

Abteilung A: Bibliographie der deutschen Zeitschriftenliteratur, 1896-1964. A supplement in 20v. covers 1861-95.

Abteilung B: Bibliographie der fremdsprachigen Zeitschriftenliteratur, 1911-1964.

Abteilung C: Bibliographie der Rezensionen und Referate, 1900-1942.

Reprinted: vols. 1-22, ns. vols. 1-25, 30-51. New York, Kraus Reprints.

13.2.18 Nineteenth century readers' guide to periodical literature, 1890-1899, with supplementary indexing, 1900-1922. Ed. by Helen Grant Cushing and Ada V. Morris. New York, Wilson, 1944. 2v.

An index to 51 periodicals. Only of peripheral philosophical interest.

13.2.19 Poole's index to periodical literature, 1802-1881. Rev. ed. Boston, Houghton Mifflin, 1891. 2v.

Supplements: Jan. 1882-Jan. 1, 1907. Boston, 1887-1908. 5v.

A subject index of 470 American and English journals.

Cumulative author index, Ann Arbor, Mich., Pierian Press, 1971. 488 pp.

13.2.20 Readers' guide to periodical literature, 1900- . New York, Wilson, 1905- .

Issued monthly (more or less) with quarterly and larger cumulations. Indexes primarily popular, nontechnical periodicals. Of limited use in preparing the ordinary philosophical bibliography, but of value in locating popular articles by philosophers or on philosophers or philosophical topics.

13.2.21 U. S. Library of Congress. General Reference Bibliography Division. Current national bibliographies, comp. by Helen F. Conover. Washington, D. C., Library of Congress, 1955. 132 pp.

An annotated list of the book trade in 67 countries.

Reprinted: N. Y., Greenwood Press, 1968.

Arab

13.2.22 Centre Documentaire International des Manuscrits Arabes. A monthly periodical of Arabic bibliography published in Arabic and French. Edited by the Centre Documentaire International des Manuscrits Arabes of Beirut, Lebanon. 1965- .

The first part concerns ancient Arabic texts; the second part is concerned with recent Arabic works.

French

13.2.23 Le catalogue de l'édition française, 1970- . Paris, VPC Livres; and Port Washington, N. Y., Paris Publications, 1971- . Biennial.

Lists French-language books in print throughout the world.

German

13.2.24 Bibliographie der Deutschen Zeitschriftenliteratur. 1896-1964.

Merged in 1965 with 13.2.17.
A comprehensive index of German periodicals.

Greek

13.2.25 Delopoulos, Kyriakos, *ed.* Greek books. 1975- . Annual. New Rochelle, N. Y., Caratzas.

A bibliography of books published in Greece.

See also: 13.1.6.

13.3 ANALYTICAL BIBLIOGRAPHY AND TEXTUAL ANALYSIS

Descriptive Bibliography

13.3.1 Aldis, H. G. The printed book. 3d ed. New York, Bowker, 1951. 141 pp.

A history of book printing and construction.

13.3.2 The bookman's glossary. 5th ed. New York, Bowker, 1975.

Includes information on the production of books, classical names of towns and cities; foreign book trade names; private book clubs; proofreaders' marks; and a selected reading list.

13.3.3 Bowers, Fredson. Principles of bibliographical description. Princeton, Princeton University Press, 1949. 505 pp.

A basic guide to descriptive bibliography. Reprinted: N. Y., Russell & Russell, 1962.

13.3.4 Cowley, John D. Bibliographical description and cataloguing. London, Grafton, 1939. 256 pp.

A textbook of bibliographical description including information on handling "awkward material."

13.3.5 Dictionary of printing terms. 5th ed. Salt Lake City, Porte, 1950. 173 pp.

13.3.6 Esdaile, Arundell. Manual of bibliography. 4th ed. rev. by Roy Stokes. London, Allen & Unwin and the Lib. Assoc., 1967. 336 pp.

1st ed. 1931.
A basic guide to bibliographies and book descriptions, with discussions of the history and makeup of the book.

13.3.7 Freer, Percy. Bibliography and modern book production; notes and sources for student librarians, printers, booksellers, stationers, book-collectors. Johannesburg, Witwatersrand University Press, 1954. 345 pp.

13.3.8 Hostettler, Rudolf. The printer's terms. St. Gallen, Hostettler, 1949. 204 pp.

Lists English, German, French, and Italian terms.

Textual Bibliography

13.3.9 **Bowers, Fredson**. Bibliography and textual criticism (The Lyell Lectures, Oxford, Trinity Term 1959). Oxford, Clarendon Press, 1964. 207 pp.

A discussion of evidence in textual criticism.

13.3.10 **Bowers, Fredson**. "Textual criticism," Encyclopaedia Britannica (1965), vol. 22, 14-19.

A succinct introduction.

13.3.11 **Cappelli, Adriano**. Lexicon abbreviaturarum; dizionario di abbreviature latine ed italiano, usate nelle carte e codici specialmente del Medio-Evo riprodotte con oltre 14,000 segni incisi, con l'aggiunta di uno studio sulla brachigrafia medioevale, un prontuario di sigle epigrafiche, l'antica numerazione romana ed arabica ed i segni indicanti monete, pesi, misure, etc. 6. ed. Milano, Hoepli, 1951. 531 pp.

Bibliography: pp. 517-31.
Supplemented by 13.3.23.

13.3.12 **Chassant, Alphonse A. L.** Dictionnaire des abréviations latines et françaises usitées dans les inscriptions lapidaires et métalliques, les manuscrits et les chartes du Moyen Age. 5. éd. Paris, J. Martin, 1884. 172 pp.

Gives manuscript abbreviations and their equivalents.

13.3.13 **Clark, Albert Curtis**. The descent of manuscripts. Oxford, Clarendon Press, 1918. 464 pp.

13.3.14 **Dearing, Vinton Adams**. A manual of textual analysis. Berkeley, University of California Press, 1959. 108 pp.

A handbook of techniques of textual criticism.

13.3.15 **Gaskell, Philip**. A new introduction to bibliography. Oxford, Clarendon Press; New York, Oxford University Press, 1972. 438 pp.

13.3.16 **Goldschmidt, Ernst Philip**. Medieval texts and their first appearance in print. London, printed for the Bibliographical Society at the Oxford University Press, 1943. 143 pp.

13.3.17 **Greg, W. W.** The calculus of variants; an essay on textual criticism. Oxford, Clarendon Press, 1927. 63 pp.

A basic guide to the technique of comparing manuscripts which "aims at nothing but defining and making precise for formal use the logical rules which textual critics have always applied" (p. vi).

13.3.18 **Kenyon, F. G.** Books and readers in ancient Greece and Rome. Oxford, Clarendon Press, 1931. 136 pp.

Treats the use of books in ancient Greece, papyrus roll books, reading in Rome, villum, and the codex.

13.3.19 **Maas, Paul**. Textual criticism. Trans. from German by Barbara Flower. Oxford, Clarendon Press, 1958. 59 pp.

A basic guide.

13.3.20 **Madan, Falconer**. Books in manuscript; a short introduction to their study and use. With a chapter on records. 2d ed. London, Kegan Paul, 1920. 208 pp.

1st ed. 1893.
"A plain account of the study and use of manuscripts" (p. v). Includes a list of books useful for the study of manuscripts.

13.3.21 **McKerrow, Ronald B.** An introduction to bibliography for literary students. Oxford, Clarendon Press, 1927. 359 pp.

2d impression with corrections, 1928; reprinted frequently.

A standard work on the making of early printed books.

13.3.22 **National union catalog of manuscript collections.** J. W. Edwards, 1962. 1061 pp. 1959/61- . Hamden, Conn., The Shoestring Press, 1962- . Annual.

Publisher varies.
A continuing series.
"Based on reports from American repositories of manuscripts."

13.3.23 **Pelzer, Auguste**. Abréviations latines médiévales. Supplément au Dizionario di abbreviature latine et italiane de Adriano Cappelli. Louvain, Publ. Universitaires; Paris, Béatrice-Nauwelaerts, 1964. 86 pp.

Supplements 13.3.11.

13.3.24 **Scriptorium**; revue internationale des études relatives aux manuscrits. 1946/47-to date. Semiannual.

Text in English, French, German, Spanish. Carries bibliographies of manuscript studies.

13.3.25 **Thompson, Sir Edward Maunde**. An introduction to Greek and Latin palaeography. Oxford, Clarendon Press, 1912. 600 pp.

Reprinted: New York, Burt Franklin.
Still a standard guide.

13.3.26 **Van Hoesen, Henry Bartlett, and F. K. Walter**. Bibliography; practical, enumerative, historical; an introductory manual. New York, Scribner's, 1928. 519 pp.

Contains chapters on subject bibliography, general reference, special bibliography, national bibliography, bibliography of bibliography, history of writing and printing, bookselling and publishing.
Bibliography: pp. 425-502.

13.3.27 **Williamson, Derek**. Bibliography; historical, analytical and descriptive. London, Clive Bingley, 1967. 129 pp.

"An examination guidebook," which reviews some of the literature on bibliography.

14. DICTIONARIES AND ENCYCLOPEDIAS

Definition of terms is a frequent first step in philosophical discussions. Unabridged English dictionaries (14.1) are useful as a source for determining ordinary and specialized usage, currently accepted meanings, derivations, and in some cases the history of individual words. Though technical philosophical meanings are frequently listed, they are not usually very detailed, and for these cases philosophical dictionaries are generally to be preferred.

Research in philosophy often involves working with languages other than one's own, to consult, verify, read, or translate texts, articles, or material written in a foreign tongue. Translations are useful for some purposes, and guides to what has been translated or what is in the process of translation are available. The translator will require dictionaries of the language in which he is working. But both the expert and the novice can use bilingual dictionaries with profit. A recommended list of these tools is contained in 14.2. The polyglot dictionaries listed in 14.3 give various foreign language equivalents for philosophical terms.

Encyclopedias offer a quick and summary presentation of a large number of philosophical topics and the biography and thought of major philosophers. Their articles are usually more comprehensive and their treatment broader and deeper than can be found even in specialized dictionaries. Encyclopedias also provide an excellent source for compiling a preliminary bibliography and for ascertaining the standard works on a topic. The general encyclopedias listed in 14.4 include the most important and the largest in the world. Their philosophical entries have for the most part been written by experts in the field and their treatment of major philosophical topics is often extensive and thorough. Many of the articles on philosophy and the bibliographies supplied in the better of these works are as good as, and sometimes superior to, those in the more specialized encyclopedias. The index should always be consulted first in any encyclopedia having one.

14.1 UNABRIDGED ENGLISH LANGUAGE DICTIONARIES

14.1.1 **Century dictionary and cyclopedia with a new atlas of the world**. Rev. and enl. ed. New York, Century, 1911. 12v.

1st ed. 1889-91.

Though based on common usage and so somewhat out of date, it is still useful for its etymologies, quotations, and references.

C. S. Peirce was the editorial contributor of many of the items in philosophy.

14.1.2 **Funk & Wagnalls new standard dictionary of the English language**. Prepared by more than 380 specialists and other scholars under the supervision of I. K. Funk, Calvin Thomas, F. H. Vizetelly. New York, Funk & Wagnalls, 1964. 2816 pp.

14.1.3 **Oxford dictionary of English etymology**. Ed. by C. T. Onions with the assistance of G. W. S. Friedrichsen and R. W. Burchfield. Oxford, Clarendon Press, 1966. 1025 pp.

14.1.4 The Oxford English dictionary, being a corrected reissue, with an introduction, supplement, and bibliography, of A new English dictionary of historical principles; founded mainly on the materials collected by the Philological Society and ed. by James A. H. Murray, Henry Bradley, W. A. Craigie, and C. T. Onions. Oxford, Clarendon Press, 1933. 12v. and supplement.

Gives the history of each word included, with many quotations exemplifying usage in various historical periods.

A supplement, ed. by R. W. Burchfield, Oxford, Clarendon Press, 1972- . 3v. projected.

14.1.5 The Random House dictionary of the English language. Jess Stein, ed. in chief; Laurence Urdang, managing ed. New York, Random House, 1967. 2059 pp.

Also contains concise French, Spanish, Italian, and German bilingual (with English) dictionaries, and a basic manual of style.

14.1.6 Webster's new international dictionary of the English language. A Merriam-Webster. William Allan Neilson, ed. in chief; Thomas A. Knott, general ed.; Paul W. Carhart, managing ed. 2d ed., unabridged. Springfield, Mass., Merriam, 1961. 3194 pp.

14.1.7 Webster's third new international dictionary of the English language, unabridged. A Merriam-Webster. Philip Babcock Gove, ed. in chief, and the Merriam-Webster editorial staff. Springfield, Mass., Merriam, 1961. 2662 pp.

New, and different from the 2d edition, with emphasis on English as it is currently used.

14.2 TRANSLATION GUIDES AND BILINGUAL DICTIONARIES

Translation Guides

14.2.1 Collison, Robert Lewis. Dictionaries of foreign languages; a bibliographical guide to the general and technical dictionaries of the chief foreign languages, with historical and explanatory notes and references. 2d ed. New York, Hafner, 1971. 303 pp.

Lists general, special, and bilingual dictionaries of the languages of Europe, Asia, and Africa.

14.2.2 Index translationum. *See* 13.2.16.

14.2.3 Delos; a journal on and of translation. 1968-to date.

Publishes translations, reports, articles, and information on translations. It is the journal of the National Translation Center (12.2.11), which aims "to support the quality, availability, and financial reward of literary translation into English of texts having cultural and artistic significance." The "clearing house" section lists translations known to be in progress and titles for which publishers are seeking translators.

The Center also awards fellowships and grants.

14.2.4 National Translations Center. *See* 12.2.11.

14.2.5 Nida, Eugene A. Toward a science of translating. Leiden, E. J. Brill, 1964. 331 pp.

Bibliography: pp. 265-320.

A discussion of meaning, communication, correspondences, and translation problems and procedures, with special reference to Bible translation.

14.2.6 Nida, Eugene A., and Charles R. Taber. The theory and practice of translation. (Helps for Translators, VIII) Leiden, E. J. Brill (for the United Bible Societies), 1969.

14.2.7 Problèmes littéraires de la traduction. (Textes des conférences présentées au cours d'un séminaire organisé pendant l'année académique 1973-74) Institut de Formation et de Recherches en Littérature, I; Louvain Univ. Leiden, E. J. Brill, 1975. 121 pp.

14.2.8 Translation Center. *See* 12.2.13.

14.2.9 **U. S. Library of Congress.** General reference and bibliography division. Foreign language-English dictionaries. Washington, D. C., 1955. 2v.

Vol. I lists subject dictionaries; vol. II, general language dictionaries.

14.2.10 **Walford, Albert John.** A guide to foreign language grammars and dictionaries. 2d ed., rev. and enl. London, The Library Association, 1967. 240 pp.

Annotated list of grammars, dictionaries, and audio-visual aids for the major foreign languages of Western Europe, plus Russian and Chinese.

14.2.11 **World bibliography of dictionaries.** Gen. Ed., Richard C. Lewanski, The Johns Hopkins Univ. Bologna Center Library Publications.

This series presently consists of *A bibliography of Slavic Dictionaries,* 4 vols. Comp. by Richard C. Lewanski. Editrice Compositori-Bologna, Istituto Informatico Italiano, 1973.

Bilingual Dictionaries

French

14.2.12 **Concise Oxford French dictionary.** Oxford, Clarendon Press. 2v.

French-English, comp. by A. Chevalley and M. Chevalley, 1934, 895 pp.; English-French, comp. by G. Goodridge, 1940, 295 pp. Frequently reprinted; also available in one joint volume.

14.2.13 **Mansion, J. E.** Harrap's standard French and English dictionary. London, Harrap, 1962. 2v.

Vol. 1, French-English, 912 pp.; vol. 2, English-French, 488 pp.
1st ed. 1934-39; American edition: Heath's Standard French and English Dictionary, 2d ed., Boston, Heath, 1939, 2v.
Generally considered the best French-En-glish, English-French dictionary.

Vol. 1 has been revised and issued in 2v., 1972. A revision of vol. 2 is in progress.

German

14.2.14 **English-German and German-English dictionary.** K. Wildhagen and W. Heraucourt. 2d ed., rev. and enl. Wiesbaden, Brandstetter; London, Allen & Unwin, 1936-65. 2v.

Helpful for translation; gives examples.

14.2.15 **Langenscheidt's new Muret-Sanders encyclopedic dictionary of the English and German languages.** Completely rev. 1962. Ed. by Otto Springer. London, Methuen; New York, Barnes & Noble, 1962-75. 2 pts. in 4v.

Pt. I (English-German), 2v.; Pt. II (German-English), 2v.
1st ed. 1908. Long considered an excellent bilingual dictionary.

14.2.16 **The Oxford-Harrap standard German dictionary.** Ed., Trevor Jones. New York, Oxford University Press, 1977- .

In progress.
Vol. 1, A-E; vol. 2, F-K; vol. 3, L-R.

Greek

14.2.17 **Greek-English lexicon.** Henry George Liddell and Robert Scott. 9th ed. rev. Oxford, Clarendon Press, 925-40. 2111 pp.

1st ed. 1843.
The standard Greek-English lexicon.
A supplement, ed., E. A. Barber, 1968. 153 pp.

Italian

14.2.18 **Hazon, Mario.** Garzanti comprehensive Italian-English, English-Italian dictionary. New York, McGraw-Hill, 1963. 2099 pp.

14.2.19 **Hoare, Alfred.** A short Italian dictionary. Cambridge, University Press, 1926. 2v.

Abridged from the A. Hoare, *Italian dictionary*, 2d ed., Cambridge, University Press, 1925, 906 pp., which is out of print.

14.2.20 **Reynolds, Barbara.** The Cambridge Italian dictionary. Cambridge, University Press, 1962- .

Vol. 1, Italian-English, 900 pp. Based in part on A. Hoare, *Italian Dictionary* (*see* 14.2.19).

Latin

14.2.21 **A Latin dictionary.** A new Latin dictionary founded on the translation of Freund's Latin-German lexicon. Ed. by E. A. Andrews, rev., enl., and in great part rewritten by Charlton T. Lewis and Charles Short. Oxford, Clarendon Press, 1955. 2019 pp.

A reprint of Harpers' Latin Dictionary, 1907.

Russian

14.2.22 **Zalewski, Wojciech.** Russian-English dictionaries with aids for translators: a selected bibliography. Stanford, Calif., Stanford University Libraries, 1977.

"Focuses on bilingual dictionaries published after 1945."

14.2.23 **Gal'perin, Il'ia Romanovich.** Bolshoi anglo-russkii slovar. Moskva, "Sovetskaia Entsiklopediia," 1972. 2v.

14.2.24 **Muller, V. K.** English-Russian dictionary. 7th ed., new rev. ed., completely reset. New York, Dutton, 1965. 1192 pp.

14.2.25 **Smirnitskii, Aleksandr Ivanovich.** Russian-English dictionary; 50,000 words appx. Comp. by O. S. Akhmanova. 7th ed. New York, Dutton, 1966. 766 pp.

14.2.26 **The Oxford Russian-English dictionary.** B. O. Unbegoun, Gen. Ed. Oxford, Clarendon Press, 1972. 918 pp.

See also: 14.2.11.

Spanish

14.2.27 **Appleton's New Cuyás English-Spanish and Spanish-English dictionary.** Rev. and enl. by Lewis E. Brett (part 1) and Helen S. Eaton (part 2) with the assistance of Walter Beveraggi-Allende. Revision ed., Catherine B. Avery. 5th ed. rev. New York, Appleton-Century-Crofts, 1972. 2v.

14.2.28 **Raventos, Margaret H.** A modern Spanish dictionary. London, English Universities Press, 1953. 1230 pp.

American Edition: *McKay's Modern Spanish-English, English-Spanish Dictionary.* New York, McKay, 1954.

14.2.29 **Simon and Schuster's international dictionary.** Diccionario internacional Simon and Schuster. English/Spanish, Spanish/English. Tana de Gámez, ed. in chief. New York, Simon and Schuster, 1973. 1605 pp.

14.2.30 **Smith, Colin.** Collins Spanish-English, English-Spanish dictionary. London, Collins, 1971. 2v.

14.2.31 **The University of Chicago Spanish dictionary.** Comp. by Carlos Castillo and Otto F. Bond. 3d ed. rev. and enl. by D. Lincoln Canfield. Chicago, University of Chicago Press, 1977. 488 pp.

1st ed. 1948.

14.3 SPECIALIZED POLYGLOT DICTIONARIES

14.3.1 **Ballestrem, Karl G.** Russian philosophical terminology. Dordrecht, Holland, D. Reidel, 1964. 117 pp.

Gives English, French, and German equivalents of Russian terms. Includes English, French, and German indexes.

14.3.2 **Inouye, Tetsujiro.** Dictionary of English, German, and French philosophical terms with Japanese equivalents by Tetsujiro Inouye, Yujiro Motora, Rikizo Nakashima. Tokyo, Maruzen Kabushiki-Kaisha, 1912. 209 pp.

14.3.3 **Miermeyer, J. F.**, *ed.* Mediae Latinatus lexicon minus. Leiden, E. J. Brill, 1976. 1138 pp.

A medieval Latin-French-English dictionary.

14.3.4 **Von Ostermann, Georg F.** Manual of foreign languages for the use of librarians, bibliographers, research workers, editors, translators and printers. See 18.5.19.

See also: 12.2.11, 12.2.13.

14.4 GENERAL ENCYCLOPEDIAS

14.4.1 **Chambers's encyclopedia**. New rev. ed. Oxford, New York, Pergamon Press, 1967. 15v.

Articles tend to be short. Major articles include bibliographies of standard works.

14.4.2 **Collier's encyclopedia**. 2d ed. New York, Crowell-Collier, 1962. 24v.

1st ed. 1949-51. 20v.
Continuous revisions. Articles on philosophy are of generally high quality.
See pp. 3-10 of vol. 24 for general bibliographical material in philosophy.

14.4.3 **Encyclopedia Americana**. New York, Americana. 30v.

1st ed. 1903-04. New ed. 1918-20; since then continuously revised. Bibliographies.
Articles on philosophy are somewhat uneven, but many are by well-known American philosophers.

14.4.4 **Encyclopaedia Britannica**. Chicago, Encyclopaedia Britannica.

1st ed. 1768-71. 14th ed. 1929; from then continuously revised until 1973. 24v. (incl.

Index). Bibliographies. Britannica of the Year, 1933- .
The most famous edition is the 11th (29v., London and New York, 1910-11).
The present edition (14.4.6) is largely rewritten; the philosophical articles are of generally high quality. A. J. Ayer, Max Black, Brand Blanshard, and Gilbert Ryle are among the contributors.

14.4.5 **The New Columbia encyclopedia**. Ed. by William H. Harris and Judith S. Levey. New York, Columbia University Press, 1975. 3052 pp.

4th ed. of Columbia encyclopedia.
1st ed. 1935.
Articles are brief; those in biography are generally better than the other articles. A useful single volume reference work on the humanities, social sciences, life and physical sciences, and geography.

14.4.6 **The new encyclopaedia Britannica**. 15th ed. Chicago, Encyclopaedia Britannica, 1974. 30v.

Propaedia (outline of knowledge), 1v.; *Micropaedia* (ready reference and index), 10v.; *Macropaedia* (knowledge in depth), 19v.
The *Micropaedia* is an index to the *Macropaedia* and a source of short references. The *Macropaedia* comprises long articles.

14.4.7 **The Random House encyclopedia**. James Mitchell, ed. New York, Random House, 1977. 2856 pp.

French

14.4.8 **Encyclopédie française**. Paris, Comité de l'Encyclopédie Française, 1935-64. 21v.

Vol. XIX: Philosophie, Religion (1957), 424 pp.

14.4.9 **Encyclopaedia universalis**. Paris, Encyclopaedia Universalis France, 1968-74. 20v.

Contents: vols. 1-16, A-Z; vol. 17, Organum; vols. 18-20, Thesaurus.

14.4.10 La grande encyclopédie. Paris, Lamirault, 1886-1902. 31v.

Very good bibliographies, especially of works in French.
A revised edition in 20v. is in progress. Paris, Larousse, 1971- .

14.4.11 Grand Larousse encyclopédique. Paris, Larousse, 1960-64. 10v.

The articles on philosophy are generally short; bibliographies are at the back of each volume.
Supersedes *Larousse du XXe siècle.*
Supplement, 1968. 918 pp.

German

14.4.12 Der grosse Brockhaus. 16. Aufl. Wiesbaden, Brockhaus, 1952-60. 12v.; Ergänzungsbd., 2v.

Good bibliographies in German, English, and other languages.
A revised ed. in 20v. is in progress, 1966- .

14.4.13 Der grosse Herder. 5. Aufl. Freiburg, Herder, 1953-56. 10v.

Supplemented by 2v., 1962.

Italian

14.4.14 Dizionario enciclopedico italiano. Roma, Istituto della Enciclopedia Italiana, 1955-61. 12v.

No bibliographies.

14.4.15 Enciclopedia italiana di scienze, lettere ed arti. Roma, Istituto della Enciclopedia Italiana, 1929-39. 36v.

5v. of supplements, 1938-61. Articles on philosophy are often long and detailed.
Bibliographies in Italian, English, and other languages.

Russian

14.4.16 Bol'shaia sovetskaia entsiklopediia. 2. izd. Moskva, "Sovetskaia Entsiklopediia," 1949-58. 51v.

Bibliographies in philosophy are usually only in Russian.
The articles are from the Marxist-Leninist point of view of the Stalinist era.
The third edition of 30 volumes is in progress, 1969- .
A translation of the third ed. is in progress: *Great Soviet Encyclopedia,* New York, Macmillan; London, Collier Macmillan, 1973- .

Spanish

14.4.17 Enciclopedia universal illustrada europeo-americana. Barcelona, Hijos de J. Espasa, 1905-33. 80v. in 81. Vols. 1-70 in 71, and 10v. supplement. Fourteen additional supplements, 1934-70.

Bibliographies in Spanish, English, other languages.
Especially good on Spanish and Latin American topics of the 19th century or earlier.

15. LIBRARY CATALOGS, DISSERTATIONS AND TRADE SOURCES

The catalogs of some of the largest libraries in the world are printed and so available in many smaller libraries. These catalogs are valuable both for completing, checking, and building bibliographies on a particular author or topic and for ascertaining where particular books may be found. The *National Union Catalog* (15.1.3, 15.1.4) and the *Union List of Serials* (15.1.8) indicate which cooperating libraries other than the Library of Congress have the book or periodical listed. This is especially useful in requesting a book through interlibrary loan.

Many works not available in their original form are available on microfilm or microcards or in photocopied or Xeroxed form. The Library of Congress, among others, makes photocopies of materials in its collections available for research use. Recent aticles unavailable through other sources can often be obtained through the Institut International de Philosophie (173 Blvd. St.-Germain, Paris 6e, France).

Doctoral dissertations frequently contain excellent bibliographies and form a part of the philosophical literature. If they are not published, however, they are not listed in the usual bibliographical journals or trade bibliographies. Many doctoral dissertations are available on microfilm or in photocopied form: others can be obtained only from the university at which they were written. The list in section 15.2 applies only to dissertations written in the United States or Canada. For lists of sources reporting dissertations accepted by universities in other countries see 13.1.6, pp. 203-08.

Trade bibliographies are another source of bibliographical information and are especially useful in discovering recent books not yet listed in printed library catalogs and not yet indexed in the general philosophical bibliographies. For more detailed information on library collections and trade bibliographies of many countries, see 13.1.6.

15.1. LIBRARY CATALOGS

15.1.1 **Library bibliographies and indexes**: a subject guide to resource material available from libraries, information centers, library schools and library associations in the United States and Canada. Paul Wasserman, Managing editor. Detroit, Mich., Gale Research, 1975. 301 pp.

15.1.2 **Young, Margaret L.** Subject directory of special libraries and information centers.

New York, Gale Research, 1975. 5v.

Vol. 4 includes the humanities and religion/theology.

15.1.3 **National union catalog**; a cumulative author list representing Library of Congress printed cards and titles reported by other American Libraries, 1953-1957. Ann Arbor, Mich., Edwards, 1958. 28v.

1958-62. New York, Rowman & Littlefield, 1963. 54v.

1952-55 imprints: an author list representing Library of Congress printed cards and titles reported by other American libraries. Ann Arbor, Mich., Edwards, 1961. 30v.

Lists cards from over 700 cooperating libraries. Supplemented by nine monthly issues, with three quarterly, annual and 5 yr. cumulations.
1963-67. Ann Arbor, Mich., Edwards, 1969. 72v.
1968-72, 119v.

15.1.4 National union catalog. Pre-1956 imprints. Chicago and London, Mansell. 1968- (in progress). 524 vols (excluding vols. 53-56, Bible) published to date. Supersedes and enlarges Library of Congress catalogs prior to 1956, including 15.1.6 and portions of 15.1.7.

15.1.5 U. S. Library of Congress. Catalog of books represented by Library of Congress printed cards, issued to July 31, 1942. Ann Arbor, Mich., Edwards, 1942-46. 167v.

Supplement: cards issued Aug. 1, 1942-Dec. 31, 1947. Ann Arbor, Mich., Edwards, 1948. 42v.
Both reprinted: New York, Rowman & Littlefield.

15.1.6 Library of Congress author catalog: a cumulative list of works represented by Library of Congress printed cards, 1948-1952. Ann Arbor, Mich., Edwards, 1953. 24v.

Reprinted: New York, Rowman & Littlefield.

15.1.7 U. S. Library of Congress catalog. Books: subjects, 1950-1954. A cumulative list of works represented by Library of Congress printed cards. Ann Arbor, Mich., Edwards, 1955, 20v.; 1955-59, Paterson, N. J., Pageant Books, 1960, 22v.; 1960, 22v.; 1960-64, 25v.; 1965-69, 42v.; 1970, 9v.; 1971, 11v., 1972, 15v.; 1973, 16v.; 1974, 15v.

Supplements issued quarterly, with annual and 5 yr. cumulations.

15.1.8 Union list of serials in libraries of the United States and Canada. 3d ed. Ed. by Edna Brown Titus. New York, Wilson, 1965. 5v.

Lists more than 156,000 titles which began publication before 1950, which are held in 956 libraries in the United States and Canada. Gives information on title, beginning date, interruptions in publication, and holdings in all reporting libraries. Continued by New Serial Titles (15.1.9).

15.1.9 New serial titles. 1950-1960; supplement to the Union list of serials. 3d ed. A union list of serials commencing publication after Dec. 31, 1949. Washington, D. C., Library of Congress, 1961. 2v.

8 monthly, 4 quarterly, and cumulative issues.
———, 1961-65. Washington, D. C., Library of Congress, 1966. 3v.
———, 1966-69, 1971. 2v.
———, 1950-70, 1973. 4v.
———, 1971-75, 1976. 2v.
———, 1976, 1977.

15.1.10 New serial titles—classed subject arrangement. Jan./May, 1955- . Washington, D. C., Library of Congress, Card Division, 1955- . Monthly.

Cumulation: 1950-65. Ann Arbor, Mich., Pierian Press, 1968.
Arranged by Dewey Decimal Classification.

15.1.11 Harvard University. Library. Philosophy and psychology. Cambridge, Mass., Harvard Univ. Library. Distr. by Harvard University Press, 1973. 2v.

15.1.12 British Museum. Department of Printed Books. General catalog of printed books. London, Trustees, 1959-66. 263v.

Primarily an author catalog, covering books cataloged through 1955. Supersedes all previous incomplete editions. Descriptions are for the most part quite full.
———. Ten-year supplement, 1956-1965. London, Trustees, 1968. 50v.
———. Five-year supplement, 1966-1970, 26v.

15.1.13 British union–catalogue of periodicals; a record of the periodicals of the world, from the seventeenth century to the present day, in British libraries. Ed. by James Douglas Stewart, Muriel E. Hammond, and Erwin Saenger. London, Butterworths Scientific Publications; New York, Academic Press, 1955-58. 4v.

—— Supplement to 1960. 1962. From 1964 there are also quarterly and annual cumulations of new periodical titles.

15.1.14 Paris. Bibliothèque Nationale. Catalogue général des livres imprimés: Auteurs. Paris, Imprimerie Nationale, 1900- .

In progress.
An author list. Each volume includes works up to the time of publication. Vol. 189 and following do not include works published after 1959. Entries are detailed.
Quinquennial supplements: 1960-69.

15.1.15 Berlin. Preussische Staatsbibliothek. Berliner Titeldrucke. Berlin, Staatsbibliothek, 1892-1944.

Title varies; also called *Deutscher Gesamtkatalog.* Weekly with quarterly and annual cumulations.
Partially cumulated and supplemented by 15.1.16 and by two *Fünfjahrs-Katalog,* 1930-34 (1935), 1935-39 (1940).

15.1.16 Deutscher Gesamtkatalog. Hrsg. von der Preussischen Staatsbibliothek. Berlin, Preussische Druckerei- u. Verlags Aktiengesellschaft, 1931-39. Vols. 1-14.

Vols. 1-14, A-Beethordnung. No more published. An author and main entry list of books published to 1930 and held by German and Austrian libraries.

15.1.17 Centro nazionale per il catalogo unico delle biblioteche italiane e per le informazioni bibliografiche. Primo catalogo collettivo delle biblioteche italiane. Roma, 1962- .

In progress.

Includes books published from 1500-1957.

15.2 DOCTORAL DISSERTATIONS

15.2.1 Guide to theses and dissertations: an annotated, international bibliography of bibliographies. Ed. by Michael M. Reynolds. Detroit, Mich., Gale Research, 1975. 599 pp.

15.2.2 U. S. Library of Congress. Catalog Division. List of American doctoral dissertations printed in 1912-38. Washington, D. C., Government Printing Office, 1913-40. 26v.

15.2.3 Comprehensive dissertation index 1861-1972. Ann Arbor, University Microfilms, 1973. 37v. in subject and author sections (1-32, subjects; 33-37, authors). Vol. 32, Philosophy and religion.

—— 1973, 5v.
—— 1974, 5v.
—— 1975, 5v.

15.2.4 Dissertations in philosophy accepted in American universities, 1861-1975. Thomas C. Bechtle and Mary F. Riley. New York, Garland, 1979.

When a dissertation is available from University Microfilms, the order number is included.

15.2.5 Doctoral dissertations accepted by American universities. Published and unpublished. New York, Wilson, 1934-56. Annual. 1933/34-1954/55.

Lists dissertations accepted by U. S. and Canadian universities.
Continued by 15.2.6.

15.2.6 Microfilm abstracts; a collection of abstracts of doctoral dissertations which are available in complete form on microfilm. Ann Arbor, Mich., University Microfilms, 1935-51. vols. 1-11.

Lists dissertations accepted by universities in the U. S. and Canada.
Continued as 15.2.7.

15.2.7 **Dissertation abstracts**; abstracts of dissertations and monographs in microform. Ann Arbor, Mich., University Microfilms, 1952- . vol. 12- . Monthly.

Beginning with Vol. 27, No. 1, it is divided into two sections: Humanities and Social Sciences (A) and Sciences (B). Issued with Key-word Title and Author Indexes for A and B cumulated separately each year as Part II of Issue 12, Sections A and B. Continued as 15.2.8.

15.2.8 **Dissertation abstracts international.** Ann Arbor, Mich., University Microfilms, 1969- . Vol. 30- . Monthly.

The name change reflects the enlargement of University Microfilm's publication program by the addition of dissertations from European universities.

A continuation of 15.2.7.

Access to doctoral dissertations has been simplified by DATRIX (Direct Access to Reference Information: a Xerox service), which is a service of University Microfilms whereby they will search and supply appropriate references to microfilmed dissertations (from 1938 on) based on the reader's individual needs and "Key Word Lists."

From 1977, there is a Part C, European Abstracts, published quarterly.

15.3 TRADE SOURCES

15.3.1 **Cumulative book index**: a world list of books in the English language. New York, Wilson, 1898- .

Issued monthly (except July and Aug.), cumulated quarterly. Permanent volumes used to cover five-year periods, then two-year periods; beginning with 1969, vols. cover one year each. As of 1929 covers all books published in English. Author, title, and subject listings.

15.3.2 **Publisher's weekly**; the industry book journal. New York, Bowker, 1872- .

A weekly list of books published. Cumulated as 15.3.3.

15.3.3 **American book publishing record.** New York, Bowker, 1960- .

A monthly cumulation of the *Publisher's Weekly* (15.3.2). Annual cumulations, 1965- .

15.3.4 **Publishers' trade list annual.** New York, Bowker, 1873- .

Annual collection of catalogs of American publishers. Gives fuller information than *Books in Print* (15.3.5).

15.3.5 **Books in print**; an author-title series index to the publishers' trade list annual. New York, Bowker, 1948- .

15.3.6 **Subject guide to books in print**; an index to the publishers' trade list annual. New York, Bowker, 1957- .

A subject guide to *Books in Print* (15.3.5).

15.3.7 **Paperbound books in print.** Semiannual. New York, Bowker, 1955- .

France

15.3.8 **"Biblio,"** catalogue des ouvrages parus en langue française dans le monde entier, Oct. 1933-70. Paris, Service Bibliographique des Messageries Hachette, 1935-71. 37v.

The French trade list, giving full information, with author, subject, and title entries. Continued by 15.3.10.

15.3.9 **Bibliographie de la France**; journal général de l'imprimerie et de la librairie. Paris, Cercle de la Librairie, 1811-71.

Weekly.

The official list of acquisitions of the dépôt légal.

Continued by 15.3.10.

15.3.10 **Bibliographie de la France/Biblio.** Bibliographie Officielle. Livres. 1972- Weekly.

Formed by combining 15.3.8 and 15.3.9.

Germany

15.3.11 Deutsche Nationalbibliographie und Bibliographie des im Ausland erschienenen deutschsprachigen Schrifttums. Leipzig, Verlag für Buch-und Bibliothekswesen 1931- .

Reihe A, weekly; Reihe B, semimonthly. Cumulates into 15.3.12

15.3.12 Jahresverzeichnis des deutschen Schrifttums, 1945/46-67, bearb. und hrsg. von der Deutsch Bücherei und dem Borsenverein der Deutschen Buchhandler zu Leipzig. Leipzig, Borsenverein, 1948- .

An annual cumulation of 15.3.11. Superseded by 15.3.13.

15.3.13 Jahresverzeichnis der Verlagsschriften. Leipzig, VEB Verlag für Buch-und Bibliothekswesen, 1972- .

Supersedes 15.3.12. Continued its numbering.

15.3.14 Deutsches Bücherverzeichnis; Verzeichnis der in Deutschland, Osterreich, der Schweiz und im übrigen Ausland herausgegeben deutschsprachigen Verlagsschriften sowei der wichtigsten Veröffentlichungen asserhalb des Buchhandels, 1911- . Leipzig, Verlag für Buch-und Bibliothekswesen, 1915- .

Five-year cumulations of 15.3.12 and 15.3.13.

15.3.15 Deutsche Bibliographie; wöchentliches Verzeichnis. Frankfurt am Main, Buchhändler-Vereinigung GMBH, 1947- . Weekly.

Cumulated semiannually into *Deutsche Bibliographie; Halbjahres-Verzeichnis.*

Frankfurt am Main, Buchhandler-Vereinigung, 1951- , which is in turn cumulated quinquennially into *Deutsche Bibliographie; Fünfjahres-Verzeichnis. Bücher und Karten,* 1945-50– . Frankfurt am Main, Buchhändler-Vereinigung, 1952- .

A competitor of the trade journals published in Leipzig (15.3.11-15.3.14), with much duplicaton.

Great Britain

15.3.16 British national bibliography, 1950- . London, Council of the British National Bibliography, British Museum. 1950- .

Weekly with four cumulations a year, and annual and five-year cumulations. Based on the copyright accessions of the British Museum.

15.3.17 The bookseller: the organ of the booktrade. London. Whitaker, 1958- .

Weekly since 1909, with monthly cumulations. Cumulates into *Whitaker's Cumulative Book List* (15.3.18); after 1970, into *Whitaker's Books of the Month* (15.3.19).

15.3.18 Whitaker's cumulative book list. London, Whitaker, 1924-69.

Quarterly, cumulating into yearly and five-yearly cumulations. The complete list of all books published in the United Kingdom, giving details as to author, title, subtitle, size, number of pages, price classification, and publisher. Subtitle varies.

15.3.19 Whitaker's books of the month and books to come, Jan. 1970- . London, Whitaker, 1970- . Monthly.

Cumulates 15.3.17.

16. BIOGRAPHICAL SOURCES

While the biographies of the more important figures in the history of philosophy are usually available in the major encyclopedias or histories of philosophy, it is often difficult to find information in these sources on relatively minor figures or on contemporary or near contemporary philosophers. Philosophical biographical sources (2.1) must frequently be supplemented by general biographical sources. National biographies are useful in searching for biographical information on particular philosophers from countries covered by such biographies.

16.1 GENERAL

Indexes

16.1.1 **Biographical dictionaries master index**, 1975-76: a guide to more than 725,000 listings in over 50 current Who's Whos and other works of collective biography. Ed. by Dennis Le Beau and Gary C. Tarbert. Detroit, Mich., Gale Research, 1975. 3v.

16.1.2 **Biography index**; a cumulative index to biographical material in books and magazines. New York, Wilson, 1947-to date.

Quarterly with annual and three-year cumulations. Wider in coverage than "Who's Who" books.

16.1.3 **Lobies, Jean-Pierre.** Index bio-bibliographicus notorum hominum. Osnabruck, Biblio, 1972- .

In progress.
An index to bio-bibliographical information in 2000 collective works covering all periods and countries.

16.1.4 **Riches, Phyllis.** Analytical bibliography of universal collected biography, comprising books published in the English tongue in Great Britain and Ireland, America and

the British Dominions. London, Library Association, 1934. 709 pp.

An index to biographies written in English.

International

16.1.5 **Biographie universelle** (Michaud) ancienne et moderne. Nouv. éd., publiée sous la direction de M. Michaud. Paris, Mme. C. Desplaces, 1843-65. 45v.

1st ed. 1811-57. 84v.
Still useful.

16.1.6 **Dictionary of scientific biography.** Includes some philosophers and theologians. *See* 21.3.1.

16.1.7 **Chamber's biographical dictionary.** J. O. Thorne. New York, St. Martin's, 1969. 1,432 pp.

"The great of all nations and all times." Includes an index of pseudonyms.

16.1.8 **Contemporary authors**; a biobibliographical guide to current authors and their works. Detroit, Gale Research, 1962-to date. Annual.

Frequency varies. An international bio-graphical source on authors in a variety of fields, including philosophy. Supplies basic personal and career data plus bibliographies and work in progress.

16.1.9 Current biography; who's news and why. New York, Wilson, 940-to date.

Published monthly, except August, and cumulated annually.
Cumulated index, 1940-70. New York, Wilson, 1973. 113 pp.

16.1.10 Dictionary of international biogra-phy. Dartmouth Chronicle Group Ltd., 1963- . Annual.

Indicates all other reference works which also contain sketches of biographies.

16.1.11 Hoefer, Ferdinand. Nouvelle biogra-phie générale depuis les temps les plus re-culés jusqu'à nos jours. Paris, Firmin-Didot, 1853-66. 46v.

A rival of Michaud (16.1.5).
Reprinted: Copenhague, Rosenkilde & Bagger, 1963-69.

16.1.12 Hyamson, Albert. A dictionary of universal biography of all ages and of all peoples. New York, Dutton, 1951. 679 pp.

1st ed. 1916.
An index to persons listed in 24 other biographical dictionaries. International in scope.

16.1.13 International who's who. 1935-to date. London, Europa Publications, and Allen & Unwin. Annual.

Short biographies of prominent persons.

16.1.14 Laffont-Bompiani. Dictionnaire bio-graphique des auteurs de tous les temps et de tous les pays. *See* 18.1.9-18.1.12.

16.1.15 Montgomery, John Marwick, *Gen. ed.* International Scholars Directory. Strasbourg, France, International Scholarly Publishers, 1973. 288 pp.

16.1.16 Webster's biographical dictionary, a dictionary of names of noteworthy persons, with pronunciations and concise biographies. Springfield, Merriam, 1972. 1697 pp.

1st ed. 1943.
Brief biographies of upwards of 40,000 persons.

16.1.17 World of learning. London, Europa Publications, 1947-to date. Annual.

Lists learned societies, research institutes, libraries, and all institutions of higher learn-ing, their administrators and senior staff. Often useful for finding addresses of profes-sors in foreign institutions.

16.1.18 Who's who in the world. Chicago, Marquis, 1970- .

16.2 BY COUNTRY

United States

16.2.1 Appleton's Cyclopaedia of American biography, ed. by J. G. Wilson and John Fiske. New York, Appleton, 1894-1900. 7v.

Reprinted: Detroit, Mich., Gale, 1968.

16.2.2 Dictionary of American biography. New York, Scribner, 1928-37. 20v. and Index.

Does not include living persons.
Four supplements, 1944-74, include per-sons who died between original publication date and 1950.
Includes bibliographies.

16.2.3 National cyclopedia of American bi-ography. New York, White, 1892- .

57 permanent volumes, plus current vol-umes of living persons, and index volumes.
The most comprehensive American bio-graphical work.

16.2.4 New York Times biographical edition; a compilation of current biographical infor-mation of general interest. New York, Times, 1970- . Loose-leaf. Monthly.

Frequency varies; originally weekly.

16.2.5 Notable names in American history: a tabulated register. 3d ed. of White's conspectus of American biography. Clifton, N. J., White, 1973. 725 pp.

1st ed. 1906.

16.2.6 Who was who in America. Chicago, Marquis, 1942- .

Historical volume, 1607-1896; vol. 1, 1897-1942; vol. 2, 1943-1950; vol. 3, 1951-1960; vol. 4, 1961-68; vol. 5, 1969-73.
A companion to *Who's Who in America* (16.2.7).

16.2.7 Who's who in America. Chicago, Marquis 1899- . Biennial.

Includes, by virtue of their position, professors at major American universities.

Canada

16.2.8 Canadian who's who. Toronto, Trans-Canada Press, 1910- .

16.2.9 Dictionary of Canadian biography/Dictionnaire biographique du Canada. Toronto, University of Toronto Press, 1966- .

In progress. Includes bibliographies.
Vol. 1, 1000-1700; vol.2, 1701-1740; vol. 3, 1741-1770; vol. 9, 1861-1870; vol. 10, 1871-1880.

16.2.10 Who's who in North America, 1976. Toronto, Quest Adventures (Canada), 1976.

France

16.2.11 Dictionnaire biographique français contemporain. 2. éd. Paris, Pharos, 1954. 708 pp.

Supplements 1-2, 1955-56.

16.2.12 Dictionnaire de biographie française. Paris, Letouzey, 1933- .

In progress.

16.2.13 Who's who in France; dictionnaire biographique. Paris, Lafitte, 1953- . Biennial.

Germany

16.2.14 Allgemeine deutsche Biographie. Hrsg. durch die Historische Commission bei der Königl. Akademie der Wissenschaften. Leipzig, Duncker, 1875-1912. 56v.

The basic German biographical dictionary. Includes bibliographies.
Reprinted: Berlin, Duncker & Humblot, 1967.

16.2.15 Neue deutsche Biographie; ein Biographisches Lexikon. Berlin, Duncker und Humblot, 1953- .

In progress.
20v. projected.
Supplements 16.2.14.

16.2.16 Wer ist Wer. West Berlin, Societäts-Verlag. 1905- .

Title, publisher and frequency vary.

16.2.17 Who's who in Germany: a biographical dictionary . . . 1956- . Munich, Oldenbourg, 1955- . Irregular. 4th ed., 1972.

Great Britain

16.2.18 Dictionary of national biography. London, Smith, Elder, 1885-1901. 63v.

Index and epitome, 1903-13. 2v. Reissue, 22v., 1908-09; reprinted, 1938. 2d-7th supplements, Oxford University Press, 1912-71. 5v.
The basic English biographical work, with bibliographies.

16.2.19 Who was who; a companion to Who's who. London, Black, 1929-72. 6v.

Lists deceased persons from the 1897-1960 volumes of *Who's who*.

16.2.20 **Who's who**. London, St. Martin's, 1849- . Annual.

Publisher varies.
Assumed its present form and coverage in 1897.

Italy

16.2.21 **Chi e?** Dizionario degli italiani d'oggi. 7. ed. Roma, Scarano, 1961. 714 pp.

16.2.22 **Dizionario biografico degli italiani.** Roma, Istit. della Enciclopedia Italiana, 1960- .

In progress.
Does not include living persons.

16.2.23 **Enciclopedia biographica e biblio-** graphica "italiana." Milano, Tosi, 1936-44. Series 4-50.

Never completed.
Divided according to professions; for philosophers see especially series XXXVIII: Pedagogisti ed Educatori.

16.2.24 **Who's who in Italy**. Milano, Intercontinental Book and Publishing, 1958.

Text in English.

Spain

16.2.25 **Who's who in Spain**. Barcelona, Intercontinental Book and Publishing, 1963- .

Text in English.

RELATED FIELDS

Since research in philosophy often involves other disciplines, the philosopher must use research tools in other fields. The aim of this section is to simplify the task of the researcher by leading him quickly and directly to the main sources of information in fields related to philosophy.

The task of the researcher is greatly facilitated when there exists a good basic guide to research in a given field. The *Sources of Information in the Social Sciences* by Carl M. White (20.1.1) is perhaps the finest example of such a guide. It consists of a separate chapter for each discipline in the social sciences which includes an essay on methodology and lists the main research tools in the field with a description and an evaluation of each work selected. It should be the first source of information consulted for research in any of the social sciences which for White includes history and education. Although the social sciences are well served by this guide, other fields are less fortunate.

Where reliable guides exist for a specific discipline, the fact is noted by indicating the entry as a useful first source of information. *Reference Sources in English and American Literature* by Schweik and Riesner (18.2.3) is a good example of such a guide.

In addition to guides to research, each section lists standard bibliographies in the field, principal encyclopedias and dictionaries, and any other major source of information that could prove useful to the researcher.

Two basic general sources that should be consulted in any field are *Guide to Reference Books* (13.1.6), 9th ed., Eugene P. Sheehy, ed. (formerly edited by Constance Winchell), and Walford's *Guide to Reference Material* (13.1.7), the British equivalent to Sheehy. The many sections, according to discipline, of the French abstract journal, *Bulletin Signalétique* (17.1.4), offer invaluable information on current publications.

When there exists in a field a bibliography of bibliographies, it is listed first. All other listings are in alphabetical order.

17. RELIGION

The field of religion offers a great abundance of reference works because of its long history, the variety of religions throughout the world, and the broad range of different viewpoints expressed. This section presents a basic selection of standard works available. The researcher is encouraged to make use of the guides listed for more comprehensive information. For the philosopher, Mitros' *Religions: A Select, Classified Bibliography* (17.1.7) is a good first source. See also Philosophy of Religion (Section 7.9).

17.1 GENERAL AND COMPARATIVE RELIGION

Guides and Bibliographies

17.1.1 **Barrows, John Graves**. A bibliography of bibliographies in religion. Ann Arbor, Edwards, 1955. 489 pp.

Entries are annotated, grouped by topics and indexed.

17.1.2 **Adams, Charles J.**, *ed.* A reader's guide to the great religions. 2d ed. New York, Free Press, 1977. 521 pp.

Bibliographic essays describing the most useful works, especially those in English, on the various religions.

17.1.3 **Berkowitz, Morris I.**, and **J. E. Johnson**. Social scientific studies of religion; a bibliography. Pittsburgh, Pittsburgh University Press, 1967. 258 pp.

17.1.4 **Bulletin signalétique**, 527: Sciences religieuses. Paris, Centre Nationale de la Recherche Scientifique, 1947- . Quarterly.

An important abstract journal, with many separate sections in the humanities, arts, and sciences, as well as in philosophy and religion.

17.1.5 **Index to religious periodical literature**. Chicago, American Theological Library Association, 1949- .

Semiannual with two-year cumulations. Includes philosophical topics.

17.1.6 **International bibliography of the history of religions**. Leiden, Brill, 1952- . Annual.

Lists articles and books, with no annotations.

17.1.7 **Mitros, Joseph F.** Religions; a select, classified bibliography. New York, Learned Publishers; Louvain, Nauwelaerts, 1973. 435 pp. (Philosophical questions series, 8)

The most useful of the guides; strong philosophical orientation; includes extensive coverage of non-Christian religions.

17.1.8 **Sheehy, Eugene P.**, *ed.* Guide to reference books. *See* 13.1.6, section BB, Religion, pp. 252-83.

17.1.9 **Walford, Albert John**, *ed.* Guide to reference material. *See* 13.1.7, v.2: Social and historical sciences, Philosophy and religion, part 2, pp. 28-74.

See also: 7.2.4, 7.9.1-7.9.3.

Dictionary

17.1.10 Dictionary of comparative religion. S. G. F. Brandon, gen. ed. London, Weidenfeld & Nicolson; New York, Scribner's, 1970. 704 pp.

Articles are signed, brief, and most are followed by bibliographies.

Collection

17.1.11 Muller, F. Max, *ed.* Sacred Books of the East. Oxford, Clarendon Press, 1879-1910. 50v.

Reprinted: N. Y., Dover, 1963-69.
Includes the most important works of Asiatic religions, translated by various oriental scholars.

17.2 BUDDHISM, CHRISTIANITY, HINDUISM, ISLAM AND JUDAISM

Buddhism

Guides and Bibliographies

17.2.1 Bibliographie bouddhique. *See 8.2.4.*

17.2.2 Hanayana, Shinsho. Bibliography on Buddhism. *See 8.2.5.*

17.2.3 Yoo, Yushin. Books on Buddhism. *See 8.2.7.*

17.2.4 Yoo, Yushin. Buddhism: A subject index to periodical articles in English, 1728-1971. Metuchen, N. J., Scarecrow, 1973. 162 pp.

Useful together with *Books on Buddhism,* 17.2.3.

Dictionaries

17.2.5 Humphreys, Christmas. A popular dictionary of Buddhism. *See 8.2.1.*

17.2.6 Soothill, William E., and Lewis Hodous. A dictionary of Chinese Buddhist terms. *See 8.2.2.*

See also: 8.2.1-8.2.9.

Christianity

Dictionaries

17.2.7 Baker's Dictionary of Christian ethics. Carl F. H. Henry, ed. Grand Rapids, Baker Book House, 1973. 726 pp.

Claims to be "authentically evangelical" (Pref.) but not to be partisan. Articles are signed and many have bibliographies.

17.2.8 Dictionnaire de spiritualité, ascétique et mystique, doctrine et histoire. Publié sous la direction de J. de Guibert. Paris, Beauchesne, 1932-.

In progress.
Finished through v.6, Gab-Gode.

17.2.9 Dictionnaire de théologie catholique. Publié sous la direction de A. Vacant, E. Mangenot et E. Amann. Paris, Letouzey, 1909-50. 15v.

Good not only for theology but also for medieval philosophy. Good bibliographies.
Tables générales, par Bernard Loth et Albert Michel. Paris, Letouzey, 1951-72. 2v.
Synthesizes and in some cases updates materials in the *Dictionnaire.*

17.2.10 Die Religion in Geschichte und Gegenwart. Handwörterbuch für Theologie und Religionswissenschaft. 3 vollig neubearb. Aufl. hrsg. von Kurt Galling. Tübingen, J. C. B. Mohr, 1956-65. 7v.

1st ed. 1909-13.

17.2.11 **Dizionario di teologia morale.** Diretto da F. Roberti. Roma, Studium, 1954. 1503 pp.

17.2.12 **The interpreter's dictionary of the Bible.** New York, Abingdon, 1962. 4v. Supplementary volume, 1976.

Identifies and explains all proper names, significant terms and subjects of the Bible, including the Apocrypha. Ecumenical approach.

17.2.13 **Lexikon für Theologie und Kirche.** 2 vollig. neubearb. Aufl. Hrsg. von Josef Hofer und Karl Rahner. Freiburg, Herder, 1957-65. 10v.

1st ed. 1930-38.
Roman Catholic.

17.2.14 **Oxford dictionary of the Christian church.** F. L. Cross and E. A. Livingstone, eds. 2d ed. London, Oxford University Press, 1974. 1518 pp.

Approach is primarily historical. Includes bibliographies.

17.2.15 **Parente, Pietro, Antonio Piolanti**, e **Salvatore Garofalo.** Dictionary of dogmatic theology. Trans. by E. Doronzo. Milwaukee, Bruce, 1951. 310 pp.

Translation of *Dizionario di teologia dogmatica*, 2. ed., Roma, Studium, 1945.

17.2.16 **Richardson, Alan.** A dictionary of Christian theology. London, SCM Press; Philadelphia, Westminster, 1969. 364 pp.

Includes bibliographies.

Encyclopedias

17.2.17 **New Catholic encyclopedia.** Ed. in chief, Most Rev. William J. McDonald, D. D. New York, McGraw-Hill, 1967. 15 v.

A supplementary volume (v. 16), 1974, updates material for period 1967-74.

"An international work of reference on the teachings, history, organization and activities of the Catholic Church, and on all institutions, religions, philosophies, and scientific and cultural developments affecting the Catholic Church from its beginnings to the present."
Includes articles on philosophy.

17.2.18 **New Schaff-Herzog encyclopedia of religious knowledge.** New York, Funk & Wagnalls, 1908-12. 12v. and Index.

Reprinted: Grand Rapids, Mich., Baker Book House, 1949-50. 13v.

Based on *Realencyklopädie*, founded by J. J. Herzog. Supplemented and to some extent revised by: *Twentieth century encyclopedia of religious knowledge.* Grand Rapids, Mich., Baker Book House, 1955. 2v.

Good bibliographies; especially useful for Protestant theology.

17.2.19 **Sacramentum mundi: an encyclopedia of theology.** Ed. by Karl Rahner with Cornelius Ernst and Kevin Smyth. New York, Herder and Herder, 1968-79. 6v.

A compendium of postconciliar Catholic theology.
Also German, French, Italian, Spanish, and Dutch editions.

Encyclopedia of theology; the concise Sacramentum mundi. New York, Seabury Press, 1975. 1841 pp.
"Contains revised versions of the major articles from *Sacramentum mundi,* together with a large number of articles from the major German works, *Lexikon für Theologie und Kirche,* and *Theologisches Taschenlexikon,* and entirely new articles" (Pref.).

See also: 4.2.7, 4.2.8.

Hinduism

Bibliographies

17.2.20 **Dandekar, R. N.** Vedic Bibliography. *See* 9.6.11.

17.2.21 **Renou, Louis.** Bibliographie védique. *See* 9.6.14.

Dictionaries

17.2.22 Dowson, John. A classical dictionary of Hindu mythlogy and religion, geography, history, and literature. 11th ed. London, Routledge and Kegan Paul, 1968. 411 pp.

1st ed. 1879.

17.2.23 Walker, George Benjamin. The Hindu world; an encyclopedic survey of Hinduism. New York, Praeger, 1968. 2v.

Dictionary of terms as well as of names, places and customs.

Islam

Bibliographies

17.2.24 Pearson, J. Index Islamicus, 1906-55; a catalog of articles on Islamic subjects in periodicals and other collective publications. Cambridge, Heffer, 1958. 897 pp.

Reprinted: London, Mansell, 1972.
1st supplement, 1956-60, Cambridge, Heffer, 1962, 312 pp.
2nd supplement, 1961-65, Cambridge, Heffer, 1967, 342 pp.
3rd supplement, 1966-70, compiled by J. Pearson and A. Walsh, London, Mansell, 1972, 384 pp.
Continued as quarterly, Vol. I- , 1977- .

17.2.25 Sauvaget, Jean. Introduction to the history of the Muslim East: a bibliographical guide. See 9.5.7.

Encyclopedia

17.2.26 Encyclopedia of Islam. New ed., ed. by C. E. Bosworth, E. van Donzel, B. Lewis, and Ch. Pellat. Leiden, Brill, 1954- .

In progress.
1978, Vol. IV, Fascicules 77-78, Khani-kin-al Khazz.
1st ed. 1911-38, 4v. in 8. Supplement, 1934-38.
A basic reference work on Islam. Editors change.

17.2.27 The shorter encyclopedia of Islam. Edited by H. A. R. Gibb and J. K. Kramers. Leiden, Brill; Ithaca, Cornell University Press, 1953. 671 pp.

Review Journal

17.2.28 The Islamic review. 1913-to date. Monthly (irregular). Ed., The Shah Jehan Mosque, Woking, Surrey.

Title varies: Feb. 1913-Jan. 1914 as *Muslim India and Islamic world;* Feb. 1914-20 as *Islamic Review and Muslim India.*
Articles, book reviews, index. A cultural journal dealing with the world of Islam.

Judaism

Bibliography

17.2.29 Shunami, Shlomo. Bibliography of Jewish bibliographies. *See* 9.5.12.

Encyclopedias

17.2.30 Encyclopedia Judaica. Jerusalem, Encyclopaedia Judaica; New York, Macmillan, 1972. 16v.

Encyclopaedia Judaica yearbook. 1973- .
Supplements and updates the basic work.
Includes bibliographies.
A basic work, comprehensive and up-to-date.

17.2.31 Jewish encyclopedia; a descriptive record of the Jewish people from the earliest times to the present day. Prepared under the direction of Cyrus Adler. New York, Funk & Wagnalls, 1901-06. 12v.

Long the standard encyclopedia in English in its field; still useful though out-of-date.

17.2.32 Jüdisches Lexikon; ein enzyklopädisches Handbuch des jüdischen Wissens . . . ,hrsg. von Georg Herlitz und Bruno Kirschner. Berlin, Jüdischer Verlag, 1927-30. 4v. in 5.

17.2.33 **Universal Jewish encyclopedia.** Ed. by Isaac Landman. New York, Universal Jewish Encyclopedia, Inc., 1939-43. 10v.

"Especially strong in treatment of American subjects and of the twentieth century" (13.1.6).

Review Journal

17.2.34 **The Jewish quarterly review.** 1888-to date. Quarterly (July, Oct., Jan., Apr.). Eds.,

A. I. Katsh and S. Zeitlin, Dropsie University, Broad and York Streets, Philadelphia, Pa. 19132.

V.1-20 (1888-1908); ns. v.1 July 1910-to date.

Cum. Index: v.1-20 (1910-1930).

See also: 9.5.11-9.5.16.

For mythology and folklore, *see* 20.2.9-20.2.13.

18. HUMANITIES

These sections present the principal bibliographies, the most useful guides, the standard encyclopedias and dictionaries, and the basic histories in literature, history and linguistics.

The *MLA International Bibliography* (18.1.6) is the most important annual bibliography for American researchers in literary fields. The Oxford companions to various national literatures offer a convenient source in English of basic information, including biographies and bibliographies.

18.1 GENERAL AND COMPARATIVE LITERATURE

Guides and Bibliographies

18.1.1 **Baldensperger, Fernand**, and **Werner P. Friederich**. Bibliography of comparative literature. Chapel Hill, University of North Carolina Press, 1950. 701 pp.

University of North Carolina studies in comparative literature, no. 1. Continued by the "Annual Bibliography" in the *Yearbook of comparative and general literature,* Bloomington, Indiana University, 1952- , v. 1- . After v. 19 (including 1969) the bibliography was discontinued.

Reprinted: N. Y., Russell and Russell, 1975, v.1-11.

18.1.2 **Bulletin signalétique**, 523: Histoire et sciences de la littérature. *See* 17.1.4.

18.1.3 **Index translationum**. Répertoire international des traductions. International bibliography of translations. *See* 14.2.2

18.1.4 **Literatures of the world in English translation**; a bibliography. New York, Ungar, 1967-70. v.1-5.

Vol. 1, The Greek and Latin literatures, ed. by George B. Parks and Ruth Z. Temple.

Vol. 2, The Slavic literatures, comp. by Richard C. Lewanski.

Vol. 3, The Romance literatures, ed. by George B. Parks and Ruth Z. Temple.

Vol. 4, The Celtic, Germanic, and other literatures of Europe. In preparation.

Vol. 5, The literatures of Asia and Africa. In preparation.

Works of philosophy are listed.

18.1.5 **Malclès, Louise.** Les sources du travail bibliographique (1950-1958). *See* 13.1.10.

Vol. 2, pt. 1-2, includes languages and literatures.

18.1.6 **Modern Language Association of America**. MLA international bibliography of books and articles on the modern languages and literatures. 1921- .

The basic annual bibliography for Americans.

Reprinted: N. Y., Kraus Reprints, 1921-1977.

18.1.7 **Sheehy, Eugene P.**, *ed.* Guide to reference books. *See* 13.1.6, section BD, Literature, pp. 293-374.

18.1.8 Walford, Albert John, *ed.* Guide to reference material. *See* 13.1.7, v.3, Generalities, languages, the arts and literature, part 8, Literature, pp. 475-626.

Dictionaries

18.1.9 Dizionario letterario Bompiani delle opere et dei personaggi di tutti i tempi e di tutte le letterature. Milan, Bompiani, 1947-50. 9v.

Appendice, 1964-66. 2v.
Lists and describes works of literature, art and music of all times and of all countries.

This dictionary has served as the model and inspiration for similar works in French and German (18.1.11-18.1.16). Together they provide comprehensive coverage of basic information on world literature: authors, works, characters, movements, historical data, and bibliographies of editions and critical works. Philosophers and their works are included.

18.1.10 Dizionario universale delle letteratura contemporanea. Direttore: Alberto Mondadori. Milano, Mondadori, 1959-63. 5v.

Covers 1870-1960, and supplements Bompiani (18.1.9).

18.1.11 Kindlers Literatur Lexicon. (Wissenschaftliche Vorbereitung: Wolfgang von Einsiedel. Chefredakteur: Gert Woerner.) Zürich, Kindler, 1965-72. 7v.

Supplement, 1974. 1375 pp.
Inspired by Bompiani (18.1.9), but completely new.

18.1.12 Laffont-Bompiani. Dictionnaire biographique des auteurs de tous les temps et de tous les pays. Paris, Société d'Edition de Dictionnaires et Encyclopédies, 1957-58. 2v.

18.1.13 Laffont-Bompiani. Dictionnaire des oeuvres de tous les temps et de tous les pays: littérature, philosophie, musique, science. 4e éd. Paris, S.E.D.E., 1962. 4v. and Index.

1st ed. 1952-54.
Abridged French edition of 18.1.9.

18.1.14 Laffont-Bompiani. Dictionnaire des oeuvres contemporaines de tous les pays. Paris, S.E.D.E., 1968.

Vol. 5 of 18.1.13.

18.1.15 Laffont-Bompiani. Dictionnaire des personnages littéraires et dramatiques de tous les temps et de tous les pays: poésie, théâtre, roman, musique. Paris, S.E.D.E., 1960. 668 pp.

18.1.16 Laffont-Bompiani. Dictionnaire universel des lettres. Paris, S.E.D.E., 1961. 952 pp.

Encyclopedias

18.1.17 Holman, Clarence Hugh. A handbook to literature. Based on the original by William Flint Thrall and Addison Hibbard. 3d ed. Indianapolis, Odyssey Press, 1972. 646 pp.

Basic and very useful; explanations of critical terms, movements and concepts in literature.

18.1.18 Preminger, Alex, *ed.* Princeton encyclopedia of poetry and poetics. Enl. ed. Princeton, N.J., Princeton University Press, 1974. 992 pp.

Orig. ed. 1965.
Comprehensive and basic; covers poetic theory, schools of criticism, and critical terms. Includes bibliographies.

18.2 AMERICAN AND ENGLISH LITERATURE

Guides and Bibliographies

18.2.1 Altick, Richard D., and **Andrew Wright.** Selective bibliography for the study of English and American literature. 5th ed. New York, Macmillan, 1975. 168 pp.

6th ed. due in 1979.
A helpful guide with some annotations.

18.2.2 Modern Humanities Research Associ-

ation. Annual bibliography of English language and literature. 1920- . v.1- . Annual.

18.2.3 **Schweik, Robert C., and Dieter Riesner**. Reference sources in English and American literature: an annotated bibliography. New York, Norton, 1977. 258 pp.

The most useful of the many guides available. A well organized and clear presentation with descriptive and evaluative annotations.

American Literature

Bibliographies

18.2.4 **Nilon, Charles H**. Bibliography of bibliographies in American literature. New York, Bowker, 1970. 483 pp.

Includes books, periodical articles and bibliographies appearing as parts of books.

18.2.5 **American literary scholarship**, an annual. 1963- . Durham, N.C., Duke University Press, 1965- .

Bibliographic essays.

18.2.6 **Gohdes, Clarence L. F**. Bibliographical guide to the study of the literature of the U.S.A. 4th ed., rev. and enl. Durham, N.C., Duke University Press, 1976. 173 pp.

Really a guide to American studies with a thorough treatment of literature.

Dictionary

18.2.7 **Hart, James David**. The Oxford companion to American literature. 4th ed. New York, Oxford University Press, 1965. 991 pp.

1st ed. 1941.
A standard work; dictionary format.

Histories

18.2.8 **Cambridge history of American literature**. W. P. Trent [et al], ed. New York, Putnam, 1917-21. 4v.

Reprinted: N.Y., Macmillan, 1972, 1v.
Out-of-date, but still important and useful.

18.2.9 **Literary history of the United States**. R. E. Spiller [et al], ed. 4th ed., rev. New York, Macmillan, 1974. 2v.

Vol. 1, History;
vol. 2, Bibliography.
1st ed., 1948 in 3v.; various reprintings.

English Literature

Bibliographies

18.2.10 **Howard-Hill, Trevor Howard**. Bibliography of British literary bibliographies. Oxford, Clarendon Press, 1969. 570 pp.

Index to British literary bibliography, 1.

18.2.11 **Cambridge bibliography of English literature**. F. W. Bateson, ed. Cambridge, University Press, 1940-57; New York, Macmillan, 1941-57. 5v.

The revised edition (18.2.13) replaces this edition in great part.

18.2.12 **The concise Cambridge bibliography of English literature**, 600-1950. 2d ed. Cambridge, University Press, 1965. 269 pp.

An abridgment of 18.2.11.

18.2.13 **The new Cambridge bibliography of English literature**. Cambridge, University Press, 1969-74. v.1-4.

V.5, Index, in progress.

The basic bibliography in English literary studies. It is thorough, but not annotated.

Encyclopedia

18.2.14 **Chambers, Robert**. Chambers' Cyclopedia of English literature. Ed. by David Patrick and rev. by J. Liddell Geddie. London, Chambers; Philadelphia, Lippincott, 1922-38. 3v.

1st ed. 1844; rev. ed. 1901. 3v. (v.1 rev. 1927; v.2 rev. 1938; v.3 rev. 1922.)

Dictionaries

18.2.15 Concise Oxford dictionary of English literature. 2d ed. (rev. by Dorothy Eagle). Oxford, Clarendon Press, 1970. 628 pp.

1st ed. 1939.
An abridgment of 18.2.16.

18.2.16 Harvey, Sir Paul. The Oxford companion to English literature. 4th ed. rev. by Dorothy Eagle. Oxford, Clarendon Press, 1967. 961 pp.

1st ed. 1932; 3d ed. 1946.

Histories

18.2.17 Cambridge history of English literature. A. W. Ward and A. R. Waller, eds. Cambridge, University Press; New York, Putnam, 1907-33. 15v.

Reprinted: 1964-68.
Out-of date, but still an important general history of the literature. Contains useful information on minor figures.

18.2.18 The concise Cambridge history of English literature. George Sampson, ed. 3rd ed. rev. by R. C. Churchill. Cambridge, University Press, 1970. 976 pp.

Orig. ed. 1941.

18.2.19 Oxford history of English literature. F. P. Wilson and B. Dobree, eds. Oxford, Clarendon Press, 1945-69. V.2, 3-4, 5-7, 9-10, 12.

In progress.
A standard work; includes extensive bibliographies.

18.3 FOREIGN LITERATURES

18.3.1 Parks, George B., and **Ruth Z. Temple,** *eds.* Literatures of the world in English translation; a bibliography. See 18.1.4.

German Literature

Bibliographies

18.3.2 Bibliographie der deutschen Sprach- und Literaturwissenschaft. Bd. 1- , 1945/53- . Frankfurt am Main, Klostermann, 1957- . Annual.

Editors vary: H. W. Eppelsheimer, C. Kottelwesch. *See* 18.3.4.

18.3.3 Goedeke, Karl. Grundriss zur Geschichte der deutschen Dichtung aus den Quellen. 2. ganz neubearb. Aufl. Dresden, Ehlermann, 1884-1966. 15v.

This is considered the most complete bibliography of German literature. Exhaustive coverage. Index in each volume, but no cumulative index.

18.3.4 Kottelwesch, Clemens. Bibliographisches Handbuch der deutschen Literaturwissenschaft, 1945-69. Frankfurt am Main, Klostermann, 1971- . Lfg. 1- .

In progress.
About 10v. projected, to cumulate and supplement Eppelsheimer and Kottelwesch's *Bibliographie der deutschen Sprach- und Literaturwissenschaft* (18.3.1).

18.3.5 Morgan, Bayard Quincy. A critical bibliography of German literature in English translation, 1481-1927. 2d ed. New York, Scarecrow, 1965. 690 pp.

Supplement for 1928-55, 601 pp.
1st ed. 1922.
Includes philosophers.

18.3.6 Smith, Murray F. A selected bibliography of German literature in English translation, 1956-60. Metuchen, N.J., Scarecrow, 1972. 398 pp.

A second supplement to 18.3.5. Includes all fields.

Dictionary

18.3.7 The Oxford companion to German lit-

erature. Oxford, Clarendon Press, 1976. 977 pp.

A basic reference source in English.

Romance Literatures

18.3.8 **Palfrey, Thomas Rossman, Joseph G. Fucilla,** and **William C. Holbrook.** A bibliographical guide to the Romance languages and literatures. 8th ed. Evanston, Ill., Chandler, 1971. 122 pp.

A basic general guide.

18.3.9 **Parks, George B.,** and **Ruth Z. Temple,** *eds.* Literatures of the world in English translation; a bibliography: the Romance literatures. See 18.1.4, Literatures of the world in English translation, v.3: Part 1, Catalan, Italian, Portuguese and Brazilian, Provençal, Rumanian, Spanish and Spanish American literatures; part 2, French literature.

French Literature

Guides and Bibliographies

18.3.10 **Bassan, Fernande, Paul F. Breed,** and **Donald C. Spinelli.** An annotated bibliography of French language and literature. New York, Garland, 1976; 2nd, rev. printing, 1977. 306 pp.

Garland reference library of the humanities, v.26.
A very useful guide in English.

18.3.11 **Cabeen, D. C.,** and **J. Brody,** *gen eds.* A critical bibliography of French literature. Syracuse, N.Y., Syracuse University Press, 1947-1968. 4v. and supplement.

In progress.
An important annotated bibliography in English.

18.3.12 **Klapp, Otto von,** *ed.* Bibliographie der französischen Literaturwissenschaft. Frankfurt am Main, Klostermann, 1960- , v.1- . Annual.

Exhaustive coverage of the field.

18.3.13 **Langlois, Pierre,** and **André Mareuil.** Guide bibliographique des études littéraires. 5e éd. Paris, Hachette, 1968. 295 pp.

Good basic guide for standard editions and critical works on major French authors.

18.3.14 **Osburn, Charles.** Research and reference guide to French studies. Metuchen, N.J., Scarecrow, 1968. 517 pp.

Supplement, 1972, 377 pp.
Not annotated.

18.3.15 **Rancoeur, René.** Bibliographie de la littérature française du moyen âge à nos jours. Paris, Colin, 1953- . Annual.

A basic bibliography in French studies.

Dictionaries

18.3.16 **Harvey, Sir Paul,** and **Janet E. Heseltine.** The Oxford companion to French literature. Oxford, Clarendon Press, 1959. 771 pp.

Reprinted with corrections, 1961.

18.3.17 **Morier, Henri.** Dictionnaire de poétique et de rhétorique. 2e éd. Paris, Presses Universitaires de France, 1975. 1210 pp.

1e éd. 1961.

History

18.3.18 **Lanson, Gustave.** Histoire de la littérature française. (Remaniée et complétée pour la période 1850-1950 par Paul Tuffrau.) Paris, Hachette, 1952. 1441 pp.

A standard work. Frequent reprints.

Spanish Literature

Guides and Bibliographies

18.3.19 **Sainz y Rodriguez, Pedro.** Biblioteca

bibliográfica hispánica. (Bibliography of Spanish bibliographies.) Madrid, Seminario "M. Pelayo" de la Fundación Universitatia Española, 1976. 4v.

18.3.20 Arnaud, Emile. Guide de bibliographie hispanique. Toulouse, Privat-Didier, 1967. 353 pp.

Useful guide; covers culture and language as well as literature.

18.3.21 Foster, David W., and V. R. Foster. Manual of Hispanic bibliography. 2d ed. New York, Garland, 1977. 350 pp.

1st ed. 1970.

18.3.22 Rudder, Robert S. The literature of Spain in English translation: a bibliography. New York, Ungar, 1975. 637 pp.

18.3.23 Simón Díaz, José. Bibliografía de la literatura hispánica. Madrid, Consejo superior de Investigaciones Científicas, Inst. "Miguel de Cervantes" de Filología Hispánica, 1950-72. v.1-10.

In progress.
2. ed., corr. y aum., v.1-6, 11, 1960-76.
Comprehensive coverage of all the Hispanic literatures.

Dictionaries

18.3.24 Diccionario de literatura española. Dirigido por Germán Bleiberg y Julián Marías. 4. ed. Madrid, Revista de Occidente, 1972. 1245 pp.

A standard work; includes biographies, with bibliographies.

18.3.25 The Oxford companion to Spanish literature. Philip Ward, ed. Oxford, Clarendon Press, 1978. 629 pp.

A very useful work in English; includes extensive bibliographic material.

Italian Literature

18.3.26 Dizionario enciclopedico della let- teratura italiana. Bari/Roma, Laterza-Unedi, 1966-70. 6v.

Some articles include bibliographies.

Other Literatures

Latin and Greek Literature

Bibliographies

18.3.27 L'année philologique; bibliographie critique et analytique de l'antiquité gréco-latine, pub. sous la direction de J. Marouzeau (et al). 1924-26- . Paris, Société d'Editions "Les Belles-Lettres," 1928- . Annual.

18.3.28 Marouzeau, Jules. Dix années de bibliographie classique; bibliographie critique et analytique. *See* 3.1.26.

Continued by 18.3.27.

18.3.29 Parks, George B., and Ruth Z. Temple, *eds.* The Greek and Latin literatures. *See* 18.1.4, Literatures of the world in English translation, v.1.

Dictionaries

18.3.30 Daremberg, Charles, and Edmond Seglio. Dictionnaire des antiquités grecques et romaines d'après les textes et les monuments. Paris, Hachette, 1873-1919. 5v. and index.

Contains long, informative articles with bibliographies. Broad in scope.

18.3.31 The Oxford classical dictionary. N. G. L. Hammond and H. H. Scullard, eds. 2d. ed. Oxford, Clarendon Press, 1970. 1176 pp.

1st ed. 1949.
A standard reference work.

18.3.32 The Oxford companion to classical literature. Oxford, Clarendon Press, 1937. 468 pp.

Dictionary format.

Oriental Literature

18.3.33 **De Bary, Theodore,** and **Ainslie T. Embree,** *eds.* A guide to Oriental classics. 2d ed. New York, Columbia University Press, 1975. 199 pp.

1st ed. 1964.
Useful annotations; covers Islamic, Indian, Chinese and Japanese works.

18.3.34 **Pearson, J. D.** Oriental and Asian bibliography: an introduction with some reference to Africa. Hamden, Conn., Archon, 1966. 261 pp.

Bibliographic essays.

18.3.35 **Sacred books of the East.** *See* 17.1.11.

Slavic Literature

18.3.36 **Zenkovsky, Serge A.,** and **David L. Armbruster.** A guide to the bibliographies of Russian literature. Nashville, Vanderbilt University Press, 1970. 62 pp.

A helpful guide to general and specialized bibliographical sources in the field.

18.3.37 **Lewanski, Richard C.,** *ed.* The Slavic literatures. *See* 18.1.4, Literatures of the world in English translation, v.2.

18.3.38 **Weber, Harry B.,** *ed.* The modern encyclopedia of Russian and Soviet literature (MERSL). Academic International Press, 1977- . Vol. 1- .

In progress.
About 50 vols., plus indexes and supplements are projected.
Many articles in v.1 include bibliographies.

18.4 HISTORY

General History

Guides and Bibliographies

18.4.1 **American Historical Association.** Guide to historical literature. George Frederick Howe, Chairman, Board of Editors. New York, Macmillan, 1961. 962 pp.

A standard work. Selective, annotated bibliographical entries, but comprehensive in coverage.

18.4.2 **Historical abstracts**: bibliography of the world's periodical literature. Santa Barbara, Calif., American Bibliographical Center, Clio Press, 1955- . v.1- . Quarterly.

Very useful bibliography; includes philosophy of history.

18.4.3 **International bibliography of historical sciences,** ed. for the International Committee of Historical Sciences. 1926- . Oxford, University Press; New York, Wilson, 1930- . v.1- . Annual.

Reprinted: N.Y., Kraus Reprints, 1963. v.1-14, 16-34.
Includes section on the history of philosophy.
V.15, to cover 1940-46, has not been published.

18.4.4 **Poulton, Helen J.** The historian's handbook: a descriptive guide to reference works. Norman, University of Oklahoma Press, 1972. 304 pp.

A very helpful guide for the researcher new to history; evaluative descriptions of basic sources.

18.4.5 **Sheehy, Eugene P.,** *ed.* Guide to reference books. *See* 13.1.6, section D, History and area studies, pp. 598-689.

18.4.6 **Walford, Albert J.,** *ed.* Guide to reference material. *See* 13.1.7, v.2, sections 93-94, History, pp. 464-586.

18.4.7 **White, Carl M.** Sources of information in the social sciences. *See* 20.1.1, chapter 2, History, pp. 83-137.

See also: 7.7.1-7.7.7.

Encyclopedia

18.4.8 Langer, William L. An encyclopedia of world history, ancient, medieval, and modern; chronologically arranged. 5th ed. rev. and enl. Boston, Houghton Mifflin, 1972. 1569 pp.

A handbook of historical facts; helpful for quick reference.

Ancient History

18.4.9 Pauly, August Friedrich von. Paulys Real-Encyclopädie der classischen Altertumswissenschaft. Neue bearb. begonnen von Georg Wissowa, et al. Stuttgart, Metzler, 1894-1974. v.1-24, 1894-1963; 2. Reihe, v.1A-10A, 1914-1972; Suppl. v.1-14, 1903-1974.

In progress.
Standard and indispensable for classical studies; articles are followed by extensive bibliographies.

18.4.10 Der kleine Pauly; Lexikon der Antike. Bearb. und hrsg. von Konrad Ziegler und Walther Sontheimer. Stuttgart, Druckenmüller, 1964-75. 5v.

A condensation of 18.4.9, with updated scholarship and bibliographies.

18.4.11 Cambridge ancient history. 3d ed. London, Cambridge University Press, 1970-75. v.1-2. Plates to v.1-2, 1977.

In progress.
1st ed. 1923-39, 12v. and 5v. plates.
Contains extensive bibliographies.

Medieval History

18.4.12 Caenegem, R. C. Van. Guide to the sources of medieval history. Amsterdam, New York, and Oxford, North-Holland, 1978. 428 pp.

Comprehensive, with annotations in a modified essay form.

18.4.13 Paetow, Louis J. Guide to the study of medieval history. Rev. ed. prepared under the auspices of the Medieval Academy of America. New York, Crofts, 1931. 643 pp.

Reprinted: N.Y., Kraus Reprints, 1964.
1st ed. 1917.
A useful general guide, though out-of-date.

18.4.14 Repertorium fontium historiae medii aevi, primum ab Augusto Potthast digestum, nunc cura collegii historicorum e pluribus nationibus emendatum et auctum. Romae, Istituto Storico Italiano per il Medio Evo, 1962-1976. v.1-4, A-Gez.

In progress.
Orig. ed. 1896.
The "new Potthast" includes philosophy.

18.4.15 Cambridge mediaeval history, planned by J. B. Bury. 2d ed. Cambridge, University Press, 1966-67. v.4 in 2v.

In progress.
1st ed. 1911-36, 8v. Bibliographies at the end of each volume.

18.4.16 Previté-Orton, Charles W. The shorter Cambridge medieval history. Cambridge, University Press, 1952. 2v.

A concise version of 18.4.15.

Modern History

18.4.17 Roach, John P. C., *ed.* A bibliography of modern history. Cambridge, University Press, 1968. 388 pp.

Highly selective companion bibliographies to *New Cambridge modern history* (18.4.19).

18.4.18 Cambridge modern history, planned by the late Lord Acton, ed. by A. W. Ward (et al). Cambridge, University Press; New York, Macmillan, 1902-26. 13v. and atlas.

"The most important general modern history," (13.1.6).

18.4.19 New Cambridge modern history.

Cambridge, University Press, 1957-70. v.1-12, 14.

In progress.
See 18.4.17 for companion bibliographies.

American History

18.4.20 Freidel, Frank, *ed.* Harvard guide to American history. Rev. ed. Cambridge, Belknap Press of Harvard University Press, 1974. 2v. (1290 pp.)

1st ed. 1954.
The standard bibliography in American history.

18.4.21 Adams, James T. Dictionary of American history. Rev. ed. New York, Scribners, 1976. 7v. and Index.

1st ed. 1940, 5v., 1961, suppl.

18.4.22 Commager, Henry Steele, *ed.* Documents of American history. 9th ed. Englewood Cliffs, N.J., Prentice-Hall, 1973. 2v.

Brief bibliographies with each document.

18.4.23 Morris, Richard B., and Jeffrey B. Morris, *eds.* Encyclopedia of American history. Bicentennial ed. New York, Harper and Row, 1976. 1245 pp.

1st ed. 1953.
A basic work; brief articles; no bibliographies. Factual information.

British History

18.4.24 Graves, Edgar B., *ed.* A bibliography of English history to 1485. (Based on: The sources and literature of English history from the earliest times to about 1485 by Charles Gross, 1915). Oxford, Clarendon Press, 1975. 1103 pp.

This standard bibliography is continued by the volumes of the *Bibliography of British history* (18.4.25).

18.4.25 Bibliography of British history: issued under the direction of the American Historical Association and the Royal Historical Society of Great Britain. 1st-2d ed. Oxford, Clarendon Press, 1928-1977. 5v.

Vol. 1, Tudor period, 1485-1603. Ed. by Conyers Read. 2d ed., 1959, 624 pp.
Vol. 2, Stuart period, 1603-1714. Ed. by Godfrey Davies. 2d rev. ed. by Mary F. Keeler, 1970, 734 pp.
Vol. 3, The 18th century, 1714-1789. Ed. by Stanley Pargellis and D. J. Medley, 1951, 642 pp.
Vol. 4, 1789-1851. Ed. by Lucy M. Brown and Ian R. Christie, 1977, 759 pp.
Vol. 5, 1851-1914. Ed. by H. J. Hankam, 1976, 1606 pp.

18.5 LINGUISTICS

Guides and Bibliographies

18.5.1 Allen, Harold B. Linguistics and English linguistics. 2d ed. Arlington Heights, Ill., AHM (Goldentree Bibliographies), 1977. 175 pp.

Not annotated, but useful.

18.5.2 Bibliographie linguistique des années 1939-1947- , publiée par le Comité International Permanent de Linguistes. Utrecht, Spectrum, 1949- . v.1- . Annual.

A comprehensive and important bibliography.

18.5.3 Bibliographie Unselbstaendiger Literatur-Linguistik (BUL-L). Frankfurt am Main, Klostermann, 1976- . Annual.

Vol. 1, 1971-1975, published 1976; vol.2, 1976 (and Nachtrage für 1974 und 1975), published 1977.
Entries from German, French, English sources.

18.5.4 Bulletin signalétique, 524: Sciences du langage. *See* 17.1.4

Title varies.
An international abstract journal.

18.5.5 **Hewes, Gordon W.** Language origins; a bibliography. 2d ed., rev. and enl. The Hague, Mouton, 1975. 890 pp.

1st ed. 1971.
Approaches to Semiotics, 44.
Includes philosophy; emphasizes the gestural theory of language.

18.5.6 **LLBA**; language and language behavior abstracts. v.1, no.1- , Jan. 1967- . New York, Appleton, 1967- . Quarterly.

Includes the philosophy of language.

18.5.7 **Rice, Frank A.**, and **Allene Guss.** Information sources in linguistics; a bibliographical handbook. Washington, Center for Applied Linguistics, 1965. 42 pp.

A basic guide.

18.5.8 **Sheehy, Eugene P.**, *ed.* Guide to reference books. *See* 13.1.6, section BC, Linguistics and philology, pp. 283-93.

18.5.9 **Walford, Albert J.**, *ed.* Guide to reference material. *See* 13.1.7, v.3, part 4, Language, pp. 202-98.

18.5.10 **Wawrzyszko, Aleksandra K.** Bibliography of general linguistics, English and American. Hamden, Conn., Archon, 1971. 120 pp.

Annotated.

Dictionaries and Encyclopedias

18.5.11 **Dubois, Jean** [et al]. Dictionnaire de linguistique. Paris, Larousse, 1973. 516 pp.

Bibliography: pp. xiii-xl.
Explains use of terms by quoting from different linguists of note.

18.5.12 **Ducrot, Oswald**, and **Tzvetan Todorov.** Dictionnaire encyclopédique des sciences du langage. Paris, Seuil, 1972. 470 pp.

Emphasis on new structural terminology.
English translation announced by Johns Hopkins University Press for 1979.

18.5.13 **Hartmann, R. R. K.**, and **F. C. Stark.** Dictionary of language and linguistics. London, Applied Science, 1972. 302 pp.

Bibliography: pp. 277-302.

18.5.14 **Meetham, R. R.**, *ed.* Encyclopedia of linguistics, information and control. Oxford and New York, Pergamon Press, 1969. 718 pp.

Includes general linguistics as well as applied linguistics and computer functions, and communications technology. Long articles with bibliographies.

18.5.15 **Pei, Mario.** Glossary of linguistic terminology. New York, Columbia University Press, 1966. 299 pp.

For the beginner as well as the advanced student.

Manuals

18.5.16 **Allen, Charles G.** A manual of European languages for librarians. London and New York, Bowker, 1975. 803 pp.

Now the standard manual used by librarians for European languages. Replaces Von Ostermann (18.5.19) in part.

18.5.17 **Meillet, Antoine**, et **Marcel Cohen**, *eds.* Les langues du monde. Nouv. éd. Paris, Centre National de la Recherche Scientifique, 1952. 1294 pp.

A standard reference work covering more than 10,000 languages and dialects. Includes an annotated bibliography.

18.5.18 **Voegelin, C. F.**, and **F. M. Voegelin.** Classification and index of the world's languages. New York, Elsevier, 1977. 658 pp.

18.5.19 **Von Ostermann, George F.** Manual of foreign languages for the use of librarians, bibliographers, research workers, editors, translators, and printers. 4th ed., rev. and enl. New York, Central Book, 1952. 414 pp.

Long the standard work used by librarians, now replaced in part by 18.5.16.

19. FINE ARTS

Included in this section is material on art and music. The items listed are all of a general nature. The dictionaries and encyclopedias (19.2) are useful as a first step in research in either area. Sheehy (19.1.7) and Walford (19.1.8) can be consulted with profit for additional sources.

19.1 GUIDES AND BIBLIOGRAPHIES

19.1.1 **Art index**, Jan. 1929- . New York, Wilson, 1930- , v.1- . Quarterly, with annual cumulations.

Subtitle: A quarterly author and subject index to publications in the fields of archaeology, architecture, art history, arts and crafts, city planning, fine arts, graphic arts, industrial design, interior design, landscape design, photography and films, and related subjects.

19.1.2 **Bulletin signalétique**, 526: Art et archéologie. Proche-Orient, Asie, Amérique. *See* 17.1.4.

19.1.3 **Chamberlin, Mary Walls**. Guide to art reference books. Chicago, American Library Association, 1959. 418 pp.

Useful though out-of-date. A new edition is in preparation.

19.1.4 **Duckles, Vincent H.**, *comp.* Music reference and research materials; an annotated bibliography. 3d ed. New York, Free Press, 1974. 526 pp.

1st ed. 1964.
A standard reference work; very useful.

19.1.5 **Lucas, E. Louise**. Art books: a basic bibliography on the fine arts. Greenwich, Conn., New York Graphic Society, 1968. 245 pp.

19.1.6 **Muehsam, Gerd**. Guide to basic information sources in the visual arts. Santa Barbara, Calif., J. Norton/ABC-Clio, 1978. 266 pp.

Information resources series.
A valuable first source; explains how to do research in the arts. Essay form; evaluates and describes sources; up-to-date information.

19.1.7 **Sheehy, Eugene P.**, *ed.* Guide to reference books. *See* 13.1.6, sections BE, Fine Arts, pp. 375-93, and BH, Music, pp.413-27.

19.1.8 **Walford, Albert J.**, *ed.* Guide to reference material. *See* 13.1.7, v.3, Generalities, language, the arts and literature, part 7, The Arts, pp. 299-474.

See also: 7.1.5-7.1.6.

19.2 DICTIONARIES AND ENCYCLOPEDIAS

19.2.1 **Encyclopedia of world art**. New York, McGraw-Hill, 1959-68. 15 v.

Signed articles with extensive bibliographies.

19.2.2 **Grove, Sir George**. Dictionary of music and musicians. 5th ed., ed. by Eric Blom. New York, St. Martin's, 1955. 9v.

Suppl. vol. 1961, 492 pp.
The standard encyclopedia of music in English.

19.2.3 **McGraw-Hill dictionary of art**. Bernard S. Myers, ed. New York, McGraw-Hill, 1969. 5v.

Includes bibliographies. Strong in primitive art and art of the Far East and Near East.

See also: 7.1.1-7.1.4.

19.3 HISTORY

19.3.1 **Pelican history of art**. Nikolaus Pevsner, ed. Baltimore, Penguin, 1953-74. v. 1-38.

In progress.
50v. projected. Volumes are not in chronological order, but in order of publication. Includes bibliographies.

See also: 7.1.17-7.1.20.

20. SOCIAL SCIENCES

Carl White's *Sources of Information in the Social Sciences* (20.1.1) is certainly the first place to look for guidance in research in any of the social sciences. Particularly helpful for research in business is *Business Information Sources* by Lorna Daniells (20.3.2), an excellent basic guide. The bibliographies in the International Bibliography of the Social Sciences series (20.2.5, 20.3.5, 20.4.6, 20.6.4) are comprehensive, current, and international in scope.

20.1 GENERAL SOCIAL SCIENCES

Guides and Bibliographies

20.1.1 White, Carl M. and associates. Sources of information in the social sciences; a guide to the literature. 2d. ed. Chicago, American Library Association, 1973. 702 pp.

1st ed. 1964.

An excellent and standard work; should be consulted as a first source for methodology in the various social sciences as well as for annotated bibliographic information. Indispensable as a research tool in the social sciences.

20.1.2 Bibliographie der Sozialwissenschaften; internationale Dokumentation der Buch- und Zeitschriftenliteratur des Gesamtgebiets der Sozialwissenschaften, 1905-67. Göttingen, Vandenhoeck & Ruprecht, 1906-68. Annual (previously monthly).

Important comprehensive bibliography. *See* 20.1.3 for continuation.

20.1.3 Bibliographie der Wirtschaftswissenschaften (vormals Bibliographie der Sozialwissenschaften), 1968- . Göttingen, Bandenhoeck & Ruprecht, 1971- . Annual.

Continuation of 20.1.2.

20.1.4 London bibliography of the social sciences. London, London School of Economics, 1931-32. 4v. Annual supplements, v.5- , 1934- .

London School of Economics. Studies in economics and political science: Bibliographies, no. 8.

The most extensive bibliography in the social sciences.

20.1.5 McInnis, Raymond G., and **James W. Scott.** Social science research handbook. New York, Barnes and Noble, 1974. 395 pp.

Essay form makes it difficult to use, but it contains much useful information.

20.1.6 Public Affairs Information Service. Bulletin of the Public Affairs Information Service (PAIS). 1st- , annual cumulations. New York, Service, 1915- , v.1- .

A useful subject index for the social sciences.

Companion volumes include: *Cumulative author index 1965-69,* and *Foreign language index,* v.1- , 1968/71- .

20.1.7 Sheehy, Eugene P., ed. Guide to reference books. *See* 13.1.6, section C, Social Sciences, pp. 429-596.

20.1.8 **Social sciences index.** v.1, no.1- . June 1974- . New York, Wilson, 1974- . Quarterly, with annual cumulations.

Continuation in part of the *Social sciences and humanities index* (*see* 13.2.12).
A very important basic bibliography.

20.1.9 **Walford, Albert J.**, *ed.* Guide to reference material. *See* 13.1.7, v.2, Social and historical sciences, philosophy and religion, part 3, Social sciences, pp. 74-298.

See also: 7.10.1-7.10.11, 7.11.1-7.11.16.

Dictionaries and Encyclopedias

20.1.10 **Encyclopedia of the social sciences.** Ed. in chief, E. R. A. Seligman. New York, Macmillan, 1930-35. 15v.

Covers the broad area of the social sciences, and includes a number of articles on philosophy.
Supplemented by 20.1.12.

20.1.11 **Gould, Julius**, and **William L. Kolb.** Dictionary of the social sciences. New York, Free Press, 1964. 762 pp.

Covers terms in current usage in political science, anthropology, sociology, economics, and social psychology. No longer current but still useful.

20.1.12 **International encyclopedia of the social sciences.** David L. Sills, ed. New York, Macmillan and the Free Press, 1968. 17v.

Good bibliographies in English, French, and German.
"Designed to complement, not to supplant, its predecessor the *Encyclopedia of the social sciences* (20.1.10)" (p. xix).

20.1.13 **Zadrozny, John T.** Dictionary of social science. Washington, D.C., Public Affairs Press, 1959. 367 pp.

20.2 ANTHROPOLOGY AND MYTHOLOGY

Anthropology

Guides and Bibliographies

20.2.1 **Abstracts in anthropology.** v.1- , 1970- . Farmingdale, N.Y., Baywood, 1970- . Quarterly.

Includes archaeology, cultural anthropology, linguistics, physical anthropology.

20.2.2 **Annual review of anthropology.** v.1- , 1972- . Palo Alto, Calif., Annual Reviews Inc., 1972- . Annual.

Supersedes the *Biennial review of anthropology*.
Essays describing and evaluating recent publications in anthropology.

20.2.3 **Anthropological index to current periodicals** (in the library of the Royal Anthropological Institute). London, Royal Anthropological Institute, 1963- .

20.2.4 **Honigmann, John J.** Handbook of social and cultural anthropology. Chicago, Rand McNally, 1973. 1295 pp.

Surveys and reviews research in anthropology; includes extensive bibliographies.

20.2.5 **International bibliography of social and cultural anthropology.** Bibliographie internationale d'anthropologie sociale et culturelle. v.1- , 1955- . Prepared by the International Committee for Social Sciences Documentation in cooperation with the International Congress of Anthropological and Ethnological Sciences. London, Tavistock; Chicago, Aldine, 1958- . v.1- . Annual.

International Bibliography of the Social Sciences Series. Publisher varies (includes UNESCO).

20.2.6 **White, Carl M.** Sources of information in the social sciences. *See* 20.1.1, chapter 6, Anthropology, pp. 307-74.

Dictionary and Encyclopedia

20.2.7 Davies, David M. A dictionary of anthropology. London, Frederick Muller, 1972. 197 pp.

20.2.8 Hunter, David E., and **Phillip Whitten,** *eds.* Encyclopedia of anthropology. New York, Harper and Row, 1976. 411 pp.

"The book deals not only with the concepts and language of anthropology, but with its theories and leading figures (both historical and contemporary) as well" (Pref.). Includes bibliographies.

Mythology

20.2.9 Diehl, Katherine S. Religions, mythologies, folklores; an annotated bibliography. 2d ed. New York, Scarecrow, 1962. 573 pp.

1st ed. 1956.

20.2.10 Internationale volkskundliche bibliographie. International folklore bibliography. Bibliographie internationale des arts et traditions populaires. 1939/41- . Bâle, Krebs; Bonn, Rudolf Habelt, 1949- . Biennial (1969/70 publ. 1972).

Supersedes *Volkskundliche bibliographie,* 1917-1937/38.

20.2.11 Funk and Wagnalls standard dictionary of folklore, mythology and legend. Maria Leach, ed.; Jerome Fried, assoc. ed. New York, Funk & Wagnalls, 1972. 1236 pp.

A reissue, with minor corrections, of the 2v. 1949-50 edition.
A standard reference tool.

20.2.12 Mythology of all races. L. H. Gray [et al], eds. Boston, Archaeological Institute of America, Marshall Jones Co., 1916-32. 13v.

Reprinted: N. Y., Cooper Square, 1964.
"The general index makes it the most useful single reference work in the field available in English" (13.1.6).

20.2.13 Thompson, Stith. Motif-index of folk-literature; a classification of narrative elements in folktales, ballads, myths, fables, medieval romances, exempla, fabliaux, jestbooks and local legends. Rev. and enl. ed. Bloomington, University of Indiana Press, 1955-58. 6v.

Orig. ed. 1932-36.
A standard work in the field.

20.3 ECONOMICS AND BUSINESS

Guides and Bibliographies

20.3.1 Business periodicals index; a cumulative subject index to periodicals in the fields of accounting, advertising, banking and finance, general business, insurance, labor and management, marketing and purchasing, office management, public administration, taxation, specific businesses, industries, and trades. New York, Wilson, 1958- . v.1- . Monthly (except August), with annual cumulations.

A basic bibliography in business.

20.3.2 Daniells, Lorna M. Business information sources. Berkeley, University of California Press, 1976. 439 pp.

An important guide to research in business; very complete. Supersedes Edwin Coman's *Sources of business information.*

20.3.3 Fundaburk, Emma L. Reference materials and periodicals in economics; an international list. Metuchen, N.J., Scarecrow, 1971-72. v.1,4.

In progress.
5v. projected: v.1, Agriculture; v.4, Major manufacturing industries; already published. V.2 will cover general economics; v.3, general business, industry, and commerce; and v.5, specific industries in services.

20.3.4 Index of economic articles in journals and collective volumes. v.1- , 1886/1924- . Homewood, Ill., R. D. Irwin, 1961- . Annual.

V.10, covering 1968, published 1971.

20.3.5 International bibliography of economics. Bibliographie internationale de science économique, 1952- . London, Tavistock; Chicago, Aldine, 1955- . v.1- . Annual.

International Bibliography of the Social Sciences Series. Publisher varies (includes UNESCO).
A comprehensive bibliography.

20.3.6 Journal of economic literature. v.1- , 1969- . Pittsburgh, Penn., American Economic Association, 1969- . Quarterly.

A restyled and completely changed version of the *Journal of economic abstracts,* 1963-68. Contains selected abstracts and reviews of recent literature.

20.3.7 Melnyk, Peter. Economics; bibliographic guide to reference books and information sources. Littleton, Colo., Libraries Unlimited, 1971. 263 pp.

Many annotations; includes economic theory.

20.3.8 White, Carl M. Sources of information in the social sciences. *See* 20.1.1, chapter 4, Economics and business administration, pp. 181-242.

See also: 1.2.8, 7.2.34-7.2.36.

Dictionaries and Encyclopedias

20.3.9 Ammer, Christine, and **Dean S. Ammer.** Dictionary of business and economics. New York, Free Press, 1977. 461 pp.

20.3.10 Encyclopedia of business information sources. Paul Wasserman, managing ed. Detroit, Gale, 1970. 2v. (689 pp.)

Lists sources of factual information in business.

20.3.11 Hegel, Carl, *ed.* The encyclopedia of management. 2d ed. New York, Van Nostrand, 1973. 1161 pp.

Covers subjects from labor relations, advertising and accounting, to public relations and personnel administration.

20.3.12 McGraw-Hill dictionary of modern economics; a handbook of terms and organizations. Douglas Greenwald, ed. 2d ed. New York, McGraw-Hill, 1973. 792 pp.

20.3.13 Munn, Glenn G. Encyclopedia of banking and finance. 7th ed., rev. and enl. by F. L. Garcia. Boston, Bankers, 1973. 953 pp.

1st ed. 1924.
Includes bibliographies.

20.3.14 O'Connell, Peter, *ed.* Economics: encyclopedia, 1973-74. Guilford, Conn., Dushkin, 1973. 278 pp.

"Comprehensive treatment of the language of economics and of the full range of its theories, practices and institutions" (Pref.). Well illustrated with charts, tables, etc.

20.3.15 Palgrave, Sir Robert H. I. Palgrave's Dictionary of political economy. Henry Higgs, ed. London and New York, Macmillan, 1923-26. 3v.

Reprinted: N. Y., Augustus M. Kelley, 1963.
A standard work, useful and authoritative, but now out-of-date.

20.3.16 Polec: Dictionary of politics and economics. *See* 20.4.10

Miscellaneous

20.3.17 Clapp, Jane. Professional ethics and insignia. Metuchen, N.J., Scarecrow, 1974. 851 pp.

Gives the complete texts of the codes of conduct of major professional organizations in the United States.

20.3.18 Samuelson, Paul. Economics. 10th ed. New York, McGraw-Hill, 1976. 917 pp.

1st ed. 1948.

The standard introduction to the field of economics.

20.4 POLITICAL SCIENCE

Guides and Bibliographies

20.4.1 **Bibliography of bibliographies in political science, government, and public policy.** Alfred Grazia, gen. ed. Princeton, N.J., Princeton Research, 1967, 1968. 927 pp.

V.3 of the Political science, government and public policy series, of the Universal Reference System, a computerized information retrieval system in the social and behavioral sciences.

Annotated and indexed. In-depth approach, but difficult to use. "A controversial series," (20.1.1).

20.4.2 **Harmon, Robert B.** Political science bibliographies. Metuchen, N.J., Scarecrow, 1973-76. v.1-2.

In progress.

20.4.3 **Brock, Clifton.** The literature of political science; a guide for students, librarians, and teachers. New York, Bowker, 1969. 232 pp.

A good first source for guidance in research methods in political science. Detailed annotations.

20.4.4 **Harmon, Robert B.** Political science; a bibliographical guide to the literature. New York, Scarecrow, 1965. 388 pp.

Supplements, 1968, 1972, 1974.
No annotations.

20.4.5 **Holler, Frederick L.** The information sources of political science. Santa Barbara, Calif., ABC-Clio, 1975. 5v.

1st ed. 1971. 264 pp.
Helpful annotations.

20.4.6 **International bibliography of political science.** Bibliographie internationale des

sciences sociales, 1953- . London, Tavistock; Chicago, Aldine, 1953- . v.1- . Annual.

International Bibliography of the Social Sciences Series. Publisher varies (includes UNESCO).
An extensive bibliography.

20.4.7 **International political science abstracts.** Documentation politique internationale. 1951- , v.1- . Oxford, Blackwell, 1951- . Quarterly.

Publisher varies.

20.4.8 **Schmeckebier, Laurence F., and Roy B. Eastin.** Government publications and their use. 2d rev. ed. Washington, Brookings, 1969. 502 pp.

1st ed. 1936.
A standard guide to U.S. documents.

20.4.9 **White, Carl M.** Sources of information in the social sciences. *See* 20.1.1, chapter 9, Political science, pp. 493-563.

See also: 1.2.8, 20.1.6.

Dictionary

20.4.10 **Polec:** Dictionary of politics and economics. Harry Back [et al], eds. 2. verb. und erw. Aufl. Berlin, de Gruyter, 1967. 1037 pp.

Very useful international dictionary; alphabetizes English, French and German terms together and uses cross-references to the counterpart entry in the other languages.

20.5 PSYCHOLOGY

In addition to the bibliographies listed in this section, the researcher in psychology has available an abundance of bibliographies on specific topics in psychology which are issued regularly by HEW and published by the Government Printing Office, Washington, D.C.

Guides and Bibliographies

20.5.1 **Louttit, Chauncey McKinley.** Bibliography of bibliographies on psychology, 1900-1927. Washington, D.C., National research council, 1928. Bulletin no. 65. 108 pp.

> Reprinted: N.Y., Burt Franklin, 1970.
> Helpful for the period covered. *See* 20.5.6 for continuation.

20.5.2 **Annual review of psychology, 1950-** . Paul R. Farnsworth, ed. Palo Alto, Calif., Annual Reviews Inc., 1950- . Annual.

> Bibliographical essays with bibliographical listings by topic in each chapter.

20.5.3 **Bibliographic guide to psychology,** 1975-. Boston, G. K. Hall, 1975- . Annual.

> Includes topics related to philosophy.

20.5.4 **Bulletin signalétique, 390: Psychologie et psychopathologie, psychiatrie.** *See* 17.1.4.

20.5.5 **Daniel, Robert S.,** and **Chauncey M. Louttit.** Professional problems in psychology. New York, Prentice-Hall, 1953. 416 pp.

> Partially a rev. and enl. ed. of Louttit's *Handbook of psychological literature,* 1932. Appendices A and B, pp. 327-74, include an annotated list of 306 reference books and 331 journals.

20.5.6 **Psychological abstracts, 1927-** . Lancaster, Pa., American Psychological Association, 1927- . v.1- . Monthly.

> Cumulated subject index, 1927-1960, 2v.
> 1st-2d supplement, 1968-71, 3v.
> Continues 20.5.1, bibliography of bibliographies, by including "Bibliographies" in the index.

20.5.7 **White, Carl M.** Sources of information in the social sciences. *See* 20.1.1, chapter 7, Psychology, pp. 375-424.

Dictionaries and Encyclopedias

20.5.8 **English, Horace B.,** and **Ava C. English.** A comprehensive dictionary of psychological and psychoanalytic terms: a guide to usage. New York, Longmans, Green, 1958. 594 pp.

> Still a standard work.

20.5.9 **Encyclopedia of psychology.** H. J. Eysenck [et al], eds. London, Search Press; New York, Herder and Herder, 1972. 3v.

> Includes bibliographies.

20.5.10 **Hinsie, Leland E.,** and **R. J. Campbell.** Psychiatric dictionary. 4th ed. New York, Oxford University Press, 1970. 816 pp.

> 1st ed., by L. E. Hinsie and J. Shatzky, 1940.
> A standard work, thoroughly revised.

20.5.11 **International encyclopedia of psychiatry, psychology, psychoanalysis, and neurology.** Benjamin B. Wolman, ed. New York, Aesculapius (Van Nostrand), 1977. 12 v.

> Now considered the most authoritative and up-to-date work in the field. Includes bibliographies.

20.5.12 **Warren, Howard C.** Dictionary of psychology. Boston, Houghton Mifflin, 1934. 372 pp.

> Still important for its historic role in making the terminology of psychology precise.

20.5.13 **Wolman, Benjamin B.,** *comp.* and *ed.* Dictionary of behavioral science. New York, Van Nostrand Reinhold, 1974. 478 pp.

> Covers psychology and related fields.

20.6 SOCIOLOGY

Guides and Bibliographies

20.6.1 **Annual review of sociology, 1975-** . Palo Alto, Calif., Annual Reviews Inc., 1975- . Annual.

Articles on current topics and research, with bibliographies of works cited.

20.6.2 Bulletin signalétique, 521: Sociologie-ethnologie. v.23- , 1969- . *See* 17.1.4.

20.6.3 Current sociology. La sociologie contemporaine. v.1- , 1952- . Paris, UNESCO, 1952- . Quarterly (varies).

Covers recent research in some specific area of sociology; includes bibliographies on the topic.

20.6.4 International bibliography of sociology. Bibliographie internationale de sociologie. 1951- . London, Tavistock; Chjcago, Aldine, 1952- . v.1- . Annual.

International Bibliography of the Social Sciences Series. Publisher varies (includes UNESCO).

20.6.5 Mark, Charles. Sociology of America: a guide to information sources. Detroit, Gale, 1976. 454 pp.

V.1, American Studies Information Guide Series.
Limited to works on American society.

20.6.6 Sociological abstracts. v.1, no.1- , 1952. New York, Sociological Abstracts, 1952- . v.1-.

Frequency varies.

20.6.7 White, Carl M. Sources of information in the social sciences. *See* 20.1.1, chapter 5, Sociology, pp. 243-306.

See also: 1.2.8.

Dictionaries and Encyclopedias

20.6.8 Mitchell, Geoffrey D. A dictionary of sociology. London, Routledge and Kegan Paul; Chicago, Aldine, 1968. 224 pp.

20.6.9 O'Connell, Peter J., *ed.* Encyclopedia of sociology. Guilford, Conn., Dushkin, 1974. 330 pp.

Short entries; many illustrations and charts.

20.6.10 Theodorson, George A., and **A. G. Theodorson.** A modern dictionary of sociology. New York, Crowell, 1969. 469 pp.

Brief definitions of terms.

21. PHYSICAL SCIENCES AND MATHEMATICS

This section lists the standard tools for research in the history of the sciences and for acquiring basic knowledge in the field.

Since current scientific and medical research produces so much information that is rapidly out-of-date, tools for research in current work in science now consist mainly of computerized data banks. Researchers should consult well-informed science librarians for the most reliable and most efficient sources of current information and for guidance in the complexities of research in this area. There also exist innumerable indexes to periodical literature in the different branches of science which are comprehensive in their listings but which are not as current as computerized sources.

21.1 GUIDES AND BIBLIOGRAPHIES

Entries are not annotated.

21.1.1 Fowler, Maureen J. Guides to scientific periodicals; annotated bibliography. London, Library Association, 1966. 318 pp.

Includes bibliographies, union lists and directories. Gives helpful and detailed instructions for finding information in the sciences.

21.1.2 Bulletin signalétique. *See* 17.1.4. (The numerous sections in the sciences are most easily found by looking in a library's card catalog.)

21.1.3 International catalogue of scientific literature, 1st-14th annual issues. Published for the International Council by the Royal Society of London. London, Harrison, 1902-21. 14v.

"While issued, this was the most important current bibliography covering all the sciences" (13.1.6).

21.1.4 Jenkins, Frances Briggs. Science reference sources. 5th ed. Cambridge, Mass., M.I.T. Press, 1969. 231 pp.

21.1.5 Lasworth, Earl J. Reference sources in science and technology. Metuchen, N.J., Scarecrow, 1972. 305 pp.

Also includes mathematics, engineering, medicine and agriculture.

21.1.6 McGraw-Hill basic bibliography of science and technology; recent titles on more than 7000 subjects compiled and annotated by the editors of the McGraw-Hill encyclopedia of science and technology. T. C. Hines, coordinating ed. New York, McGraw-Hill, 1966. 738 pp.

Subject headings correspond to the entries in the *Encyclopedia of science and technology* (*see* 21.1.14). Though prepared as a supplement to the encyclopedia, it is helpful as a separate guide.

21.1.7 Parke, Nathan Grier. Guide to the literature of mathematics and physics including related works on engineering science. 2d rev. ed. New York, Dover, 1958. 436 pp.

1st ed. 1947.

A useful guide with a bibliography of 5000 titles.

21.1.8 **Sheehy, Eugene P.**, *ed.* Guide to reference books. *See* 13.1.6, section E, Pure and Applied Sciences, pp. 691-829.

21.1.9 **Walford, Albert J.**, *ed.* Guide to reference material. *See* 13.1.7, v.1, Science and technology, 615 pp.

See also: 7.8.1, 7.10.1-7.10.11.

21.2 DICTIONARIES AND ENCYCLOPEDIAS

21.2.1 **Chambers's dictionary of science and technology.** T. C. Collocott, ed. London, Chambers, 1971; New York, Barnes and Noble, 1972. 1328 pp.

A complete revision of, and successor to *Chambers's Technical dictionary*, 1st-3d eds., 1940-58.

21.2.2 **Harper encyclopedia of science.** James R. Newman, ed. Rev. ed. New York, Harper, 1967. 1379 pp.

1st ed. 1963 in 4v.
Bibliography: pp. 1282-97.
Includes articles on logic and the history and philosophy of science.
Also covers astronomy, biochemistry and biophysics, biology, chemistry, geology, mathematics, meteorology, physics, and technology.

21.2.3 **McGraw-Hill dictionary of scientific** and technical terms. Daniel N. Lapedes, ed. in chief. New York, McGraw-Hill, 1974. 1634 pp.

"Almost 100,000 definitions, is a major compendium of the vocabulary of science and technology" (Pref.).

21.2.4 **McGraw-Hill encyclopedia of science and technology;** an international reference work. 4th ed. New York, McGraw-Hill, 1977. 15v.

Supplemented by the *McGraw-Hill yearbook of science and technology,* 1961- .
All bibliographies are updated.
Covers most of the sciences in a relatively nontechnical manner.

21.2.5 **Van Nostrand's scientific encyclopedia.** D. M. Considine, ed. 5th ed. New York, Van Nostrand Reinhold, 1976. 2370 pp.

Much attention given to energy and environmental problems.

21.3 BIOGRAPHY

21.3.1 **Dictionary of scientific biography.** Charles C. Gillispie, ed. in chief. New York, Scribner's, 1970-76. v.1-14.

In progress.
v.15, supplement, and v.16, index, are in preparation.
Published under the auspices of the American Council of Learned Societies. There are no articles on the careers of living persons. Includes bibliographies on the person and his work.

22. PROFESSIONS

Only three professions are dealt with in this chapter: education, law, and medicine. There is a good deal of work in the philosophy of these professions currently being done. The sources in law are complex; but there are excellent tools available (listed in 22.2) which can guide one in research in law. The situation in medicine is not as good from this point of view. Some of the basic resources are listed in 22.3.

22.1 EDUCATION

Guides and Bibliographies

22.1.1 Berry, Dorothea M. A bibliographic guide to educational research. Metuchen, N.J., Scarecrow, 1975. 150 pp.

Emphasis on recently published sources; descriptive annotations.

22.1.2 Bulletin signalétique, 520: Sciences de l'éducation. *See* 17.1.4.

22.1.3 Burke, Arvid J., and **Mary A. Burke.** Documentation in education. New York, Teachers College, 1967. 413 pp.

A basic guide to the literature.

22.1.4 Current index to journals in education. v.1, no.1/2- , Jan./Feb. 1969- . New York, Macmillan Information, 1969- . Monthly, with semiannual and annual cumulative indexes.

Published in cooperation with the U.S. Office of Education's Educational Resources Information Center (ERIC) program. (*See* 22.1.6).

Includes brief summaries of articles indexed. Serves as a companion to ERIC's monthly *Resources in education* (22.1.6).

22.1.5 Education index, Jan. 1929- ; a cumulative subject index to a selected list of educational periodicals, proceedings, and yearbooks. New York, Wilson, 1932- . Monthly (except July and August).

Annual cumulation.
Now less complete than the *Current index to journals in education* (CIJE). *See* 22.1.4.

22.1.6 Resources in education. v.10- , 1975- . Washington, D.C., U.S. Department of Health, Education and Welfare, 1975- . Monthly.

Formerly, *Research in education,* v.1-9, 1966-74.
This and 22.1.4 comprise the printed equivalent of the Educational Resources Information Center (ERIC) data base accessible to computer searching. (*See* 22.1.8.)

22.1.7 Sheehy, Eugene P., *ed.* Guide to reference books. *See* 13.1.6, section CB, Education, pp. 437-55.

22.1.8 Thesaurus of ERIC descriptors. 7th ed. New York, Macmillan Information, 1977. 451 pp.

"The basic tool for access to the store of information (computer based) in ERIC through *Resources in education,* the *Current index to journals in education,* and other specialized bibliographies" (20.1.1). *See* 22.1.4 and 22.1.6.

22.1.9 **Walford, Albert P.**, *ed.* Guide to reference material. *See* 13.1.7, v.2, section 37, Education, pp. 240-61.

22.1.10 **White, Carl M.** Sources of information in the social sciences. *See* 20.1.1, chapter 8, Education, pp. 425-92.

See also: 7.6.1-7.6.5.

Dictionaries and Encyclopedias

22.1.11 **Cyclopedia of education.** Ed. by Paul Monroe with the assistance of departmental editors and more than 1000 individual contributors. New York, Macmillan, 1911-13. 5v.

Contributors included John Dewey, Paul Carus, Morris Cohen, and A. O. Lovejoy. Now dated.

22.1.12 **Encyclopedia of education.** Lee C. Deighton, ed. in chief. New York, Macmillan, 1971. 10v.

Emphasis on American education; includes bibliographies.

22.1.13 **Encyclopedia of educational research.** Robert L. Ebel, ed. 4th ed. London, Macmillan, 1969. 1522 pp.

1st ed. 1941.

22.1.14 **Good, Carter V.**, *ed.* Dictionary of education. 3d ed. New York, McGraw-Hill, 1973. 681 pp.

1st ed. 1945.
A scholarly work; standard in the field.

22.1.15 **International encyclopedia of higher education.** Asa S. Knowles, ed. in chief. San Francisco, Jossey-Bass, 1977. 9v.

Information on national systems of education in 198 countries and territories. Includes bibliographies.

22.2 LAW

Research in law is a highly specialized activity. Fortunately there are several basic guides on the methodology of legal research, such as Morris Cohen's *Legal Research in a Nutshell* (22.2.2) and *How to Find the Law* (22.2.3), and Pollack's *Fundamentals of Legal Research* (22.2.6), which should be consulted for basic sources of legal information and for guidance in how to use the sources.

The primary sources for legal research are the many bound volumes of statutes (laws passed by legislative bodies), cases (interpretations of statutory or common law handed down by courts), and administrative regulations (rules promulgated by duly constituted administrative agencies). Legal encyclopedias, such as the *Corpus Juris Secundum* (22.2.13), offer a broad overview of the law and are an important secondary source of information. The *Index to Legal Periodicals* (22.2.5) indexes the articles in law reviews and bar journals.

Guides and Bibliographies

22.2.1 **Cohen, Morris L.** [et al]. Law and science: a selected bibliography. Cambridge, Harvard University, Science, Technology and Human Values (a quarterly review), 1978. 141 pp.

"Focuses on ethical and social dimensions of science and technology."

22.2.2 **Cohen, Morris L.** Legal research in a nutshell. 3d ed. St. Paul, Minn., West, 1978. 415 pp.

1st ed. 1968.
A good introduction to legal research. Text is simple and concise.

22.2.3 **Cohen, Morris L.**, *gen. ed.* How to find the law. 7th ed. St. Paul, Minn., West, 1976. 542 pp.

Orig ed. 1931.
A basic work; extremely helpful to the non-legal researcher and the beginner in law.

22.2.4 **Friend, William L.** Anglo-American legal bibliographies: an annotated guide. Washington, D.C., U.S. Government Printing Office, 1944. 166 pp.

Reprinted: South Hackensack, N.J., Rothman.

22.2.5 **Index to legal periodicals**, 1908- . Published for the American Association of Law Libraries. New York, Wilson, 1909- .

Monthly indexes with annual cumulations. The *Current index to legal periodicals* (v.1- , 1968-) is issued weekly by the *Washington Law Review*, Seattle: "Mimeographed index to be used only until the printed edition of *Index to legal periodicals* appears."

Index to foreign legal periodicals complements the *Index to legal periodicals.*

22.2.6 **Pollack, Ervin H.** Fundamentals of legal research. 4th ed. by J. Myron Jocobstein and Roy M. Mersky. Minneola, N.Y., Foundation Press, 1973. 565 pp.

1st ed. 1956.

An important and basic reference work in law.

22.2.7 **Price, Miles Oscar,** and **Harry Bitner.** Effective legal research; a practical manual of law books and their use. New York, Prentice-Hall, 1953. 633 pp.

Reprinted: South Hackensack, N.J., Rothman, 1969.

A basic guide which discusses procedures and literature.

22.2.8 **Schanck, Peter C.** A guide to legal research in the University of Michigan Law Library. Ann Arbor, University of Michigan Law Library, 1976. 89 pp.

The information is useful and basic for all law libraries.

22.2.9 **Sheehy, Eugene P.,** *ed.* Guide to reference books. *See* 13.1.6, section CK, Law, pp. 553-72.

22.2.10 **Szladits, Charles.** Bibliography on

foreign and comparative law; books and articles in English. New York, Parker School of Foreign and Comparative Law, Columbia University, 1955. 526 pp.

Supplements, 1953-59; 1960-65; 1966-71 (2v.); 1972.

22.2.11 **Walford, Albert J.,** *ed.* Guide to reference material. *See* 13.1.7, v.2, section 34, Law, pp. 180-213.

See also: 1.2.8, 7.11.6, 7.11.8-7.11.10, 7.11.16.

Dictionaries and Encyclopedias

22.2.12 **Black, Henry Campbell.** Black's Law dictionary; definitions of the terms and phrases of American and English jurisprudence, ancient and modern, with guide to pronunciation. Rev. 4th ed. by the publisher's editorial staff. St. Paul, Minn., West, 1968. 1882 pp.

1st ed. 1891: A dictionary of law.

The standard law dictionary. Front matter includes the Code of Professional Responsibility and the Canons of Judicial Ethics.

22.2.13 **Corpus Juris Secundum:** a complete restatement of the entire American law as developed by all reported cases. By William Mack and Donald J. Kiser. St. Paul, Minn., West, 1936-58. 101 v. + 5 General index volumes.

5th reprint, 1975. Cumulative Annual Pocket Part (latest, 1978).

"America's Great Law Encyclopedia. Based upon the authority of all the reported cases from 1658 to date."

22.2.14 **Oran, Daniel.** Law dictionary for non-lawyers. St. Paul, Minn., West, 1975. 333 pp.

22.3 MEDICINE

Guides and Bibliographies

22.3.1 **Blake, John Ballard,** and **Charles Roos.**

Medical reference works, 1679-1966; a selected bibliography. Chicago, Medical Library Association, 1967. 343 pp.

Medical Library Association publication, 3.
Supplement 1, 1970, 46 pp.; supplement 2, 1969-1972, 174 pp.

22.3.2 **Index medicus.** Washington, D.C., National Library of Medicine, 1960- . v.1- . Monthly.

Cumulates annually into the *Cumulated index medicus.*
A comprehensive international index.

22.3.3 **Sheehy, Eugene P.,** *ed.* Guide to reference books. *See* 13.1.6, section EK, Medical sciences, pp. 801-22.

22.3.4 **Walford, Albert J.,** *ed.* Guide to reference material. *See* 13.1.7, v.1, section 61, Medicine, pp. 246-83.

See also: 7.2.23-7.2.33.

Dictionary and Encyclopedia

22.3.5 **Encyclopedia of bio-ethics.** *See* 7.2.27.

22.3.6 **Stedman, Thomas L.** Stedman's Medical dictionary. 23d ed. Baltimore, Williams & Wilkins, 1976. 1678 pp.

1st ed. 1911.
A standard work with frequent revisions.

History

22.3.7 **Garrison, Fielding Hudson.** Introduction to the history of medicine, with medical chronology, suggestions for study and bibliographic data. 4th ed., rev. and enl. Philadelphia, Saunders, 1929. 996 pp.

Reprinted: 1960.
"The most valuable reference history in English, covering the whole history of medicine from the earliest times to the 1920s" (13.1.6).

INDEX

This index includes author and subject entries and most, but not all, title entries. In general titles of journal articles have been omitted, as well as titles of collected works of an individual philosopher, which may be found under the author entry.

INDEX

Bergson, H.: bibliography, biography, journal, works, 79

Berkeley, G.: bibliography, biography, society, works, 51

Berkowitz, M. I., and J. E. Johnson. Social scientific studies of religion, 98, 191

Berlin, I. Karl Marx, 66

Berlin, J. B. Mouvement philosophique en France, 112

Berliner Titeldrucke, Preussische Bibliothek, Berlin, 182

Bermont, H., and D. St. J. Thomas. Getting published, 153

Bernard of Clairvaux, St.: biography, works, 38

Bernoulli, E. A. Franz Overbeck und Friedrich Nietzsche, 69

Bernstein, T. M. Careful writer, 149

Berry, D. M. Bibliographic guide, 217

Bertman, M. A. Research guide in philosophy, 7

Bertrand Russell Society, 86

Bertrand Russell's dictionary, L. E. Dennon, 86

Besterman, T. World bibliography of bibliographies, 169

Bett, H. Nicholas of Cusa, 44

"Biblio," 183

Bibliografia Argentina de filosofia, 109

Bibliografia critica degli studi Plotiniani, B. Marien, 28

Bibliografia Crociana, E. Cione, 80

Bibliografía de estética, N. Pinilla, 91

Bibliografia de Giordano Bruno, V. Salvestrini e L. Firpo, 39

Bibliografía de la literatura hispánica, J. Simón Díaz, 201

Bibliografía de Ortega, U. Rukser, 85

Bibliografía filosófica, L. Martinez Gómez, 113

Bibliografia filosofica italiana, 113

Bibliografia filosofica italiana dal 1900 al 1950, 113

Bibliografía filosófica méxicana, 109

Bibliografía filosófica méxicana, E. Valverde Téllez, 109

Bibliografia filozofii polskiej, Polska Akademia Nauk, 114

Bibliografia filozofii w Polsce, A. Grzegorczyk and L. Kasinski, 114

Bibliografia ragionata, E. Zampetti, 113

Bibliografía suareciana, P. Múgica, 45

Bibliografia vichiana, B. Croce, 75

Bibliographia, O. Schafer, 40

Bibliographia Augustina, E. Nebreda del Cura, 35

Bibliographia Augustiniana, C. Andresen, 35

Bibliographia Cartesiana, G. Sebba, 52

Bibliographia degli scritti di Giovanni Gentile, V. A. Bellezza, 82

Bibliographia Franciscana, 38

Bibliographia logica, W. Risse, 95

Bibliographia patristica, 31

Bibliographia philosophica 1934–1945, G. A. De Brie, 9

Bibliographia S. Alberti Magni, A. Walz and A. Pelzer, 34

Bibliographic guide, D. M. Berry, 217

Bibliographic guide to psychology, 213

Bibliographic index, 169

Bibliographic review of the history of philosophy, D. Pesce, 7

Bibliographic style manuals, M. R. Kinney, 150

Bibliographical description, J. D. Cowley, 171

Bibliographical guide, C. L. F. Gohdes, 198

Bibliographical introduction, H. O. Christopherson, 63

Bibliographical procedures and style, U. S. Library of Congress, 151

Bibliographie, O. von Klapp, 200

Bibliographie, S. Nafisy, 37

Bibliographie bouddhique, 105, 192

Bibliographie critique, 11

Bibliographie critique, G. E. Voumvlinopoulous, 113

Bibliographie d'Aristote, M. Schwab, 25

Bibliographie d'esthétique, 90

Bibliographie de l'anarchie, M. Nettlau, 101

Bibliographie de l'antiquité classique, S. Lambrino, 23

Bibliographie de la France, 183

Bibliographie de la France/Biblio, 183

Bibliographie de la littérature française, R. Rancoeur, 200

Bibliographie de la philosophie, 10

Bibliographie der deutschen Sprach-und Literaturwissenschaft, 199

Bibliographie der Deutschen Zeitschriftenliteratur, 171

Bibliographie der sowjetischen Philosophie, 114

Bibliographie der Sozialethik, A. Utz, 94

Bibliographie der Sozialwissenschaften, 208

Bibliographie der Wirtschaftswissenschaften, 208

Bibliographie des oeuvres de Karl Marx, M. Rubel, 66

Bibliographie des oeuvres de Leibniz, E. Ravier, 62

INDEX

INDEX

Mourelatos, A. P. D. Pre-Socratics, 24
Mouvement philosophique en France, J. P. Berlin, 112
Muehsam, G. Guide to basic information sources, 206
Múgica, P. Bibliografía suareciana, 45
Muirhead, H. H., and S. Radhakrishnan. Contemporary Indian philosophy, 117
Muirhead library of philosophy, 147
Muller, A., et al. Orientalische Bibliographie 1887–1911, 117
Muller, F. M. Sacred books of the east, 192
Muller, K., und G. Kronert. Leben und Werk von G. W. Leibniz, 63
Muller, V. K. English-Russian dictionary, 177
Munn, G. C. Encyclopedia of banking, 211
Murdoch, I. Sartre, 87
Murphey, M. C., and E. Flower. History of philosophy in America, 110
Music
  bibliographies, 206
  dictionaries, 206–7
  encyclopedias, 206–7
  history, 207
Music reference, V. H. Duckles, 206
Mythology, 210
Mythology of all races, 210

Nadel, G. H. Studies in the philosophy of history, 97
Nafisy, S. Bibliographie, 37
Nagel, E., and R. Brandt. Meaning and knowledge, 102
Nakhnikian, G., and W. P. Alston. Readings in 20th century philosophy, 78
Natanson, M. Philosophy of the social sciences, 100; Social dynamics of George Herbert Mead, 84
National Council for Critical Analysis, 161
National cyclopedia of American biography, 186
National Forum for Philosophical Reasoning in the Schools, 161
National Information and Resource Center, 164
National register of scholarships and fellowships, 163
National Translation Center, 161, 175
National union catalog, 180; Pre-1956 imprints, 181
National union catalog of manuscript collections, 173
Natural law forum, 127
Nature and scope of social science, L. I. Krimerman, 100

Nature of law, M. P. Golding, 100
Nauchnye doklady vysskei shkoly, 140
Nauman, St. E., Jr. Dictionary of American philosophy, 109
Nebreda del Cura, E. Bibliographia Augustina, 35
Negley, G. Utopian literature, 100
Nettlau, M. Bibliographie de l'anarchie, 101
Neue deutsche Biographie, 187
Neue Hefte für Philosophie, 138
Neuhausler, A. O. Grundbegriffe der philosophischen Sprache, 15
New American philosophers, A. Reck, 110
New Cambridge bibliography of English literature, 198
New Cambridge modern history, 203
New Catholic encyclopedia, 193
New Columbia encyclopedia, 178
New encyclopedia Britannica, 178
New encyclopedia of philosophy, J. Grooten and G. J. Steenbergen, 17
New introduction to bibliography, P. Gaskell, 172
New Schaff-Herzog encyclopedia of religious knowledge, 193
New scholasticism, 108, 127
New serial titles, 181
New serial titles—classed subject arrangement, 181
New titles in bioethics, 94
Newman, J. H.: works, 68
Newsletter for Society for the Study of Mind/Brain/Machine, 103
Newsletter of the American Philosophical Association Committee on Philosophy and Medicine, 143
Newsletter of the Center for Process Studies, 89, 143
Newsletter of the committee on philosophy and medicine, 94
Newsletter of the International Society for Neoplatonic Studies, 143
Newsletter on science, technology, and human values, 143
New York Public Library. Check list of cumulative indexes, 119
New York Times biographical edition, 186
New York Times manual of style, L. Jordan, 150
Niccolo Machiavelli, A. Gerber, 42
Nichol, J. Francis Bacon, 38
Nicholas of Cusa: bibliography, biography, concordance, works, 43–44
Nicholas of Cusa, H. Bett, 44
Nicholson, M. Dictionary of American-English usage, 150; Manual of copyright